PUEBLO, HARDSCRABBLE, GREENHORN

The Greenhorn Valley near the Taos Trail crossing.

PUEBLO
■
HARDSCRABBLE
■
GREENHORN

The Upper Arkansas, 1832–1856

by
Janet Lecompte

University of Oklahoma Press: Norman

Lecompte, Janet, 1923–
    Pueblo, Hardscrabble, Greenhorn.

    Bibliography: p.
    Includes index.
    1. Arkansas Valley—History.   I.   Title.
F782.A7L36   978.8'53   77-18616
ISBN 0-8061-1462-2

Copyright 1978 by the University of Oklahoma Press, Publishing
Division of the University. Manufactured in the U.S.A.
First edition.

Preface

IN THE QUARTER-CENTURY between 1832 and 1858 there were more than a dozen distinct trading posts and settlements along a hundred-mile stretch of the Arkansas River and its tributaries in the present state of Colorado. The men who lived in these settlements were the first white settlers, farmers and stockmen of the Rocky Mountain West. Their influence on the development of the West was both obvious and subtle. Striking was their effect on the Indians who moved in large numbers to the Arkansas to trade with them, causing a displacement of other tribes, a rearrangement of alliances and a change in cultures. The first Mexicans to live north of New Mexico settled in the Arkansas Valley, where many of their descendants still live. Three hundred Mormons spent a winter near the settlements and carried on to Salt Lake City skills and perhaps attitudes learned from their neighbors on the Arkansas. United States Army expeditions passed the settlements and procured guides, provisions, and animals essential to their operations. When gold seekers arrived they found the Indians tamed by contact with the early traders, and friendly for just long enough to allow new towns to become well-established. At first the gold seekers lived on produce from the Arkansas Valley; later they themselves farmed, using techniques of agriculture and husbandry already tested by the Arkansas Valley pioneers. The narrative that follows is about these settlements and the men and women who struggled to make a living—or more precisely, a good life—out of the wild Indians, stubborn soil and thin grass of this difficult valley.

For source material I have been dependent upon libraries and their staffs. Very important has been the Cragin Collection in the Pioneers' Museum, Colorado Springs; my mother, Dorothy Price Shaw, introduced me to history while we were arranging these papers for the Museum. Equally important have been the Barclay

Papers, made available to me in microfilm first by Agnes Wright Spring, former Colorado State Historian, and later by Dolores Renze at the Colorado State Archives, and used here with gracious permission of the Bancroft Library, Berkeley, California. Former librarians of the Colorado State Historical Society Library, Frances Shea and Laura Allyn Ekstrom, opened to me the files of that library, as have their successors, Enid Thompson and Kathleen Pierson. The Denver Public Library's Western History Department has been vital to my work, thanks to Ina Aulls, Alys Freeze, Opal Harber and Jim Davis. Most of my general library research has been done at Tutt Library of Colorado College, whose successive librarians and research librarians, Louise Kampf, Ellsworth Mason, Reta Ridings, and George Fagan, have spent hours finding things for me. At the Bancroft Library in Berkeley, California, George P. Hammond and his staff were wonderfully helpful, as were Haydée Noya at the Henry E. Huntington Library in San Marino, California, Archibald Hanna and his staff at the Beinicke Library at Yale University, and Earl E. Olson at the Church Historian's Office in Salt Lake City. Without the help of my dear friend Frances Stadler and her staff at the Missouri Historical Society in St. Louis, I could never have worked my way through even the fraction I have seen of that Society's manuscript collections. Ruth Rambo helped me at the Museum of New Mexico in Santa Fe, and Myra Ellen Jenkins at the State Records Center and Archives at Santa Fe. At the National Archives in Washington I have been especially indebted to Jane F. Smith; at the Oregon Historical Society to Priscilla Knuth; at the Library of Pacific University to Elsie M. Lundborg; at the McClelland Library at Pueblo, to Claire Knox and Joanne Dodds; at the Kansas State Historical Society, to Louise Barry.

My special thanks go to four people who read and criticized the manuscript:

—Dale L. Morgan, whose painstaking reading uncovered not only errors of fact but awkwardness of style, and who added generous contributions from his own vast knowledge.
—David J. Weber, for his warm encouragement and specific information.
—Ann H. Zwinger, for her vigorous efforts to pluck out pedantry.
—my daughter Ellen, who read with love, corrected with skill, laughed at my jokes and made it all seem worth the doing.

There is one other to whom I am deeply indebted—LeRoy

Hafen—whose patient research and collecting of source material is the rock upon which all students of Colorado history must build. His pioneer work in the field is reflected on every page of this book, and his kindness to me has been inexhaustible.

I must thank Arthur R. Mitchell for permission to reproduce his wonderful old photographs; as well as Paul Albright, James Arrott, Harvey Carter, Jeanette Coonsis, Edwin C. Crampton, Lorene and Kenny Englert, Jon Frost, Pat Lamme, Savoie Lottinville, Andrew Marshall, Annie R. Mitchell, Peter Ortega, Edward F. Rizer, Reverend John A. Sierra, Marshall Sprague, Lester F. Turley, Fred Voelker, Fred Walters, Luther Wilson, Myron Wood, and members of my patient and loving family—Oliver, Jenny, Ellen, Louisa, Charley, Tom, and Peter Lecompte, and Mickey Shaw. There are scores of other librarians, county clerks, city engineers, abstracters, old-timers and fellow historians who have generously given me their time. I hope I have not wasted it.

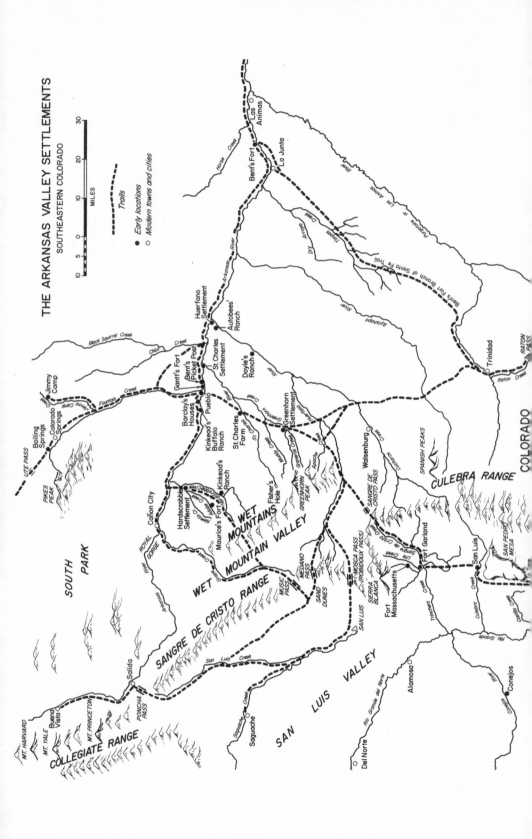

THE ARKANSAS VALLEY SETTLEMENTS
SOUTHEASTERN COLORADO

MILES

Trails

● Early locations

○ Modern towns and cities

COLORADO

UTE PASS

PIKES PEAK

SOUTH PARK

Black Squirrel Creek

Chico Creek

Jimmy Camp

Boiling Springs

Colorado Springs

Jimmy Camp Creek

Fountain Creek

Gantt's Fort

Bent's Picket Post

Huerfano Settlement

Autobees' Ranch

St Charles Settlement

Doyle's Ranch

Barclay's Houses

Kinkead's Buffalo Ranch

Pueblo

St Charles Farm

St Charles River

Greenhorn Settlement

Arkansas River

COLLEGIATE RANGE

MT. HARVARD

MT. YALE

Buena Vista

MT. PRINCETON

Salida

PONCHA PASS

Saguache Creek

Saguache

Del Norte

Hardscrabble Settlement

Kinkead's Ranch

Maurice's Fort

Cañon City

ROYAL GORGE

Hardscrabble Creek

WET MOUNTAINS

Fisher's Hole

WET MOUNTAIN VALLEY

GREENHORN PEAK

Greenhorn Creek

Adobe Creek

SANGRE DE CRISTO RANGE

MUSIC PASS

MEDANO PASS

SAND DUNES

MOSCA PASS (ROBIDOUX PASS)

SIERRA BLANCA

Fort Massachusetts

Ute Creek

Sangre de Cristo Creek

SANGRE DE CRISTO PASS

Walsenburg

SPANISH PEAKS

CULEBRA RANGE

Fort Garland

San Luis

SAN PEDRO MESA

Conejos

Alamosa

SAN LUIS VALLEY

San Luis Creek

San Luis Creek

Rio Grande del Norte

Rio Grande

Trinchera Creek

Culebra Creek

Costilla Creek

Taos

Horse Creek

Arkansas River

Las Animas

Bent's Fort

La Junta

Purgatoire or Las Animas R.

Timpas Creek

Arroyo

Dry Creek

Bent's Fort Branch of Santa Fe Trail

Trinidad

Raton Creek

RATON PASS

Apishapa River

Huerfano River

COLORADO

Contents

Illustrations

PUEBLO, HARDSCRABBLE, GREENHORN

George S. Simpson. Courtesy of A. R. Mitchell, Trinidad, Colorado.

1
George Simpson
Learns a Trade

IN THE LATE AUTUMN OF 1840 a gathering of farmers in western
Missouri listened to a fur trader named Robidoux tell some truths
and myths about California. He spoke of its perennial spring and
boundless fertility, its friendly people, its thousands of wild horses
and cattle, and a climate so healthy that natives of Monterey went
eighteen miles into the country just to watch a man shake with ague.
Convinced, fifty-odd Missourians brought their wagons to the Kansas River in May, 1841 to begin their journey to paradise. They had
little idea where California was and not the slightest notion how to
get there. With the luck of fools, they were joined at their rendezvous by a party of missionaries and hunters guided by the mountain
man Thomas Fitzpatrick who agreed to show them the way. Single
file they all started out together. The missionaries were in four carts
and a small wagon; the others were in eight wagons drawn by horses
and mules, with five big ox-drawn wagons lurching along at the
rear.[1]

Setting out in a brand-new mule wagon furnished with every
camp comfort by loving parents was George Simpson, just
turned twenty-three years old. George was a slightly built,
pleasant looking youth with an eager, friendly manner, and sufficient wit and education to enjoy the company of many of his
distinguished fellow travelers. Among them were Father Pierre-
Jean DeSmet and his assistants Father Nicolas Point and Gregory
Mengarini, on their way to found a mission among the Flathead
Indians; the Reverend Joseph Williams, an elderly fire-and-
brimstone preacher seeking Indians to convert; Talbot Green, who
under another name had defrauded a Philadelphia bank; a British
nobleman named Romaine on a pleasure trip with his Herculean
hunter, John Gray. Of these interesting men, George Simpson
chose to cultivate not his equals in education but the old half-
Iroquois John Gray, who became Simpson's principal companion as

3

they crossed the plains to Fort Laramie. In later years, Simpson wrote that from John Gray he "received much information and many lessons in wood craft and I may say Indian craft before I parted from him the last time in 1841. . . ."[2]

George Simpson's preference for John Gray was characteristic of him—everything about mountain men fascinated him. He admired their fringed buckskin costumes, their endless stories of adventure told with peculiar humor and exaggeration, their courage and self-sufficiency, and their contempt for the restraints and social absurdities of civilization. From the trappers with the emigrant party Simpson got a taste of trapperhood. At Fort Laramie he met more mountain men and proceeded to charm them with his ready acceptance of their high odor and tall tales, finally eliciting an invitation to join them. "Come along, sonny," said old Bill Williams, "you are as green as a gosling and as soft as a boiled turnip, but I'll make a beaver trapper of you in a few seasons."[3] On the morning of June 24, when the wagon company of emigrants continued its journey up the North Platte, George Simpson remained at Fort Laramie with his new trapper friends, intending no doubt to accept Bill Williams' invitation.[4]

Old Bill Williams was the embodiment of all the rustic virtues and vices that Simpson found irresistible. Williams had the added interest of being an old acquaintance of Simpson's cousin-by-marriage, George C. Sibley, factor (agent) at Fort Osage in the days when western Missouri was wild frontier. Originally from North Carolina, Williams had drifted west to Fort Osage as an itinerant Baptist preacher. There he became a missionary and trader among the Osage Indians, marrying into the tribe and fathering two little girls. In 1825 he left his family to accompany George Sibley on an expedition to mark the Santa Fe trail, and, except for brief and unsatisfactory visits, he never went home again. At Taos he was introduced to beaver trapping. From then on he believed that "to be a successful beaver trapper was to have arrived at the acme of human ambition."[5] He signed himself "Master Trapper" ("M.T." for short) and remained passionately faithful to his vocation, if to little else. His dirty buckskins, thin craggy face and whiny voice became the delight of travelers, few of whom could resist writing about him. Dick Wootton, who knew him well, said he was "warm-hearted, brave and generous"; Matt Field called him benevolent and honest, but also surly, abrupt, and eccentric. Documents of the period show that Williams honored few debts and was loyal to neither white man nor Indian.[6]

4

Simpson met other trappers at Fort Laramie. Levin Mitchell was a big fellow, florid-faced and red-haired (Mexicans called him "Colorado") who had been a trapper since 1830. He had lived briefly with the Comanches while trying to discover their secret gold mine. When Simpson met him he had a Sioux squaw, whom he later discarded for a Mexican girl. Mark Head was a trapper whose stupidity had carried him into numerous scrapes which luck and reckless daring carried him out of, bruised and mutilated but none the wiser. Louis Ambroise was a half-Iroquois from St. Louis who had come to Taos in 1824, married a local girl, become a Mexican citizen and then left home and family for a trapper's life in the mountains. Charley Raymond, even younger than Simpson, was a Canadian whom Francis Parkman later hired at Fort Laramie. Parkman described him as heavyset, stupid and self-confident, and discharged him for unsatisfactory conduct.[7]

Such was a sampling of the men George Simpson met at Fort Laramie in the summer of 1841, most of them a cut below the average trapper in intellect and character. By 1841 beaver trapping as a full-time occupation was dead. Intelligent trappers had assumed some kind of leadership in the mountains, as the proprietor of a trading post, or as guide. Some had gone home, or settled in Oregon or New Mexico. Others had taken a respectable job with a trading company. The small percentage of ex-trappers who remained in the mountains, unable to shake off the habits of their former lives, were the dregs of the romantic breed that intoxicated George Simpson. In better days they had earned two or three hundred dollars a year which they often gambled away in a single night or drank up in a bibulous week at summer rendezvous. They had formed incomplete attachments to Indian women, leaving fatherless and embittered half-blood children in all the tribes of the West. Like animals, they thought only of the food, shelter and pleasures of the moment, and with animal skill they went about satisfying their simple needs. Those who had attempted to go back to their homes in Missouri or Kentucky found themselves incapable of shouldering the responsibilities they had so long rejected, and they returned to the mountains for good, muttering about the indignities a free man had to suffer in "society."[8]

At the 1839 rendezvous the American Fur Company announced the end of its mountain business, which meant the end of organized trapping. Destitute and demoralized, some of the trappers turned to horse stealing. Led by Levin Mitchell and Philip Thompson, a group including Bill Williams, Dick Owens, Bill New and others went to

Fort Hall, a Hudson's Bay Company post where they had been treated kindly in the past, and stole all the fort's horses. On the way back to Brown's Hole, they stopped for a night with an old Shoshone Indian who fed and lodged them. As they left in the morning, they stole all his horses. Trappers at Brown's Hole and Fort Uintah on Green River made them give up their booty. The thieves, joined by others, went on to California where they stole several thousand horses from missions and ranches. On their way back to the Rocky Mountains, half the horses died in the desert. Bill Williams, in an act of typical improvidence, sold his remaining horses at Bent's Fort for four or five gallons of whiskey.[9]

Aware as he must have been of the trappers' shortcomings, George Simpson indulgently excused them: "What at first appeared rough and outré in their manners and character soon lost that distinction by association, and as my knowledge of their many sterling qualities increased, I became attached not only to their persons, but to their erratic and seemingly purposeless lives."[10] Perhaps the idea of providing some sort of home for these strays, and an alternate vocation to trapping, occurred to Simpson as early as his stopover at Fort Laramie.

The "erratic and seemingly purposeless lives" of these men struck a familiar chord in young Simpson's sensitivities, for his own life was no better regulated. George Semmes Simpson was born May 7, 1818, at a forty-four acre farm at Bridgeton, near St. Louis, Missouri. He was the son of Dr. Robert Simpson, an Army doctor from Maryland, and the well-bred Miss Brecia Smith of Rome, New York. Dr. Simpson settled down with his bride in St. Louis, practicing medicine and running a drug store. As his remarkable energy and intelligence became manifest, he served in civic capacities, such as postmaster, town trustee, tax assessor and sheriff, as cashier of several banks, and as a state legislator on an antislavery ticket. Before he died in 1873 at the age of 88, he had become a successful merchant, earning enough to support his son George in comfort all his days. For the rest of his life, George's stipend was doled out to him in an annual remittance.[11]

George was the fourth of seven children, but the first to survive infancy, which may explain why his parents pampered him. He grew to be a good-looking boy with some talent; his famous cousin-by-marriage, George Sibley, took an interest in his writing. Nothing was spared to give him a fine education, but pursuing a profession was beyond his capability. In later years he wrote that if he had followed wise counsel he would have remained at home and "might now be a third class lawyer with a big family and a little practice, or a member of the legislature."[12]

In spite of his personal attractions, superior education and the security of his family's position in St. Louis, George began drinking hard as a youth. When he tried to kill himself with laudanum after an unhappy love affair, his father decided to send him west with the first party of emigrants to California.

At Fort Laramie George would have liked to go trapping with Bill Williams and the rest of his new friends. In later years, he may have done so, for he wrote a series of sketches purporting to describe just such an expedition. But in 1841 Simpson went no further west than Fort Laramie where he met Robert Fisher, an Indian trader for Bent, St. Vrain & Company and a very different man from the romantic, restless trappers. Fisher was nine years older than Simpson, a big, quiet man who was intimately acquainted with the dull realities of life in the West. Instead of joining the trappers, young Simpson made the sensible decision to go to Bent's Fort with Robert Fisher and others, to learn the Indian trade.[13]

The road leading south from Fort Laramie to Bent's Fort along the foot of the Rocky Mountains passed near the favorite camping places of the Indians. After leaving Fort Laramie on the North Platte River, George Simpson and his party went south to the South Platte River where they passed four Indian trading posts within twenty miles of one another, all built of adobe in the form of a hollow square. Only Fort George, belonging to Bent, St. Vrain & Company, was a bustling, prosperous post. The other three showed the effects of excessive competition. Sarpy & Fraeb's Fort Jackson was abandoned and falling into ruin; Fort Vasquez, sold by Sublette and Vasquez to Lock and Randolph in 1840, was now operating with the lassitude of imminent failure; and Fort Lancaster was run by the little ex-Army officer, Lancaster P. Lupton, who would declare bankruptcy within the year.[14]

At the mouth of Cherry Creek, where Denver was subsequently located, they came upon an Arapaho village. Its white conical buffalo-skin lodges covered several acres of the South Platte bottoms. The Arapahos gave the traders a vociferous welcome, a feast of boiled puppy dog, and, to George Simpson, an invitation to stay in the lodge of the chief, Little Raven. Pushing on, they ascended

Cherry Creek to its source in the pine forest of the Platte-Arkansas divide. On the other side, they had a broad view of the grassy plains of the Arkansas Valley, dominated on the west by Pikes Peak, a head taller than any other mountain in the escarpment known as the Front Range. East of the foot of Pikes Peak was a semicircle of pine-covered bluffs enclosing a little valley with a never-failing spring in it. The valley would soon be known as Jimmy's Camp in memory of Jimmy Daugherty, one of the trappers Simpson met at Fort Laramie, who was murdered at the spring by a Mexican companion in the winter of 1841–42. The travelers continued on the trail south to Fountain Creek, named *Fontaine qui bouille* (fountain-that-boils) for a pair of bubbling mineral springs on its banks where it debouches from the mountains at the present site of Manitou, Colorado. Forty miles down Fountain Creek they came to its junction with the Arkansas.[15]

What George Simpson saw at the mouth of the Fountain in the summer of 1841 was a cluster of trading posts for the Arapaho Indians. The buildings were all empty, for trade was conducted only in winter. One post belonging to Lancaster P. Lupton was a hollow square of cottonwood logs set upright in a three-foot-deep trench. Along its inside walls were "houses" or rooms plastered with mud. Nearby was a second stockade post built in the winter of 1836–37 by Robert Newell, a Bent, St. Vrain & Company employee, and a third was built by Sarpy & Fraeb in the winter of 1837–38. These wooden "houses" were for seasonal use only, and there would be more just like them down the Arkansas, known as "Smith's Houses," "Hatcher's Houses," "Wilson's Houses." They would not last long. If the Indians did not burn them in sheer mischief, travelers used their wood for camp fires, or traders built other posts with their timbers.[16]

At the mouth of the Fountain, George Simpson and his party turned east, following the trail along the north bank of the Arkansas. Six miles east of the Fountain they passed Gantt's Fort, another abandoned trading post. In contrast to the ephemeral wooden posts, Gantt's adobe building would stand for another twenty years, a bulwark against the ravages of man and nature. Its stability was a lesson to George Simpson and other fort builders.

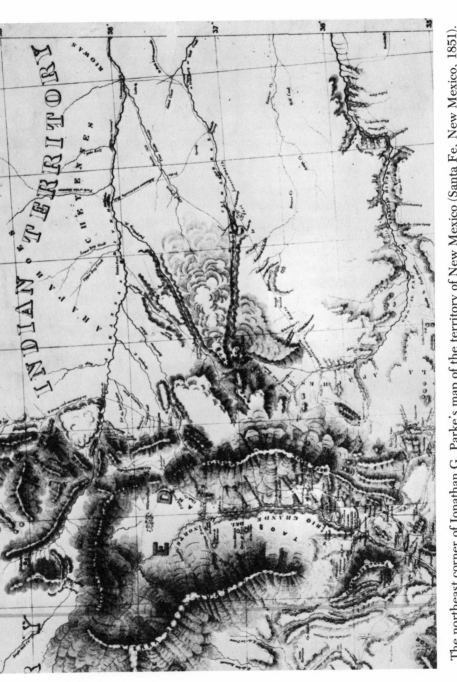

The northeast corner of Jonathan G. Parke's map of the territory of New Mexico (Santa Fe, New Mexico, 1851). Courtesy of the National Archives.

Gantt's Fort was built by John Gantt, an ex-Army officer dismissed from the service in 1829 for falsifying pay accounts. In 1831 Gantt and his partner Jefferson Blackwell came West at the head of a party of trappers. In September, 1832 Gantt was camped on the Arkansas. Near the mouth of the Purgatory, he set his men to building "winter quarters"—probably two or three log houses enclosed by a stockade. During the winter of 1832–33 he traded with some Cheyennes and Arapahos for buffalo robes. By sweetening whiskey he persuaded these previously teetotal Indians to drink it, thereby laying the foundation of the whiskey trade on the Arkansas.[17]

Gantt's business was extensive enough to invite competition. It was his misfortune that the competition he attracted was Bent, St. Vrain & Company. By December, 1832, that company had begun to build Fort William, a stockade post on the north side of the Arkansas about nine miles below the mouth of the Fountain. There twenty-five-year-old William Bent, a junior partner, traded with whatever Indians turned up at his post. His first success was with the Cheyennes, who remained on the Arkansas in the winter of 1833–34 to trade with Bent instead of returning, as they usually did, to the rest of their tribe on the Upper Missouri River.[18]

Now Gantt felt the pressure of competition. In May, 1834, in order to capture some of William Bent's trade, Gantt imported Mexican brick-layers from Taos to make adobes for a fort, which he located on the north side of the Arkansas six miles below the mouth of the Fountain and three miles west of Fort William. He called the post Fort Cass, for the United States Secretary of War. While it was under construction, eight lodges of Shoshones came to trade with Gantt. On July 29, 1834, William Bent and his ten employees, one of them Robert Fisher, attacked the Shoshones, killing three, wounding one and an Arapaho by mistake, scalping the dead, capturing two women and dividing the plunder by lot. It was an early and unusually bloody example of the kind of competition William Bent would offer his rivals on the Arkansas.[19]

John Gantt was the first to make a business of trading with the Indians on the Arkansas. He was probably the first to use wagons instead of pack mules to ship the buffalo robes east to market and the trade goods west to his fort (wagons were a requisite of the buffalo robe trade on the Arkansas, which was not navigable). He was also the first to introduce the Cheyennes and Arapahos to the joys of liquor, and the first to build an American fort of adobe. Gantt was

A wagon-train corral as illustrated in H. L. Conard, *"Uncle Dick" Wootton* (1890). Courtesy of Denver Public Library Western Collection.

immensely important to the Indian trade on the Arkansas, but he was not strong enough to withstand the Bents.

During the winter of 1834–35, Gantt gave up his fort and his trading business. Bent, St. Vrain & Company then abandoned its picket post near the mouth of the Fountain, and moved seventy miles down the Arkansas, to be closer to the buffalo range and to the Indians whose livelihood depended upon that animal. The fort they built, probably begun late in 1834, was of adobe.[20] From that time on many posts in the West were built of adobe, which was fireproof, bulletproof, handsome, durable and comfortable—an altogether better building material than the soft wood locally available.

The very construction of these adobe posts had its sociological consequences throughout the Indian country. Only Mexicans were skilled at forming and laying up adobe brick. Hence Mexicans were imported for this purpose and retained for other purposes, such as trading, herding horses, and packing mules. In the 1830's and 1840's hundreds of Mexicans were employed on the Arkansas, South Platte, North Platte, and at adobe posts in the far west such as Fort Boise, Fort Walla Walla, and at military posts of a later era. The building of adobe posts became in good measure responsible for the bilingual and bicultural nature of the Arkansas Valley settlements, then and now.

George Simpson followed the trail along the north side of the Arkansas River to Bent's Fort, where he would spend the winter. When Simpson first saw Bent's Fort in the summer of 1841, its owners had been almost unchallenged in their trading operations on the Arkansas for nearly eight years. The brutality that William Bent had shown towards Gantt and the Shoshones in 1834 had softened to a benign and regal paternalism over the Arkansas Valley. Bent's Fort was a warm and friendly haven for travelers, one of the few places in the West where a cultivated man could enjoy books, good wine, and the conversation of other cultivated men. In these golden years the Bents were good to young men whose families they knew in St. Louis, even ne'er-do-wells like George Simpson. From the Bents and their employees, Simpson learned the only vocation he ever knew. And how did he repay his kind hosts and patient instructors? By setting himself up in competition to them, and building a trading post in their own back yard!

2
At Bent's Fort,
1841–42

AS GEORGE SIMPSON CAME down the Arkansas in his fancy little mule wagon, he saw the massive beauty of Bent's Fort rising out of the flat Arkansas bottom, in utter harmony with its setting, being made from the same prairie soil on which it stood. Its smooth mud walls were fourteen feet high; bastions at opposite corners were four feet higher still. The only opening was a central gate' of heavy planks over which an enormous United States flag strained at its ash pole in the constant summer breeze. Sentries paced back and forth on top of the walls carrying loaded muskets. From the bastions guards trained their spyglasses on the slightest puff of dust disturbing the prairie.[1]

The gate, big enough to admit wagons, led to the plaza or courtyard inside the walls. Around the plaza were houses—a two-story warehouse, a row of single-story rooms for the owners and their families, a large trading room where Indians threw their robes across the counter and bartered for goods and hardware, ornaments and flour. But not for whiskey. To the side of the gate was a little opening in the wall where clerks passed small quantities of the dangerous stuff out to Indian chiefs.

There were clerks' offices, servants' quarters, and sleeping rooms for visitors. In the dining hall, aristocratic Ceran St. Vrain, dressed in a frilled shirt and frock coat, entertained visitors at a table spread with silver and fine linen, garnished with goblets of claret wine. The second story had a room with a billiard table and a bar. Here the four Bent brothers, dressed like Indian chiefs in fringed buckskin embroidered with dyed porcupine quills, made their guests mint juleps with ice from an icehouse near the river and fresh mint that grew on its banks. The roofs of the rooms were gravelled; they made a pleasant place to stroll and gaze at the blue, vaporous outlines of mountains in the distance. The fort was a complete facility, a melding of necessities and amenities. In addition to the blacksmith shop and carpenter shop for the needs of the business, there was a tailor shop and barber shop for the comfort of the inhabitants and guests. But lest anyone forget the essential function of the post, in 1845 the Bents placed a huge and graceless wooden robe press in the center of the courtyard, a monument to their commerce.

The east wall of the fort struck out at an angle enclosing a pie-shaped yard for poultry, cows, sheep and goats, and for various tamed creatures of the plains—a white bear, two or three buffalo calves, and cages of wild birds. South of this triangular yard was an enormous roofed shed covering eighteen Conestoga wagons. Beyond the main wall to the south was a corral for horses, mules and oxen, surrounded by an eight-foot wall planted on top with cactus to discourage scalers.

The Bent brothers and Ceran St. Vrain were from highly respected St. Louis families. Charles Bent, the eldest, had been a trader and partner in the Missouri Fur Company from 1823 to 1828. When that company was dissolved, Charles bought an outfit for the Santa Fe trade and in 1829 set out for New Mexico with his next-younger brother, William. The manifest competence of Charles Bent was such that he was elected captain of the caravan even though he had never taken the route before. Of medium stature, rotund figure, black hair and steel-grey eyes, he had sharp intelligence, great vigor, passionate prejudices and a wicked wit that earned him both friends and enemies. William Bent, darker and smaller than his brother, was just as strong-willed, shrewd and energetic. Both were tough and devious in their business behavior, but courteous to their friends and loyal to their country—for they had been raised as gentlemen.[2]

Charles and William Bent never went back to St. Louis except on business trips. In the winter of 1830–31, while William was trapping in the Gila River region with three other young men, Charles formed a partnership with Ceran St. Vrain of Taos. St. Vrain was a burly, puffy-faced man descended from lesser Flemish nobility. Since 1825 he had traded American goods at Taos and Santa Fe, endearing himself to everyone with his rare combination of gentleness and courage, compassion and dignity. For the first year or so the partnership of Bent and St. Vrain was limited to transporting and marketing goods for the Santa Fe

William Bent in 1835. Courtesy of Pioneers' Museum, Colorado Springs.

trade. In 1832 Bent, St. Vrain & Company entered the Indian trade on the Arkansas, and by August, 1835 the company had completed Bent's Fort (properly, Fort William) on the north side of the Arkansas twelve miles above and opposite the mouth of the Purgatory. William Bent was its manager, and later he became a partner in the company along with the younger Bent brothers, George and Robert. Marcellin St. Vrain, Ceran's younger brother, managed Fort St. Vrain and traded for the company, although he was not a partner.[3]

From the establishment of Bent's Fort until the building of the Pueblo trading post in 1842 the history of the Arkansas Valley was quite simply the efforts of Bent, St. Vrain & Company to control whatever business the region afforded. According to Cheyenne tradition, Bent's Fort was built to trade with the Cheyennes, but the Bents had no such limited aspirations. Their first license of 1834 shows that they also meant to trade with Sioux, Kiowas, Snakes (Shoshones), Arapahos, and Arikaras. Having destroyed his chances of trade with the Shoshones by his attack on them in 1834, William Bent set out to woo the Comanches with a visit to the Red River of Texas in 1835. The Comanches and their allies, the Kiowas, were at war with the Cheyennes and refused to visit Bent's Fort. William's later attempts to trade with the Navajos and Utes were also unsuccessful.[4]

In the summer of 1837 the company built its second adobe post, Fort George (better known as Fort St. Vrain) on the South Platte River, in opposition to three other adobe posts already built within twenty miles of it. In the struggle for survival, Bent, St. Vrain & Company won. By the time George Simpson passed the posts, Fort Vasquez was a crumbling ruin, Fort Lancaster was moribund, and Fort Jackson was empty, having been bought out by William Bent in 1838. When he bought Fort Jackson, William made a cartel with its financial backers, the St. Louis firm of Pratte, Chouteau & Company. Henceforth, traders of Pratte, Chouteau & Company were to limit themselves to trading north of the South Platte River, traders of Bent, St. Vrain & Company were to stay south of that river, and the Bents were to buy all their supplies from, and sell all their furs to, Pratte, Chouteau & Company. The ink was hardly dry on the agreement when William Bent violated it, being caught by the bourgeois (manager) of Fort Laramie in the act of luring sixty lodges of Northern Cheyennes to the South Platte with three wagon-loads of liquor. Bent also made offers of employment to traders of the other company. For this sly and unscrupulous act he was apparently forgiven; the agreement with the Chouteau company remained in force until Bent, St. Vrain & Company went out of business ten years later.[5]

The mainstay of the Bents' Indian trade were the Cheyennes, whose friendship William Bent had secured in 1837 by marrying a Cheyenne chief's daughter. He took the marriage seriously;

when his first wife died, he married her sister, in accordance with Cheyenne custom. Bent's intimacy with the Cheyennes doubtless worked to his disadvantage with other tribes, especially the Comanches, Utes, Shoshones, and Kiowas, who were all enemies of the Cheyennes. During the summer of 1840, the Cheyennes and Arapahos made peace with the Comanches and Kiowas. This event, long desired by the Bents, more than doubled the number of Indians the Bents traded with and the number of robes they sent back east. In 1842, Bent traders John Hatcher and Robert Fisher built a log post on the South Canadian River among the Kiowas and Comanches. In the winter of 1845-46, the log post was succeeded by an adobe one a few miles down the river, the ruins of which later became famous as "Adobe Walls."[6]

Bent, St. Vrain & Company had other interests. Charles Beaubien kept a store for them at Taos under the direction of Charles Bent and Ceran St. Vrain, both of whom lived with their families in that town. From Taos they made yearly and sometimes twice-yearly trips to Missouri for goods, usually taking their wagons via Raton Pass and Bent's Fort. Many other Santa Fe traders followed their route, patronizing the Bent's Fort store and other facilities, and adding to the growing profits of the business. By 1843, Charles Bent had acquired an interest in three large Mexican land grants: The Vigil and St. Vrain Grant including much of the land south of the Arkansas and east of the mountains in present Colorado; the Beaubien and Lee, or Sangre de Cristo Grant, including a large part of the San Luis Valley; and the Beaubien and Miranda, or Maxwell Grant, including a large part of northeastern New Mexico. On the latter grant Charles Bent put a herd of cattle and attempted to start settlements, which, had they not failed, might eventually have made him a land baron on the scale of the mighty hacendados of Mexico.[7]

By 1842 Bent's Fort reigned supreme in the Arkansas Valley. Competing posts were so short-lived that almost no records of them remain. The only one to survive in the literature of the period was Fort Leche, a peculiar little fort and settlement located a scant five miles upstream from Bent's Fort in the summer of 1839. It called itself "Fort Independence," but it was known locally as "Fort Leche" or "Milk Fort" (because the inhabitants drank goat's milk) or simply as "El Pueblo," meaning "the town." Visitors described it as a hollow square of adobe enclosing about thirty whitewashed rooms, where ex-trappers and Mexicans lived with their families. They kept all sorts of animals—dogs, burros, goats, cats, tame raccoons, tame antelope, tame buffalo calves—as well as horses and mules which they drove into the courtyard at night to share a fitful slumber with the inhabitants. The men of the settlement made a marginal living by hunting, trading with Indians, and growing a little corn in an irrigated field near the fort. They imported their flour and whiskey from Taos. Indeed, it was a superabundance of the latter article to which one traveler attributed the failure of the settlement. By 1840 or 1841 Fort Leche was gone, levelled, forgotten. No later travelers mention seeing even the ruins of it, indicating that it was built not of honest adobe brick but of jacal, a specious substitute of poles and intertwined twigs plastered with mud. Fort Leche was the first *settlement* on the Arkansas. To some of the men at Bent's Fort, it looked like a good idea, badly executed. Three years later the concept would appear again, in another "Pueblo."[8]

Bent's Fort was at the height of power and importance when George Simpson wintered there. He was one of between twenty and a hundred employees, depending upon the season. Fifteen or twenty men accompanied the wagons back east with peltry in April, returning in July or August with goods. Eight more were constantly employed in hunting buffalo, which ranged fifteen to thirty miles east and north at this time, and a few years later as far as a hundred and fifty miles from the fort. A horse-guard opened the corral gate every morning, freeing eighty to a hundred horses and mules to graze under the alert eyes of the sentries until sundown, when they were driven back into the corral.[9]

Inside the fort was a retinue of domestic employees as varied and exotic in this wilderness as a collection of orchids. Fat, jolly Josefa (called Josie or Chepita) Tafoya of Taos was the housekeeper, laundress, candlemaker, midwife, and social hostess at balls and taffy-pulls. Her husband, Ben Ryder, was a Pennsylvania carpenter whose principal duty was the repair of wagons. The cook was a Negro named Andrew Green, whose brother Dick was Charles Bent's personal servant. By 1844 Chepita and Ben Ryder had left, and Dick's black wife Charlotte succeeded Andrew as cook, proclaiming herself "de onlee lady in de dam

Charles Bent. This painting was done at St. Louis in 1844. It hung for years in the Taos home of Bent's daughter, Teresina Scheurich. A copy was made from the original for the New Mexico State Capitol, from which this photograph was made in the early 1900's. Courtesy of Pioneers' Museum, Colorado Springs.

Injun country." In the early forties the blacksmith was also a
Negro; the tailor was a Frenchman from New Orleans; the
muleteers were Mexicans from Taos; and all around the courtyard strutted the Indian wives of the occupants, "in all the pride
of beads and fofarrow, jingling with bells and bugles, and happy
as paint can make them," adding to the Babel of tongues and the
spectrum of human complexions.[10]

As George Simpson soon discovered, the heart of the great
fort was the Indian trade, and its arteries were the traders,
whose traits combined the tact of an ambassador with the nerves
of a lion-tamer. Accompanying these traders, Simpson went out
to Indian camps with wagonloads of goods and learned the business.[11] The best of the Bent traders were men of strong character. Robert Fisher, the solid, serious man who had brought
Simpson to Bent's Fort, was, in Simpson's words, "simple
minded and honorable in his dealings, but obstinate and com-
bative when roused to anger."[12] Born in Virginia in 1807, Fisher
had come to New Mexico by 1824. He was living in Taos when
Ceran St. Vrain took pack mules with supplies to the Arkansas to
build the picket post in late 1832, and he may have been along
on that trip. He was present at William Bent's 1834 attack on
the Shoshones, and had worked for the Bents ever since.
Fisher's frequent companion was John Hatcher, small, lively,
good-natured and talkative; together they opened the post
among the Kiowas and Comanches on the South Canadian River.
One of the Bent's best Cheyenne traders was John Simpson
Smith. He was a small, well-educated man, a brilliant linguist
and interpreter for treaty councils, but his character was soured
with a streak of bitterness and cynicism. William LeGuerrier or
Guerrier (called "Bill Garey") was from St. Louis and, like John
Smith, he had a Cheyenne family. He was as illiterate as his Indian wife, but an honest and successful trader. Lucien Maxwell,
from a French-Louisiana family of Kaskaskia, Illinois, was a dark
and stocky young man of withdrawn and almost sullen disposition. In the early forties, Maxwell traded with the Arapahos near
Fort St. Vrain, spending much of his time at Taos with his wife,
the daughter of the Bents' Taos storekeeper, Charles Beaubien.
William Tharp of St. Louis was another Cheyenne trader and a
first cousin of Ceran St. Vrain.[13]

In varying degrees all these Bent men were connected with
George Simpson in years to come, but none so closely as Joseph

Doyle and Alexander Barclay. Doyle, originally a Virginian and a few years older than Simpson, had begun working as a trader for the Bents by at least 1839. Barclay, a well-educated Englishman, had been bookkeeper and storekeeper for the Bents since 1838. Both Doyle and Barclay had spent several years in St. Louis before coming West, where it is possible they knew Simpson. But it was not until the winter of 1841–42 that their three lives began to intersect, and before long they would be woven together like a braid.

Occasionally there were trappers at the fort, trading otter, beaver, bear, and muskrat skins to the Bents in return for guns, powder, lead, traps, goods, provisions, and whiskey. One party of trappers, some of whom Simpson had met at Fort Laramie in early summer, arrived at the fort from the mountains in the fall of 1841. Among them were Levin ("Colorado") Mitchell, Bill New, Kit Carson, Frederick (a Swiss trader with the Crow Indians) and a Shoshone named Cut-nose. On the Arkansas a hundred miles above Bent's Fort, Mitchell and New had been stripped by Indians of everything they owned and had arrived at the fort ten days later as naked as plucked chickens. Mitchell and Carson were hired for the winter as hunters for the fort, but the others probably drifted back to the mountains.[14]

Bent's Fort was not primarily a trappers' rendezvous; its principal business was not in beaver pelts but in buffalo robes. Before Bent's Fort was built, the fur trade centered on the Upper Missouri. Every year between 1815 and 1830, about 26,000 buffalo robes and 24,000 beaver pelts were sent to market from Missouri River trading posts. Before the price of beaver fell in the early 1830's a pack of beaver skins weighing a hundred pounds consisted of sixty to eighty skins and was worth $400; a pack of ten buffalo robes weighing the same was worth only $30. Traders on the Upper Missouri packed their St. Louis-bound boats with beaver, filling any empty spaces with the less valuable buffalo robes. Until John Gantt arrived on the Arkansas, there was no organized trade with the Cheyennes, Arapahos, Kiowas, Comanches and other Plains Indians, for their only product was buffalo robes.[15]

When John Gantt first came up the Platte River to trap on the Missouri in 1831, the situation was changing. As eastern and European markets finally became saturated with beaver, the price began to fall. At the same time, demand for buffalo robes

Bent's Fort in 1844–45, drawn from memory by Will Boggs sixty years later. The sketch shows the following features of the fort: the billiard room on the roof of William Bent's rooms; Ceran St. Vrain's room on the roof of the dining hall and kitchen; the stair or ladder leading to these rooftop rooms; the large stone warehouse for goods and robes; the corral on two sides; and a small porthole where liquor was passed through to Indians outside (this trade stopped in 1844, Boggs says). To the right or north of the fort was an oval Indian race track, and in the lower righthand corner an old Indian burial scaffold. Courtesy of Pioneers' Museum, Colorado Springs.

increased, along with their value. When the Bents built their adobe post, buffalo robes were worth $5 to $6 apiece in St. Louis, and the Bents' business grew steadily. At the picket post in 1834 they employed twenty-nine traders and held trade goods worth $3,877.28 by invoice. At the adobe post in 1838 they employed thirty-one traders and held $11,888.05 worth of goods. By 1842 they employed fifty-four traders and carried $12,169 worth of goods; their returns that year were eleven hundred packs of buffalo robes, almost five hundred packs of beaver, muskrat and otter, and over three hundred buffalo tongues for eastern dinner tables.[16]

The winter of 1841–42 was the best the Bents ever had. The Indians made so many robes that there were not enough wagons to take them to market. All hands were set to making bull-boats (great baskets of bent saplings covered with buffalo-bull hides) to float the furs at least part way down the Arkansas. Alexander Barclay was in charge of the bull-boat navy from Bent's Fort. From Fort St. Vrain, more bull-boats with surplus furs were sent down the South Platte in charge of Baptiste Charbonneau. Even such light craft as bull-boats, drawing only a few inches of water, were unable to navigate either the Arkansas or the South Platte. Somewhere in western Kansas the boats from Bent's Fort scraped the sandy bottom of the Arkansas and finally stuck fast in the river bed. Barclay ordered the men to unload the furs and guard them on shore, while he went on to St. Louis to report the misadventure. On the South Platte the same thing happened. Baptiste Charbonneau unloaded his stranded furs on an island where he and his men camped for the summer.[17]

As a consequence, buffalo robes were too scarce that year to meet the demands of fur buyers in St. Louis. And in the West there was a shortage of trade goods because a steamboat had sunk in the Missouri River near Independence with $80,000 worth of goods, or one-third of the fall outfit for the entire Indian country. Furthermore, the spring of 1842 saw the height of a depression which had ruined merchants in Missouri. Fur traders in the West were also going bankrupt. Lancaster Lupton sold his Fort Platte on the North Platte River and his Fort Lancaster on the South Platte, and was hired by his creditors, Hiram Rich and Albert Wilson, as manager of Fort Lancaster. Lock and Randolph abandoned nearby Fort Vasquez in the same year, and its former owners, Andrew Sublette and Louis Vasquez, gave up their sinking business and left the mountains.[18]

Sublette was probably reluctant to leave. His brother William wrote in the fall of 1842, "there is now the greatest opening I have ever seen as peltries of all description is plenty and cheap—for want of goods . . . the prettiest opening in the Indian trade that a man could wish, and if I had of had the wherewith you would have seen me on the headwaters of the Platte this winter . . . ."[19]

Furs were plenty, goods scarce, and competition light. If Sublette did not have the "wherewith," young George Simpson did, through the generosity of his indulgent parents. Even before Sublette wrote these words, there was a new trading post at the mouth of the Fountain, ready to take advantage of that "prettiest opening."

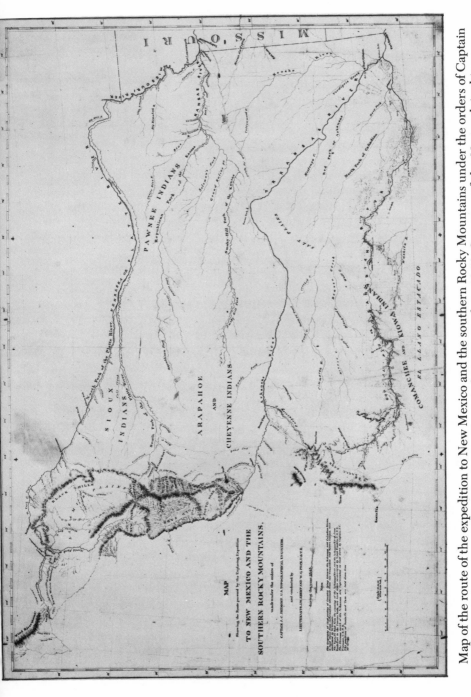

Map of the route of the expedition to New Mexico and the southern Rocky Mountains under the orders of Captain J. C. Frémont conducted by J. W. Abert and W. G. Peck in 1845. Courtesy of the National Archives.

3
The Mouth
of the Fountain

JUAN DE ULIBARRI, a Spaniard from Santa Fe who visited the mouth of the Fountain in 1706, wrote in his journal that the Napestle (as all the Indians called the Arkansas River) was more than four times as large as the Río del Norte and bathed the best and broadest valley yet discovered in New Spain. The land was extremely fertile, he wrote, with beautiful open stretches abounding in cottonwoods, plums, cherries, and wild grapes.[1]

In 1820 an American exploring expedition under Major Stephen H. Long camped near the very place where Juan de Ulibarri had crossed the Arkansas, a few miles above the mouth of the Fountain. Major Long's journalist described the Arkansas river bottom as beautiful, but he thought the scenery around it was "dreary and disgusting," a desolate plain covered with withered grasses. Long's journalist dismissed the region as wholly unfit for cultivation and uninhabitable.[2]

These two descriptions of the Arkansas Valley reflect the backgrounds and experiences of the men who wrote them. Juan de Ulibarri came from a land at least as arid as the Arkansas Valley, where rainfall was stored, and river water was diverted from its channel to irrigate cultivated fields; where timber was scarce and had to be hauled from the mountains; where houses were made of mud bricks dried in the sun. To the Spaniard the Arkansas Valley was the best land he had ever seen. In his mind's eye he could picture an irrigated garden extending along the banks of the Arkansas for hundreds of miles. Major Long, on the other hand, came from a country where fields had to be cleared of timber, where houses and fences were made of logs, where rivers flowed deep and strong, and where rain was as dependable as sunrise. Major Long saw the Great Plains as "a barrier to prevent too great an expansion of our population westward," and on his map he located the Arkansas Valley in a region labeled "Great American Desert."[3]

It was Ulibarri's vision, not the American's, that became a prophecy fulfilled.

The junction of Fountain Creek (*Fontaine qui bouille*) and the Arkansas at present Pueblo, Colorado, is a place of considerable geographic and historical interest. Puny though it may be, Fountain Creek is the Arkansas's largest tributary from its source in the high mountains near Leadville, Colorado to a point halfway across Kansas, a distance of 550 miles. The land around the junction of these rivers is flat and barren, but close by the Rocky Mountains soar a mile into the sky and bring a thousand miles of Great Plains to an abrupt and breathtaking end. The mountains are immutable, yet ever changing; their patches of aspen greening in spring, bronzing in autumn, and graying in winter; their slopes coated a brilliant white after a snowstorm; their summits crimson in the dawn. But for all their splendor, the mountains near Pueblo were only a backdrop for the drama acted out on the bleached plains below.

The Arkansas and Fountain rivers are shallow streams bordered with rushes and coarse grass, thinly timbered with cottonwoods and willows, hemmed in by barren bluffs of sandy loam. Beyond the bluffs to the west is an expanse of almost naked sand, leading to foothills dotted with dwarfed piñon, scrub oak and pine. To the east are the arid beginnings of the Great Plains, gouged by deep gullies and covered with sparse clumps of grass, sage, and greasewood, yucca and prickly pear; prairie dog towns and anthills, jackrabbits, horned toads, and rattlesnakes.

The Arkansas River and its tributaries are torrents at their mountain sources. When they reach the plains they slow down and begin to deposit pebbles and sand. As they continue to lose momentum, the streams meander and form islands in ever wider and shallower beds. In dry years the water sinks into the river beds and disappears altogether for miles at a stretch. The Arkansas River sometimes vanishes at Garden City, Kansas, where its sandy bed is over a thousand feet wide. Forty miles east, at present Dodge City, is the ancient ford of the Arkansas, where travelers from Francisco Vásquez de Coronado to the Santa Fe

Fountain Creek, or *Fountaine qui bouille,* near its junction with the
Arkansas. Major Long found it "dreary and disgusting," but an earlier
Spanish visitor thought it "the best and broadest valley in New Spain."
Photograph: Myron Wood, Colorado Springs.

Railroad's *Super Chief* have made safe and easy crossings. Between Garden City and Dodge City were other fords, including the Cimarron Crossing made famous by Santa Fe traders.

The average annual rainfall at Pueblo is between eleven and twelve inches. In a good year, when the rain falls at proper intervals, there is enough moisture to grow a little corn or winter wheat, and not much else. There are many years when the "average annual rainfall" does not fall when needed, or in the amounts required, as manifested by the abandoned dryland farms with broken windmills, collapsing farmhouses, and rusted machinery buried in dust blown from stubbled fields.

But, spread the waters of the river over the bottoms and uplands, and the Arkansas Valley springs to verdant life. At one time the Arkansas Valley of Colorado had about eight hundred irrigation systems. Some of the ditches were seventy feet wide and a hundred miles long, extending out from the river as far as twenty miles. These ditches watered over four thousand farms, producing wheat, oats, alfalfa, seed-flowers, sugar beets, garden vegetables, and tree fruits. In recent years the amount of water appropriated for irrigation purposes has decreased, and so has the number of farms. But crops still mature quickly in the high, thin atmosphere, and Arkansas Valley fruits and vegetables are still noted for their flavor.

The prairie also has its uses. The mouth of the Fountain is the western limit of the short-grass country, where foot-high gramma grass sends up oblong shoots like little brown flags, and curly buffalo grass grows in clumps only three to five inches high. For all their sparse and dry appearance, these short grasses provide more reliable pasture than the tall, thick prairie grasses of Minnesota, Iowa, and Missouri. The water-filled stems of the eastern grasses freeze in autumn and fall flat to the ground, useless as forage. Short grasses cure in the August sun and retain their strength and nutrition all through the winter.

Moisture that makes grass thick and tall in the Mississippi Valley also causes greater snowfall. Close to the mountains, snow is light and infrequent. When the winter sun radiates through the thin air, or a warm west "chinook" wind rushes down the mountain slopes, snow quickly disappears. At the foot of the mountains in Colorado, winter is dry, and days are warm when the sun shines, even if nights are cold. To men from the miasmas of the Mississippi Valley, the rigorous winters of New England, or the cheerless leaden skies of the Great Lakes region, the sunny climate at the mouth of the Fountain was a delight. So was the high level of health maintained by both men and beasts, in an era when good health was not taken for granted.[4]

What prehistoric people lived at the mouth of the Fountain has not been determined. The journals of the first white men in the region mention no Indian villages and few buffalo, for the great herds of buffalo grazed on the more abundant grass to the east and northeast. Moreover, the mouth of the Fountain is deep in a pocket, shut in on three sides by timbered elevations. To the south are the high, eastward-stretching mesas of the Raton Mountains; directly west are the formidable barriers of the Front Range and Wet Mountains, separated by the deep and narrow Royal Gorge of the Arkansas; to the north is the Platte-Arkansas Divide, a pine-forested ridge extending eastward onto the plains for twenty-five miles. It was a trap, and buffalo avoided it; so did Indians. They stayed out on the open plains, where grass was thicker, the Arkansas was easier to ford, and paths were level and direct.[5]

Consequently, the earliest Spaniards—looking for the kind of gold-plated civilizations found by Cortez and Pizarro—ended up not at the mouth of the Fountain but at Indian villages far east of the mountains, on the plains of western and central Kansas. In 1541 Coronado was led by his Indian guide to Quivira in central Kansas, an assemblage of grass huts of the Wichita Indians—who grew corn, beans, and squash; hunted buffalo on foot; and possessed, to the Spaniards' intense disappointment, not a single piece of gold. Fifty years later Francisco Leyva and Antonio de Humaña also found Quivira, and were killed somewhere beyond it—Leyva by Humaña, and Humaña by Indians. Their deaths without the last sacraments of the church supposedly gave the Purgatory a Spanish name, *El Río de Las Animas Perdidas en Purgatorio* (The River of Souls Lost in Purgatory), but evidence suggests that these particular souls left their earthly remains far east of the Purgatory.[6]

Don Juan de Oñate led a third expedition to Quivira in 1601 and established once and for all that there was no gold here. In 1609–10 Santa Fe was founded at the foot of the Sangre de Cristo Mountains in New Mexico. Later villages dotted the banks of the Rio Grande, cheek by jowl with the mud towns of the sedentary Pueblo Indians, who became vassals of the Spanish king and helped their Spanish neighbors fight off the constant attacks of nomadic Indians. Henceforth, Spanish expeditions to the Arkansas Valley were only for the defense of the tenuous settlements. Juan de Ulibarri went to the Arkansas in 1706 to bring back Pueblo Indians who had run away to Apache villages; Valverde's campaign of 1719 was to attack the nomadic Comanches, whom he failed to find; Villasur's campaign of 1720 was to locate French intruders, with whom he fought a battle on the River Platte disastrous to the Spaniards.[7]

Throughout the eighteenth century, Frenchmen from the Mississippi Valley pushed ever closer to the Spanish settlements. They established trading posts and arsenals among the Indians, even as far west as the Comanches, who had driven the Apaches south from the Arkansas Valley. About 1750 one group of traders from French Louisiana built a trading post at a Comanche village at the foot of the mountains on the "Río Case," to trade not only with Indians but also with Spaniards. The Spaniards arrested them and confiscated their goods, but freed them when their trading post was judged to have been located in French Louisiana, being east of the mountains and below the sources of the Arkansas.[8] This was perhaps the first trading post at the mouth of the Fountain.

In 1763 French Louisiana was ceded to Spain, and the French who lived and traded there became Spanish subjects, posing no threat to Santa Fe. Comanches, however, continued to harass New Mexican settlements. In 1779 Governor de Anza mustered over five hundred soldiers, marched to the Arkansas, and, at the foot of what is now Greenhorn Peak, killed the haughty Comanche chief Cuerno Verde and routed his forces. In 1787 Spanish workmen built a "house of poles" on the Arkansas for six hundred lodges of Jupes Comanches. The town was known as *San Carlos de los Jupes*, and was probably located six miles east of the Fountain at the mouth of the St. Charles River. After three months' residence there, the Comanches abandoned the town, but they remained at peace with the New Mexicans for sixty years afterwards.[9]

After the Louisiana Purchase in 1803, the Arkansas River was understood to be the international boundary between the United States and New Spain. Lieutenant Zebulon M. Pike was sent by the United States in 1806 to explore the new territory as far as the source of the Arkansas. On the Arkansas, opposite the mouth of the Fountain, Pike built a log breastwork. There his party camped for six days while their leader attempted and failed to reach the summit of the famous mountain named for him. Later Pike and his men were captured by Spaniards, taken to Mexico, and then sent home again. Pike's report, published in 1810, mentioned the scarcity of manufactured goods in Mexico and the abundance of mules. This sent merchants from the Missouri frontier scurrying to Santa Fe to trade goods for mules. Foreign trade was prohibited in Mexico, and most of these early Santa Fe traders were captured and imprisoned. In 1819 the Florida Convention between the United States and Spain firmly established the Arkansas River as the international boundary. That year the Spaniards built a fort in the Sangre de Cristo Pass on the headwaters of the Huerfano River, south of the Arkansas, to keep Americans out. The fort was attacked by Indians and abandoned before 1822.[10]

In 1821 New Mexico declared her independence of Spain, and threw open her borders to foreign commerce. In this year William Becknell and fellow-adventurers from Franklin, Missouri came up the Arkansas to trade for horses and mules with the Arapahos, as other groups of Missourians had done for the past decade. Finding no Indians, Becknell's men followed the Purgatory to Raton Pass, and over the pass to Santa Fe, where they found a ready market for their trade goods. Raton Pass was rocky, steep, and filled with bushes, and Becknell avoided it on his return to Missouri, going by the Cimarron River. Next year Becknell brought a wagon of goods over this level Cimarron route and, in doing so, established both the Santa Fe trail and the Santa Fe trade.[11]

Had he stayed on the Arkansas in 1821, Becknell would have found the Arapahos, who had pushed the Comanches out of the Arkansas Valley to the south and east. The Arapahos would have been eager for Becknell's trade. Their name meant "trader"; trade was their principal business and greatest joy. As the Santa Fe trade flourished in the early 1820's, white traders no longer came to the Arkansas, where the Arapahos languished, hungry for trade. In 1825, when William Ashley and his trappers appeared on the South Platte, sixty or seventy Arapaho warriors left the Arkansas in deep snow to pay him a visit, but only three

The Wah-to-yah or Spanish Peaks as sketched by Richard Kern in 1853 for E. G. Beckwith's Pacific Railway Survey *Report.* Courtesy of Denver Public Library Western Collection.

managed to get through. Shortly afterwards the Arapahos turned against white men, attacking trappers in the mountains and caravans on the Santa Fe trail.[12] What caused the hostility is unknown, but what brought peace again on the Arkansas was John Gantt's sweetened whiskey.

Whether from scarcity of Indians or excess of white traders, trading posts at the mouth of the Fountain did not prosper. John Gantt's adobe post brought peace with the Indians, but not success to its owner. Nor was William Bent's picket post a success, nor the wooden winter houses of Robert Newell, Lancaster Lupton, and Sarpy & Fraeb, which probably attracted as little Indian trade as they did contemporary mention. The future of the place lay in different directions—as a center for storage and shipment of furs and trade goods, as a depot for contraband liquor, as a home for traders' families, and as a location for farming and stockraising.

All that now remains of two and a half centuries of Spanish attempts to exploit the Arkansas Valley are a few dusty journals of expeditions; a few relics, like the fragment of chain mail found near Lindsborg, Kansas; and a few place names: *Sangre de Cristo* (blood of Christ) for the southern Rocky Mountains in Colorado and New Mexico, which, according to legend, glowed red in the dawn (or perhaps in the sunset) as de Anza (or perhaps Valverde) watched in pious awe; *Huerfano* (orphan), the little volcanic butte rising in isolation beside the river that borrowed its name; *Río de las animas perdidas en Purgatorio* —*Purgatoire* to the French, Purgatory to American traders, "Picketwire" to homesteaders; *Cuerno Verde* (Greenhorn) as a name for the peak and for the southern branch of the St. Charles River. Behind the *conquistadores* trudged the common folk, the soldiers and traders—who bestowed common names like *chico* (little), *cuchara* (spoon), *salado* (salty), *ratón* (mouse), *Sierra Mojada* (Wet Mountains). A few Indian names survive in the Arkansas Valley from Spanish times: *Huatolla*, Spanish spelling of a Comanche word meaning "breasts of the world," left untranslated by prudish Americans as "Wah-to-yah," or rejected in favor of "Spanish Peaks"; and *Apishapa*, a Ute or Comanche word meaning "stinking water." Three of the biggest rivers north of Santa Fe—*Río Napestle* (Arkansas), *Río Almagre (Fontaine qui bouille), and Río Chato* (South Platte)—lost their Indian and Spanish names and retained ones the French had given them, as if to emphasize the fact that although Indians and Spaniards were here first, men from the Mississippi Valley prevailed.

4
The Founders

SOMETIME DURING THE WINTER OF 1841–42 George Simpson and Robert Fisher met with other men and planned the Pueblo. Like Fort Leche, its inglorious precursor, the post would be owned not by a corporation, partnership, or single trader, but by a company of independent traders. Each trader would build, buy, or rent a house within its walls, where he might live with his wife and children, keep milk cows and chickens, cultivate a piece of land in the Arkansas bottom during the summer, and trade with Indians during the winter. The post would provide not only a means of livelihood but a way of life. Such was the vision of its founders.

When Bent traders left Bent's Fort for the east with their wagons in the spring of 1842, George Simpson sent with them an order of trade goods to be filled by his father in St. Louis and delivered on the Arkansas. By July or August, when the goods arrived, Simpson, Fisher, and their associates meant to have a fort built to receive them. In the meantime, Simpson and Fisher made the three-day trip to Taos on horseback. There Fisher married María Rumalda López on May 8, 1842, while Simpson presumably hired masons.[1] On their return from Taos they were joined by their associates, and they all began to build the post—or so we assume, for there is no record of it. Nor is there any record explaining how ownership of the fort was divided up among these original proprietors, or in what way they divested themselves of this interest, as they all seem to have done within a few years.

Who were Simpson's and Fisher's associates? According to Simpson's wife, their names were Mathew Kinkead, Francisco Conn, and Joseph Mantz. The latter can be disposed of forthwith, as the first of many unemployed trappers to make Pueblo a

35

stopover in their nomadic lives. By 1845 Mantz had drifted off and was heard of no more. But Mathew Kinkead and Francisco Conn cannot be dealt with in a few words, for they were men of importance in the history of the Arkansas Valley.[2]

Kinkead was not only a founder of Pueblo but also the first cattle rancher of the Great Plains and the first to bring white women there, in the persons of his beautiful wife and two charming stepdaughters. Yet he remains a shadowy figure, seldom referred to by others and never speaking for himself. His ranch on the Arkansas was begun in the summer of 1841, six miles above the mouth of the Fountain, but it attracted almost no contemporary notice. Even the Indians ignored it, perhaps because Kinkead persuaded them to leave him alone, for he had vast experience with Indians. He had, as well, an assortment of other skills learned in forty-six years on the frontiers of Kentucky, Missouri and New Mexico, and a gift for speculation that made most of his ventures profitable.[3]

Kinkead was born in Madison County, Kentucky, in 1795. As soon as the Kentucky backwoods began settling down to comfortable farms, the Kinkeads packed up and moved to a wilder land. Always on the savage edge of the frontier, Mathew's family and their Kentucky neighbors—Becknells, Turleys, Conns, and Carsons—gradually drifted west to the lush wilderness in central Missouri known as Boonslick. By 1812 five or six hundred Boonslick pioneers were scattered about the wooded countryside, and they were as tough as any people who ever lived. Surrounded by hostile Indians, they cleared their land, built cabins, shot game, grew corn and flax, made furniture and candles, spun wild nettles and wove fabrics, distilled whiskey, raised large families, praised the Lord, and taught their children to read. At the beginning of the War of 1812 the Kinkeads and their friends built Fort Kinkead, a stockade enclosing log cabins, where they lived for three years. During Indian attacks the fort was defended by twenty-nine men and boys, among them Mathew Kinkead, his father David, and his brother John.

After the war David Kinkead helped found the town of Franklin, Missouri, near Fort Kinkead, where in 1821 the Santa Fe trade began. By 1825, perhaps a year earlier, Mathew and John Kinkead brought goods to Santa Fe. Mathew sold his goods and became a partner in a distillery at Taos, where he lived for nine more years. During the winter of 1826–27 he earned his place in the many biographies of Kit Carson by sheltering that young runaway apprentice from Franklin.

In 1830 a thirty-year-old Missouri carpenter named Edmond Conn joined the brothers Kinkead at Taos. By now Mathew Kinkead was a naturalized citizen of Mexico, and he sponsored Conn's application for citizenship. When Conn was baptized a Roman Catholic in 1834, he took the name "Francisco" and so he was henceforth known in New Mexico.

In February, 1834 Kinkead and Conn applied for a grant of land in the lovely little valley at the headwaters of the Mora River in northeastern New Mexico. Even before the grant was made in 1835, Kinkead and Conn had moved there with several hundred other settlers from the Taos valley. They called their town *Santa Gertrudis de Mora*, or simply *Mora*. All of them promised to farm with guns in their hands, since there would be constant harassment from Indians.

At Taos or Mora, Kinkead met a young woman named Teresita Sandoval. Born at Taos in 1811 to Gervasio and Ramona (Barela) Sandoval, Teresita became the wife of Kinkead's neighbor at Mora, José Manuel Suaso. By 1835 they had four children; Juana María, aged seven; María de la Cruz, aged four; José Tomas, aged two; and baby Rufina. Teresita must have been a beautiful woman at twenty-four, for when she was over forty she was said to be "pretty as a peach." She was stubborn and hot-tempered, and as many men hated as loved her. But she was also intelligent and courageous, and willing to share the drudgery and terrors of a frontier life with her man—until a man she liked better turned up, as Kinkead did in the winter of 1835.[4]

On November 29, 1835 Teresita gave birth at Taos to a fifth child, who was baptized two days later as Juan Andrés Suaso, legitimate son of María Teresa Sandoval and José Manuel Suaso. Soon afterwards the little boy was known as the son of his real father and called Andrés or Andrew Kinkead. Teresita left Suaso to live with Kinkead, and a year later she bore Kinkead a daughter Rafaela. José Manuel Suaso sold his land in Mora in 1838 to Francisco Conn. By 1844 he had died, leaving Teresita free to marry again, but it is doubtful she ever did.[5]

On March 29, 1838 Mathew Kinkead sold his land and house in Mora for three hundred sheep and a yoke of oxen. He kept

Jesús Silva and "Uncle Dick" Wootton, 1885. Courtesy of the Museum of New Mexico, Santa Fe.

his undivided interest in the common pasture further down the
Mora River, where he continued to graze his sheep, and probably to make his home, until provoked by anti-American feelings
in New Mexico to go elsewhere.

Since the fall of 1840 rumors of an invading army from the
Republic of Texas had kept New Mexico in a state of nervous
apprehension. During the tense spring and summer of 1841 all
Americans, whether naturalized citizens or not, were suspected
of collaborating with the enemy. They were treated coldly and
subjected to various annoyances, threats, and even injuries.
Francisco Conn was told, when he complained of the quality of
local justice, that he could march his troubles off to the Supreme
Court in Mexico City. David Spaulding was charged an exorbi-
tant fee for a marriage license. American merchants in Santa Fe
wrote the United States Secretary of State that their lives and
property were in danger from an angry populace and the malice
of Governor Manuel Armijo. Mathew Kinkead and other Americans living on the exposed northeastern frontier of New Mexico
had reason to fear not only the New Mexicans but also the Texans, reported to be a desperate band of brigands.[6]

In the spring of 1841 Kinkead decided to move. He hired
Dick Wootton to take his sheep from the Mora Valley to
Westport (Kansas City) and trade them for milk cows. The latter
were to be delivered to Kinkead at the ranch on the Arkansas,
where he meant to establish a "buffalo farm."

In later years Dick Wootton claimed that buffalo farming was
his own idea. When he was a hunter for Bent's Fort, he came
across twin buffalo calves whose mother had been killed by the
hunters. The gentle little creatures followed him back to the
fort, where he put them to suck on a good-natured milk cow. As
his buffalo calves thrived, Dick got the notion of taming them
and selling them in the east to zoos or curiosity shows, or to rich
men who would exhibit them on their estates in this country and
Europe.[7]

Dick was a spinner of yarns. A tall, strong, boisterous lad from
Virginia, he had worked for the Bents since 1836 when he was
twenty years old, all the while dreaming of other projects for
making money. His autobiography, *"Uncle Dick" Wootton*, is an
account of his shrewd and imaginative, if not always profitable,
schemes, as well as a compendium of adventures which were
either products of that same imagination or actual events in the

life of somebody else. In his chapter entitled "Buffalo Farming" he appropriates the experiences of Mathew Kinkead as his own and never mentions Kinkead.

Despite his claim, Wootton was not the first to domesticate buffalo. For hundreds of years Indians and Mexicans had lassoed buffalo calves as they fell behind the herd during a hunt and taken them home to tame. The Aztec emperor Montezuma had a buffalo bull in his zoo in 1519. By 1832 experiments in New Mexico purported to show that tamed buffalo could draw a plow faster than oxen, and a man in Kentucky kept a pair of buffalo at his farm for crossbreeding with draft cattle to make a hardier stock. But Wootton was probably correct in saying that raising buffalo to sell had not been done before.[8]

By the fall of 1841 Mathew Kinkead's buffalo farm was in operation. Its site was a spot on the Arkansas six miles above the mouth of the Fountain. At this place the grassy, timbered bottom south of the river was a mile wide in the middle, protected by high bluffs and closed off at both ends by an abrupt narrowing of the bluffs, making the valley nearly cattle-tight. It was an outstanding natural corral, the very place cattleman Charles Goodnight established headquarters for his Rock Cañon Ranch twenty-odd years later. Kinkead and his hands built a large adobe barn sixteen to eighteen feet wide and three times that in length, and waited for Dick Wootton to return from the east with milk cows for the ranch or buffalo farm.[9]

Francisco Conn was probably Kinkead's partner and Dick Wootton his employee in the first year of the venture. Then or later Kinkead brought his wife Teresita to this wild and dangerous place. For several years Teresita accompanied Kinkead out on the plains in April or May with a few milk cows to steal newborn buffalo calves from their mothers. When the calves were a year old they were sent to the frontier settlements of Missouri, where they sold for $100 apiece. The buffalo farm on the Arkansas lasted until the fall of 1843, when Kinkead and Conn gave it up and moved again.

If Kinkead sold his forty-four yearling buffalo calves in the spring of 1842 for $100 apiece (the numbers are Wootton's), he had a gross profit of over $4000. A part of this capital probably went into the construction of the new trading post at the mouth of the Fountain.

John Brown. Portrait on the cover of his *Mediumistic Experiences of John Brown, the Medium of the Rockies* published in 1897.

Another builder, but not owner, of the fort was John Brown, who had spent the winter of 1841–42 at Lancaster Lupton's log post on the Fountain near the Arkansas. Lupton's post was probably abandoned in the spring of 1842. Brown then helped build the Pueblo, as he later wrote.[10]

There is no reason to doubt John Brown's statement. A different matter entirely is the similar claim of James P. Beckwourth in his ghostwritten autobiography published in 1856. This flamboyant mulatto mountain man was so famous a liar that one must resist the temptation to reject all his statements, for there is usually a grain of truth in them. Beckwourth was born in Virginia in 1798 and moved to St. Louis with his wealthy father and twenty-two Negro slaves. The autobiography does not reveal that both Jim and his mother numbered among the slaves. At St. Louis he was apprenticed to a blacksmith, but ran away to the mountains. For nearly twenty years he trapped and traded while living with the Crow Indians. In the fall of 1842 he went to Taos, married a woman he called Louise Sandeville in his book, and took her directly to the mouth of the Fountain.[11]

According to the autobiography, Beckwourth and his wife reached the Arkansas about the first of October, 1842. There they erected a trading post and began a successful business. Very shortly afterwards they were joined by fifteen to twenty free trappers and their families. Uniting their labors, they built an adobe fort sixty yards square. By the following spring the settlement had grown, and they named it Pueblo. Many of the men raised very good crops the first season, "such as wheat, corn, oats, potatoes and abundance of almost all kinds of vegetables."[12]

The fact is, Beckwourth did not build either a trading post or an adobe fort in October, 1842. By October the Pueblo had already been in existence several months. Nor was the fort sixty yards square, which would have made it one of the largest in the West. Nor could Beckwourth have known how the crops matured the following summer, for he left in the spring of 1843 not to return for three years. Behind him at Pueblo he left his wife and apparently a daughter Matilda as hostages to the truth of his story that he was ever there at all. His wife's name was Luisa Sandoval, but church records of Taos show no marriage between them. During Jim's absence, according to his autobiography, another man brought Luisa a forged letter purporting to be from Jim declaring that he no longer cared for her and releasing her

James P. Beckwourth. Courtesy of Denver Public Library Western Collection.

from marital obligations toward him. Luisa married the other man, probably in the same informal way she had married Jim. On Jim's return she regretted her new marriage and offered herself back. The gallant Jim declined. When Jim's book containing this unpleasant story was published in 1856, Luisa and her husband—none other than John Brown—were living comfortably in California with their ten children. If John and Luisa Brown could have denied the story, they never did so publicly, perhaps because it had a grain of truth in it.[13]

Luisa Sandoval, then, was one of the first white women in the upper Arkansas Valley. So were Rumalda López Fisher and Teresita Sandoval Suaso and her daughters. Juana Suaso, the eldest, was not to be a child much longer. By November, 1842, a month before her fifteenth birthday, she was married to George Simpson. Two years later her sister Cruz married Joe Doyle, fusing many Anglo-American and Mexican elements in the Arkansas Valley settlements.

These women and others were the justification for the villages. Without them Pueblo, Hardscrabble, and Greenhorn would have been mere trading posts where men led half-lives, separated from the emotional security and domestic enjoyment of their families. The site and architecture of the various structures were chosen with the convenience of the women in mind. Social customs and culture were derived principally from the distaff side. Trading, hunting, and farming methods of the men were influenced by their women. This was the way of life envisioned by the founders, as they sought a stability and continuity as yet unknown in the Rocky Mountain West.

5
The Arkansas Pueblo

THE FIRST CONSIDERATION in the location of a trading post was access to customers, markets, and sources of supply. At the mouth of the Fountain a variety of Indian customers were no more than a few days away. The post was located on lands claimed by Arapahos and close to Ute camps in the mountains and Cheyenne camps at Big Timber down the Arkansas. It was the nearest point in United States territory to the village of Taos, which would furnish not only more customers but also flour and whiskey as trade items. For taking furs to market and bringing back trade goods, there was a fine, level wagon road down the Arkansas and along the Santa Fe trail to Westport (now Kansas City), whence steamboats ran regularly on the Missouri River to St. Louis. Many trails joined at the mouth of the Fountain—trails east to the United States, south to the Mexican settlements, and north to the trading posts on the South Platte and beyond. To be sure, there was a flaw in the location that would in the end prove fatal to the development of the fort and to the Arkansas Valley, for the mountains to the West were an unbreachable barrier. But in 1842 who would have dreamed that the site should have been on a direct route to the Pacific Ocean?

In locating the post, the founders looked for a spot near the three indispensable needs of dwellers of the prairie:—grass for animals, wood for fires, water for man and beast. For cooking, cleaning, and clothes washing, the fort had to be close to the river, because there was to be no well within its walls. For the convenience of travelers it had to be near the principal ford of the Arkansas. The gravel-bottomed ford was at the top, or north, extremity of a sharp meander of the Arkansas, half a mile west of Fountain Creek. The founders put their fort on the northwest side of this meander, about two hundred yards from the bank of the river and the same distance southwest of the ford.[1]

Once the site was marked, the men dug foundation trenches, and the Mexican masons made adobe bricks of clay. The bricks were puddled with a binder of dried and chopped grass. As the adobe mixture became the consistency of mortar, the masons packed it into wooden frames, leveled off the top, and emptied the bricks onto the ground to dry in the sun. The bricks were of no standard size (those at Bent's Fort were eighteen inches long, nine inches wide, and four inches thick), and each mason could make about two hundred and fifty a day. Using mortar of the same puddled mud, the masons laid the bricks up thicker at the bottom to allow for ground-level erosion. Like all adobe buildings, the walls of Pueblo had an inward lean, unnerving to the easterner from the land of plumb lines and proudly perpendicular walls. Women finished the wall with a coat of adobe, spreading the mixture with the palms of their hands.[2]

According to George F. Ruxton, who spent several months in and around Pueblo in 1847, no part of its walls were higher than eight feet. A resident of the fort said that the top of the wall was no higher than the roofs of the houses built inside it. Francis Parkman described a line of slender wooden pickets strung along the top of the wall, which by 1846 were half broken down. As a further defense measure there were two round, portholed bastions at the northeast and southwest corners of the building. In other forts, bastions were four or five feet higher than the walls, but, as Ruxton indicated, Pueblo's bastions were no more than eight feet high.[3]

Facing the river on the east side of the fort was a gate, which by 1846 "dangled on its wooden hinges so loosely, that to open or shut it seemed likely to fling it down altogether," as Parkman wrote. This creaky affair had two doors made of double layers of strong planks—probably of cottonwood cut on the site, a miserable building material which shrank, warped, and splintered. Later buildings on the Arkansas used pine, even though the logs had to be hauled from the mountains. The gate was at least six feet wide, to admit wagons, and it was the sole entrance to the *placita*, or courtyard.[4]

Like most structures used for defense against primitive weapons, the Pueblo was a quadrangle with houses built against an exterior wall and a gate to close the enemy out and the horses in. Its contemporaries called it a "small" fort. Its exact dimensions are unknown and probably unknowable, for its foundations have been washed away by flood or destroyed in excavations for other buildings in the modern city of Pueblo.[5] A frequently published picture of the Pueblo, drawn by a commercial artist in the east about 1880, shows the fort with a high, portholed, castellated wall. The picture is

Model of the Pueblo, El Pueblo Museum, Pueblo, Colorado. Reconstructed from the same evidence used in this book, but with different details, especially in the bastions and gates, and with different proportions than the evidence would seem to indicate. Courtesy of the State Historical Society of Colorado Library, Denver.

entirely fanciful; the walls of Pueblo were neither portholed nor castellated.[6] Nor in general was the post well suited for defense. The walls were too low for protection against a concerted attack, and there was no well to provide water in case of siege. The founders of the fort apparently had little expectation of attack. During Pueblo's years as a fur trading post, its architecture justified its builders' faith, for it was never threatened. When it was finally captured in 1854, neither battlements nor portholes would have saved the occupants, who simply threw open the gate and invited the enemy in.

The Pueblo was less a fort than a typical New Mexican country house, built as a center for agriculture and husbandry, and for family life. The *placita* had many uses. It served as a pen for hogs and poultry, and for larger animals in an emergency. It stored the little wagons and carts that carried traders' goods to Indian camps and sometimes the traders' big Conestoga wagons that hauled robes to market. When the weather was good, business was probably conducted in the *placita*, and goods exchanged in the bright sunlight instead of in the dark little rooms. The *placita* undoubtedly contained a big adobe oven shaped like a beehive (*horno*), where women baked bread, parched corn, and burned lime for whitewash while their children played amidst the rich odor of animals and manure. In the winter the *placita* was a sun trap where one might sit comfortably out of the wind, leaning against a warm adobe wall.

Lining the *placita* were rooms or "houses." There is no agreement as to how many rooms there were, nor what proportion of them were public or private.[7] Forts owned by a single company had large storage rooms or warehouses, trade rooms, parlors, dining halls, and kitchens for common use, but Pueblo traders lived with their families in their own houses, where they did their cooking, eating, sleeping, and trading. One communal room was the blacksmith shop. The forge and anvil were in a room with a door, instead of in the open under a shed roof as in other *placitas*. The blacksmith shop was primitive, or its blacksmith was far from the master of his trade, for Alexander Barclay's diary shows that the inhabitants went to Bent's Fort for repairs on their wagons, plows, and guns. By 1847 John Hawkins, nephew of the inventor of the Hawken rifle and an expert gunsmith, lived at Pueblo and solved the gun repair problem.[8] Other common facilities were the bastions (where firearms and ammunition were kept), chicken coops, corncribs, irrigation ditches, and the corral.

In large posts the corral was outside the main wall and had its own gate. At Pueblo the corral occupied the southeast portion of the *placita*, and was made of pickets or logs set upright. Horses and mules were driven into the *placita* through the main gate and then into the corral, where their odors, flies, and fearful night whinneyings were shared by the inhabitants.[9]

The houses were probably not all constructed at the same time or of the same material. The earliest rooms were of adobe and were built against the outer wall as soon as it was completed. There was at least one log room as well. Doorways were narrow and so low that a man had to stoop to enter. Doors were made of cottonwood planks, which by 1847 had warped and shrunk so badly that one could see

"Old Adobe Fort." An illustration in George Rex Buckman's article on Pueblo in *Lippincott's Magazine* (December, 1800) bearing very little resemblance to the actual fort. Courtesy of Denver Public Library Western Collection.

into the rooms through the cracks. The sill was probably six inches off the ground, to keep water out. Some of the rooms may have had tiny windows ("little bigger than the ventilator of a summer hat," said George F. Ruxton of the typical adobe house). Bent's Fort had glass panes in some of its windows, but most other adobe houses had windows with panes of selenite or mica. Pueblo, being a "rude" fort, may have had only wooden shutters inside the rooms to close the openings, or no openings at all.[10]

The floors of the rooms were not of wood. In all New Mexico at this time there were said to be only two plank-floored rooms. Wooden planks and beams were hand-hewn and so valuable that they were

bequeathed in wills and made a prominent part of real estate transactions. At the Pueblo floors were native soil stripped of grass and
spread with a layer of adobe. Floors were sprinkled with water two
or three times a day, and swept until they were as hard and dustless
as concrete. Coverings on the floors may have been cowhides,
bearskins, or the rough New Mexican homespun called *jerga*.[11]

Inside walls were plastered with adobe by the women and
whitewashed with *jaspe*, a compound of selenite burned in the oven,
mixed with water, then spread on the walls with bare hands, and
brushed with pieces of sheep skin. The whitewash rubbed off freely;
to keep it from powdering everything in the room, the lower half of
the wall may have been covered with brightly colored calico, as was
common in better New Mexican houses. In a corner, raised on a low
hearth, was the little fireplace with its quarter-round hood, against
the back of which sticks of wood were leaned together to burn
quietly and frugally. The narrow flue was lined with thin adobe
bricks. Many charred vigas and roof sheathings of old New Mexican
houses show that flue fires were common, but they were seldom
dangerous because of the fireproof sod or adobe roof. The chimney
rose above the roof by only a few courses of adobe brick or rocks and
was topped with an old *olla* (a pottery water jar) with the bottom
broken out.[12]

The ceiling was supported by vigas or pared logs, whose ends
protruded from the front walls of the houses and were used to hang
strings of chili peppers and bundles of many-colored Indian corn.
On top of the vigas was a layer of peeled saplings covered with a foot
of adobe. The roofs were inclined slightly to promote runoff, or were
drained by short wooden troughs extending beyond the walls to
prevent a steady stream of water from digging a trench down the
walls of the house. Perhaps at Pueblo as at other Arkansas Valley
settlements the roof was used to plant vegetables, safe from the
trampling of horses and the inroads of rabbits. It was also used for
drying strips of venison out of reach of dogs and other carnivores.[13]

The rooms were small, limited in width to the length of the vigas,
which was ten to fifteen feet. A room could accommodate an entire
family because there was little furniture. Food was served on pon-
chos spread on the floor. The men sat on folded buffalo robes and
were served by the women, who ate later. In the center of the
poncho would be an earthen bowl containing soup, a thin mush
called *atole*, or a more solid mixture of beans, meat, corn, onions and
chili peppers. Each man would dip into the bowl with a tortilla

"A Mexican Ranch." This country house resembles the Pueblo more than the imaginary fortification pictured in "Old Adobe Fort" above. From Colonel Henry Inman, *The Old Santa Fe Trail* (1897).

doubled between his fingers, and cut meat from the roast with his hunting knife.[14]

During the day the women chatted together and smoked their *cigarillos* seated cross-legged on the floor. Who needed forks or plates, tables or chairs? There were no bedsteads at Pueblo, or in almost any other New Mexican house before the American invasion. The family slept on the floor on buffalo robes or on thin wool mattresses (*colchones*) brought from New Mexico. In the daytime the *colchones* were rolled up against the wall and covered with a piece of *manta* or printed muslin to form a comfortable settee. On warm summer nights *colchones* were probably spread outdoors under the stars, as they were at Greenhorn in 1853.[15]

Clothing and other possessions, as well as the trader's stock of goods, were kept in chests and boxes ranged around the walls. Near the little fireplace were a few cooking tools, baskets, pottery vessels and water jars, perhaps an iron skillet and kettle, and a trivet to hold the pot over the coals. In the corner would be a metate for grinding corn, a hen sitting on a nest, a cat, or the family dog. On the walls hung strings of the dried chili peppers and onions which went into every meal, as well as the trader's powder horn, extra rifle, and "possibles sack" in which he kept the little necessities of a journey. Propped up by the door was a broom, a good stout stick with a bunch of dried gramma grass bound to the end.[16]

Such rooms could be kept clean and comfortable. Whitewashing was applied to the walls frequently, as was a new layer of adobe to the floors. Though dark, the rooms were as cheerful and bright as color could make them, with calicos and *manta*, gaudy pictures of saints, and tin-framed mirrors against the white walls. Perhaps there were strips of *manta* stretched under the vigas as a false ceiling to catch the dust filtering down from the adobe roof.[17]

How much did the fort cost to build? In materials, practically nothing, for everything was made from what the plains and mountains furnished free. As for labor, how much is a man's time worth when he is building his own house? Mexican laborers, called peons, were paid a maximum of $10 per month. If the fort took two months for ten peons to build, $200 in goods at the highly inflated "mountain prices" would cover their wages. The fort or rooms inside it changed hands occasionally, but the prices are never quoted. After comparing the size and crudity of the Pueblo with other posts of the period whose market values are recorded, the owners should have accepted an offer of a few thousand dollars for it with gratitude.[18]

The earliest name for the trading post was Pueblo. The word means "town" in Spanish; in New Mexico it often referred specifically to the permanent Indian villages whose pinkish-brown adobe walls rose from the river bottoms and mesa tops as though they had grown from them. Perhaps the founders were thinking of these indigenous villages when they named their fort. Sometimes the fort was called "the Arkansas Pueblo," or "Pueblo Almagre" in reference to "Rio Almagre," the Spanish name for Fountain Creek. At least once Pueblo was called "Pueblo Colorado" (both *almagre* and *colorado* mean a dirty shade of red).[19]

"Fort Pueblo," with its ambiguous translation of "fort town," was an invention not of the Spanish-speaking people who lived there but of visitors. When soldiers and emigrants poured into the West in 1846, some of them picked up the misnomer. "Fort Pueblo" did not become an established name until the need arose to distinguish between it and the town that grew up around it. In the winter of 1858–59 about two hundred miners settled at the mouth of the

Indian Pueblo of Taos, South House. Many architectural elements here were used in early Arkansas Valley buildings. Note the beehive ovens in the foreground. From A. F. Bandelier, *Final Report on Investigations in the Southwest*, Part 1 (1890), Papers of the Archaeological Institute of America, American Series, III.

Fountain and called their shacks and tents "Pueblo." By February, 1859 the miners had named their settlement "Fountain City," a name it kept for a few years before settling down to "Pueblo" again. Thenceforth the old post has been known as "Fort Pueblo."[20]

There were other names for the fort in recognition of someone's ownership of all or part of it: "Fort Spaulding," "Fort Juana," "Robert Fisher's Fort," "Spaulding and Fisher's Fort." The fort was also known as "the lower Pueblo," to distinguish it from Hardscrabble which was called "the Upper Pueblo." On some maps it was called "*Pueblo de San Carlos*," and a few scholarly settlers called it "*Napesta*," the Indian and Spanish term for the Arkansas River. But the name by which the little fort was known to its inhabitants was simply Pueblo.[21]

6
Lives of
Limited Enjoyment

BY SEPTEMBER 21, 1842 the Pueblo was built and occupied. On that date Rufus Sage, an Indian trader and former newspaper reporter, passed the fort and wrote:

At the delta, formed by the junction of Fontaine qui Bouit with the Arkansas, a trading fort, called the Pueblo, was built during the summer of 1842. This post is owned by a company of independent traders, on the common property system; and, from its situation, can command a profitable trade with both Mexicans and Indians. Its occupants number ten or twelve Americans, most of whom are married to Mexican women, while everything about the establishment wears the aspect of neatness and comfort.[1]

Sage's description tells a great deal about the Pueblo in the fall of 1842. As yet there was no farming, although in an earlier paragraph Sage described the Arkansas Valley as showing "a fitness for agricultural purposes." Nor were Pueblo's large herds of cattle and horses yet in evidence, nor the "drifters" and "outlaws" that later offended its critics. The pickets on top of the wall had not yet half broken down nor the gate warped out of fit. Sage liked the place. It wore the aspect of neatness and comfort because it was clean and new.

By "common property system" Sage appears to mean that there was no single owner. The walls, bastions, corral, and gate were owned in common by Kinkead, Conn, Simpson, Mantz, and Fisher, and the expenses of maintenance were shared. The irrigation ditch, not yet built, would be dug and maintained as a community project probably under the management of Kinkead and Conn, whose farming experience in New Mexico had taught them about irrigation systems. Farming lands in the river bottom were not considered property since there was plenty for all, and grazing lands on the prairie were undivided.

Less than a year later the "common property system" seems to have suffered the fate of all such ideologies. In 1843 the fort was known as "Robert Fisher's Fort," and the houses around its plaza belonged to various of its occupants or were rented to them. Simeon Turley had a store at the fort run by an employee.[2] That same summer George Simpson was licensed to trade at "Fort Juanna a point on the Arkansas river about a mile above Fountaine qui bouille."[3] The name was a whimsical tribute to his bride and referred, perhaps, to his house within the fort.

By December, 1843 Mathew Kinkead and Francisco Conn had left the Pueblo, abandoned their buffalo farm and moved to Hardscrabble. By March, 1844 George Simpson also had moved there. If they sold their houses, or an undivided interest in the fort itself, they left no records of it. Real estate transactions on the Arkansas were private and unrecorded, for property owners had no legal title to either land or improvements, as we shall see.

By 1843 David W. Spaulding had come from New Mexico and bought an interest in the fort from Robert Fisher, or from the founders who had moved to Hardscrabble. For the next two years the post was called "Fort Spaulding" or "Spaulding and Fisher's Fort."[4] Alexander Barclay bought some houses at Pueblo at one time or another, which he sold to A. C. Metcalf in November, 1847. The post was said to have been owned by J. B. Doyle and Simeon Turley after it was abandoned in 1855. Years later, Charles Autobees summed up the matter of Pueblo's ownership (with mistakes in dates) thus: "From the year 1839 until 1854 it was generally occupied for trading purposes and passed through a number of hands."[5]

Considering the American aptitude for self-government, it is surprising that the occupants of Pueblo did not immediately elect one another to various offices and draw up a set of rules to live by. One deterrent to community organization was the continual absences of the men which prevented them from serving consistently in any capacity. Decisions that affected the community were settled in spontaneous town meetings. Business dealings were handled directly, and a man's word was as good as his deed. Murder seems to have been the only crime dealt with communally; it was punished by banishment from the settlement. There was no recourse to law, for courts and enforcement officers were seven hundred miles away. Even when such officers were close at hand the people of Pueblo withdrew and lay silent—for it will be seen that Pueblo was an outlaw settlement engaged in illegal pursuits.[6]

Sage's estimate of Pueblo's population was "ten or twelve Americans, most of whom are married to Mexican women," but it cannot be assumed from this that the population was about twenty souls. Ruxton counted "three or four Taos women and as many squaws of every nation" as comprising the "female society" of the Upper Arkansas, and he noted also "little dusky buffalo-fed urchins who played about the corral of the fort." If there were ten women in the fort we must allow a fair sprinkling of buffalo-fed urchins—say a minimum of ten. Each proprietor had a peon or two—assume a minimum of ten Mexican "hands" and already the population has risen to forty or more. Some of the peons had wives and children, so the population of the settlement was many times the number of its male proprietors.[7]

Contemporary estimates of Pueblo's population vary because the population was fluid. Men were frequently absent, out hunting, trading with Indians or emigrants, buying whiskey and flour at Taos, getting wagons or guns repaired at Bent's Fort, or taking furs back to St. Louis. Conversely, some of the men Rufus Sage counted among the proprietors may have been only visitors for a night, a week, a month. It is no wonder that Sage's "ten or twelve Americans" of September, 1842 is fewer than Beckwourth's "fifteen or twenty trappers" of a month later; Parkman's single American at the Pueblo in the summer of 1846 does not agree with a visiting Mormon's estimate of six or eight mountaineers in the fall of the same year. A more mobile set of people never existed, and trying to enumerate them is like counting ants in an anthill.[8]

When the men were home they were likely to be out hunting on the plains or in the foothills, alone or with one or two companions. Hunting was both a necessity and a joy, pursued with relentless vigor at all seasons of the year. To this incessant hunting, Alexander Barclay attributed the good health of the community.[9]

The most hunted animals were antelope, properly called pronghorns because they are only distantly related to the true old-world antelope. Mountain men called them "goats," a translation of the French *cabri* by which the animals were first known to French-Canadian voyageurs. In size and form they rather resemble dun-colored goats, with large, liquid brown eyes and short, hollow, backward-curving horns which they shed every year. But in motion

"Calling Up Antelopes." The hunter's white flag draws the curious animals into gun range. From Randolph B. Marcy, *The Prairie Traveler* (1859).

they lose their goatishness and float over the prairie as lightly as a puff of wind, jumping obstacles in great airy leaps. Despite their speed and powerful sense of hearing and smell, antelope were then so abundant on the Arkansas and so easy to hunt that they were not considered game. Barclay's diary records a day in which he killed an antelope but found no game. Their curiosity often proved their undoing. A red rag on a stick would bring them within rifle range and a man on his back waving his legs in the air would lure them to approach and investigate. The flesh of the antelope was considered tough and flavorless. Plains Indians would not eat it until buffalo became scarce, but the men of the Arkansas Valley settlements hung up the carcasses in cribs to age and the women cooked them—even if everyone preferred venison.[10]

The real game was deer, either the white-tail (red) or the much larger black-tail (mule), whose meat was savored and whose skins provided tunics and fringed trousers for mountain men and Indians. But shooting a deer was not an everyday occurrence on the Upper Arkansas. Barclay's diary records only five deer killed by him in over two years, although he doubtless shot many he did not record. As for elk, they were not much hunted for their meat was considered stringy and strong-flavored. But their hide was tough and had its uses, the covering of packsaddles, for instance. Buffalo were not a staple at the Upper Arkansas settlements. By the mid 1840's, the Great Plains buffalo herds were one or two hundred miles to the east, although there were still buffalo in some mountain valleys, particularly in Bayou Salado (South Park).[11]

Rifles at Pueblo were not leveled solely at four-footed animals. Barclay's diary records shooting wild turkey, especially those he found in his fields at harvest time. Rufus Sage spent several nights hunting turkeys on the St. Charles River by moonlight. Ducks and geese were shot in the spring if they happened to fly overhead, and grouse were pursued if their hoarse cries emerged from the deep grass in the river bottoms. They made a tasty supper, but no effort was expended in hunting them. Once Barclay shot an eagle to make a fan from its feathers.[12]

The Arkansas had plenty of fish, and fishing became a springtime diversion after the ice in the river went out around the first of April. Catfish and hickory shad were abundant and of good size. In 1839, Thomas Farnham caught a catfish weighing a pound between Bent's Fort and the mouth of the Fountain. Lieutenant Abert caught a seventeen-inch shad at Bent's Fort in 1846 and remarked in his diary that at Pueblo, where the water was clear, trout were speckled with red. George Ruxton fished the river at Pueblo one day in the spring of 1847 and pulled out ten trout, hickory shad and suckers in as many minutes, but from that time on, he got nary a nibble. Pueblo men accounted for this by saying that fish migrated upriver as soon as the ice broke and that Ruxton just happened to dip his line at the very moment a shoal of fish swam by.[13]

There were bears on the Upper Arkansas and most of them, to hear the mountain men tell it, were grizzlies, the great lumbering beasts whose coats were brushed with silver giving them a shaggy, grizzled look. A glimpse of one was enough to frighten the wits out of any man familiar with their viciousness. Every hunter in the mountains had his story of an encounter with a grizzly, and the denizens of Pueblo were no exception. Dick Wootton tells of one of the most serious grizzly battles at Pueblo: One day while hunting near the settlement, Dick Owens and John Burroughs met a grizzly. Both shot, both missed, and the bear charged. They ran for the nearest tree, a small bushy juniper. Owens managed to climb to the top of the tree, but Burroughs had hardly cleared the ground when the bear caught him by the foot and dragged him down. Burroughs lay perfectly still and allowed the bear to maul him until it left him for dead. The bear then went after Owens in the tree. While Owens and the bear fought a hand-to-paw battle, the badly-wounded Burroughs managed to reach his rifle, load it, and shoot down the bear. Both men were crippled for life after the encounter.[14]

Hunting and fishing were recreation as well as necessity, and beaver trapping in the early 1840's was more for sport than gain. Barclay's diary tells of an occasional nostalgic trapping trip made by former mountain men, like the one Calvin Briggs and Sabourin took in 1846. They caught seventeen beaver in the middle of July when pelts were almost worthless. At this time even winter pelts had dropped in price to ninety cents a pound at St. Louis. But, until the United States soldiers showed up in the West with their greenbacks in 1846, a good winter pelt would still bring a price in the mountains, as currency if not as fur. Bill Williams got four dollars a pound for his beaver at Bent's Fort in 1843, and Marcelino Baca traded two beaver skins for $10.62 worth of merchandise at Lancaster Lupton's store at Pueblo in December, 1846.[15]

When there were visitors at Pueblo, such as Frémont's men in 1845, there was target shooting. Pueblo men probably insisted on high stakes for every one of them was a crack shot. Among themselves, however, ammunition was expended for more serious purposes, and there were no such contests recorded.[16]

For pure recreation men played cards and drank. The most popular card games were euchre and poker and the beverage most copiously consumed was Taos whiskey. Card games sometimes went on all day. Gambling debts were paid in beaver skins or, after 1846, in greenbacks. Drinking was either a pastime unto itself or it accompanied fandangos and was the cause of fights afterwards. Barclay's diary records several monumental frolics lasting for days or weeks involving many men staggering around the settlements, shooting off guns, quarreling, maiming and, on occasion, murdering.[17]

The most popular entertainment was the fandango, a dance party given two or three times a week, attended by all classes from proprietor to peon, and by all ages from babes–in–arms to toothless grandmothers. Anyone could give a fandango who had access to a big–enough room. At nine or ten in the evening the musicians took their places at one end of the room. The ladies perched on benches or divans along the walls, rolling their *cigarillos* and chatting, dressed in fresh white *camisitas* (off–the–shoulder blouses) and bright-colored *enaguas* (short, full skirts), powdered and perfumed, and gleaming with gold and silver ornaments. As the music struck up, the gentlemen formed a line across the center of the hall. They began clapping their hands, and the ladies rose and faced them. Then the couples whirled away in the intricate sets of the dance, sometimes with a rapidity quite painful to watch.[18]

Music was provided by guitars and violins, or occasionally by other instruments such as triangles, mandolins or *tombes* (little Indian drums). Most of the musicians knew a dozen tunes; in New Mexico the same melodies were played by the same musicians at church services, marriages, and funerals. Everyone knew the dances: *La Cuna* (the cradle), *El Italiano, El Jarabe* (familiar now as the Mexican Hat dance), and the quiet, slow waltz danced to the lovely song, *La Paloma* (the dove). Some of the dances told stories. Matt Field witnessed a waltz that resembled a battle. The dancers separated into two divisions. After singing a few words of defiance, they clapped their hands, stamped their feet, and waltzed off towards, around, and through the other couples, accompanying the music with short yells and other sounds of battle.[19]

During the dancing a singer (male or female) sometimes sang the words of the songs or improvised verses complimentary, or gently mocking, to persons present, which, depending upon the wit of the singer, drew shouts of laughter from the company. After a set the music stopped, and everyone lit up their *cigarillos*. The gentlemen left their ladies at the benches, or bought them treats at a table where candy, cakes, and wine were sold by the owner of the room, at double the usual price to recompense him for the wear and tear on his establishment. The dance continued well past midnight and (especially when there was gambling) sometimes into the dawn.

On the Arkansas, fandangos included not only the graceful dances of the Mexicans but also "such a medly of steps as is seldom seen out of the mountains—the halting, irregular march of the war dance; the slipping gallopade, the boisterous pitching of the Missouri backwoodsman, and the more nice gyrations of the Frenchman."[20] Pueblo had its fiddle, as George Ruxton remarked, and Greenhorn had its fiddler, known as "José the fiddler," who may have earned his eight dollars a month by little more than his proficiency with the instrument. But José's profits were scanty, for at each of the two fandangos he was reported to have attended, he was charged $1.50 and $1.75, probably the cost of buying sweets or liquor.[21]

Alexander Barclay's diary mentions many fandangos: "Fandango at Bussards' Roost"; "Fandango at Mormontown, Metcalf the soul of fun"; "Metcalf & Blackhawk or someone else gave fandango to which everybody who felt like it went"; "Tesson struck his lodge but stayed all night to give fandango"; and, most descriptive of all, "Fandango—all drunk as usual and fuss."[22] What was for Mexicans a decorous evening of dancing frequently turned into a drunken brawl when Americans and their whiskey were present. George Ruxton described a fandango at Taos in 1846 that was invaded by Americans, divested for once of their greasy buckskins but not of their hunting knives and pistols. As the Mexicans stood aside, Americans would seize their partners with the grip of a grizzly bear and whirl and twirl, jump and thump, whooping unearthly yells as they stamped through an Indian scalp dance. They had the floor all to themselves, and if a Mexican chanced to step into the dance he would be sent sprawling by a galloping mountaineer. During the lull the Americans would gulp down gourds full of whiskey and so would their ladies. When everyone became drunk and rowdy, out would come the knives and pistols[23]—and that was what Barclay meant by "fuss."

Such were the manly amusements. Others less vigorous were sponsored by the ladies—berry-picking, visiting, or simply strolling along the river bank on a mild afternoon. The accoutrements of civilization were limited. Books and newspapers were rare; fine wines, fancy clothes, and even the most elementary items of furniture were lacking. But there was abundance of the good and simple things of life—food, health, comfort, and companionship—and sufficient dangers and excitements to preclude the blight of boredom. Alexander Barclay wrote at Hardscrabble in 1845, "We pass a life of sufficient though limited enjoyment, our wants are few, and as we witness no instance of ostentation and luxury in our neighbours we have nothing to create envy, thus we have only to repress occasional recollections of the superfluities of civilized life to be contented with our own."[24] In this setting of broad plains, clean rivers, mountains full of game, and skies full of birds, there was space and time for men to move around, experiment, and change. Life was pared down to its essentials, which set the spirit free.

There was another kind of freedom in the Arkansas Valley. Defying the bigotry of their era and upbringing, these people lived intimately with men and women of other races, adopting what they needed from other cultures and casting aside the rigid conventions of their own. They dressed in Indian buckskins and moccasins, treated illnesses with Indian remedies, hunted and traded like Indians, while living in Indian lodges. They used Mexican irrigation ditches, plows, and mules; built Mexican houses; ate Mexican food; danced Mexican waltzes; and were married in Mexican or Indian ceremonies as the case required. They imported American cows, horses and wagons, goods and tools. They learned to speak many languages, using not only words but also signs, and their ability to communicate generally brought them peace. On the Arkansas, for a few precious years, men and women of various races and backgrounds lived together and enjoyed a high degree of personal liberty. If some remnant of this tolerance and freedom persists in the Arkansas Valley, or in Colorado, or even in the whole Rocky Mountain West, it may be in part the legacy of the early settlements on the Arkansas.

7
A Woman's Life
on the Arkansas

IT WAS THE LADIES who made Pueblo a unique establishment—a settlement as well as a trading post. There were no American women on the Arkansas until the Mormons brought their families in the fall of 1846. Before that, all the women were Indian or Mexican.

Indian women were used to hard work. Their duties included preparing skins and buffalo robes, erecting lodges or other forms of shelter, gathering and cooking food, hauling wood for fires, making clothing. The Indian wives of the Americans came in different shapes, shades, and sizes, from different tribes and parts of the West, with different languages and customs. Strikingly different individuals are two trappers' wives described by George Simpson. The only thing these women seemed to have in common were trapper husbands who doubtless deserted them when the journey was over. Nancy was a good–natured Piute from the barren Great Basin. Simpson described her as fat, lazy, and silent but not sad, for her full, round face and sparkling eyes told of peace within and contentment with her lot. To her mind—if mind she had in that bullet head of hers—the contents of the camp kettle were much to be preferred to the lizard and grasshopper diet on which she had been reared. Her chief duty and only occupation, so far as Simpson could see, was to mend the moccasins and buckskins of anyone who brought them to her for repairs. Her husband provided her with a pinto pony, but when horses were scarce, she became the pack animal, waddling along with a bundle of her personal effects strapped across her shoulders, upon which was piled the camp kit—a three-gallon kettle, coffee pot, large tin pan, and a wooden bowl, which she wore over her head like a hat. When, in the eyes of her lord and master, she misbehaved, he took a willow switch to her, but if he asked her if she would like to return to her parents, who had probably traded her for a Mexican blanket, she answered "Nary."[1]

The other Indian wife described by George Simpson was Maurice

LeDuc's Shoshone squaw, "a marvelous, ill-favored member of the tribe. Large, angular and with features, if not absolutely repulsive, as harsh as her temper was crabbed and cross-grained. 'Her voice was theatrically loud and masculine was her stride.' That's the mildly drawn pen–portrait of Ka–wot,—Anglice—'got none.' Medusa! what a name: but how expressive of the utter absence of personal attractions. Nancy was no beauty, but she looked a Venus besides this emobiment of ugliness."[2]

Nancy and Ka–wot were probably dumped when the trappers left the mountains and took up residence at trading posts. Indian women who were mere slave laborers were good enough for trappers but not for traders. A woman's brute strength and willingness to work were not as prized at trading posts, where the settled life and secure source of food required less labor. What was more important was a woman's social qualities and her influence in a tribe with which her trader-husband did business. William Bent's successive marriages to a chief's daughters were of utmost importance to the company in keeping peace with the Cheyennes; John Poisal's wife, Ma–hom, was sister of the Arapaho leader, Left Hand, and her Indian family camped frequently around Pueblo and kept the peace. Ma–hom was probably something of a beauty, as the good looks of her brother and her daughters would indicate.[3]

There were Indian women aplenty at the Arkansas Valley settlements but, probably because of language and cultural differences, they did not seem to participate fully in the social life of the community. Nevertheless, many of the Indian wives were given all the respect and privileges due to white wives. When the settlements on the Arkansas broke up, the Shoshone sisters called Susan and Sarah Ann who married Calvin Briggs and John Burroughs respectively, went with their husbands and children to California, where they all lived together in a respectable frame house in Dry Creek Township on the Consumnes River. Later on, the Burroughs family returned to John's original home in Kentucky, that the children might get better schooling. Lancaster Lupton's Cheyenne wife and their many offspring accompanied him to northern California where they became substantial members of the community of Arcata. Marcelino Baca and his Pawnee wife, a woman of grace and dignity, brought their children to live in the Mexican village of Río Colorado. Charles Autobees' Arapaho woman, Sycamore, was his constant companion for twenty years. He had a Mexican wife and family as well, who

A Cree Indian woman and a Snake (or Shoshone) Indian woman, drawn by Bodmer for *Maximilian's Travels*. The handsome Shoshone girl illustrates, perhaps, why the Shoshones were preferred over other Indian women by Arkansas Valley men. Courtesy of Denver Public Library Western Collection.

considered Sycamore "not regular wife—out-of-door wife in a tent," but a wife all the same. William Guerrier and John Smith both had Cheyenne wives and children, whom they lived with until death did them part.[4]

These were stable marriages between white men and Indian women. Other Pueblo men were careless of their Indian mates. Levin Mitchell had a Sioux wife when George Simpson first met him at Fort Laramie in 1841, but by the time Mitchell was living at

Pueblo his wife was a Mexican girl named Luz Argüello. After Maurice LeDuc got rid of Ka–wot, he had a Sioux wife, Marguerita. He took Marguerita and their children to live in the little Mexican village of San Geronimo, near Mora. There he fell in love with thirteen-year-old Elena Mendoza and married her in the local church. Marguerita packed her possessions on a horse and walked back with her children to the Sioux nation.

Thomas Fitzpatrick wrote in 1847 that there were about sixty men in Pueblo and Hardscrabble, nearly all having wives and some having two from various Indian tribes, including the Blackfeet, Assineboine, Arikara, Sioux, Arapaho, Cheyenne, Pawnee, Shoshone, Sanpete and Chinook. These women lived in lodges raised near the fort, which they found more familiar and far more comfortable than the drafty cubicles within the fort walls. Even Mexican wives were known to have lived in Indian lodges on the Arkansas, as did the wives of John Hawkins at Pueblo and of William Tharp at Big Timber below Bent's Fort. [5]

Indian women had been taught many more of life's weary chores than their light-skinned sisters from Taos and Mora. In the words of one old Pueblo man, a Mexican girl was taught to do just three things, "to grind corn on a rock, make tortillas and dance." [6] But the Mexican women who came to Pueblo did far more than that. Since there was no well in the courtyard women made daily trips to the river, carrying water back in large jars on their heads. They washed clothes in the river using the root of the soapweed and spreading the clothes to dry on bushes. They sprinkled and swept the floors of their rooms several times a day. Every day they ground corn and chili peppers used in tortillas and *atole*. They took care of the smaller domestic animals, kept fires going, whitewashed rooms and plastered walls, dried the meat their hunter-husbands brought back, planted and tended little gardens. They made clothes for themselves and their children, although not always the buckskin garments and blanket coats their husbands wore. Alexander Barclay, former corset maker, cut out and sewed his own buckskin shirts and trousers, and made them for other men in the community on occasion. Moccasins, worn by most traders and their wives at the settlements, were made by Indian women and sold for fifty cents to a dollar and a half a pair. [7]

Most of the Mexican women at Pueblo, as well as the hired hands, were from Taos. Taos was a frontier town. Its people seem to have been hardier and more independent than their southern countrymen, willing to leave their families, their church and priest and the graves of their ancestors to live hundreds of miles north among the savages and Americans. Taos had importance to the Arkansas Valley settlements all out of proportion to its size. From Taos came indispensable items such as whiskey, flour, and news. To Taos the Arkansas Valley settlers went for visits, marriages, and baptisms. Because of their close ties with Taos the Arkansas Valley settlements had a flavor far more Mexican than American, with a culture of saint's days, fandangos, Spanish language, Mexican music and food.

A woman at Pueblo had more responsibility for the safety of her children and herself than did her Taos counterpart, for her husband was likely to be gone much of the time. She learned to ride a horse with a baby in her arms, shoot a gun, drive a team, talk to an Indian, sleep in the mountains, and suppress her terror when something went wrong. There are a few descriptions of Pueblo women in situations of danger: Maria Whittlesey, when surprised by Indians miles from home, tied her baby to her with her *reboso* (shawl) and ran her horse back to safety; Teresita rode with Mathew Kinkead out on the plains to the buffalo herd to capture newborn calves, risking the fury not only of the buffalo cows but of the Indians; Luisa Brown, pursued by Apaches, grasped her little son tightly about the neck and forced her horse to jump a deep arroyo; Juana Simpson, with her baby in her arms, was tossed off her horse into the snow at the top of Sangre de Cristo Pass and smiled as she struggled to get up; shortly afterwards that same indomitable young lady was given her husband's gun belt when Utes were sighted in the valley below, with the understanding that she would shoot herself before submitting to capture. These are not pictures of delicate little women who knew only how to grind corn, make tortillas, and dance.[8]

After other settlements were founded on the Upper Arkansas, the ladies made many visits between them, and had occasional outings at Bent's Fort. At least one Pueblo woman, Luz Trujillo Metcalf, was visiting at Bent's Fort when Colonel Kearny paid his famous call with the Army of the West in 1846. Saints' days on the Arkansas were sometimes celebrated with feasts and fandangos. Every fall Pueblo had a fiesta with the usual food, drinking, and dancing. One of the dances was a sort of Indian dance to the beat of a small drum. Afterwards the local strongman, Jesús María Gallegos, would tie all the drunks together in bunches of three or four to prevent murder-

Thomas Suaso, son of Teresita Suaso Barclay. Courtesy of A. R. Mitchell, Trinidad, Colorado.

ous assaults upon each other. Gallegos also provided entertainment by lying on his back and lifting a man in each hand.[9]

Pueblo had a high level of health to which climate, diet and exercise all contributed. George Simpson wrote, "The climate is delightful, salubrious." Barclay described the Arkansas Valley settlements as having no epidemics or local infections, and Ruxton claimed to know a hundred cases of hopeless lung disease restored to health in the "pure and bracing air of the Rocky Mountains."[10]

Children at Pueblo who survived infancy were husky and healthy, for they ate quantities of meat, green and dried vegetables, milk, butter, eggs, dried beans, and chili peppers, a diet excelling in nutrition the diet of the average American child of today. Even the coarse, dirty Taos flour of which their bread was made exceeded in health benefits the refined variety used in more civilized places, then and now. These children lived on horseback, learning at an early age to herd animals and to hunt, spending their days in the fresh air and sunshine.

When there was illness at Pueblo, the people resorted to simple remedies and hoped for the best. There was no doctor and very little medicine. At Bent's Fort in 1838 Barclay reported that there was no medicine of any kind, although by 1848 the fort's medicine chest contained "calomel, camphor, Lees pills, Sedlitch powder, etc."[11] According to Barclay's diary, Pueblo had castor oil and calomel, and Hardscrabble had calomel and salts, which probably did as much good or harm as the "secret elixirs" then peddled by quack doctors back east. The Indians of the settlements used various herbal concoctions, as well as their undeniably effective steam baths, achieved with a tent of tanned buffalo hides (*apishamores*) inside which water was poured over stones heated in a fire of cedar chips. Barclay treated his gout by steaming his foot, wrapped in wet blankets, over a fire of cedar boughs, and with poultices of mustard and onions.[12] John Poisal used "eye-water" for his chronically irritated eyes, as did José Jimines, who stopped at Pueblo in February, 1843 for the purpose of obtaining "eye-water."[13] Other troubles were probably treated with folk remedies such as boiled rattlesnake oil for the measles, or the sign of the cross painted on an afflicted part.[14] By far the most common ailment on the Arkansas was the hangover, for which there was no more relief than there is today.

Despite general good health, people died, mostly women in childbirth and their infants. Childbearing was hazardous

69

everywhere, but especially in isolated communities like the Arkansas Valley settlements. Pueblo was fortunate for a time to have a good midwife, Josefa (Chepita) Tafoya. She came to Pueblo in 1844 or 1845 from Bent's Fort, where she had been housekeeper and her husband, Ben Ryder, the carpenter. Three of her own children were born at Pueblo, and she eased the birth of many another baby there. Barclay's diary from 1845 to 1848 notes six deaths, three of natural causes (as far as we can tell), and three the victims of murder. During the same period he records four births.[15]

There is no mention of a graveyard connected with any of the settlements. Those who died appear to have been buried on high ground wherever the bereaved relatives chose. Ed Tharp's grave was on the *loma* or bluff east of the Fountain. Rumaldo Córdova was buried on top of a hill near the Huerfano settlement, where he died. Victims of the 1854 massacre were buried where they fell, five of them in a common grave in front of the Pueblo. When the first settlers of the city of Pueblo arrived, they saw some old graves on Tenderfoot Hill west of the Fountain above its mouth, which may have been the site of the Mormons' graveyard in 1846–47.[16]

There was no graveyard at Pueblo for the same reason there were no baptisms, marriages, or funerals. The nearest priest was at Taos, and he never visited the Arkansas Valley settlements. Babies died unbaptized and were buried in unconsecrated ground; devout Catholics lived together and had children, then made the trip to Taos to be married and have their children baptized. Festivals of the church and saints' days were celebrated without the blessing of a priest, or not celebrated at all, a great loss for the good Catholic women to whom these fiestas had been a source of pleasure, and the sacraments a source of spiritual security.

American husbands would not always have understood and sympathized with the deprivations suffered by their Mexican wives caused by the lack of sacraments. It was a common opinion of non-Catholic Americans in New Mexico that every priest was a corrupt and vicious shepherd, leading a flock of stupid and hypocritical sheep. No one was more violent on the subject than Charles Bent, who wrote about the Mexicans (three years before he became their governor) as follows:

Thare religion consistes intirely in outward show, they have no idea a sinsear devotion—they are taught to belive that thare priestes are the only

"A Kitchen Scene." From Josiah Gregg, *Commerce of the Prairies* (1845). The cooking facilities here are more elaborate than those at Pueblo, where there were only little corner fireplaces to cook at. The girl spinning the stick between her palms to mix the chocolate is typical, as are her friends grinding corn on the metate and patting the tortillas into shape. The strings of peppers on the wall were also a common feature. Courtesy of Denver Public Library Western Collection.

meadiator betwean the supriem being and themselves, and eaven in this, you can acheave great benifits (nominly) by a lavish present of gold, thare valler consists of Boasting and show whare thare is no dainger . . . The Mexican caracter is made up of Stupidity, obstinacy, Ignorance duplicity and vanity.[17]

Bent's judgement on Mexicans was not unusual; Josiah Gregg, Rufus Sage, George Ruxton and other writers described them in similar terms. On the Arkansas most Mexican men were of the peon class, and the Americans saw them as "a poor, cowardly, despicable, thievish, gambling set—little removed from the Indian, and only fit to drudge, break wild horses and mules, and herd cattle and sheep."[18]

Scorn was the attitude of many Americans toward Mexican women as well. Charles Bent had an eleven-year connection with María Ignacia Jaramilla, a beautiful woman of good Taos family, sister of Kit Carson's wife, Josefa. Although Ignacia was free to marry and so was Bent, he never married her. Their five children were given their mother's name at baptism, and their father was recorded as "unknown." Ceran St. Vrain lived successively with three different women, each of whom bore him a child, "father unknown." St. Vrain loved his children and provided handsomely for them, but he left Luisa Branch, his last mistress, an annuity of $300 in his will payable on condition of "her good behavior" and her relinquishment of their child, Felicita. George Bent's will left his mistress, María de la Cruz Padilla, his property in Taos on condition that "she is living with me at the time of my death," and that she give up their two children to be raised in St. Louis, which she did after he died in 1848. Both wills show a concern for the children, but contempt for the mothers.[19]

These are by no means isolated or unusual examples. Birth records of New Mexico show countless babies who were given their mothers' names, their fathers recorded as "unknown." Sexual freedom and concubinage were taken for granted in New Mexico, where relatively few couples married. No shame or blame was attached to women bearing children out of wedlock, nor did the children carry a stigma for their illegitimacy. Like good Anglo-Saxons from the land of the moral double standard, Americans blamed this "immorality" on the women: "The standard of female chastity is deplorably low," wrote one; "the women deem chastity no virtue," wrote another.[20]

Morals aside, most American men found the women of New Mexico "joyous, sociable, kind-hearted creatures almost universally liberal to a fault, easy and naturally graceful in their manners, and really appear to have more understanding than the men."[21] Ruxton found them "an ornament to their sex, and to any nation," and Sage declared they presented "a striking contrast to their countrymen," being kind and affectionate, mild and affable, if deficient in "common chastity."[22]

Some marriages at Taos and Pueblo, both consecrated and free-union, were surely made in heaven. No word of reproach could be leveled at the marriage of Kit and Josefa Carson, of Lucien and Luz Maxwell, of Joe and Cruz Doyle. Even the slightly tarnished Luisa

Sandoval settled down to a lifetime of faultless domesticity with John Brown.

Juana Simpson was the very model of a faithful and patient wife, although her marriage too began without sanction of the church. George and Juana, aged 24 and 14 respectively, wanted to be married in the fall of 1842, but the nearest priest was at Taos, a hundred and seventy miles away over snow-covered mountains. Instead, the young couple went to Bent's Fort where, according to family tradition, they found a man who had been a notary public in Missouri and displayed his seal to prove it. With this semblance of legality they were content, and on November 30, 1842 they signed a statement (Juana with an "X") that they agreed to live together as man and wife. The document, properly witnessed, certified by the notary, decorated with a stamped gold seal and a blue ribbon, became a treasured keepsake in the Simpson family. Two years and a baby daughter later, they finally got to Taos to be married by the priest and to have the child baptized.[23]

At both Taos and Pueblo, some women were considered less than respectable. One was Antonia Luna, described as half-witted. She had lived at Taos with Jim Beckwourth, then with Kit Carson who dropped her instantly when she told him she preferred Beckwourth as a lover. Bill Williams was another of her lovers before she ended up at Pueblo as William Tharp's woman and mother of his two children.[24]

At Hardscrabble, Candelaria Sena, a dark-skinned woman from Taos, had a brief fling with a man named LaFontaine before her "husband," Wells, was struck with a fit of jealousy and murdered her and her lover. Then there was the unmitigated tramp, Nicolasa, who was Rube Herring's girl most of the time, fighting with him constantly and flirting with his friends. She was said to have caused three duels, one at Fort Lancaster between Herring and Henry Beer in 1841, one between John Brown and "Seesome" at Greenhorn, and a third between Jim Waters and Ed Tharp at Pueblo in 1848.[24]

Such were the women of Pueblo, from best to worst, a cross section of a small community. On the frontier these Mexican women became the courageous companions of their tough and adventurous men. Teresita and her daughters, Luisa Brown, Luz Trujillo Metcalf and many others, typified the pioneer woman just as truly and nobly in their *rebosos* as did the much better publicized covered-wagon heroines in their poke bonnets.

8
A Company
of Independent Traders,
1842–44

TRADE WAS THE BUSINESS of the Pueblo. Pueblo men traded with anyone who had anything to buy or sell—with Indians, Mexicans, emigrants, trappers, travelers, one another. Their most important customers were Indians, who were considered at peace when Pueblo opened business. This peace was apparent in the Kinkead buffalo farm of 1841–43 which the Indians allowed to exist even though they considered a white man who appropriated their buffalo in the same light a cattleman viewed a rustler; in the fact that Teresita, Kinkead and Conn went out on the plains unmolested to catch buffalo calves; in the architecture of the Pueblo with its minimal provisions for defense; in the confidence with which the men of Pueblo brought their wives and children into the Indian country.[1]

There was peace in the Arkansas Valley as long as white men who came there were not trappers, miners, farmers, ranchers, or settlers. These the Indians would not tolerate, for they used resources of the land which, by Indian tradition and United States law (the "Trade and Intercourse Act" of 1834), were reserved for the Indians. But if the white men were traders, they were welcomed and allowed to use as much land as needed for their support. All the Indians loved to trade, and as a rule they protected white traders among them. During the trading period on the Arkansas (1832–55) Indians numbered in the thousands; white men numbered perhaps two to five hundred. At any time the Indians could have forced white traders out of their country by besieging trading posts, attacking supply trains, killing men and horses. But they never did, because their desire for white men's goods overpowered their aversion to the white man's presence.

When Hugh Glenn, Jacob Fowler and their twenty trappers marched up the Arkansas in January, 1822, it did not matter that the seven hundred lodges of various tribes of Indians they met outnumbered them roughly 1,750 to 1—the Americans clearly had the upper hand. At Glenn's refusal to stay and trade for horses, the chief of the Arapahos burst into tears and flung himself on his bed. At the mouth of the Fountain the trappers built two successive forts and horse pens on either side of the river to protect themselves from "Spaniards." The Indians could have demolished these flimsy picket buildings in an hour, killing the occupants and taking their trade goods. But they did not, for it would have deterred other Americans from coming to trade with them.[2]

The Arapahos were the best customers of Pueblo men and among the most avid traders of the plains. Before they had horses, the Arapahos had lived for centuries on the Northern Plains, gathering fruits and roots, hunting buffalo on foot, and moving from camp to camp using dogs for pack animals and for drawing baggage on poles (travois). By historic times they had formed an alliance with the Cheyennes which has never dissolved. Both Arapahos and Cheyennes were relatively tall and light-skinned and of Algonquian linguistic stock, but there the similarity ended. They could not understand each other's spoken language, and their customs and religions were quite different, as in many cases were their political alliances.

In the eighteenth century the Arapahos began to obtain horses from other Indians and, horseborne, they made visits to the Spanish settlements about 1800 to trade or steal more horses. Around 1810 half the tribe or over three hundred lodges (1,500 souls) left the Black Hills of Dakota and moved permanently to the plains along the foot of the mountains in present eastern Colorado "because there were more horses and a milder climate," an Arapaho chief explained. There they were visited occasionally by American trappers seeking horses to trade, and by their allies, the Cheyennes. In 1833 William Bent lured about half the Cheyenne tribe to the Arkansas to trade, and they often camped near Bent's Fort. Bands of other plains tribes roamed the Arkansas Valley, including Kiowas, Kiowa-Apaches, Comanches, Shoshones, Blackfeet, Sioux, Pawnees, Arikaras and Crows, but only at the indulgence of the Arapahos and Cheyennes. Except when the Utes ventured out of the mountains to steal horses, there was peace on the Arkansas.[3]

Whatever their reputation for peace, Indians were not as welcome at Pueblo as they would have been at a trading post where there were no women or children. A New Mexican woman had been taught from childhood to fear Plains Indians. When a band appeared, sometimes outnumbering the men of the fort, she could be

An Arapaho village photographed by William S. Soule in the late 1860's or early 1870's. Courtesy of National Anthropological Archives, Smithsonian Institution.

forgiven for hiding her children among the trade goods, moving chests against doors and trembling like an aspen until they had left. When Indians came, they brought deerskins, buffalo robes, moccasins, and bows and arrows which they traded for flour, goods, tools, and whiskey. They went away quietly, taking nothing but corn from the fields which the men of the settlement invited them to stuff into their saddlebags, knowing they would do so anyway. In later years Indians turned their horses into the fields before they left, not merely to forage the animals but to impress upon the white man that the land he farmed was Indian land, and the fruit of the fields was Indian property.[4]

At Pueblo, each man was in business for himself, keeping his trade goods in chests and boxes lining the four walls of his room.[5] He had no need for the shelves and counter that constitute a store, for he rarely did his trading at the fort. If he had a store at Pueblo, it was probably what we would call a storeroom.

Pueblo traders did most of their trading at Indian villages, which they reached either with wagons, if the village was known to be on a road, or with pack animals. The Arapaho villages most frequently visited by traders were north of the Pueblo along the foot of the mountains, at Jimmy's Camp, at Bijou Basin on the Platte-Arkansas divide, at the mouth of Cherry Creek where Denver is now located, or near the South Platte trading posts.

On the South Platte in July, 1843 an Arapaho village described by Theodore Talbot was situated on a level plain, its lodges pitched here and there in no particular order. The lodges were of buffalo hides sewn together and stretched over lodge poles in the shape of a cone. Measurements varied greatly, but the majority of lodges were about ten feet in diameter at the bottom and twelve feet high, their sides secured to the ground with pickets. A hole near the bottom of the lodge with a flap to close it served as a door. Another opening at the top served as a chimney for the fire built directly underneath. The smoke was controlled by flaps manipulated from the outside by long sticks. The interiors of better lodges were lined with cloth or handsomely ornamented skins to a height of three or four feet, and around the perimeter were spread buffalo robes and blankets. Many Arapaho lodges had attached doghouses made of wickerwork covered with skins, housing a score of dogs (Arapahos were dog eaters). Near the outside entrance to the lodge was a tripod on which a warrior's shield, lance, battle-axe and other war implements were hung.[6]

An Indian village, wrote Theodore Talbot, was the scene of bustle and excitement. Women scurried here and there, fetching wood and water, cooking, and dressing skins. Young girls helped their mothers or played ball, while the men lounged around gambling or talking politics. Sometimes a hunter more enterprising than his fellows would arrive laden with meat. Boys of the village guarded and attended to the horses, while others practiced with their savage weapons, or engaged in athletic games and boyish pranks. Now and then some eloquent old man who served as the village newspaper would call out the news of the day in his loudest voice. At sunset the horseherd was driven up to the village, and the most valuable animals were picketed near their owners' lodges to prevent capture in an enemy attack. As night fell, sentinels were placed outside the village.

A trader in the village was received graciously, directed to the chief's lodge, and given the best place there, at the back behind the fire, for his coming was a source of great delight. At his arrival a crier went out through the village to announce him and to give an account of his goods and what he wanted to trade them for. Business was conducted with dignity and deliberation. The trader waited patiently while the Indians felt his goods, contemplated each purchase for as long as an hour, and haggled politely over each set price. At the end of the transactions the trader's wagon was loaded with robes. Off he went to his fort, well pleased if he had emptied the village of its robes. He left the Indians supplied with copper kettles, guns and ammunition, sugar, coffee, corn, flour, cloth for men's shirts and women's dresses, beads for ornamenting buckskin garments, horse-trappings and parfleches, and vermilion for beautifying the skin of young ladies and braves. Usually the trader left a barrel of whiskey with a chief as a gift to be enjoyed by all the village in a joyous bacchanal. If the results of the orgy were more serious than a general hangover, the trader was by that time far away.[7]

Traders' goods came from St. Louis, from Taos, and from the trade itself. Every spring around the middle of April a number of traders acting for themselves and for partners who remained at Pueblo, took wagons loaded with buffalo robes and tongues, deerskins, beaver and other furs to Westport Landing, now a part of Kansas City, Kansas. There the furs were loaded onto steamboats bound for St. Louis, where they arrived around the last two weeks in May. At St. Louis the furs were sold and goods were bought from wholesalers

"The Trapper," by Frederic Remington. An illustration in Francis
Parkman, *Oregon Trail* (4th edition, 1892).

Taos, New Mexico. Courtesy of Denver Public Library Western Collection.

and commission merchants. Back onto a steamboat went the goods, bound for Westport; there they were loaded on the traders' wagons for their trip to Pueblo. Traders usually left Westport for the return journey about the last week in July, arriving in September after a trip of thirty to thirty-five days. Partnerships in a wagonload of merchandise, usually worth from $1,500 to $2,000, were common, and partners appeared to change frequently.[8]

Once or twice a year Pueblo traders would make the trip to Taos to buy whiskey, flour, dried vegetables, cats, pigs, and so forth, and to bring back the news, that item of inestimable value to the isolated little settlements. At Taos traders bought on credit; in the early days they paid with beaver skins. After the Mexican War they bought with greenbacks or specie brought into the country by soldiers and emigrants, or they used drafts, which were circulated almost as freely as paper money.

In the Missouri Historical Society is a draft that perfectly illustrates the mobility of drafts. It was issued to Baptiste Gordier for

$300 at rendezvous on Green River, August 19, 1835, by Andrew Drips as agent for Fontenelle, Fitzpatrick & Co. Baptiste Gordier took it to Fort William (Bent's Fort) and endorsed it over to Bent, St. Vrain & Co. on November 17, 1835. An agent of Bent, St. Vrain & Co. took it to Taos where it was endorsed over to D. Waldo & Co. on January 29, 1836. At Taos, Waldo & Co. endorsed it over to James Glenday, who took it with him to the next trappers' rendezvous on Green River in August, 1836. There it was made over to Fontenelle, Fitzpatrick & Co. who had issued it in the first place. From there it was returned to St. Louis and given honorable retirement, having traveled several thousand miles and done $1,500 worth of business in a year's service.[9]

Rufus Sage remarked that Pueblo was well situated for trade with Mexicans. Mexican traders usually came from Taos, which had developed a set of Indian traders long before there were Americans on the Arkansas. After Pueblo was built, there was constant traffic on the Taos trail over Sangre de Cristo Pass. Hordes of Mexican traders went far north of their previous limit on the Arkansas River, showing up at Fort Laramie and even beyond.[10]

Traders from Taos traveled with pack mules loaded with dark, unbolted flour, coarsely ground corn meal and raw whiskey, all products of their own valley. They also brought dried onions, squash and chili peppers, as well as *piloncillos,* the little pillows of brown sugar imported from Mexico, and *biscochos,* hard-crusted rolls with the long-lasting properties of hardtack but a much better flavor. They had Navajo blankets and silver trinkets the Indians liked. In barter Mexican traders took buffalo robes, deerskins, furs, meat, moccasins, bows and arrows, guns and ammunition, coffee, calico, tobacco—and old clothes. Thomas J. Farnham traded his dress coat, pants, overcoat, and shirts for three horses at Fort Leche in 1839, his Mexican buyer demanding either clothes or cash.[11]

Trade between Mexicans and Americans had less order and dignity than trade with Indians. Rufus Sage describes a party of twelve or fifteen Mexican traders from Taos as "a miserable looking gang of filthy half-naked ragamuffins" who showed up at Fort Lancaster on the South Platte in September, 1842. They wanted twenty dollars per *fanega* for their flour and meal, which the men of Fort Lancaster thought was worth four to six dollars per *fanega* (who would in turn sell it to emigrants at Fort Laramie for twenty-five cents a pint, or twenty-five dollars per *fanega*!). The Americans agreed to pay the

Mexicans' price, if they would accept inferior buffalo robes in exchange. The Mexicans refused. The Americans insisted. The Mexicans retired a short distance and camped. The Americans made a rush for the Mexicans' horses and drove them off. The Mexicans seized their guns. The Americans did likewise, and a Mexican was shot through the chest. Both sides retired for the night. The next day they came to terms, the Americans returning the Mexicans' horses, and the Mexicans lowering their prices.[12]

Probably in the first year of the fort's existence Pueblo traders discovered the Oregon or California emigrant, a class of customer that would be increasingly important to them. The great migration to the west coast started in 1841 with the very company that brought George Simpson to Fort Laramie. That year Simpson found trappers and traders at Fort Laramie and Fort Platte, some of whom were later closely connected with the Pueblo, and there was doubtless barter. After Simpson left, the emigrants went on to Green River where they spent a whole day trading with mountain men, gagging at the mountain prices and jacking up their own prices proportionately. The emigrants offered gunpowder at one dollar per cup, lead at a dollar and a half per pound, sugar at one dollar per cup, good Mackinaw blankets at eight dollars to fifteen dollars apiece, cotton shirts at three to five dollars, rifles at thirty to sixty dollars. The mountain men offered dressed deerskins at three dollars, deerskin pants at ten dollars, beaver skins at ten dollars, moccasins at one dollar, flour at fifty cents per cup, tobacco at two dollars per pound. At these mutually outrageous prices, neither side could complain of being overcharged.[13]

News of the emigrants' propensity for trade at Green River in 1841 doubtless flew like rumor to all the independent traders in the West. There may have been some traders from the new post at Pueblo to greet the 1842 emigrants. The second emigration consisted of about 125 people and a considerable number of cattle. These emigrants had made the mistake of loading as much household furniture and possessions as they could cram into nineteen large, heavy wagons. When they arrived at Fort Laramie and were told that the country ahead was "entirely swept of grass," they sold some of their wagons and cattle at prices they had paid for them in the United States, receiving in exchange sugar, coffee and worn-out horses at mountain prices. At Fort Laramie they sold thirty head of cattle and eighty more at Fort Platte, some of them fine Durham or short-horns. Or they traded two sore-footed oxen for one sound animal, a pattern that would long be followed in the emigrant trade, and one which served to increase the herd at Pueblo. By the summer of 1843 Pueblo had "a fine stock of cattle" which probably came from dealings with emigrants on the Oregon Trail.[14]

The 1843 emigrants profited by the misfortunes of their predecessors. Instead of packing heavy wagons with household goods, they packed light wagons with provisions. When they reached Fort Laramie they were so well-stocked with food that they traded away some of their flour and coffee for other things, presumably with Pueblo traders. By 1843 the business of supplying emigrants, although only in its third year, was of sufficient promise for James Bridger to establish Fort Bridger, a small store with a blacksmith shop on Black's Fork of Green River. There was not a summer after 1843 that Pueblo traders did not hang about Fort Laramie, Fort Platte, Fort Bridger, and points between, lying in wait for the emigrants.[15]

In the early years of the Pueblo, a small part of its trade was with trappers. A persistent misconception of writers has been that the Pueblo was established and maintained as a trappers' rendezvous, a center for the beaver trade. On the contrary, it was peopled by ex-trappers forced by the collapse of the beaver trade to find other means of livelihood. Among them were John Hawkins, Marcelino Baca, Jim Beckwourth, Maurice LeDuc, Calvin Briggs, John Burroughs, Asa Estes, Bill New, Levin Mitchell, Rube Herring, John Brown, and Jim Waters. Only Bill Williams and the Delaware Indians—Jim Dickey, Jim Swarnock, Big Nigger and Little Beaver—were known to have pursued trapping after 1842, and they probably marketed some of their furs at Pueblo.[16]

There was still beaver in the streams of southern Colorado and Utah, on the Gila River and its tributaries in Arizona in the 1840's. The product of these southern streams was called "Santa Fe beaver," a pelt markedly lighter in color than the dark Hudson's Bay skins. For a few years, "Santa Fe beaver" was popular in European fur markets. From 1841 to 1844 P. Chouteau Jr. & Co. bought all the "pale fur" Arkansas Valley traders could collect. But in the spring of 1844, the Bents sent only four packs of beaver to St. Louis, marking the end of the beaver trade on the Arkansas.[17]

There was also a little trade with free trappers in the mountains. In the winter of 1842 and 1843, Alexander Barclay traded with trappers near South Pass in Wyoming. In the spring of 1843 he was ready to take another outfit to trappers, but in the meantime beaver had fallen in price from four and a half dollars per pound in 1842 to

"March of the Caravan" on the Santa Fe Trail. From Josiah Gregg, *Commerce of the Prairies* (1845). The squarish black buggy in the lead could be Ceran St. Vrain's dearborn. Courtesy of Denver Public Library Western Collection.

three dollars in 1843. Barclay meant to hold the beaver he had received in trade until the price went up, but the price did not go up, and Barclay relinquished his business.[18]

Those who did not actively engage in trade were farmers or stockmen. Pueblo built up a large herd of cattle from trade with emigrants, as well as from the original herd of forty-four milk cows brought from the east to serve as foster mothers to buffalo calves. Pueblo's dairy herd produced "an abundance of excellent milk" for Frémont's expedition in 1843, and were of such quality that Charles Bent purchased some animals that summer to take east to his farm in Missouri. The cattle herd continued to increase until by 1846 it was so large that it had eaten all the grass for miles around the fort. Husbandry, in short, was a major concern at Pueblo.[19]

Farming was not a major concern, at least in Pueblo's first years, nor was it at earlier Arkansas Valley posts. Bent's Fort once had an irrigated cornfield on a low piece of land between the fort and the river, but before the corn was ripe, Indians destroyed it. The field had long been abandoned when Lieutenant Abert remarked in 1846 on its still-visible irrigating ditch. Fort Leche, five miles west of Bent's Fort, had irrigated fields in 1839. But no white settlement on the Arkansas did serious farming until Pueblo was founded, and Pueblo's farming was secondary to its trading.[20]

By the summer of 1843, Pueblo's cornfield had been located northwest of the fort in bottom lands now covered by the city of Pueblo, but there is no further description of it.[21] A most annoying gap exists in the record of Pueblo's farming, but in glorious compensation a day-by-day, disaster-by-disaster account of a summer of farming on the Hardscrabble survives, and will be presented in a subsequent chapter. Suffice it to say that in Pueblo's later years farming became more and more important, providing corn to trade to other settlements as fodder for the greatly increased number of horses and oxen in the west.

Trade was, in fact, the first and foremost business of the Pueblo. If there was farming, its purpose was to produce a trade item. If there were cattle, a market for them existed among the emigrants on the Platte or the other traders on the Arkansas. If there was trapping, it was for skins to barter at Taos for whiskey, which was to trade to Indians for buffalo robes, which were to trade to outfitters for trade goods—and on and on. The men at Pueblo were traders from beginning to end.

"Fort Laramie." From Frémont's *Report of the Exploring Expedition to the Rocky Mountains in the year 1842*. . . . Note the pickets along the top of the wall, which probably influenced George Simpson and his friends in constructing the Pueblo. Courtesy of Denver Public Library Western Collection.

9
The Liquor Trade

IN THE SPRING OF 1843 George Simpson left his bride at Pueblo and went to St. Louis to buy goods for the next winter's trade. At the end of June he applied to David D. Mitchell, Superintendent of Indian Affairs at St. Louis, for a trading license. After furnishing a $5,000 bond, Simpson left the Superintendent's office with the bond. In the meantime, the clerk made out a license to "George S. Simpson" for one year's trade "at Fort Juanna a point on the Arkansas river about a mile above Fountaine qui bouille, with the Arrapahoes & such other Indians as may frequent said point," with capital in the amount of $423.63 and five men employed.[1]

By the first of July Simpson had not returned to Superintendent Mitchell's office to pick up his license. Mitchell had heard that Simpson was already on his way west "without any authority whatever to trade in the Indian country," and, Mitchell suspected, with every intention of selling liquor to the Indians. Mitchell wrote his agent at Council Bluffs that if Simpson passed there, he and his party were to be seized and prosecuted.[2] But Simpson had left St. Louis well before, and he arrived safely at Pueblo. There is no record that he ever again applied for a trading license, for he could sell whiskey to Indians just as well without it.

Selling whiskey to Indians was one of the chief concerns of the Pueblo. Most of Pueblo's whiskey came from Taos, from the distillery of Simeon Turley, another backwoodsman from Boonslick like Mathew Kinkead whose frontier childhood afforded him knowledge of many basic crafts, including the manufacture of whiskey. Turley came to Taos in 1830 and opened a store and distillery. Shortly afterwards, he built a flour mill and distillery on Arroyo Hondo Creek twelve miles north of Taos, where in 1836 an ex-trapper from St. Louis named Charles Autobees came to work for him as a traveling salesman. Leading mules packed with flour and whiskey—the latter in ten-gallon casks on either side of a mule—Autobees went up the San Luis Valley, over the Sangre de Cristo Pass to the plains, then north to the trading posts on the South Platte River. There he traded his whiskey and flour for skins, robes and drafts on St. Louis banks and returned to Arroyo Hondo the way he had come.[3]

In 1841 Turley's business was bad; he had trouble collecting money due him and paying his own creditors. In desperation he started a ranch on his land near Arroyo Hondo to ride out the bad times. It was a short ride. Within two years Turley's whiskey business was booming, and he was well on his way to becoming one of the richest men in New Mexico.

A considerable source of Turley's sudden success undoubtedly was his early participation in the affairs of Pueblo. Tom Autobees, son of Charles, said Turley had an interest in the fort and a store there. By 1843 Robert Fisher and David Spaulding were Turley's agents at Pueblo. Charles Autobees continued to bring Turley's flour and whiskey over the Sangre de Cristo Pass and north to the forts on the South Platte, but now, instead of packing the furs back to New Mexico, he sent them in a wagon from Pueblo to Missouri. In April, 1843 Turley wrote his brother Jesse that he was sending his wagon east from "Robert Fisher's Fort" with two hundred buffalo robes and some beaver. In 1844 Autobees traded some of Turley's whiskey and flour at Fort Lancaster for cows, calves and steers which ended up either at Pueblo or at the Arroyo Hondo ranch.[4]

By 1845 there are no more records of Charles Autobees packing whiskey to the Arkansas and South Platte, nor of Turley's store at Pueblo. That year Turley sent Charles Autobees to St. Louis to buy goods for the Santa Fe trade. From then on, Turley's whiskey was so popular that he did not need a salesman or delivery service. Traders from the north now made the trip to Turley's Mill to buy their whiskey, packing it back through the mountains on their own mules.[5]

Whiskey was by far the most compelling item a trader had to sell an Indian. The Cheyenne Indians told Colonel Dodge in 1835 at Bent's Fort that "in arranging the good things of this world in order of rank . . . whiskey should stand first, then tobacco, third, guns, fourth, horses, and fifth, women."[6] After the first drink, as Indian Superintendent William Clark noted in 1831, "not an Indian could

Ruins of Turley's Mill, Arroyo Hondo, New Mexico. Courtesy of Oliver Lecompte.

be found among a thousand who would not sell his horse, his gun, or his last blankets for another drink."[7]

Whiskey was not only the most popular but the most profitable trade item. Traders bought pure alcohol at St. Louis in 1837 and 1838 for about a dollar a gallon and sold it in the mountains for $4 per pint or one buffalo robe. John Brown bought whiskey for his Greenhorn store for $2.25 per gallon and sold it for $1 per pint to the men of the settlement. But the pint sold to the Indians was even more profitable, for it was sold not as pure alcohol or pure Taos whiskey. Depending on the tribe, the whiskey was diluted four to nine times its strength with water, and sometimes was drugged to avoid the inevitable difficulties when the Indians became drunk. The margin of profit was such that no trader could afford not to sell whiskey, no matter what his scruples might be.[8]

Despite the enormous profits there were enormous drawbacks to this trade, not only for the Indians but for the traders. During drunken orgies the Indians committed mayhem and murder not only on their own people but on the white trader, who might be killed and his trading house destroyed. Liquor caused quarrels among the Indians, during which the village broke up into warring factions; the men neglected to hunt and their families starved. In the year 1841 David D. Mitchell, St. Louis Superintendent of Indian Affairs, estimated that 120 Indians in his jurisdiction, mostly heads of families, had died in drunken brawls; in 1842 he increased the estimated number of dead to 500.[9]

It is no wonder then that selling liquor to Indians was against the law. The law covering the period of the Arkansas Valley settlements was the Trade and Intercourse Act of June 30, 1834 which, if enforced, would have protected both the Indians and the trader in the Indian country. The Indian country in 1834 was defined as all that part of the United States west of the Mississippi, and not within the states of Missouri or Louisiana, or the territory of Arkansas, and also, that part of the United States east of the Mississippi river, and not within any state to which the Indian title has not been extinguished. The Indian country of the 1840's included all or part of the present states of Wisconsin, Minnesota, Iowa, Kansas, Oklahoma, North Dakota, South Dakota, Wyoming, Colorado, Idaho and Montana. Within this huge territory, which the Indian rightly thought of as his own land, the statute provided that the white man should neither hunt, range stock, nor make settlement. The trader was entitled, through a license issued by the Superintendent of Indian

Affairs, to bring to Indian lands such goods as he could sell, excepting whiskey, and take away such items as he could barter for, including furs and horses and excluding traps, guns, Indian cooking utensils and Indian-made clothing. No one but a regularly licensed trader or agent of the government had any business in the Indian country without a passport.[10]

Pueblo violated almost all the provisions of the Intercourse Act, and every one of its inhabitants was breaking the law. Those responsible for establishing the settlement could have been fined $1,000 each. Most of its traders could have been fined $500 and their merchandise confiscated for trading without a license. All the foreign or Mexican population could have been fined $1,000 each for entering the Indian country without a passport, as could all the unlicensed traders from the United States. Also subject to fine were mountain men and their Mexican ladies wearing Indian moccasins; men caught in the act of trapping or hunting game; owners of cattle, horses and mules ranging near the post; and of course traders selling liquor to Indians. The whiskey sellers could have been arrested, held by a military force for five days, then removed to Missouri and proceeded against for libel by the nearest United States court. If convicted, half their goods and peltries would go to the informer, half to the United States.[11]

The Intercourse Act should have prevented a settlement like Pueblo from springing up in the wilderness and thriving for eight long years. During nearly every year of its existence there were army officers or Indian agents passing by the post or within seventy miles of it who were authorized by the Intercourse Act, or some liberal interpretation of it, to arrest violators and confiscate their goods. For nine months during the Mexican War, three hundred United States soldiers were stationed half a mile from the post—enough men to haul off all the people, whiskey, livestock, and goods. In fact, the liquor trade all over the west could have been eliminated in a season with a military post on the Arkansas, another on the Upper Mississippi, and five energetic agents on the Platte and Missouri. Why was it not done?

The answer is, neither the government, its agents, nor the traders wanted it done. To deny American fur traders the use of liquor would have prejudiced the United States' chances of obtaining Oregon, a dearly sought object of many men in high political office. Without liquor, the American traders could not have opposed the Hudson's Bay Company, whose goods were duty-free, cheaper, and of better quality. Should American traders have been forced to withdraw from the waters of the Columbia, not only that territory but the Upper Missouri River would have fallen under British control, and, under the strange conditions of joint ownership of the far northwest, the land itself would revert to the British in time. So ran the argument, which was impressive enough to excuse the government's failure to enforce the law prohibiting the sale of liquor to Indians.[12]

To government agents, enforcement of the Intercourse Law seemed impossible. St. Louis Superintendent Mitchell declared in 1842 that the ways of smuggling liquor into the Indian country were so various that all the officers and troops in the United States could not prevent its introduction, for there was no end to the ingenuity of the whiskey traders. Even if the smuggler were caught, he simply lost his goods, paid his fine and was smuggling again in a short while, because the penalties were negligible compared to the profits of his trade. Usually he escaped any penalty at all, for he had to be brought with witnesses to Missouri and tried in the civil courts which met only a few weeks of the year. The honest and faithful officer who had apprehended him—a rare bird indeed!—would discover that witnesses had disappeared or changed their stories, that he lacked proof that the liquor was not for the trader's personal use, or that the substance he had poured out on the ground was really liquor. If he were not that man of rare honesty, he would accept the bribes offered by the traders, which were likely to be larger than his salary.[13]

The traders themselves could hardly afford to discontinue the use of whiskey, for nothing so efficiently separated the Indian from his robes. Heads of the big fur companies—McLoughlin, Astor, Crooks and Chouteau, whose future depended upon the ability of the Indians to hunt buffalo and make robes—deplored the use of alcohol, and in principle prohibited it within their own companies. But in practice they condoned the actions of their traders who, as soon as opposition traders appeared, rolled out their kegs and poured whiskey down Indian gullets like mother birds feeding their young.[14]

In the fall of 1841 Pierre Chouteau, Jr., whose St. Louis house had taken over the western business of the American Fur Company, decided to destroy the liquor trade and his competitors with one well-aimed shot by demanding enforcement of the Intercourse Act. He wrote his intentions to the Commissioner of Indian Affairs in the fall of 1841. Together they had worked out a plan by the summer of 1842: At various points on the Missouri River, agents and companies of dragoons would stop and search all boats and wagons. A special agent fully empowered to act against whiskey sellers would be appointed to tour the Indian country with a company of dragoons to stop the sale of any liquor that might have slipped through.[15]

Chosen as special agent was Andrew Drips, with many years' experience in the fur trade both as an American Fur Company brigade leader and as a leader of competitors' brigades. By his fellow mountain men he was known as "a good, honest old beaver trapper." D. D. Mitchell said he was "an intelligent, enterprising man." But he was also described as a mere pawn of the big company, who sent word to the company's posts that he was coming, to give them time to hide their liquor.[16]

There was little enthusiasm for Chouteau's plan in the upper echelons of the government. In fact, the Indian Department, the War Department and Congress seemed to put as many obstacles as possible in its way. At the start Congress delayed approval of Drips' appointment from July to October, 1842, allowing whiskey merchants to duck past the guards and hurry to their upriver posts to sell liquor to the Indians, or to hide it before Drips arrived. By the time Drips reached the Upper Missouri in November, the region was crawling with whiskey traders and awash in alcohol.[17]

Undaunted, alone except for an interpreter, Drips started off along the Missouri to visit Sioux villages and their traders. Naturally, he found no liquor, nor, without dragoons, could he have enforced the law had he found any. He strongly recommended that dragoons be sent to accompany him next summer on a tour to Bent's Fort and trading posts on the Platte and Missouri. But when Superintendent Mitchell and the Commissioner of Indian Affairs made a formal request for dragoons, the Secretary of War answered tersely, "The request cannot be complied with." That was the end of any hope for strict enforcement of the Intercourse law.[18]

In the spring of 1843 Mitchell was forced to admit that Drips's efforts had so far been unsuccessful, but by September his outlook had brightened. In his annual report, he announced that Drips's labors and those of the more sensible and sober Indians had done much toward destroying the liquor trade. The trading season of 1843–44 justified his optimism. When John Richard brought liquor cross-country from St. Louis, traveling at night and avoiding all roads, he cached it on the prairie near Fort Platte and defied Drips's bright young deputy, Joseph V. Hamilton, to find it. Hamilton never did find it, but he clung like a burr to Fort Platte the whole winter long, and kept not only John Richard but a number of Taos traders from selling liquor to the Indians. As a result, seven hundred lodges of Sioux wintering on the Platte drank not a drop of whiskey and made twelve hundred packs of robes, as opposed to their average of eight hundred packs.[19]

In the same way, Drips's own presence on the Missouri curtailed the liquor trade there. Pierre Chouteau, Jr. did his part by defying his own employees in refusing to allow them liquor for their trade despite their angry and impassioned demands. Some liquor got through, but on June 1, 1845 Drips wrote that the illicit trade in whiskey had almost disappeared from the Upper Missouri. The competition had also disappeared. During 1845, P. Chouteau Jr. & Co. bought out its opposition, mortally wounded by the liquor ban, on the Missouri and Platte. All in all, Drips had done his duty, both to his commission and to his former employers, reducing the use of liquor and eliminating the competition. If he was rightly denounced for serving two masters, it can at least be said that he served them both well.[20]

Drips's efforts to contain the use of whiskey on the Upper Missouri were relatively successful, but his attempts to stop the importation of whiskey from Taos through Pueblo and Hardscrabble were not. In the spring of 1845 he dipped his pen in a well of frustration and wrote:

I would particularly call the attention of the department to a description of Traders who reside in the vicinity of the Mexican country, on the waters of the Arkinsas, they cultivate corn &c, which they trade to the Indians for Robes & Skins, with which they proceed to St. Fee & Taos and barter for whiskey Flour &c. these latter articles they again bring to the Indians with whom they trade in opposition & much to the detriment of the regular Licensed Traders, they defy a U.S. agent and for want of a proper force of the latter, at his command, permits those people to act with impunity. They reside in two villages, one on the American & the other within the Mexican line, they are a mongrel crew, of Am., French, Mexicans and half Breeds, and generally speaking are unable to procure employment for past misconduct; in fact, they are no better than outlaws.[21]

Bent, St. Vrain & Co. had been a party to the decision of Pierre Chouteau, Jr. to stop using liquor. When Marcus Whitman passed

Bent's Fort in December, 1842 he spoke highly of the beneficial effects of the Bents' new dedication to temperance; their trade, said Whitman, was good and the prospects promising. But by March, 1843 the news from the Arkansas was that business at Bent's Fort was anything but good, and only the Bents' trade with the Comanches on the South Canadian would bring them through.[22]   '

Charles Bent knew what the trouble was. On New Year's Day, 1843 he or his clerk wrote Superintendent Mitchell about "several renegade Americans" who had built houses at the mouth of the Fountain in United States territory where, "without any license from any authority, they procure whiskey in the Mexican country, which they keep on hand continually, for the purpose of trading with the Indians in the country, to the great injury of the Indians and of licensed traders." Bent wrote that Pueblo was a harbor for Mexican traders who brought whiskey and other articles to that place.[23]

There was more self-righteous indignation in Bent's words than a dispassionate view of Pueblo. The "renegades" were men he had known well at St. Louis, Bent's Fort, and Taos, and the illegal commodity they were selling had been a staple of his own trade until a few months before Pueblo was established. If Charles Bent felt he had to tattle on Pueblo, it was not on moral principle but because Pueblo traders with their whiskey were doing better than Bent's traders without it.

Bent had every expectation of seeing Pueblo crushed, if not by Andrew Drips and his dragoons, then by an even more potent weapon—a military post on the Arkansas at the mouth of the Fountain. Bent's hopes were based upon proposals to Congress introduced in 1838 by Dr. Lewis F. Linn, junior senator from Missouri and protégé of Missouri's senior senator, Thomas H. Benton. Dr. Linn began by stating that title of the United States to Oregon was indisputable (a highly disputable statement), and demanding the military occupation of that territory. By 1841 the idea had gained some support in Congress, and on January 8, 1841 Linn introduced a bill providing for land grants to settlers in Oregon and a chain of military posts from Fort Leavenworth to the Rocky Mountains to protect emigrants on their way west. The proposals were widely discussed, and it seemed likely they would be accepted.[24]

In the fall of 1842 Senator Linn asked Manuel Alvarez, United States Consul at Santa Fe, to ask Charles Bent's opinion as to the best location for a post. Bent was charmed to oblige. With every appearance of disinterest, he suggested a location at the junction of the "Fontan Que Biaule" with the Arkansas, which he declared was equidistant from the North Platte and the Santa Fe trail and would thus afford protection to both Oregon emigrants and Santa Fe traders. In the heart of the Indian range, Bent wrote the Senator, the location had the added advantage of being directly on the Mexican border and in a position to prevent the Mexicans from exciting Indians to commit depredations on the United States frontier in case of war. The answer was typical of the wily Bent who knew full well that only an Oregon emigrant with a broken compass would ever travel to his promised land via the Arkansas, and that the "heart of the Indian range" was actually several hundred miles to the east of Pueblo (where, in fact, the first of the chain of military posts was finally built in 1849). [25]

Delighted with the way things were going, Bent could not refrain from crowing to the Mexican authorities at Santa Fe that the United States was about to establish a line of military posts along the Arkansas to mark the boundary, and (his imagination in full bloom) extending from the Arkansas to the South Platte. This information was received with trepidation and forwarded immediately to the Mexican Minister of War, where it was added to a file of frightened reports dating from the 1700's regarding foreign posts on the Arkansas. [26]

Bent also wrote the Superintendent of Indian Affairs on January 1, 1843 that the only way to stop the liquor trade from Mexico would be to establish a military post on the Arkansas "at some suitable point near the mountain," but he did not suggest the mouth of the Fountain, nor did he say that this location would be of any value in controlling the natives in the "heart of the Indian range," for he was aware that Superintendent Mitchell, an old mountain man, knew better. [27]

Senator Linn introduced his bill early in the 1842–43 session of Congress; it passed the Senate but was dropped in the House. Dropped also from that time on was Charles Bent's pretense that the military post at the mouth of the Fountain would be of any aid to Oregon emigrants. In May, 1843 he wrote Superintendent Mitchell that the only way to prevent New Mexico traders from bringing whiskey to Indians in the United States was a military post "on or near the line between the U. States and Mexico." Two months later, his good friend Manuel Alvarez wrote Daniel Webster, Secretary of State, about the transient Mexican whiskey peddlers, and about a village of Americans above Bent's Fort which sold the Indians at least as much liquor as the Mexicans did. Alvarez suggested that some arrangement be made with the Mexican government to prohibit the transportation of alcohol across the mountains into the United States, and in this Bent and Alvarez got surprising support from their most bitter enemy, Padre Antonio José Martínez of Taos, who complained to President Santa Anna of American posts on the boundary between the countries which demoralized the Indians by selling them liquor and inducing them to steal horses from the New Mexican settlements.[28]

By the end of 1843 Senator Linn was dead, and so was his Oregon Bill. That summer a thousand emigrants made their way to Oregon and in effect won that land for the United States without need of either military posts or land grants. Neither Bent, Alvarez, nor Superintendent Mitchell ever succeeded in getting a military post for the mouth of the Fountain. The only military post established there before Fort Reynolds was built in 1868 was a paper one, erected by several hurried historians on a foundation of unwarranted assumptions.

It started with a letter of Joseph V. Hamilton who had heard that there were dragoons on the Arkansas (as indeed there were, two hundred miles east of Pueblo at the Cimarron Crossing, to provide escort for Santa Fe traders). Hamilton wrote from the North Platte on November 4, 1843 that "there is a company of dragoons stationed at the Messrs. Dent & Senevern Fort on the Arkansas, I have no doubt for the purpose of stopping those whiskey peddlers from the Spanish country."[29] Hamilton's piece of wishful thinking induced H. M. Chittenden to write sixty years later, in his *American Fur Trade of the Far West*, that "the practice of smuggling liquor from Santa Fe to the headwaters of the Arkansas and Platte rivers had become a regular business and led the War Department to station a company of dragoons on the Arkansas in 1843."[30] Forty years later another researcher, after reading Chittenden's statement, and being familiar with letters of Charles Bent referring to "Fort Spaulding" and to the military post on the Fountain, concluded that Fort Spaulding was the very military post in question: "Subsequently," he stated, "Fort Spaulding was constructed in the location Bent recommended. . . ."[31] A map at the end of the book in which this statement appears, shows "Fort Spalding" as a United States military post located on the south side of the Arkansas in Mexican territory!

10
A Dry Year
in the Whiskey Trade
1843

FROM THE SUMMER OF 1842 until the summer of 1843, Pueblo's trade was excellent; that much can be inferred from Charles Bent's extraordinary efforts to destroy the post. Its early success was based primarily upon smuggling liquor from Taos, an illegal business which the United States government, as Bent discovered, was unable or unwilling to stop. But a series of events having little to do with either Charles Bent or the United States government succeeded for a time in curbing Pueblo's commerce in Taos whiskey. For this catastrophe the men of Pueblo could in part blame their old trapping comrade, Charles Warfield.

Warfield, the son of a New Orleans merchant, was a most personable young man, handsome, agreeable and witty. By 1833 he was a trapper on the Upper Missouri, and by the time he left the mountains eight years later, he was thoroughly acquainted with most of the trappers and traders who later settled at Pueblo.[1]

In 1841 Warfield went to St. Louis, then left for Texas with his wife. In Indian Territory his wife died, and Warfield went on to Texas alone. There he lived for a year, soaking up the fervent nationalism and the hatred of Mexico which permeated that turbulent republic.[2]

In 1836 Texas had won her independence from Mexico, to the wild applause of most Americans who saw in Texan defiance of tyranny a reflection of their own struggle of 1776. When the Texans invaded New Mexico in 1841, they were captured and treated roughly. Again they had the support of the people of the United States. The Texans were to count heavily on this support in their next foray into Mexico. Based, like the Texan Santa Fe expedition of 1841, on a preposterous claim of Texas to all of New Mexico east of the Rio Grande, the new expedition proposed to capture Mexican wagon trains laden with specie as soon as they crossed the Arkansas, and then go on to capture Santa Fe. Half the booty was to go to the men of the expedition, half to the insolvent government of Texas. For this adventure, Charles Warfield was chosen as leader.[3]

Given a colonel's commission by Sam Houston on August 16, 1842, Warfield was authorized to commission other officers and to raise a force on the Missouri frontier and at trading posts in the mountains. Houston commissioned another colonel, Jacob Snively, to recruit 250 Texans and meet Warfield and his forces at the Arkansas Crossing (near present Dodge City, Kansas) for the purpose of waylaying the annual caravan from Missouri, which this year consisted mostly of Mexicans.[4]

Warfield went to St. Louis and then to Westport, beating the Missouri frontier for recruits. When he had signed up fifty or sixty men, including John McDaniel who was to lead them, he gave them instructions to meet him at the Arkansas Crossing. Warfield left Westport on October 30 with mountain man Tim Goodale and went west along the Arkansas visiting trading posts to persuade his old trapping comrades to join him.[5]

By February, 1843 he had reached Fort Lancaster with two men and the bullet-pierced, tattered flag of the Republic of Texas that had flown over the battlefield at Corpus Christi in 1836. At the sight of the flag, two Mexican employees shinnied up the fort flagpole in terror. The emotional impact of the Lone Star banner and the fluency and fair promises of the affable colonel captured ten or fifteen men at Fort Lancaster for the Texans' cause, and they all set out to rendezvous at the mouth of the Purgatory in March.[6]

On their way they camped on the south side of the Arkansas opposite Pueblo. Four of them visited the fort where they took over a room, drank whiskey, and got brawling drunk. In their giddy exaltation, they forced José María Jimines to swear allegiance to the Republic of Texas, and they bragged how they would cut off the heads of public officers of New Mexico and seize the goods of the *ricos*. The men of Pueblo called a meeting in another room to discuss how to get rid of their unmanageable guests. Finally, David Spaulding confronted the Texans and asked them why they had come here. They answered that they meant to do whatever damage they could to New Mexico. Spaulding said he could not approve their plan, because his livelihood depended upon trade with New Mexico, and his wife and those of his companions were from New Mexico. He ordered them to leave immediately, or the Pueblo men would disarm them and throw them out.[7]

Early the next morning, Spaulding left for Taos bearing a letter from Robert Fisher to Simeon Turley, a rare and interesting document about Pueblo in March, 1843:

Fort Spaulding March 13th 1843
Mr. Simeon Turley
  Dear Sir,
      Mr. Towne has just arrived from Taos. He met Antonio Vijil who told him that I had taken his liquor from him. That is a lie. He asked me to take charge of it, as there was no chance of his getting over to the Platte. This I can prove by every person in the fort both Americans and Spaniards. He also said that we were all Texians and that Geo. Simpson was a Texian officer. All this is false. There is a party of Texians on this river four of them came here and wished some of us to join them but we refused. I understand that Antonio Vijil threetend to raise a party and attack this place. He may come, but he must know that the Fort is in the Territory of the United States and if the Mexicans enter it, in arms with hostile intentions our Government will consider it a declaration of war. An Express is ready to start to the U. States as soon as they commence hostilities. The liquor A. Vijil can get whenever he wants. He wished to sell out to me but I told him that I did not want it and then he asked me to take care of it for him which I did. Tomorrow Jas. Waters will pay me what he owes you and I will speak to him about the cow. He has been waiting for an opportunity to send the mules in. The first chance he will send them. Spaulding will tell you about the trade &c. I had a notion to go to the Platte but I can't get over. I will have about 200 robes I mean Robes that have been paid to me for you. I have traded about 17 Robes worth of tobacco. I went to the Indians but the company (Bent's) [paid] in tobacco and I quit trading it. The Indians won't trade liquor now. I traded 5 animals and lost your big legged horse - he was stolen.
      The cows are doing well and some are beginning to have calves. Before I can do anything about the cows in there I can't tell until Spaulding comes out. We are determined to stay here and mind our own business.
      Write every opportunity.

Robert Fisher [rubric][8]

At Taos, Spaulding and José María Jimines testified to Warfield's activities on the Arkansas, in order to absolve Pueblo from any involvement with these freebooters. They presented to the Alcalde the letter of Robert Fisher as tangible proof of Pueblo's innocence and as a deterrent to attack by the Mexican trader Antonio Vigil and his friends. The threat of United States retaliation was, of course, mere bravado. United States officials considered Pueblo an outlaw settlement entirely undeserving of protection, let alone worth going to war over. The letter and a translation ended up in the files of the Mexican Secretary of Defense.

On May 6, Colonel Warfield was again at the mouth of the Fountain looking for volunteers without success. After he left for Bent's Fort he sent a letter back to Pueblo addressed to the British trader Alexander Montgomerie, offering him a lieutenant colonel's commission and an allowance of ten pesos a day. Montgomerie not only declined but hurried off to Santa Fe to give another account of Warfield's movements to Mexican authorities.[9]

Warfield arrived at the Purgatory rendezvous to find that only twenty-five mountain men had showed up. The company under John McDaniel, numbering only fifteen, had met Antonio José Chávez at the Little Arkansas and robbed and murdered him. After dividing up Don Antonio's money and turning his servants free, McDaniel's men returned to Independence, where their leaders were arrested for robbery and murder and executed in 1844.[10]

Without the McDaniel forces, Warfield and his twenty-three mountain men decided they were too few to take Santa Fe. Instead, they drifted down to the vicinity of Mora, New Mexico, where they pounced on a party of buffalo hunters camped on Coyote Creek, killing three, wounding three, and stealing seventy horses. The outraged gentry of Mora organized, counterattacked, recovered the horses, and captured five of Warfield's men. The rest of the Texans, carrying their saddles, walked back to the mouth of the Purgatory where they disbanded.[11] Warfield joined the Snively forces who were lying in wait for the Mexican caravan at the Arkansas Crossing.

The murder of Antonio José Chávez and the senseless attack on the citizens of Mora were not only crimes but blunders, turning the tide of American sympathy against the Texans. When the Mexican caravan and its United States escort of dragoons under Captain Philip St. George Cooke arrived at the Arkansas Crossing on June 30, Captain Cooke crossed the river and disarmed Snively and his men. The Texans returned to their own Republic and the Mexican caravan passed on to Santa Fe in peace.[12]

In the meantime, a vanguard of predominantly Taos Indians under Governor Armijo, which was to escort the caravan from the Arkansas to Santa Fe, had been defeated by the Texans near the Arkansas and eighteen of the Indians were killed. In July angry Taos Indians rose in a mob, sacked the tithe granaries in the valley of Taos, and plundered the stores and houses of wealthy foreigners.

Consequently, Americans at Pueblo were afraid to buy their staples at Taos that summer. Before fall there were Mexican decrees against commerce with foreign nations, and a scarcity of New Mexican products throughout the West.[13]

One of the first to feel the pinch was Lieutenant John Charles Frémont. Bound for California, he had expected to find provisions and mules at Fort St. Vrain, brought from Beaubien's store at Taos. One of Frémont's hunters was Lucien Maxwell, son-in-law of Beaubien. Frémont commissioned him to go to Taos and buy ten or twelve mules, pack them with provisions and take them to Pueblo, where Frémont would meet him. Maxwell left Fort St. Vrain for Taos on July 6, Frémont and his men following the next morning on their way to Pueblo.[14]

Traveling south by the wagon road to the settlements on the Arkansas River, Frémont approached Pueblo and began to meet denizens of the place. In the afternoon of July 13 he passed "the encampment of a hunter named Maurice, who had been out on the plains in pursuit of buffalo calves, a number of which I saw among some domestic cattle near his lodge."[15] Shortly afterwards a party of buckskin-clad mountaineers galloped up on good fat horses. Frémont recognized several of them as New Englanders whom he had seen the year before on the South Platte, camped with their Indian wives and half-blood children. These were probably Calvin T. Briggs and John Burroughs, and their surveillance of Frémont's party was a routine check to see if the visitors were government agents looking for whiskey.[16]

At noon on July 14, Frémont and his detachment of fifteen men camped at the mouth of the Fountain, where Frémont wrote:

A short distance above our encampment, on the left bank of the Arkansas, is a *pueblo,* (as the Mexicans call their civilized Indian villages,) where a number of mountaineers, who had married Spanish women in the valley of Taos, had collected together, and occupied themselves in farming, carrying on at the same time a desultory Indian trade. They were principally Americans, and treated us with all the rude hospitablity their situation admitted; but as all commercial intercourse with New Mexico was now interrupted, in consequence of Mexican decrees to that effect, there was nothing to be had in the way of provisions. They had, however, a fine stock of cattle, and furnished us an abundance of excellent milk.[17]

At Pueblo, Frémont learned that Maxwell and two other men were thought to have fallen into the hands of the Utes. Despairing of

J. C. Frémont. An engraving by J. C. Buttre from a photograph by Brady. Allan Nevins dates it 1856, when Frémont was a candidate for President (*Frémont, the West's Greatest Adventurer*, New York, 1928). Courtesy of Donald Jackson.

getting mules and provisions from Taos, Frémont hired Kit Carson to ride from Pueblo to Bent's Fort, buy mules there and meet Frémont at Fort St. Vrain. At Pueblo Frémont also hired Charles Town (or Towns, as Frémont calls him) as voyageur. On July 16 Frémont left for Fort St. Vrain, whence he would go on to California.[18]

On his return from California a year later, Frémont passed the Pueblo at sunset on June 29, 1844, and "had the pleasure to find a number of our old acquaintances." He added that "the little settlement appeared in thriving condition; and in the interval of our absence another had been established on the river, some thirty miles above," which is the first official notice of Hardscrabble.

Frémont's party occupied the same camp as the year before, and in the morning they proceeded down the Arkansas towards Bent's Fort and home.[19]

Frémont obviously amended his journal after the events described, for the Mexican decrees interrupting commercial intercourse were not in existence when he first visited Pueblo. However, Santa Anna had not been slow to take such measures in order to stop the Texan invasions. On June 17, 1843, it was decreed that no quarter should be granted to foreigners who invaded the territory; on August 7, that all customs houses on the frontier should be closed; on September 23, that no goods could be sold at retail by foreigners except those who were naturalized, married, and living with their families in Mexico.[20]

Santa Anna's decrees stopping the Santa Fe trade were no more popular with New Mexicans than with Americans. For twenty years the economy of New Mexico had been fostered by the Santa Fe trade, and without foreign commerce New Mexico was threatened with political and economic collapse. Both American traders and New Mexican officials knew that some trade and foreign enterprise must go on, and it did, with suitable variations from the norm. As usual, Dick Wootton brought goods from Bent's Fort to Charles Beaubien's store at Taos, but now he came and left in the dead of night. Beaubien's and Bent's land grants were ordered to be suspended and their settlements destroyed, but the order was quietly rescinded and the settlements, although officially nonexistent, were allowed to remain. Simeon Turley's whiskey reached the South Platte forts and Pueblo as usual, but in curtailed amounts.[21]

Beaubien and Turley were longtime merchants and naturalized citizens whom the local government allowed to slip under Santa Anna's fence because their money and business would be sorely missed. In the case of American merchants not so rich or trusted, the law was rigidly enforced, and some of the more enterprising Yankee minds were hard at work on the problem. On December 26, 1843, Santa Fe trader Josiah Gregg wrote from New York to his fellow-trader Manuel Alvarez in Paris, telling him of the closing of the frontier ports. He predicted that there would be a revolution if the ports were not soon opened, and suggested a way to turn the situation to good account by "stocking a shop" at the closest point to Santa Fe on the *Napesta* (Arkansas) River.[22].

Josiah Gregg was too late. His idea had already occurred to

Mathew Kinkead—naturalized, married to a Mexican—who had moved across the Arkansas and had stocked a shop where he was trading American goods for Mexican. By December Kinkead's Mexican goods had reached the Upper Missouri, where they infuriated the hardworking Indian Agent, Andrew Drips:

There is on the south fork of Platte a nest of traders who get ther supplys from the Spanish country sich as corn Flour Spanish Blkts Shells &c which is a great injury to the lic^d traders If ther is not a stop put to it our traders will have to leave the country for they are not able to complete with those unlicen^d pedlers. There is at present two towns of them sort of traders one on a fork of the Arkansas & one other lately built on the Spanish line the setlers is genneraly French Americans & Spanards I am inform^d that a man by the name of Kincaid is the principle person in the new village in the Spanish Territory.[23]

Mathew Kinkead had moved to the Hardscrabble River some thirty miles west of Pueblo in the fall of 1843. At the foot of Hardscrabble canyon where the river leaves the mountains, he built a house of upright logs and established his "shop." Less than a year later his trading business probably came to an end, for on March 31, 1844 Santa Anna rescinded the unpopular decree closing ports of entry. News of the reopening of the customs houses reached Pueblo in May, 1844, and Kinkead's store would then have been superfluous, but its proprietor did not move away.[24]

After the store closed, Kinkead's business on the Hardscrabble was a cattle ranch. North of his log headquarters, down the Hardscrabble, were corrals for his stock and jacal cabins for his employees, who were Calvin Briggs and John Burroughs with their Indian families, a man named Wells who lived with a girl named Candelaria Sena, and three French Canadians named Maurice LeDuc, La Fontaine and Gagnier. At his ranch Kinkead had domestic cattle and pigs, but apparently no buffalo calves.[25]

The three Frenchmen working for Kinkead probably came from a nearly defunct adobe trading post nearby. It was located in the foothills four or five miles northwest of Kinkead's house, on a point of land fringed with scrub pine and scrub oak, just above the junction of Adobe Creek and Mineral Creek. French ex-trappers had built it probably in the late 1830's when trapping became unprofitable. Its trade was with the Utes, whose trail between the plains and their summer camps in the Wet Mountain Valley passed close by. There is no contemporary reference to this fort, a fair indication of its unimportance. Even its name has passed into oblivion. By the time Kinkead settled down near it, it was called "Buzzards' Roost" for the turkey buzzards that nested there, or "Maurice's Fort" for the last man to live in it. The Mexicans called it *el cuervo*, perhaps an abbreviation of *el nido del cuervo*, the crow's nest. The Frenchmen's trade at Buzzards' Roost was not successful. By 1842 William Le-Blanc, one of the founders, had moved to New Mexico, and Maurice LeDuc was catching buffalo calves for Kinkead. But the fort on Adobe Creek was used off and on for years to come, with Maurice LeDuc as its most frequent occupant.[26]

By December, 1843, when news of Kinkead's "shop" reached Andrew Drips on the Upper Missouri, there were already two trading posts in the Hardscrabble Valley. Kinkead's venture must have been successful, for it was soon imitated and challenged. By February, 1844, George Simpson, Alexander Barclay, and Joseph Doyle were making plans to establish a third trading post within six miles of Kinkead's. By March they had moved, "traps and all," to the new settlement. They called it *San Buenaventura de los tres Arrollos*, a fancy name which would soon surrender to the more descriptive "Hardscrabble."

11
Hardscrabble
in a Wet Year
1844

THIRTY MILES WEST OF PUEBLO at the mouth of the Hardscrabble, the Arkansas Valley bluffs press in on the river. Between the Wet Mountains to the south and the foothills of the Front Range on the north, the Arkansas Valley is only twenty-five miles wide. On either side of the river the uplands are sandy, prickled with greasewood and cocklebur and ragged with arroyos. Major Long's gloomy journalist noted the "meagre and gravelly soil" and concluded that this "dreary expanse of almost naked sand . . . must for ever remain desolate."[1]

San Buenaventura de los Tres Arrollos was located in the midst of this "dreary expanse,"·on the west bank of the Hardscrabble just above its junction with Newlin Creek and below the junction of Newlin and Mineral Creeks—the "tres arroyos." Local farmers say there is no better land in Colorado than this flat river plain where two crops of alfalfa, watered by springs and wells that have never gone dry, are cut every summer. But without springs and wells farming here would be perilous, for the Hardscrabble River is not a steady source of water.

Rising in the Wet Mountains, the Hardscrabble rushes from its sources to the plains through a canyon lined with walls of yellow rock, hence its Spanish name, *Rio de Peñasco Amarillo,* and through foothills covered with scrubby white oak, hence one of its American names, "White Oak Creek." As the foothills flatten, the river loses momentum, spreads into thin strands over a sandy bed, and in some seasons disappears altogether, leaving the dry creek bottom to meander through the prairie. In some years the bed of the Hardscrabble becomes a road in summer, and a rough road it is, filled with rocks brought down the canyon in roiling yellow spring floods, with exposed roots of cottonwoods and dead branches broken off in wet spring snows.

When Frémont passed the Front Range of the Rockies in July, 1843 the high mountains were covered with snow. As he travelled down the Fountain towards the Arkansas his narrative fairly dripped with springs and rain showers and abounded in green prairies, brilliantly flowered meadows and other indications of unusual moisture. Frémont saw the Arkansas Valley in a wet year. Compare Stephen Harriman Long's description of the Arkansas Valley in the typically dry year of 1820, when the prairie turned brown and crackled underfoot, when dust dulled the color of the grass, streams were dry beds of scorching sand and flowers were the stiff yellow blossoms of drought. If Stephen Long's description kept people away from the region, as it is reported to have done, Frémont's was just as influential in drawing them to it—and the difference was little more than a dry year and a wet one.[2]

The year 1844 was another wet one on the Hardscrabble. Although the winter had been mild and dry, there was abundant snow in April and high water on the Arkansas with evidence of a flood at Pueblo where driftwood hung in tree branches and tree trunks leaned downstream at half-pitch.[3] In 1844 the valley of the Hardscrabble was green and grassy, bright with wild flowers, shaded with handsome stands of cottonwood and willow—with a promise of fertility and lush pasture. The three owners of the plaza on the Hardscrabble were men with intelligence and a sense of history who could look ahead to the end of the Indian trade and beyond it to the eventual settlement of the Arkansas Valley. Their village, *San Buenaventura de los Tres Arrollos*, was perhaps to be the first civilized wedge driven into the wilderness. Its failure as a wedge was apparent as soon as it acquired the name "Hardscrabble."

San Buenaventura de los Tres Arrollos was located and its houses built and populated by seventy people between February 12 and March 31 in the wet year of 1844. George Simpson began a letter to his cousin George Sibley in February, 1844, which dwelt dismally upon Simpson's difficulties in making a letter interesting, upon his rambling and disjointed style, upon his regret that he had spent his life in idleness instead of learning to write letters—a bored and boring production of a self-conscious youth writing a duty letter to an older relative. He laid the letter aside for a month and a half. When he resumed it, his life had become vital and exciting and so had the letter:

San Buenaventura de los tres Arollos

March 31ˢᵗ It is some time since I wrote the above - Since then I have moved, "traps and all" - I am now resident in the Republic of New Mexico — The "settlement" where I now live has been located and peopled within the last six weeks. It can number already about 70 souls - I have a plenty of good land and have built me a very substantial *house* Next week I commence ploughing - This is a delightful climiate -

April 10ᵗʰ I wish that you would send me some apple seed - and indeed all kinds of seed that you grow - I will send some of this country's productions next spring. There is fruit of different kinds here in abundance, - such as Plums, (exc*elle*nt) cherrys, (sorter) strawberries (good) currants and gooseberry (do) and Service Berries (de-licious Game - Boffelo, Elk, Black and white-tail deer, - grizzly Bear (crowders) and turkies; but they are not call'd game in this country - I don't intend to go to the States this spring. Indeed I am not going home until I make *something* Give my Respects to Cousin Mary, Aunt and Medora and Alby and Miss Rocester and - Everybody - I am writing by fire light and I have 2 other letters to finish to night for ~~they~~ the bearer starts early in morning, so I must say fare well; - wishing you health and hapiness and a kindly remembrance of your affectionate and respectful cousin

Geo S Simpson

Write to me   )
as soon   )
as possible   )

P.S. Your old acquaintance W S Williams Master Trapper left here a few days ago for t'other side of the "big Hills"[4]

The sonorous name *San Buenaventura de los Tres Arrollos* gave way to simpler names, first to "San Carlos de Napeste" as on Simpson's marriage record in October, 1844, and to "Saint Charles" or "San Carlos" as used in 1848 by J. C. Frémont and Lancaster Lupton.[5] But the name that eventually stuck to the river long after the adobes of the settlement had been absorbed into the earth was Hardscrabble. George Simpson tells how it came to be so called: "A small number of trappers and traders had, in the spring of 1844, combined for the purpose of farming on Hardscrabble, in a small way, and a very small way it was—one American plow, procured from the "States" by the writer the year before, with a half dozen hoes among nine of us, it was rather hard scrabbling to get in a crop—hence the name of the settlement."[6]

Pueblo was founded as a trading post with a little farming to be

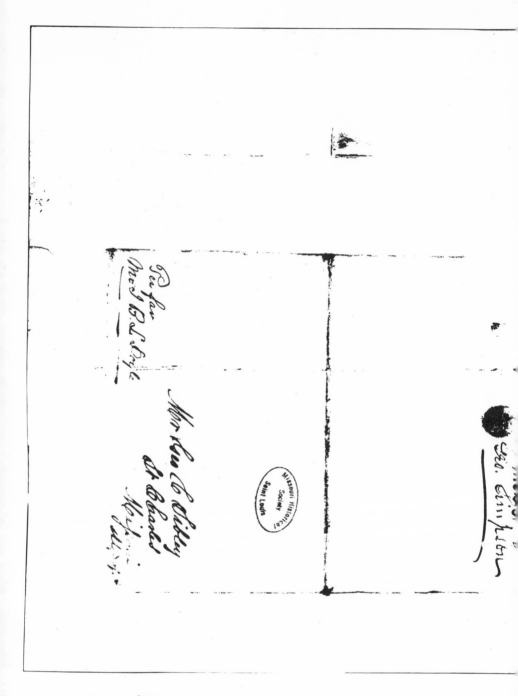

Letter of George S. Simpson to his cousin George Sibley, February 7–April 10, 1844, telling of the founding of the Hardscrabble settlement. Courtesy of Missouri Historical Society, St. Louis.

Arkansas River Lat 31°23' - Lon 31½   St Louis Mo   Feb 7th on 8th 1844

Well, my dear sir, I confess that I have been a sad delinquent,—
I have no excuses to offer,—but humbly sue for forgiveness - I promised
you that I would keep a kind of diary or Journal for your es-
pecial amusement and edification(?) Some one has given a definition
of the word "promises"; to wit - "things made to be broken",—or for "duns"
Jeremy Diddler was of this opinion - But as I am not of the Diddler
School I shall hasten to escape from a "protest" by offering this
meager epistle in the way of interest, whilst the principal
is renewed indefinitely, drawing the same interest annually
or semi-anually as opportunities may offer for remittance .
Now in this I shall promise you neither edification nor amusement
I have few resources to draw upon,—or it may be that I have been
so long in this country that what appears ~~amusing or~~ interesting or peculiar to a new-comer is to me somewhat dull and common
place   One who makes Nature his study, whether animate or
inanimate will here find numerous subjects for speculation
12th - I am a desultory man - Even in writing I am addicted
to a rambling and disjointed Style - For that, my exercises
in composition, in my School days were often condemned - It
must be a species of mental disease - I often think it grew
from a misapprehension of the rules of Rhetoric - nothing
When very young I learnt much by rote and understood ^nothing   My mind

too feeble then to comprehend, nevertheless, formed its own erroneous construction – And impressions formed in early years are so ma[ny] cross readings in the Book of Wisdom – (My humble Opinion) Verily I must have look'd but seldom into that same boo[k] or I would not have wasted many of the best years of my life in idleness and —— but n'emporte – I am a Philos[opher] in some respects, – And I think that some of Soloman's Proverbs are much better than others (I did not say more [sen]sible)

San Buenaventura de los tres Arollos

March 31st It is some time since I wrote the above – si[nce] then I have moved, "traps and all" – I am now resident in [the] Republic of New Mexico – The "settlement" where I now live ha[s] been located and peopled within the last six weeks It can n[ow] be already about 70 souls – I have a plenty of good l[and] and have built me a very substantial house Next week I c[om]mence ploughing – This is a delightful climate –

April 10[th] I wish that you would send me some app[le] seed – And indeed all kinds of seed that you grow – I will send some of this country's productions next spr[ing] There is fruit of different kind here in abundance – su[ch] as Plums (excellent) cherrys (sorter) strawberrys (good) Currants and gooseberry (do) and Service Berrys (de[licious]) Game, = Boffelo, Elk, Black and white-tail deer, gr[isly] Bear (Crowders) and turkies; but they are not call'd Ga[me] in this country – I don't intend to go to the States this sp[ring] Indeed I am not going home untill I make somethin[g] Give my Respects to Cousin Mary, Aunt and Medora an[d] Abby and Miss Rouster and – Everybody – I am wri[ting] by fire light and I have 2 other letters to finish to night

~~they~~ the bearer starts early in moring so I must say fare well;= wishing you health and hapiness and a kindly memberance of your affectionate and respectful cousin

Geo S Simpson

write to one
as soon
possible
} P.S. Your old acquaintance W S Williams

Master Trapper left here a few days ago for t'other side the "big hills" done in the summer; Hardscrabble was founded as a farm with a little trade to be conducted in the winter. The difference between the posts reflected changes on the Arkansas between 1842 and 1844. In the spring of 1844, trade was slow due to decreasing buffalo and the difficulty of obtaining Taos whiskey and flour. Hardscrabble was not a trading post but a settlement where men could live with their families on meat and vegetables they raised themselves, independent of the political and economic factors that controlled the lives of Indian traders.

One factor ignored by the founders of Hardscrabble was the ownership of the land they settled on. Barclay wrote in 1852 that Hardscrabble had been situated south of the Arkansas River under the impression that Mexico allowed and encouraged foreigners to settle her lands—a willful misconception.[7] Mexico did indeed make land grants to foreigners, but only to those who had become Mexican citizens and were responsible men of good character, capable of contracting to make settlements on the land and to pay for improvements. The men of Hardscrabble were not considered responsible either by the United States or Mexico, nor had they even attempted to obtain a Mexican grant. They simply moved onto the land and built their houses, and the Mexican government was not officially aware of their trespass for a year and a half.

The purpose of Hardscrabble was farming, according to an article in a St. Louis newspaper in the spring of 1845. The article described Hardscrabble as a settlement of about twenty-five old trappers and hunters and their Snake (Shoshone) wives whom they much preferred to Plains Indian women. They had built houses and raised considerable quantities of corn, which they traded to Indians for furs, robes, and other articles. The Indians parched the corn, pounded it into meal in skin bags, and made bread of it, but the Hardscrabble settlers had only a few poor hand mills to grind corn for their own use. The men of Hardscrabble were very expert riflemen, well practiced in the usages and warfare of Indians. They lived a rough, hard, romantic life but were hospitable to visitors.[8]

Alexander Barclay also wrote a description of Hardscrabble in 1845, admitting to the farming of maize, but declaring that the principal occupation of the twenty or thirty white men at the post was husbanding hundreds of head of cattle, as well as hogs and chickens.[9]

According to Simpson, Hardscrabble was a farm; according to Barclay, a cattle ranch. According to neither was there contraband trade in liquor or other goods; nor were there any women—pure or sullied, black, white, or red. Naturally so, for Barclay and Simpson were writing to proper lady relatives. But Andrew Drips and Thomas Fitzpatrick both mountain-men-turned-Indian-Agents, spared no one's feelings in giving an entirely different picture of Hardscrabble and Pueblo. They wrote of unlicensed traders who defied U.S. agents; of a "mongrel crew" no better than outlaws, unable to procure employment because of past misconduct; of idlers and loafers and smugglers of liquor; of men with Indian wives from every tribe in the West, some having two. Their picture of the Arkansas Valley settlements was as repugnant as Barclay's and Simpson's was charming—and the truth lay in between.[10]

Like Pueblo, Hardscrabble was a *placita,* an open space surrounded by houses, the whole enclosed by an adobe wall. Maurice LeDuc was said to have described it as "thirteen low, flat, earth-roofed adobe houses on one side of a projected square or plaza, which was completed by an adobe wall." The description may well be accurate, but unfortunately Maurice spoiled his credibility by describing one of the houses as a church where Mexicans of the settlement performed their marriage ceremonies, after a night of dissipation and a bizarre procession with friends shooting off guns and making grotesque gestures. Maurice was probably thinking of festivities connected with San Juan's Day, for there was no church on the Arkansas—no priest, no marriages.[11]

The population of Hardscrabble, like that of Pueblo, is nearly impossible to determine because it constantly fluctuated. In 1844 and 1845 the population was estimated variously as "seventy souls," "twenty-five families," and "twenty or thirty whites." In 1847 the combined population of Pueblo and Hardscrabble was said to be one hundred and fifty, sixty of them men. George Simpson wrote that there were nine farmers at Hardscrabble the first season. Mrs. Simpson named seven of them: George Simpson, Alexander Barclay and Joseph Doyle, owners; John Poisal, hunter; Marcelino Baca, hunter and trader; and two Mexican laborers, Juan and Francisco Martín.[12]

Alexander Barclay was the leader of the colony, a man whose dignity and intellect were respected by everyone—"a very quiet, cool and considerate gentleman."[13] Born in England on May 21, 1810, he was raised with a sister and brother by his mother, his father having proved improvident. Although the children were well educated, they lived in genteel poverty and at maturity they had to support themselves. Alexander was determined to be independent, to make his fortune, to become a man of property and to live like one—the theme ran through all his letters and impelled all his actions. [14]

Barclay's first business was making corsets for London ladies, at which he was a failure. When he could find no other employment he considered suitable, he decided to leave England. In the spring of 1833, he sought his fortune in Canada, locating at a farm on the eastern shore of Lake Huron near Goderich, Ontario. He lived in a windowless log cabin, chopping an eight-acre farm out of a dense and dreary forest, harvesting potatoes that froze like stones in his cellar in the twenty-below-zero winters, nursing his sickly cattle through hot and humid summers swarming with venomous insects. By October, 1836 he had had enough. He sold his land and left for St. Louis, swearing never to be a farmer again. [15]

Alexander Barclay was tall, broad-shouldered and strong, an attractive figure of a man. He was also intelligent and well-read. He wrote in an ornate but lively and witty style, and he was accomplished in drawing and watercoloring. His good manners and sense of humor made him popular when he first went to St. Louis, then a sophisticated little city of 15,000 souls. In St. Louis Barclay discovered that ladies wore silks and satins, feathers and laces; that their beauty was aided by paint and false curls; that mere laborers in America dressed as well as businessmen in England. His $600-per-annum salary barely covered the expense of keeping up with these fashionable folk, and the charms of St. Louis began to pall in the autumn of 1837. He found the local belles pert and arrogant, and he compared them unfavorably with the gentle, practical, modest British girls he had known. He complained that his health was poor. In the spring of 1838 he quarreled with his employers, quit his job and began grumbling in his letters about the mosquitos and the heat. By the middle of July, 1838 he had accepted a two-year position with the Bent brothers as keeper of books and stores at their trading post on the Arkansas. He hoped thereby to satisfy his curiosity about snow-covered mountains, grizzly bears, panthers and Indians, and to save from his salary four or five hundred dollars. It never occurred to him that he would spend the rest of his life in the West; someday, surely, he would go home to England, as a man of property. [16]

At Bent's Fort, his duties kept him so busy and so close to the fort that he had no time to investigate panthers and grizzly bears, and he

Alexander Barclay. From the Barclay Papers, Bancroft Library, Berkeley.

became dull and querulous. He complained that there was no educated company at the fort; that his only pastimes were rifle practice, horseback riding, chess and backgammon; that the owners were away too much, leaving him with full responsibility; and that although he was better educated they would not admit him to their friendship. He wrote that he was too proud to take an Indian wife, and he refused a lovely Cheyenne girl whose father had asked one horse too many for her. He boasted that he had escaped the folly of taking a squaw or Mexican woman, but he did not deny he was lonely.[17]

At Bent's Fort, Barclay was no more satisfied than he had been in Canada or St. Louis, and he groped for a way to make his fortune and return to England. In 1839 he and his brother George, a London printer, hit upon a scheme of stocking an English park with buffalo. When this plan was dropped, Barclay wrote that he intended to raise buffalo calves and sell them in Canada for $100 apiece, and he went so far as to buy five milk cows to suckle the calves before he changed his plans again. Then he meant to raise beef cattle and buffalo calves together, apparently in partnership with Kinkead and Conn, but his would-be partners declined. A few months later he had another scheme of raising buffalo calves, and while this was still in his mind, he gave the Bents notice in the spring of 1842 that after transporting their peltry back to St. Louis he would leave their employ.[18]

Barclay left Bent's Fort in April, 1842 with bull-boats full of buffalo robes. Somewhere in western Kansas the water sank into the sands and the bull-boats were stranded. Leaving his men to guard the furs, Barclay hurried on to St. Louis. At the offices of P. Chouteau Jr. & Co. he was refused any funds or credit, which destroyed his hopes of buying cows for his buffalo farming venture. Instead, he bought trade goods, a light wagon and a pair of mules and set out for the west. He spent the winter around Fort George (Fort St. Vrain) on the South Platte, intending to trade the coming spring at the sources of the North Platte with trappers in the mountains. But by the end of December he was at Bent's Fort, still undecided whether to return to the South Platte or make a trip over the mountains to Mexican Territory. In the spring of 1843 he went to the North Platte to trade with trappers, as he had planned to do. After that, or perhaps even before, he came to Pueblo to live.[19]

There is a question as to whether Barclay's decision to live at Pueblo was based primarily on hopes of successful speculation or on a glimpse of a fascinating woman. Barclay himself says he first saw

Teresita in 1842; he is not specific as to the day or month he saw her, but the sight of her he never forgot. Eleven years later he drew a sketch of her as she had first appeared to him, coming up from the river with a tub of laundry on her head. She was dressed in the style of Mexican country women—in a white, off-shoulder chemise, a full, short scarlet skirt and a long blue reboso covering her bosom and shoulders and falling nearly to the ground in back. She wore white stockings and ankle-high moccasins. Her dark hair was parted in the center, looped behind both ears and secured with ribbons. She had large eyes, dark heavy eyebrows, a straight and rather large nose and a pointed chin. Her figure was short and stocky, even a little thick-waisted by today's standards. Barclay's sketch of her does not capture all the beauty she must have had, nor was it altogether her beauty which Barclay, in the misery of her absence, recalled so poignantly:

To confirm that my heart with weakness still leans towards her, I send you the copy of a portrait I have drawn of her, from memory, since she left, it is not so faithfull a likeness as I could wish, but near enough to be recognized by all well acquainted with her, it is the garb and guise she wore eleven years ago when I first saw and admired her, there is something in the Mexican attire that recalls the Scotch lass with her pladie; and the domestic virtue of her avocation, returning from the river where she had been washing, impressed me with her industry & economy, of which I never had any subsequent cause to complain. It is hard to forget!![20]

Before the spring of 1843, Barclay had settled at Pueblo where his vaunted pride in his bachelorhood was being undermined by his admiration for Teresita. Bursting with a new interest in life, Barclay left for the States on April 29, 1843 with George Simpson and other traders and the season's furs. They arrived at Westport on June 7 and took the steamboat to St. Louis. Two weeks later, with furs sold and supplies purchased, they were aboard the steam boat *Mary Tompkins* heading west to Independence where they had left their mules and wagons. On the steamboat Barclay wrote his brother a not-quite-honest account of what was on his mind; he wrote that he still hoped to find eventual happiness in marriage but that he was too old—thirty-three last May.[21]

Too old, indeed! His eventual happiness with Teresita was prevented not by his age but by the fact that she was another man's wife, an impediment that, as Teresita had already demonstrated, was far from irremovable.

The other partner in Hardscrabble was Joseph Bainbridge Lafayette Doyle, a very different kind of man from either Barclay or Simpson. Like them he was well-educated for his era, "the equivalent of high school" said an acquaintance. But his mind did not embrace the fancies and fantasies to be found in his friends' correspondence. Letters written by Joe Doyle are plain and to the point and all business, like the man himself. He was honest, forthright and generous. In later life as a wealthy landowner on the Huerfano River in Colorado he was famous for giving help to those who needed it. His obituary said, "He had at all times a piece of good land, seed and teams for any man who was broke and wished by labor to repair his lost fortune . . . No honest, industrious man can say that he ever went to the deceased for aid and did not receive it." Doyle's portrait shows him to have been a fine-looking man with handsome, clean-cut features and bright, intelligent eyes.[22]

Joseph Doyle was born July 10, 1817 at Mountain Pleasant (now Mount Jackson), Shenandoah County, Virginia, the son of Alexander and Jane (Evans) Doyle. Alexander Doyle had been a captain of the militia in the War of 1812 but resigned his commission in 1814 to sell town lots at Mount Pleasant. He became a merchant and served as postmaster and as trustee for the New Market Academy in 1817, where his son Joseph may have gone to school. In the early 1830's the family moved to Belleville, Illinois across the Mississippi from St. Louis. As a boy of eighteen in 1834 Joseph Doyle was remembered by a Belleville friend as being mischievous but never dishonorable, and a fine pistol shot.[23]

By 1839 the Doyle family had moved to St. Louis. Joseph, now twenty-one, signed up with the Bents and left for Bent's Fort in late July, 1839. He worked for the Bents for five years. In the summer of 1842 he went to St. Louis with the Bent wagons, and again in the summer of 1843, this year with John Hawkins, Levin Mitchell, Ben Ryder and William Tharp, all later denizens of Pueblo and Hardscrabble. In the spring of 1844, Doyle left the Bents' employ

Teresita Suaso Barclay, as drawn by Alexander Barclay in 1853. She was returning from the Arkansas River with a tub of freshly washed laundry on her head when Barclay first saw her. This is how he remembered her eleven years later when he made this drawing. Barclay Papers, Bancroft Library, Berkeley.

Joseph Doyle. From H. L. Conard, *"Uncle Dick" Wootton* (1890). Courtesy of Denver Public Library Western Collection.

and joined Simpson and Barclay in their Hardscrabble venture. He left Hardscrabble on April 10, 1844 and traveled east with Alexander Barclay. At St. Louis he was paid his year's salary by the Bents at the store of their agent, P. Chouteau Jr. & Co. After he returned to Hardscrabble in the fall of 1844 he never again worked for anyone but himself, and eventually he made a fortune.[24]

Another important man at Hardscrabble was the Mexican trader and hunter, Marcelino Baca. Born in Taos about 1808, Baca spent nine years on the Upper Missouri and was described by George Ruxton as "the best trapper and hunter in the mountains and ever first in the fight." Strikingly handsome, over six feet tall, and "in form a Hercules," Baca despised his Mexican background—"no dam Spaniard, but 'mountainee man', wah!," he says in Ruxton's *Life in the Far West.*[25]

Baca acquired his wife in an interesting way. About 1838 he blundered into Pawnee lands on the Platte River, was taken captive and prepared for ritual sacrifice. During the ceremony strips of his flesh would be cut off and roasted as the Indians danced about him. Before this painful event could take place, the chief's daughter begged her father to spare his life. Marcelino was released and took his Pawnee Pocahantas as his wife, giving her his mother's name of Tomasa. Their first child was a son, José, born on the South Platte in 1839; their second was a son named Luis, born at Fort Laramie in 1841; and their third was a daughter, Elena, born at Hardscrabble in 1846 and later the wife of Charles Autobees' son, Mariano. Baca was a leading man, a *rico* at Hardscrabble; later he lived not in the settlement but in a house on a point of land an eighth of a mile southwest of the Hardscrabble plaza.[26]

The other principal resident of Hardscrabble named by Mrs. Simpson was John Poisal. He was born in Kentucky in 1810 and by 1831 he had come to Santa Fe where he was jailed briefly for smuggling goods. Three years later he was working for John Gantt at Fort Cass on the Arkansas. By this time he had taken an Arapaho named Ma-hom (Snake Woman) to wife, who bore him five children. Before Poisal came to live at Hardscrabble as hunter for the post, he had thrown in his lot with his wife's people, and particularly with his wife's brother, the magnificent Left Hand, a huge and handsome Indian. At Hardscrabble Poisal camped outside the settlement with his Arapaho relatives, whom Barclay came to call "Poisal's Indians." Poisal's daughters confounded the old belief that Indian half bloods favored the Indian side. Although they were brought up more with

Indians than whites, they had light complexions and acquired the mannerisms of white belles, which they probably learned at the many fandangos and social events at Hardscrabble. They all married white men.[27]

Important happenings of Hardscrabble's first year were births and marriages and the hullabaloo that attended them. On June 2, 1844 Isabel Simpson was born to George and Juana Simpson and was later proclaimed by the proud father to be the first white child born in what is now the state of Colorado. The same glory was later claimed for various Mormon children born at Pueblo in 1846–47. The gold rushers of 1858–59 also had their entry for the baby derby—one Emory Young. It all depended upon how "white" the child had to be to qualify, for many half-Indian children were born in Colorado well before 1844. Whether or not she won the derby, Isabel was a beautiful child who would grow to be a lovely woman, like her mother.[28]

To the Indians Isabel was an object of great wonder. George Simpson tells how hundreds of Indians came to see her, crowding around her cradle; how they held a war dance in her honor by the light of huge bonfires; how a medicine man passed by the cradle to bless the baby, Indian-style. The squaws evinced a puzzling interest in the size of the baby's feet, which was subsequently explained when they showered her with tiny moccasins.[29]

The baptism of the child was of prime importance to the young parents, both Roman Catholics. Their plans were to take the baby to the priest at Taos and to be married in the church at the same time. Late in September they left for Taos on horseback with baby Isabel carried by her mother in a sling made of a reboso. Also in the party were Juana's sister Cruz and Joe Doyle, who intended to be married, and Asa Estes as hunter, and three Mexicans to pack and drive the mules. On the first day they reached the St. Charles River just south of Pueblo, where they were caught in an unseasonable snow storm. For the next seven days they traveled only sixty miles through wind and snow, nursing their camp fires at night to keep the baby warm. They were saved from hunger by three deer which were driven into their camp by the blizzard and shot by Estes. After the storm subsided they reached the top of the Sangre de Cristo Pass, where the men dismounted and beat a road through the snow drift. At this place Juana's horse, Comanche, stumbled and fell, throwing

Juana and the baby into a snow bank. Juana was unconcerned; in the words of her admiring husband, "she came up smiling with her babe in her arms, regained the track unaided, and when her horse was extricated, resumed her place in the cavalcade as if nothing had happened to disturb her serenity."[30]

On the other side of the Pass they saw in the San Luis Valley below a Ute village moving up Ute Creek with a large number of cattle and sheep. Without a word George handed Juana his belt containing a pistol and hunting knife. She buckled the belt around her waist, having discussed with her husband many times what she should do if faced with worse-than-death captivity among the Indians. They hid in the willows by the stream until nightfall. Then they crept out of their hiding place and rode twenty-five miles in darkness and silence to the Culebra River. At the village of Río Colorado the next day they learned that the Utes they had seen had killed several herders of that village and three travelers on their way to Taos.[31]

On October 6 they arrived at Taos and began festivities connected with a baptism and two marriages. The most urgent was the baptism, which was performed in the Nuestra Señora de Guadalupe Church on October 13, 1844. María Simpson, four months old, daughter of Jorge S. Simpson and Anna María Suaso, granddaughter of Roberto Simpson and María Bricia and of José Manuel Suaso and María Teresa Sandoval, was baptized by Padre Antonio José Martínez. Godparents were Antonio Archuleta and María López. The next day Isabel's parents were married by the same famous priest, with Luis Lee (Stephen Louis Lee of St. Louis) and his wife Luz Tafoya as sponsors. Immediately afterward José Doyle was married to María de la Cruz Suaso, with Charles Beaubien and his wife as sponsors.[32]

By November the newlyweds were back at Hardscrabble, and an infectious miasma of romance hung low over the Arkansas Valley and did its noxious work in the heart of Alexander Barclay, the smug bachelor who two years earlier had considered himself too old for such nonsense. In November, 1844 Barclay went to Bent's Fort, borrowed $50 from Tom Boggs, and returned to Hardscrabble. There, sometime in December, he was joined by Teresita, aged thirty-three, a grandmother and "pretty as a peach."[33]

In the spring of 1845 Barclay received a challenge to a duel which he accepted and backed his opponent off the field. It was his second challenge, and he was delighted with himself. Barclay does not say whether his challenger was the aging man whose beautiful wife he had stolen, for he was reporting these duels to his brother George with whom he did not discuss affairs of the heart.[34]

Barclay doubtless believed he had won a great prize in the handsome Teresita. Mathew Kinkead must have concurred, for he seemed hardly to stir from his ranch after her departure. An entry in Barclay's diary on October 2, 1846 indicates the strain, when Barclay went to Kinkead's ranch and met his rival face to face for the first time in two years. Barclay's diaries and letters duly record his quarrels with Teresita, their near-separations and the final tragic period when she left him. But the connection, lasting for ten years, was a deep and emotional relationship that changed the lives not only of Barclay and Teresita but of others.

This was Hardscrabble in a wet year, a happy valley of green fields and wild flowers and rushing brooks, redolent of love and romance, bursting with hope that the joy of the new settlement would last forever. But there were many dry years ahead.

12
Oh Give Me a Home
Where the Buffalo Roam
1845

SINCE JOHN GANTT SEDUCED the Arapahos and Cheyennes with whiskey in 1832, the principal business of the Rocky Mountain West had been trade in buffalo robes. In 1843 and 1844 this trade decreased because of a growing scarcity of buffalo and a lessening demand for robes. As a result, some of the smaller trading houses gave up. Other trading posts were abandoned because of Ute attacks. In 1844 and 1845 the Arkansas Valley became a refuge for displaced traders, just as it had been a home for unemployed trappers in 1842.

Buffalo had always seemed limitless on the western plains. Thomas Fitzpatrick told Frémont that from the time he first came to the Rocky Mountains in 1824 until the year 1836, a traveler from any point along the base of the mountains to the Missouri River and down to the frontier settlements of Missouri was never out of sight of buffalo. Then the herds began to shrink eastward from the foot of the mountains and westward from the frontier of Missouri. The mass of them lumped together like quicksilver into three great divisions— the northern herd near the Canadian border, the southern herd in Texas, and the middle herd centering on the Republican River in eastern Colorado and western Kansas. By 1845 Pueblo men had to go one or two hundred miles east to catch sight of a buffalo. The reason was obvious: Frémont estimated that 1,800,000 buffalo were killed every year by Indians and white men, some for food, shelter and raiment, some for their robes, some for their tongues, and some for nothing more than sport.[1]

As buffalo and Indians became threatened with extinction (they were expected to disappear together), there was a little flurry of interest in them. Probably the only place that raised buffalo for sale was the Kinkead buffalo farm at Pueblo, but from 1841 to 1845 there were a number of men on the plains catching their own calves. In April, 1841 a party of seventeen men went on a hunting excursion along the Arkansas, returning east a year later with thirty-seven young buffalo, an antelope, and an elk, which they intended to sell in New York City or in Europe. In the summer of 1843 several parties from Missouri went out on the plains to capture buffalo calves, and several eastbound wagon trains had buffalo calves to sell in the frontier settlements.[2]

Buffalo calves were not the only native creatures brought east for exhibition. In February, 1844 Indian agents were ordered to stop white men from taking Indians off reservations for exhibition purposes. In spite of this order, in the summer of 1844 fourteen Iowa Indians were exhibited in England and France, where three of them died. Nine Osages were exhibited in Baltimore in May, 1844 by a Missouri entrepreneur who abandoned them in Louisville, Kentucky. The Indians finally made their way back to St. Louis, emaciated and half naked.[3]

The most famous collector of Western Americana, flora and fauna division, was Sir William Drummond Stewart, the energetic Scotsman who had been making pleasure trips to the Rocky Mountains since 1833. On his last trip in 1843 he took back a sample of everything portable in his beloved West—antelope, deer, mules, buffalo, a Cheyenne scalp, large and small Indian lodges, two hundred cedar logs ("as free of knots as possible" was his order), a serviceberry bush and numerous seeds to sprout on his native heath. The crown of his collection was a real Rocky Mountain trapper in the person of Charles A. Warfield, who had recently disgraced himself among most of his fellow mountain men by turning Texan.[4]

Arranging Sir William's tours and helping him collect his souvenirs was the former fur trader William Sublette. Sublette's brother Solomon was also a collector and spent the summer of 1844 in the mountains trying to bag antelope and mountain sheep for the Sublette farm near St. Louis. From Solomon's letters we learn of other men collecting wild animals—Marcellin St. Vrain and his companions "Ward & Shavano" (Seth E. Ward and Baptiste Charbonneau) and "T. Goodell" (Tim Goodale) who had been in the mountains for more than three years trying to catch mountain sheep.[5]

By October, 1844 Solomon Sublette had been joined by yet another brother, Andrew, who came west for his health. Andrew moved along the Arkansas following the buffalo herd with his cart, lodge, three mules, five horses and two "Spaniards," apparently collecting buffalo calves and "not making much but enjoying good

"A Herd of Buffalo in Western Kansas." From William A. Bell, *New Tracks in North America* (1869). Courtesy of Denver Public Library Western Collection.

health." Andrew's peregrinations took him to Pueblo in the fall of 1844 and again in the spring of 1845—and perhaps many times. On April 6, 1845 he wrote, "the whites and Spaniards are settling on this River near the mountain raising cattle and corn there is now about twenty families they were out after buffalow a fiew days since and had thirteen horses and mules taken from them by Indians."[6]

By the fall of 1844 when Andrew Sublette was at Pueblo, Kinkead's buffalo calf farm had been out of business for a year, and its proprietors had been conducting a cattle ranch on the Hardscrabble. Kinkead was an astute speculator and knew when to get out. Not so Alexander Barclay. Barclay entered the buffalo calf business at a time when it was becoming not only unprofitable but dangerous. In the spring of 1843 Barclay bought twenty-one buffalo calves for $30 to $35 a head, probably from Kinkead and Conn. With eight of the calves Barclay left Pueblo in April for the East, confident that he could sell his curiosities for $100 apiece. He drove his little buffalo herd to central Missouri, but not finding a market for them, he left them with a Boone county farmer who agreed to pasture them for a year at a charge of $8 apiece. Then Barclay went on to St. Louis and made arrangements with Robert H. Betts, commission merchant, to sell the animals for $100 a pair. He bought his trade goods and left St. Louis for Pueblo about the first of July.[7]

The next spring Barclay went east again with the rest of the calves he had bought at the Pueblo buffalo farm. On June 26, 1844 he wrote his brother that he still had seventeen buffalo on hand, but that now he had another idea. He would catch some rarer wild animals and sell them to an exhibitor who had assured him that he would receive $1,500 per annum for his share of the exhibition proceeds (even the gullible Barclay suspected this was an exaggeration). Again he left the buffalo in Missouri to be pastured, for again they found no buyer.[8]

In the spring of 1845 Barclay was greeted at Independence with the gloomy news that Indians had attacked the buffalo he had left in Missouri, only six remaining unhurt. He deplored the fact that he could not identify the Indians and therefore could not claim reimbursement from the government (his claim would have been rejected anyway, since taking buffalo from the Indian country was a violation of the Trade and Intercourse Act). So he sold the six remaining calves to the first bidder, pocketed the meager proceeds and went on to buy goods in St. Louis, finally free of the buffalo calf business.[9]

In the spring of 1845 Barclay was lucky to have lost nothing more than his little herd of buffalo, and the men of Pueblo were lucky to have lost no more than thirteen horses and mules during the buffalo hunt recorded by Andrew Sublette. For several years past, Indians had been furious at white men for destroying their buffalo and taking their game back east. In the summer of 1843 Pawnees attacked a group of buffalo calf hunters on Pawnee Fork and killed two men. That same summer a party of Arapahos threatened Rufus Sage's caravan because it was accompanied by tame buffalo. In the following spring the Indians warned that they meant to kill all young buffalo the white men attempted to take to the States, for they thought the decrease in the number of buffalo was caused by adult animals following their calves eastward. The number of buffalo calves taken east by white men could not have been, all told, more than a few hundred—a fraction, for instance, of the thousands of calves killed on the Upper Missouri by snow that fell in a single day in May, 1843. But Indians were acutely aware, as white men were not, that the buffalo belonged to the Indians. If Indians killed buffalo to sell the hides to white men it was permissible for white men to buy from them, but when white men hunted buffalo themselves they were poachers and thieves.[10]

So the Indians fought the buffalo hunters by attacks, by threats and by complaints to United States officials. In the spring of 1844 the Cheyennes sent a hatchet-jawed chief named Slim Face (Mi-ah-tose) to St. Louis with the Bent wagons to protest to the Superintendent of Indian Affairs that white men were stealing Indians' buffalo and peddling whiskey on Indian lands. After talking to the Superintendent, Slim Face sat down on a St. Louis street with a stick which he notched for every passerby. When the stick was full of notches he threw it away and began counting, and he counted and counted until finally he gave up. The message that he probably took back to his people was the infinite number of white men and the hopelessness of expecting any help from them in preserving the buffalo—or the Indian.[11]

As the scarcity of buffalo became noticeable, so did the lack of demand for buffalo robes. The trading season of 1843–44 was characterized by these strangely unrelated conditions. Traders on the Missouri were ordered to buy every robe that was offered. Solomon Sublette reported that there were more goods for sale in the country than there were robes to trade for them. Yet a trader at Fort John (Laramie) wrote P. Chouteau Jr. & Co. that he was "sorry to hear after all our trouble here to get Robes that they are of so little value," and an agent in Germany reported that sheep skins were competing with buffalo robes in northern Europe and that he could no longer sell robes on the continent.[12]

By the next year the robe trade on the Arkansas was in serious trouble. The winter of 1844–45 was mild and dry and the grass was parched. In consequence, buffalo ranged far east and south of the Arkansas. By summer Bent's Fort was so low on buffalo meat that there was none to spare for travelers. The Cheyennes had left the

Arkansas for the Cimarron looking for buffalo but were forced to return in a starving condition because they had found none. The Indians had nothing to sell, and the white men's goods went begging. Ceran St. Vrain wrote from Bent's Fort that he had not gone to trade with the Kiowas during the winter for lack of men and animals, and that unless the Kiowas visited Bent's Fort, half the company's trade goods would be left on hand.[13]

It was the worst season the Bents had known. When their wagons left about April 25, 1845 they carried east only two hundred packs of buffalo robes (as compared to seven hundred the year before). Pueblo's and Hardscrabble's independent traders had done nearly as well as the mighty Bents. On April 10, 1845, several weeks earlier than usual because of the mildness of the weather, six wagons left Pueblo carrying 187 packs of furs and robes under the management of William Tharp and Alexander Barclay. Leaving Barclay at Independence to tend to his buffalo calf business, Tharp went on to St. Louis, arriving May 25 on the steamboat *Nimrod.* Barclay arrived at St. Louis a week or so later, bought his trade goods in partnership with Joseph Doyle, and on June 11 took the steamboat *John Aull* back up the river to Independence. At Council Grove, Barclay's wagons joined those of Tharp and other traders to form a caravan. Near the Little Arkansas, Barclay and two others left the caravan to hunt buffalo and were given a merry chase back to the wagons by some Indians whom Barclay took to be Osage. One of his companions lost his sense of direction and Barclay, behind him on a mule, guided him to safety by shouting "Right! Left! Ahead! Faster!" Rumors of Texans (synonymous with robbers since the 1843 invasion) and drought on the Cimarron route prevented the train from crossing the Arkansas at the Cimarron Crossing, and all the wagons came up to Bent's Fort, arriving around the 27th of July.[14]

Both 1844 and 1845 were bad years for the fur trade. Many of the posts dealing in buffalo robes failed, and their traders ended up at the Arkansas Valley settlements. On the Upper Missouri, agents of P. Chouteau Jr. & Co. spent the summer of 1845 buying out opposition companies who could obtain neither robes nor, thanks to Andrew Drips, the liquor to trade for them. On the South Platte Marcellin St. Vrain shut the gates of his Fort George (Fort St. Vrain) in the spring of 1844 intending to keep the fort open only for the winter trade, but in the summer of 1845 he closed up the fort for good. And in the late fall of 1844 Fort Lancaster was abandoned by its testy little proprietor.[15]

Lancaster P. Lupton was "a pleasant, well informed little man but a victim of intemperance,"[16] a failing which probably had something to do with his ending up at Pueblo penniless and furious in December, 1844. Born in New York in 1807, he graduated from the United States Military Academy at West Point in 1829, served his stint as a soldier and came west with Colonel Dodge as a dragoon in 1835. The next year he resigned from the dragoons after being threatened with court-martial for criticizing President Jackson at a dinner party ("I attribute the Most of the Difficulties Here to the intemperate use of Ardent Spirits," wrote his commanding officer).[17]

Again Lupton came west, this time as an Indian trader at Fort Laramie on the North Platte. In 1837 he moved to the South Platte and built Fort Lancaster with the financial help of Hiram Rich, then a trader of Liberty, Missouri. Fort Lancaster did very well. In 1841 Lupton and Rich built two more posts—Fort Platte a mile from Fort Laramie on the North Platte and a log post on the Arkansas. But these posts did not do very well.[18]

In 1842 Lupton declared bankruptcy. Fort Platte was sold to Pratte and Cabanné; Fort Lancaster became the property of Hiram Rich and his partner Albert G. Wilson, postmasters and merchants at Fort Leavenworth. By 1843 Wilson had come west to trade not only at Fort Lancaster but at Big Timber below Bent's Fort, at a post known as "Wilson's Houses." Lancaster Lupton still traded at Fort Lancaster, but the arrangement was not a happy one. In 1844 Wilson and Lupton had a serious disagreement over Wilson's refusal to pay Lupton's Westport creditor when presented with a statement. In a rage, Lupton wrote out an account charging Wilson for the use of everything in the fort, for $800 in repairs to the building, for numerous articles loaned to Baker, sold to Metcalf and lost by Brown, and for his own services during the winter of 1843–44, which he never got around to evaluating. By December, 1844 Lupton had left for Pueblo, and Fort Lancaster was probably abandoned then or soon after.[19]

At Pueblo Lupton found that another of his business transactions had been dishonored. In hot indignation he wrote a letter dated Fort Spaulding, December 13, 1844, reproaching Charles Town because Mr. Maxwell could not procure Lupton a mule at Pueblo which Town had promised him, and he would have been without an animal to fetch his family from "below" had Brown not loaned him a mule.[20]

The abandonment of Fort Lancaster left a number of Lupton's suppliers and traders out of a job, and many of them came to Pueblo

Lancaster P. Lupton. Courtesy of State Historical Society of Colorado Library, Denver.

or Hardscrabble. Lucien Maxwell, an independent trader, was at Pueblo when Lupton arrived in December, 1844. So were James Grieve, a man named Brown who was doubtless John Brown, as well as Charles White, Charles Kinney and V.J. (Rube) Herring, all of whom appear to have worked for Lupton until the end of 1844 and to have lived at the Arkansas Valley settlements after that date.[21]

Perhaps the most interesting survivor of the collapse of Fort Lancaster was Archibald Charles Metcalf, a tall, handsome, lively New Yorker who had first come west with John Richard as a whiskey trader on the North Platte in the 1830's. By the beginning of 1841, he spent part of his time hunting and trapping on Greenhorn Creek south of the Arkansas, where in later years he would spend even more time. In 1843 Metcalf took a load of whiskey to the Sioux near Fort Laramie, unaware that the United States government was finally cracking down on liquor peddlers. Hardly had Metcalf opened his wares when James V. Hamilton, government agent, forced his hasty retreat to Fort Lancaster. Metcalf sold his goods to Wilson at the fort and took a job with Rich and Wilson selling liquor to the Cheyennes, where government agents had not penetrated.

By 1845 Metcalf had spent enough time at Taos to have fallen in love with María de la Luz Trujillo, fifteen-year-old daughter of José Francisco Trujillo and his wife María Natividad Sandoval. To marry Luz, Metcalf renounced his Episcopal faith and was baptized at the Guadalupe Church at Taos. On April 30, 1845 Luz and Metcalf were married and came directly to Pueblo. For two years Luz lived on the Arkansas while her husband was in and out, pursuing his trade with the Utes, Cheyennes and Arapahos. At that time, Luz's widowed mother, María Natividad Sandoval was also living at Pueblo with Asa Estes, as was Luz's brother Vicente Trujillo. Occasionally Luz accompanied her husband on short trips. Once they camped at Manitou Springs on the upper Fountain River while Metcalf traded whiskey and coffee for robes with the Cheyennes and Arapahos. Fifty-five years later Luz recalled that she made very good bread using the charged mineral waters of the springs as leavening.[22]

At about the same time that Fort Lancaster went out of business, two other posts were abandoned because of Ute hostility, and their traders came to live on the Arkansas. Both trading posts belonged to Antoine Robidoux and were for trade with trappers and Ute Indians. One was Fort Uintah or Robidoux on a fork of the Uintah River near

Lucien B. Maxwell. From H. L. Conard, *"Uncle Dick" Wootton* (1890).
Courtesy of Denver Public Library Western Collection.

its junction with Green River in present northeastern Utah; the other was Fort Uncompahgre on the Grand (Gunnison) River below the mouth of the Uncompahgre River near present Delta in western Colorado. To supply these posts, Robidoux brought goods from St. Louis in light horse carts up the Arkansas and over Robidoux (Mosca) Pass into the San Luis Valley and over Cochetopa Pass to the Gunnison. Long afterwards it was said that the Utes were not happy with Robidoux's business methods, for he sent his own men to trap beaver instead of buying the skins from the Indians, and for this reason the forts were attacked. Contemporary sources show that this was not the whole story.[23]

In September, 1844 Governor Martínez of New Mexico started a war with the Utes. What happened, according to the Governor's report, was the following. In the fall of 1843, Governor Armijo allowed the Frenchman José Portelance and the Englishman Alexander Montgomerie to raise a company of volunteers to invade the territory of the Navajos, then at war with the Mexicans. Their raid was not successful. On their return they fell upon a band of friendly Utes, killing ten, taking three captive, and driving off their horses and mules.

On the afternoon of September 7, 1844 six Ute chiefs and over a hundred braves, mounted, armed and drawn up in battle array, arrived at Santa Fe demanding retribution for the outrage. The next day the six chiefs were admitted to Governor Martínez's office for a talk. When an argument started, the governor knocked Chief Panasiyave to the ground with a chair, killing him. The governor's servants, honor guard and other citizens ran into the room, and through the window came more Indians. In the ensuing fray seven Utes died. The rest of the Indians gathered in the plaza, armed and threatening, but then retreated. As they passed through Abiquiu the Utes made a charge upon its citizens and killed ten. Then they retired to the mountains, determined to make war on the Mexicans.[24]

During their war the Utes made a bloody shambles of Robidoux's Fort Uncompahgre. In late September two men from the fort, José Francisco Trujillo and Calario Cortéz, went out to check their beaver traps in the river. They were fired on by Utes from the top of the bluffs and Trujillo was killed. Cortéz ran back to the fort where he found the bodies of seven Mexicans. All the Indian women at the fort had been carried into captivity. Cortéz took off afoot for Taos, arriving fourteen days later without shoes, coat or provisions.[25]

The Utes had spared the one American at Fort Uncompahgre and sent him to Antoine Robidoux at Fort Uintah with the message that Robidoux's peltry was safe and that the Indians had no desire to harm him or other Americans. The Mexicans at Fort Uintah were terrified; seven of them stole mules, rifles and other equipment and fled to Hardscrabble.[26] There Alexander Montgomerie heard their story on his return from a buffalo hunt and went to Taos to notify Mexican authorities. The authorities blamed the massacre on the Americans. After castigating Montgomerie for hunting without a license, they reviled Robidoux for selling guns to the Utes and encouraging the Indians to attack New Mexican settlements.[27]

Robidoux employees who ended up at the Arkansas Valley settlements were Manuel Ruis, Esquípula Salasar (mentioned frequently in records of the settlements as "Scapoodlar," "Estapoola" and other variants), Manuel Pais, Miguel Ruibali, a Paiute slave named José, and Felipe Archuleta.[28]

Pueblo and Hardscrabble were collecting men from other places, too. Bent, St. Vrain & Co. employed forty-four traders in 1842, twenty-nine in 1843. At least some of the fifteen Bent traders who were not rehired in 1843 came to Pueblo. John Hawkins, a trapper since the early thirties and an employee of the Bents in 1842–43, was at Pueblo by 1847 at the latest and probably earlier. Ben Ryder and his wife Josie (Chepita) came to Pueblo about 1844, as did William Tharp and William Guerrier.[29]

Other new men on the Arkansas before 1846 were the two Englishmen William Adamson and Alexander Montgomerie; the half-Indian hunter Pascual Rivière (Blackhawk); Tim Goodale, the mountaineer from Illinois; John B. Guerin; Jim Waters; Antoine Cournoyer; Jim Cowie; Bill Garmon; a man named Cosper; and the four Delaware Indians—Little Beaver, Jim Swarnock, Big Nigger and Jim Dickey.[30]

In 1845 some of the new settlers founded a new town south of Pueblo where the grass was consistently higher and lusher than at either Pueblo or Hardscrabble, and where the little stream that watered the valley seldom went dry. The new town, named for the Comanche chief whom De Anza had outsmarted at this place sixty-six years earlier, was called Greenhorn.

The Store at Greenhorn

GREENHORN (*Cuerno Verde*) was the name of a Comanche chief so called for his monstrous headdress, who was defeated in battle by the great Spanish Governor De Anza in 1779 at about the place where the store at Greenhorn was later located.[1] The beautiful little valley of Greenhorn Creek is broad and rolling pasture, lying directly under 12,000-foot-high Greenhorn Mountain, the tallest peak in the Wet Mountain Range. The stream is nothing but a rock-bottomed brook two feet wide and three or four inches deep, but its proximity to its mountain source usually keeps it flowing in summer and fall with sufficient water to irrigate the narrow bottom lands. The trail from Pueblo to Taos over the Sangre de Cristo Pass crossed the Greenhorn at a point where the river banks were nearly level with the water, and the slopes rose smoothly to the tops of bluffs on either side. On this trail, south of the river, was the Greenhorn settlement—if settlement it could be called. In 1847, George Ruxton described it as one adobe hovel and several Indian lodges where two or three mountain men lived a life of pleasant indolence with their Indian wives.[2]

The valley of the Greenhorn had been used by mountain men three or four years before there was any settlement. Archibald Metcalf, John Brown, Bill New and Marcelino Baca seem to have had some sort of base there as a hunting and trapping camp or as a grazing tract for their horses and mules. But real settlement did not occur until the spring of 1845 when John Brown started his store.[3]

We have encountered John Brown before, building a log stockade post for Lancaster Lupton near the mouth of the Fountain; taking over Jim Beckwourth's cast-off wife, Luisa Sandoval; working for Lupton at Fort Lancaster in 1844. But a recital of John Brown's fugitive appearances in the records cannot capture the peculiar flavor of this simple, gullible and good man.

John Brown was simple, but no simpleton. In later life he became a wealthy citizen of San Bernardino County, California, important enough to rate a long biography in a county history. The account says he was born in Worcester, Massachusetts, on December 22, 1817. As a boy he rafted on the Mississippi, was shipwrecked off Galveston, fought at the battle of San Jacinto, and spent two years at Fort Leavenworth, before embarking on a fourteen-year career as hunter and trapper in the Rocky Mountains. "His bear and Indian encounters and hair-breadth escapes," says the account, "would fill a volume fully as interesting as 'Kit Carson's Travels' or Washington Irving's 'Captain Bonneville.' "[4]

When it came time for John Brown himself to fill a volume of his adventures, nothing in his book approached the dime-novel excitement of "Kit Carson's Travels." Entitled *Mediumistic Experiences of John Brown, the Medium of the Rockies*, his work is a very personal and modest account of his life as a spiritualist. As a young man, it relates, John Brown set out from St. Louis with a company of trappers. They came up the Arkansas and built a log post at the mouth of the Fountain "near where the old Fort Pueblo was first erected, which, in after years I helped to build." Here the trappers were joined by six Delaware Indians ("a band of desperadoes") with whom they went trapping in the Blackfoot country.[5]

About this time John Brown acquired his "Spirit Guide," who appeared to him for three years while he was in and about Pueblo, foretelling the future and rescuing John from disaster. One time the Spirit Guide appeared to Brown just in time to save him and his friends Estes and Stone from two grizzly bears. Another time when Brown was camped with Owens and Goodale at the foot of Pikes Peak, the Spirit Guide showed him a vision of an emigrant family named Washburn arriving at Pueblo with "Mr. Waters," who had with him a grey mare brought from the east for Mr. T. Goodale. When Brown and his friends returned to Pueblo they found that the vision pictured exactly what had happened. On another occasion, while living in a lodge with Briggs and Burrows, John Brown was informed by the Spirit Guide that he would throw a stone and break his mule's leg, which happened in spite of his efforts to control himself.[6]

In his little book Brown tells of these occurrences reverently and without a trace of humor, but the men of Pueblo probably had many a hearty laugh over the solemn Brown and his ectoplasmic friend, and they labored mightily to thwart the Spirit Guide's predictions. Finally it came to Brown's attention that his companions were

The Greenhorn Valley near the Taos Trail crossing. Ruts of the trail may be seen faintly at the extreme left of the photograph. Greenhorn Mountain is the high point in the background. Somewhere in the bottom land was the Greenhorn settlement. Photograph: Janet Lecompte.

making bets behind his back on the outcome of the predictions. Brown was deeply hurt. The climax came when Timothy Goodale proposed to Brown that he be given exclusive knowledge of the Spirit Guide's forecasts in return for half the wager winnings. Brown indignantly rejected the proposition, and the Spirit Guide was so offended that it told John to have nothing more to do with Tim Goodale. From that time on it ceased to haunt John, appearing only at rare intervals. [7]

John Brown's *Mediumistic Experiences* was just what its title implies. It has little more to say about Pueblo than is indicated above, and Hardscrabble and Greenhorn are not mentioned at all. Fortunately John Brown left us another piece of his handiwork, an account book of his Greenhorn store which is as full of names and dates as the other is lacking in them.

Brown began his account book in April, 1845, presumably when he began his business. The land Brown chose to settle was then thought to be a part of the enormous land grant made in 1843 by Governor Manuel Armijo to Cornelio Vigil and Ceran St. Vrain, residents of Taos. The grant was bounded roughly by the valley of the Purgatory on the east, by the Arkansas on the north, and by the mountains on the west and south. Brown may have gotten permission from Vigil and St. Vrain before he built his store, or received some financial help from them in starting his business, for one of the conditions of the grant was that the grantees encourage settlement upon it. When a Mexican inspector toured New Mexico in 1845, he denounced Hardscrabble for existing on Mexican soil without a vestige of authority; he did not mention Greenhorn, perhaps because it had that vestige of authority. [8]

For the first year and a half Brown's store was a primitive affair, perhaps no more than a "camp," as Barclay's diary describes it in March, 1846. Brown apparently bought his merchandise at Pueblo and sold it to passing traders, hunters and travelers. His stock of goods encompassed only the bare essentials of life in the Arkansas Valley—horses, corn, beans, deerskins, buffalo robes, parfleche, knives, soap, razors, combs, domestics, linsey, manta, calicos, thread, shirts, drawers, hats, tin pans, rope, caps and lead. His merchandise was so limited that it did not include coffee, sugar or flour—but not so limited that it did not include whiskey and tobacco, the most popular of his sale items. His biggest transaction in 1845 was with Blackhawk, a half-blood Indian trader also known as Pascual Rivière, who bought 112 pounds of iron and sold Brown seven gallons of whiskey. [9]

Then Brown began to enlarge his inventory of goods and his list of customers. Early in the summer of 1846 he went to the North Platte to trade with emigrants and to bring back some new trade items for his store at Greenhorn. In the fall he acquired more goods, probably selected from the fresh merchandise brought back from St. Louis in Pueblo traders' wagons. From then on, his store catered to more sophisticated tastes, with sugar, coffee, flour, pants, shoes, vests, coats, scissors, ribbons, buttons, hooks and eyes, playing cards, sheets of paper, stockings, silk handkerchiefs, bed-ticking, awls, axes, hoes, files, gunpowder, bar-lead. Now Brown's store served not only transients but local traders and farmers. William Bent was a customer; he sent "E Garry" to Brown's store to sell goods and to buy a steer in May, 1846, and in November Bent's brother George bought 1½ *fanegas* of corn. Charles White, a steady if perhaps troublesome customer, bought large quantities of whiskey in pints and half-pints, the small amounts indicating it was for personal and immediate use. Other customers were Cosper, Frank the Dutchman, James Grieves, William Adamson, Girteau, Lewis Belheres, Harrison, Antoine Conoia, Joseph Bridger and Richard (or "Reubin") Herring.[10]

Brown's store was for the white man, not the Indian. The only Indians mentioned in the account book are Jim Dickey, Sickamore (Charles Autobees's Arapaho squaw), "Mirs Burns" (probably John Burroughs's Shoshone wife) and the Indian wife of E. Romero. These ladies were paid for moccasins which they made to order for fifty cents to a dollar a pair. There was little commerce in buffalo robes, none at all in beaver pelts. Goods sold at the store were given in exchange for work, for whiskey or goods, for corn or butter, or for cash. At some unnoted time, Brown added up the specie he had on hand, and it was quite a coin collection, containing doubloons, gelders, sovereigns, Mexican dollars and gold pieces. His total came to $680.67½, a large amount of coin for that era.[11]

Luisa Brown was active in the store, collecting money, lending articles when Brown was away, buying butter from peons, handling the expenses of fandangos and selling whiskey and tobacco at those social events. In the fall of 1847 the Browns slaughtered a fat hog; the candles and soap that were henceforth sold in John Brown's store were probably made from the lard by his industrious wife.[12]

The store at Greenhorn was not busy enough to satisfy the energies or ambitions of John Brown. In the spring of 1846 he hired more men and set them to making an irrigating ditch and a farm. By harvest time the fields at Greenhorn were producing corn and watermelons. The amount of corn grown was not sufficient for the needs of the community, and in October Brown paid Charles White $45 for nine or ten *fanegas* grown somewhere else. In 1847 Brown broke new ground and planted a field to wheat. However small the crop may have been, it was probably the largest in the Arkansas Valley, for other settlements grew corn. By 1847 Brown had also acquired a large number of cattle and horses and a large number of peons to herd them. From then on the store at Greenhorn was patronized mostly by the peons.[13]

Brown's biggest financial plunge was making new adobe houses and building a grist mill. In September and October, 1846, he set four or five peons to making adobe bricks and building houses, paying them from $3 to $5 for the "dobies" and about the same for the labor—not, of course, for a day's work, but for the whole completed job. On November 30, 1846, Charles White was paid $9 for three doors he had made, indicating that the new houses were ready for occupancy.

Greenhorn now resembled not a camp but the other Arkansas Valley settlements. It consisted of adobe rooms joined together with no other opening than a single low door which a six-foot man would have to stoop to enter. On the flat roofs women grew tiny crops and people gathered on the approach of strangers. Inside, the only articles of furniture were benches against the wall covered with blankets and pillows, and wool mattresses rolled up to serve as settees by day and spread out as beds by night.[14]

Brown's biggest speculation was the grist mill, the first in the Arkansas Valley. The mill was a testament to its builder's faith that the Arkansas Valley settlements would be permanent, for building a mill was costly and difficult. It was constructed between December 1846 and February 1847 by Jessa Degraves and two helpers— "White" (probably Charles White, the whiskey-drinking carpenter) and "Jones" (later identified in the accounts as Calvin "B.A." Jones, a lazy, talkative, witty mountain man who first turned up at Pueblo in 1846).[15]

Dick Wootton remembered the mill as "a building of logs, the machinery rude, the burr stones hewn out of granite."[16] John Brown of Walsenburg (no relation to the Greenhorn Brown) remembered that the millstones were down by the creek as late as the 1860's, long after the building had caved in and disappeared. The mill was little used until the wheat crop of 1847 was harvested, after which it was kept humming all the time grinding quantities of flour. Brown sold his flour for 6¼¢ per pound or $8 per *fanega* (1.6 bushels) to traders such as George Lewis, A. C. Metcalf, Joseph Bridger, James Waters, C. Kinney and Blackhawk. Farmers from Hardscrabble and Pueblo—Conn, Waters, Lupton—brought their own wheat or corn to be ground at the mill at the rate of 50¢ for 4 *almudes* (an *almud* was 1/12 of a *fanega*) or $1 per *fanega*. Even when the customer bought flour already ground at Brown's mill, he usually brought his own container, as was indicated when Blackhawk bought 72 pounds of flour "bag and all" for $4 in 1848.[17]

Brown had a number of hired hands, most of them herding his cattle and horses. Thirty-eight men were named in the account book as his hired hands, three of them hired in 1845, twenty-four in 1846, eight in 1847, and two in 1848. Of this number only three stayed longer than a few months. The hired hands from New Mexico were

called "peons," but there was a world of difference between these
free laborers and the peons at the great haciendas of Mexico, who
were given a fixed wage of from $3 to $6 a month and a ration, and
were paid in articles of clothing or other necessities at prices which
kept them in continual debt to their masters.[18]

New Mexican laborers who came north to work at American
trading posts as horse or cattle guards, mule packers, drivers or farm
hands, earned $6 to $10 a month. They were paid in goods and the
goods were high–priced, but no higher to the peons than to American customers. Storekeepers on the Arkansas did not allow workers
to charge more than their salary would cover so that when they left
they owed little or nothing to the store. John Brown occasionally
paid his more dependable peons in cash, and he paid them extra for
certain chores such as making bricks and building houses or collecting salt, which they had to pack out from the saline in South Park.[19]

John Brown's hired hands were not underpaid even by the standards of civilization. A saying at that time was that "a dollar a day is a
white man's pay," but most laborers in the States got only 50¢ or 75¢
per day and had to pay board and room out of it. On the Greenhorn,
a man with a little initiative could live for practically nothing,
growing his own corn, shooting his own meat, and sleeping in an
Indian lodge (if he were lucky enough to have an Indian wife) or
under a buffalo robe on the prairie. Note, for instance, that Luisa
Brown bought her butter (at 50¢ to $1 per pound) from peons,
indicating that some of them owned a cow.[20]

A man could live well enough off the land, but he had to use great
discretion in making purchases or collecting salary at the store. A
day's work for Charno, for instance, was worth 37½¢ and would buy
half a plug of tobacco, a yard of calico or domestic, three sheets of
paper, or a pint of lard. Tucksender was paid 50¢ a day, which would
buy him a coarse comb, a common deerskin, an *almud* of flour or
corn, half a pint of whiskey, four cheeses, four watermelons, a knife,
two decks of playing cards, half a pound of gunpowder, a pound of
lead or a hundred caps, two dozen buttons or hooks and eyes, a
candle, two pieces of soap, four balls of thread, or a pair of plain,
undecorated moccasins. If, after a few months of work, a peon
"runoff" or "left" (the words defining the formality of his departure),
he had usually drawn enough merchandise from the store to make
his stay on the Greenhorn worthwhile.[21]

In January, 1847 George F. Ruxton visited Greenhorn, which he
described as two or three Indian lodges and "one adobe hovel of a

more aspiring order." As he crossed the creek, an American mountaineer galloped up, clad in a buckskin hunting shirt and pantaloons with long fringes hanging down his arms and legs, his rifle over the horn of his saddle. As this was the first white man Ruxton had encountered since leaving the Canadian River, he was as delighted to see him as the mountaineer was to learn the news from the Mexican settlements. At Greenhorn lived two or three French-Canadian hunters with their Assinaboine and Sioux squaws. They led a lazy life with no cares to annoy them, for game was abundant and the rich soil grew a sufficiency of Indian corn. Ruxton foresaw that this valley would one day become a thriving settlement. Its soil could grow all kinds of grain, and the abundant and excellent grass could pasture any quantity of stock. [22]

Ruxton goes on to say that, "there is a general tendency among the mountain men to settle in the fruitful valleys of the Rocky Mountains. Already the plow has turned up the soil within sight of Pike's Peak . . . ."[23] Ruxton was referring to Pueblo and Hardscrabble, both within sight of that conspicuous mountain. Ruxton's view that the Greenhorn Valley would one day become a thriving settlement was a popular one regarding all the settlements of the Arkansas Valley. The building of Brown's grist mill manifested confidence in the region's future, as did a remark of Alexander Barclay in a letter of December, 1845 that his imports now included more agricultural implements than Indian trade goods. [24]

There was little fear of Indian attack, as shown by the structural design of buildings in the Arkansas Valley which, progressing from Bent's Fort through Greenhorn, had ever fewer provisions for defense. But this sense of security was a false one. From our lofty perch of hindsight we can see that these intimations of permanent settlement were to be blown away in the next few years by the Mexican War and its aftermath of Indian hostility. Otherwise, Pueblo might have been the first permanent settlement in present Colorado.

On the other hand, it is doubtful whether, Indians or no Indians, Pueblo and her sister towns could have stood firm until reinforced by the real settlers who poured into the country in 1858. For the men of the Arkansas Valley settlements were speculators, and the slightest shift in the economic balance sent them scurrying to the weighted side of the scale. At any rate, they never had a chance to prove their stability. For American soldiers were on the march out of the East, bringing destruction with them.

14
Soldiers on the Arkansas
1845–46

ON MAY 13, 1846, THE UNITED STATES declared war on Mexico. For nearly two years troops of the two nations fought each other in Mexico, on the borders of Texas and in California. Guerrilla bands engaged United States troops at Taos, only 175 miles from Pueblo. At Bent's Fort, seventy miles from Pueblo, Kearny's Army of the West camped in August, 1846, and left commissary officers and a hospital unit stationed there for many months afterwards. Only half a mile from Pueblo a detachment of troops—Mormons sworn in as United States soldiers—camped from August, 1846 until May, 1847. But at the settlements on the Arkansas people hardly raised their eyes to see the soldiers marching past and manifest destiny being acted out in their front yards.

Charles Bent was one of the few Americans in New Mexico deeply concerned about the coming war. Being the wily, designing man he was, he had probably begun to map out his political future in 1845 as soon as he heard that James Polk had been elected to the presidency of the United States on a platform promising the acquisition of Texas, California and New Mexico. Wrote Bent, "I am fearfull that this election will cause difficulty between [Mexico] and our country," and of course he was right.[1] After Polk's election, Texas was invited to join the Union, despite the fact that it was still considered a department of Mexico by Mexicans and by some Americans. The invitation was accepted in June, 1845, while Mexico continued to assert that such an act would force her into war to regain her strayed province. With war half expected in the summer of 1845, two United States military expeditions were sent west, each with a most ambiguous set of instructions.[2]

Colonel Stephen Kearny's 1845 march to the Rocky Mountains with 250 dragoons was ostensibly to protect the Oregon emigrants and Santa Fe traders, and to awe the Indians. Unofficially the dragoons sought to prove the utility of a band of mounted men operating on the plains far from their supply base, as opposed to a string of military posts located at fixed intervals along the trails as advocated by Dr. Linn, Senator Benton and Lieutenant John C. Frémont. But the men of Kearny's expedition, as their journals show, were meant also to gather information for troops in the coming war and to be ready to march into New Mexico or California should war break out.

They could not have chosen a year when their presence on the plains was less welcome. About twenty-five hundred emigrants struggled west that year with over seven thousand head of horses, mules and cattle. Consequently there was hardly a blade of grass or a single buffalo along the trail from the frontier to Fort Laramie. To make things worse, it was a summer of searing drought. Almost no snow had fallen all winter long. When spring came the grass did not send up its shoots, and by midsummer the dead clumps crunched underfoot like dry leaves. There was no forage for animals, no game for men—and no joy at the prospect of 250 dragoons, all well mounted, followed by extra horses, thirty cattle, twenty-seven sheep, twenty-one supply wagons and two mountain howitzers, raising the dust and consuming the scarce grass and game.[3]

Thomas Fitzpatrick was Colonel Kearny's guide, and among the guests was George Simpson, whose brother-in-law was Lieutenant Andrew Jackson Smith of Kearny's command. Out to Fort Laramie they marched, passing an endless procession of emigrant wagons and dodging the barren spots where emigrants had camped. At Fort Laramie, Colonel Kearny met with Indians, and again at South Pass. The Indians received their presents graciously and promised to be good. Satisfied, the dragoons returned to Fort Laramie and then went south to the Arkansas, seeing neither buffalo nor Indians in all this wide, parched region.[4]

On July 26 they approached Pueblo. They came within fifteen miles north of it on the Fountain. Then they turned southeast across the prairie, meeting the Arkansas fifteen miles below Pueblo. They were hot, dry and hungry, reduced to one day's ration, and in a hurry to reach Bent's Fort, where two years earlier Captain Cooke had ordered provisions to be deposited when he anticipated having to spend the winter on the Arkansas with his dragoons.[5]

Not the slightest mention of Pueblo appears in any of the dragoons' accounts although its nefarious business seems to have been on their minds. Kearny himself describes "a number of white men, from our own States, who have nominally their residence near Taas

[sic] and Santa Fe, and who come frequently into the Indian country between the upper Arkansas and the Platte, between 'Bent's fort' and 'Fort Laramie;' bringing whiskey with them, which they trade to the Indians; consequently causing much difficulty and doing much harm."[6] Captain Cooke of Kearny's command describes the road as connecting "a chain of trading posts, where whiskey and gunpowder are bartered for robes and tongues."[7] Colonel Kearny was well aware of his rights and duties regarding whiskey peddlers in the Indian country: on meeting some Taos traders on the Arkansas, he confiscated their liquor and arrested them without hesitation.[8] But Pueblo and its whiskey were left alone, perhaps because of the dragoons' urgent need for the rations at Bent's Fort, or perhaps because, with war on the horizon, even such a disreputable community as Pueblo might prove to be a frontier stronghold or a base for troops.

At Bent's Fort Colonel Kearny again talked to Indians and then dashed home, forgetting that he was supposed to give aid and succor to Santa Fe traders, who had even less use for it than Oregon emigrants. The dragoons may have awed the Indians a little and given a modicum of comfort to the emigrants, but their real accomplishment was the affirmation that mounted men could travel 2,066 miles in 99 days, living off a desiccated prairie; that Stephen Kearny was an exceptionally able commander; and that the Indians were not likely to give an army much trouble. The dress rehearsal was a success.[9]

If Colonel Kearny's summer campaign of 1845 had motives other than the protection of emigrants and Santa Fe traders, Captain Frémont's expedition that same summer was not merely a survey of the Arkansas River, Great Salt Lake and California mountain passes. Frémont hints in his *Memoirs* that "eventualities of war were taken into consideration," and that his survey party might end up as troops fighting in California.[10] Both the main body and a detachment of the expedition would make armed invasions of Mexico's borders, and would be subject to death without trial if apprehended, according to Santa Anna's edict of 1843 after the Texan invasion. But Frémont considered the dangers to be inconsiderable compared to the rewards, which were nothing less than the acquisition of California for his country and power and glory for himself.

Across the dry plains Frémont set off in June, 1845. With him were fifty-odd men, each provided with a Hawken rifle, two pistols, a riding horse and one or two pack animals. There were also 150 loose horses and mules and 250 head of cattle. At Bent's Fort the command reorganized and took on more men, among them Kit Carson and Richard Owens (who had abandoned their farm on the Little Cimarron to join their old commander), and eight or twelve Delaware hunters, including James Swanock. Here Frémont detached Lieutenant J. W. Abert and thirty-five men to survey the Purgatory River, Raton Pass, the waters of the Canadian and False Washita—all in Mexican territory. Lieutenant Abert found Raton Pass a "rough and rock-strewed road," but a road all the same and one over which next year's invading forces would pass, an eventuality not unforeseen by Lieutenant Abert, who noted more than once in his journal the possibility that the United States might succeed in extending its territory to the Rio Grande.[11]

Frémont's party went on to Pueblo, arriving August 20 and camping there until August 23. On August 22 Frémont conducted a shooting match with a dozen fine Louisville rifles as prizes. The target was eighty yards distant, and each man had three shots at it, the winner to have first pick of the guns. Thomas Martin was the first winner, and he sold his rifle on the spot for $80. Martin described a merry incident of his stay at Pueblo, when a spark from the pipe of a French engagé named Merque fell into his open powder horn. The powder horn exploded with a loud report. Startled, the Frenchman and Martin dashed to the bushes shouting "Indians!" to the amusement of the rest of the company.[12]

At Pueblo Frémont bought supplies from Alexander Montgomerie, Joe Doyle and Andrew Sublette and traded his wagons for about two hundred pack animals. Then he went on to Hardscrabble, where on August 25 he bought a cow from Mathew Kinkead and hired Lucien Maxwell and Manuel Ruiz to accompany him.[13]

At Hardscrabble, Bill Williams loped up on an old mare, his yellow hair sticking out in every direction, his shirt flying loose and his greasy leather pantaloons shrunk to his knees. His face was streaked with vermilion in the Indian manner, and he was accompanied by a fat young Mohave girl. Old Bill regaled Frémont's artist, Edward Kern, with stories of his life on the frontier as a preacher and his conversion to trapping. His greatest coup, he told Kern, was robbing California ranches of four thousand horses, which he brought across the desert to Bent's Fort and sold for four or five gallons of whiskey.[14]

With Bill Williams guiding them as far as Great Salt Lake, Frémont and his men went on. In California, Frémont made himself conspicuous in the seizure of the territory for the United States. When he refused to accept General Kearny's authority, he was arrested, marched back to St. Louis and finally court-martialed in Washington. But Pueblo had not seen the last of him.

Frémont never produced a report of this expedition. He wrote his wife a letter from San Francisco in January, 1846, part of which was quoted in St. Louis newspapers. Wrote Frémont, "By the route I have explored I can ride in thirty-five days from the *Fontaine qui bouille* river to Captain Sutter's and, for wagons, the road is decidedly better." An editorial note to Frémont's published letter explained that the *Fontaine qui bouille* was Boiling Spring river in English: "This is the outside settlement on the Arkansas, about seventy miles above Bent's Fort, where old retired hunters and traders, with Mexican and Indian wives, and their children, have collected into some villages, called by the Mexican name for civilized Indian villages, pueblos, where they raise grain and stock."[15]

In the fall of 1845, long after Kearny and Frémont had passed Pueblo, more troops threatened to visit the Arkansas—Mexican ones this time—because the fact of Hardscrabble's existence had finally come to the attention of Mexican officials. Undoubtedly Hardscrabble had been known at Taos and Santa Fe from its beginning, but the authorities, dulled by the harsh realities of New Mexican politics, managed to ignore the settlement. Then in 1844 Manuel Armijo, the efficient native governor, was replaced by General Mariano Martínez y Lejanza, who in his zeal to improve the chronically hopeless situation in New Mexico began making political mistakes. In the fall of 1845, General Francisco García Condé, the military inspector, arrived in New Mexico to remove General Martínez.[16]

Shortly after his arrival, General García Condé discovered that there were foreigners illegally settled at Hardscrabble, at Poñil on the Beaubien and Miranda Grant, and at the junction of the Mora and Sapello Rivers (La Junta de los Ríos), as his ludicrous report indicates:

On my trip to the frontier I was informed that in the settlement called Peñasco Amarillo, or Tierra Amarilla, near the Napeste River, the foreigners Matias Quinques, José Espolen, Luis Lachoné, Jorge Simon, José Doyle, N. Con and others whose names are unknown, have located, with permission of the government, they claim. And beyond Taos in the settlement known as Poñil, there is also a farm belonging to Don Carlos Hipolite Beaubien, where he has several foreigners employed and has as associate Don Carlos Benton, owner of the fort located beyond the Napeste, and who are against the best interests of the Republic. I am assured that while Señor Martínez occupied the office [of governor] he ordered this farm destroyed, but afterwards his order was forgotten and the farm is growing, with danger to our frontier. At La Junta de los Ríos there are also several foreign owners of land; if they are North Americans their efforts must be halted, and their right to occupy the land investigated. Let them take their chances in Texas, if they will be allowed to do so. No less dangerous is the free intercourse between the forts [on the Arkansas] and our settlements, where foreigners come without passports and without the knowledge of authorities, to whom, according to law, they should present themselves. I suggest placing troops at the most remote points, even though unfortunately they will have to be foot-soldiers, since there are no horses or accoutrements for them.[17]

What a pathetic, frustrated document is this—a government too weak to uproot dangerous foreigners from their squatter settlements; subordinates who "forgot" orders which they were incapable of carrying out; foreigners coming and going across the borders as they pleased, and no possibility of stopping them except by troops rendered totally ineffective by having no horses! Such was the force of Mexico's threat of soldiers on the Arkansas.

After García Condé's departure, the settlers at Hardscrabble were ordered to present themselves at Taos by October 26 with documents proving their possession of the land they occupied. October 26 came and went; no Anglo-American strangers presented themselves with or without documents, "a delay most harmful to the public interest and most insulting to the Supreme Government." Having delivered themselves of this ringing condemnation, the authorities proceeded to forget General García Condé's order.[18]

New Mexican authorities continued to express their disapproval in various ways. When Sabourin and another Hardscrabble man arrived at Taos around the end of January, 1846 they were "denounced" by some petty official.[19] Mexican threats were received at Hardscrabble; on May 12, 1846 Barclay wrote in his diary that Spaniards were reported on their way to destroy the settlement and that its men were preparing for battle. Next day the report proved to be nothing but rumor.[20]

In the ordinary course of events the Mexicans might have succeeded eventually in destroying Hardscrabble, whereupon its inhabitants would merely have crossed the river to United States Territory and resumed their business. But the course of events was anything but ordinary. In August Colonel Stephen Kearny and his Army of the West marched to Santa Fe and raised the American flag over the Governor's Palace without firing a shot. Before he went on to capture California, Kearny set up a civil government for New Mexico with Charles Bent at its head. Bent was perhaps the strongest and most capable American in New Mexico, but as governor he may have been a poor choice because his contempt for his constituents had become apparent in his many confrontations with officials and clergy at Taos.[21] Bent was murdered by a mob of Taos Indians and Mexicans in January, 1847, leaving the Territory in the hands of a succession of United States clerks, colonels and Indian agents, whose ineptitude would finally mean the end of the Arkansas Valley settlements.

On the Arkansas the greatest concentration of soldiers ever seen there had gathered by the first of August, 1846 at a camp nine miles below Bent's Fort. News of the march of Kearny's Army of the West, seventeen-hundred strong, had reached Taos and Santa Fe well before its arrival. Some of the ladies of these towns, uncertain of their safety in New Mexico as wives of Americans, came to Bent's Fort. There was also a small delegation of ladies from Pueblo, of whom we have only the name of Luz Trujillo Metcalf. Luz and the other women, true to their sympathetic natures, organized a fandango in honor of the officers who were about to conquer their homeland.[22]

A supply of women for fandangos at Bent's Fort was not Pueblo's only contribution to the war effort. In the early months of the war Pueblo was a center for trade in horses and mules. Business was conducted mostly with the United States Army, which was notably careless in the husbanding of animals. While the Army of the West was camped below Bent's Fort, its horses were turned loose upon the prairie on July 27, 1846 under guard. At some fearful scent or sound a few of the horses took fright and dashed off across the plains, followed by the rest in a surging, panting body. The guards found some of them as far as fifty miles away, and about sixty-five disappeared altogether. A week later Francis Parkman's party found three in poor condition and bitten by wolves. Alexander Barclay found more, as did others who lived on the Arkansas, but only a few were ever returned to the quartermaster at Bent's Fort.[23]

The quartermaster immediately set about replacing the lost animals. Fortunately, Pueblo had recently received enough horses to fill his needs. On May 28, 1846, Jim Beckwourth, Jim Waters, LaBonte, Mark Head, Calvin Jones and others arrived from California with a large herd of horses stolen from California ranches. Beckwourth said that when they arrived at "my fort on the Arkansas" or "my plantation" (as he called Pueblo), they had a thousand horses, a remnant of the eighteen hundred "stray horses we found roaming on the California ranchos." Beckwourth took his horses down the Arkansas to meet Colonel Kearny, who greeted him warmly and listened with amusement to Beckwourth's story that when he heard war had broken out, he stole some of the enemy's horses as an act of patriotism.[24]

When Norris Colburn and a man named Cooper arrived at Pueblo at the beginning of July they encountered Jim Waters, who said that on his way home from California with the stolen horses the Piutes had killed six to eight horses every night, and that he lived on horse meat alone for two months. Colburn probably bought some of Waters' and Beckwourth's horses, but he did not keep them long. After he left Pueblo for Santa Fe, the Apaches stole thirty-four mules and a horse from Colburn and six mules and a horse from his companion.[25] The Apaches also stole twenty horses from Greenhorn belonging to Maurice LeDuc, John Brown and Murray, to add to the numerous transfers of horseflesh on the Arkansas between May and August, 1846.[26]

Neither John Brown nor Alexander Barclay wasted more than a dozen words on their reactions to the Mexican War. John Brown's only contribution to the war literature was a funny little quasi-legal statement in his account book written in December, 1846, perhaps reflecting his anxiety over the change of allegiance in the Greenhorn Valley. Here it is, in all its magnificent brevity and pith:

> John Brown for 1846 no all men by these
> presents that I John
> Brown am living on
> Greenhorn Creek.[27]

Alexander Barclay happened to be at Bent's Fort when news came that Colonel Kearny's dragoons were on the march from Fort Leavenworth, and his diary mentioned that event in July, 1846. But

"Troops Going to Mexico," 1847. Frederic Remington's illustration in Colonel Henry Inman, *The Old Santa Fe Trail* (1897). Notice at the far left the buckskin-dressed, bearded mountain man serving as scout. Courtesy of Denver Public Library Western Collection.

it was August 22 before Barclay got news of Kearny's troops arriving at Bent's Fort, and by that time the soldiers had already marched into Santa Fe. Consequently his diary never records the dramatic moment of conquest. Distant as he was from the sounds of bugles and cannons and from newspapers to report the momentous happenings, Barclay turned his attention to matters at hand—trading with the Utes and Plains Indians, herding his cattle and farming.[28]

15
Trade
1845–47

BETWEEN 1845 AND 1847 ARKANSAS VALLEY traders expanded their territory in many directions—to the South Platte, where they dickered with the Arapahos, Northern Cheyennes, and Sioux; to the North Platte near Fort Laramie, where they traded with Sioux and with California emigrants; to the Utes at the sources of the Río Grande del Norte and Arkansas; to the winter camps of the Cheyennes and Arapahos in Big Timber on the Arkansas thirty miles below Bent's Fort; and to the Navajos far to the southwest. Their Taos whiskey was turning up all over the West, to the consternation of the Indian Agent. He wrote that the Indians had been plundered and demoralized by a band of unlicensed traders, who procured their liquor at Taos, New Mexico, some of whom were Mexicans and some citizens of the United States.[1]

The agent was partly in error, for not all these rascals were unlicensed traders. Joe Doyle and John Guerin obtained a license from the Superintendent of Indian Affairs at St. Louis on July 2, 1846 permitting them and seven employees to trade for a year with the Cheyennes, Sioux, Arapahos, Utes, and any other Indians, at Big Timber on the Arkansas, at the mouth of the Fountain, on the South Platte at a point about two miles above the mouth of the Cache la Poudre, and on the North Platte about two miles below the mouth of the Laramie. Alexander Barclay was not mentioned in Doyle's license because he was a British citizen, but he was Doyle's partner, and his capital was involved in the $2,662.00 worth of trade goods. The other licensed trader from Pueblo was William Tharp, Doyle's partner of the previous year, who was authorized to trade at Big Timber, on the South Platte five miles from the mouth of the Cache la Poudre, on the North Platte at the mouth of Horse Creek, and in Bayou Salado (South Park), with eight men and goods worth $2,175.72.[2]

They worked hard, these traders. Weeks of preparation and days

of arduous travel often netted little profit, as was the case with
Barclay's ventures to the North and the South Platte in the winter of
1845–46. In the fall of 1845 Barclay sent a wagonload of goods to the
North Platte with Levin Mitchell, who returned in December with
goods not traded. Stoically, Barclay unpacked the wagon and put the
goods away in his Pueblo store, to be used in a later trading trip.[3]

Even before Mitchell returned, Barclay was preparing for another
trip to the Platte. He made six packsaddle trees (wooden crosspieces
fitted over mules' backs to which merchandise was tied) and hunted
a bull elk for leather to cover the trees. After that he made up the
packs and plaited grass rope to use as halters. On January 13, 1846
Barclay and Teresita's brother, Benito Sandoval, left Hardscrabble
on what Barclay termed the Laramie expedition, although they
never reached the Laramie River.

It was a miserable trip. The winter was so cold that on the
Arkansas a Bent employee out riding his mule froze stiff in the saddle
and fell off dead.[4] Beyond the South Platte Barclay and Sandoval
met some Arapahos who threatened them with extinction, probably
because Barclay had just returned from a trade with their enemy the
Utes. On Lodgepole Creek snow began to rage around them, con-
tinuing until they arrived at the Spring Branch of Horse Creek.
Down Horse Creek they struggled into the steep-walled, ravine-
filled valley of Goshen's Hole. A series of blizzards detained them in
this dismal canyon, where they camped from February 1 until
March 1 with other Pueblo traders—Joe Doyle, William Tharp,
Levin Mitchell, Bill New and Dick Wootton. Doyle and Tharp had
already sold all their goods. The 120 lodges of Indians they had
traded with were now on the South Platte trading with Marcellin St.
Vrain, and Barclay and Sandoval may have obtained no robes at all
on this trip.[5]

On March 2, 1846 Barclay and Sandoval left Goshen's Hole for
home. They took a single pack mule, leaving the remaining animals
and wagons for the other traders to bring home. After more
snowstorms they reached Pueblo on March 15 and Hardscrabble
shortly after. Joe Doyle did not arrive home until March 24, having
left all the wagons mired in deep snow on the Platte-Arkansas
Divide. Doyle sent Gurteau with five yoke of oxen from Hardscrabble to pull out the stalled wagons. As soon as the wagons arrived at
Pueblo, Barclay and Doyle came down from Hardscrabble, settled
up with New, Mitchell, and Wootton, and began packing the furs on
wagons for the trip east to market.[6]

"Starting Out as Trapper and Trader." From H. L. Conard, *"Uncle Dick" Wootton* (1890). A Mexican on horseback looks on as a mule is packed with bales of goods. Boots such as these and cloth trousers came into use after the Mexican War. The bearded mountaineer in the foreground still wears a buckskin shirt. Courtesy of Denver Public Library Western Collection.

By 1846 Pueblo and Hardscrabble traders were everywhere, even in that most sacred of Bent preserves, the winter camps of Cheyennes and Arapahos at Big Timber. Corn was a trade item even more popular than whiskey this year. The summer had been dry; grass had been destroyed by horses and cattle belonging to thousands of soldiers and contractors for the Army of the West. Soldiers, traders, and Indians alike bartered fiercely for corn fodder grown at Pueblo and Hardscrabble.

William Tharp spent the whole winter of 1846–47 among the Cheyennes at Big Timber. Doyle's men were busy, too. For two months Guerin, Adamson, and Doyle made relays to the Cheyennes at Big Timber with wagon-loads of corn, which they traded not only for buffalo robes but for horses and mules, sought by quartermasters at Bent's Fort and in New Mexico. Then in January, 1847 the focus of trade shifted to an Indian village on the Platte, tribe and location unknown, to which Doyle, Cowie, Guerrier, Adamson, and Craighead took their wagons loaded with corn and goods. Tharp, still trading at Big Timber, sent his man Murray to the same village on the Platte, and by spring Tharp had traded more robes than he ever had before. It was said that Tharp's profit for the winter's trade would have amounted to $5,000, had he lived to get his robes to market. [7]

Trading with the Utes was relatively new to Arkansas Valley traders and fraught with peril. The Utes were continually at war with the Plains tribes, frequently at war with the Mexicans, and jealous of the affinities of the Arkansas Valley men for their enemies. The Utes were small, dark, thickset Indians of Shoshonean linguistic stock, a different people altogether from the tall, light-skinned Cheyennes, Arapahos and Sioux whom they hated. They had lived in the mountains of Colorado and Utah many centuries before the Spaniards came. In their beautiful mountain country they were nomads, living in buffalo-skin lodges, hunting small game and deer for food and raiment. They learned to tan deerskins to velvety perfection—the "white skins" of John Brown's account book, costing twice as much as ordinary deerskins, were of Ute manufacture. When first discovered by Spaniards, the Utes hunted buffalo in the San Luis Valley. After buffalo disappeared from there, they hunted in the Arkansas Valley or South Park, where they frequently met their enemies and gave battle.

The Utes were among the first Indians to obtain Spanish horses

160

"On the Arkansas," by Rengler of Denver. This is farther down the Arkansas than the site of the Pueblo, probably in Big Timber where the Cheyennes had their camps among the cottonwoods. Courtesy of Denver Public Library Western Collection.

and to breed them. Their horses were small, elegant creatures which they traded to the Comanches in Northern Colorado and Wyoming. About 1700 the Comanches, now fully horseborne, galloped south to wrest the Arkansas Valley from the Apaches. Throughout the eighteenth century, the Utes, Apaches, Comanches, and Spaniards fought continually over possession of the Arkansas Valley, with and against one another in varying alliances. And the Arkansas Valley, like most battlefields, was largely unoccupied during this turbulent period.

When they were not at war during the eighteenth century, Utes and Spaniards traded with each other. By 1750 the Spaniards had become dependent upon this trade. Ute deerskins and the women and children they stole from the gentle Diggers or Piutes to be used as house servants became the only trade items New Mexicans could offer for barter in Sonora and New Biscay. Peace with the Utes was sought abjectly by the Spaniards as a concomitant of trade, but for another reason as well. In times of war the Utes attacked settlements north of Santa Fe where cattle, sheep, horses, corn and wheat were raised. The results were disastrous to the food supply of all New Mexico. Even in times of peace the Utes stole cattle and sheep and demanded tributes of corn. The Mexicans treated the Utes with craven respect; toward the Mexicans the Utes showed nothing but contempt. [8]

Not so toward the Americans. When American traders showed up in Santa Fe in 1821, the Utes greeted them eagerly and begged them to trade, offering their splendid spotted ponies, their cattle, mules, sheep, and the privilege of unlimited trapping in their beaver-rich mountain valleys. American trappers were not slow to respond. Provost, Ashley, Smith, and their men prowled the Ute country from 1824 to 1827, and other trappers followed them. But any trading the white men did with the Utes was for horses or other necessities; their trade was merely incidental to trapping. [9]

The first to build trading posts for the Utes was Antoine Robidoux, a St. Louis French Creole who became a naturalized Mexican. He established Fort Uintah and Fort Uncompahgre on Mexican soil in the mid or late 1830's. In 1839 the Bents' trading license showed that they meant to challenge Robidoux's trade at the "Uentee on the Colorada River." When Bent traders arrived on the Uintah, the Utes received them coldly, demanded tribute and forced them to leave without trading. Next spring the Utes came to Bent's Fort to trade. Hostile in mien, they crowded into the courtyard in overwhelming numbers with bows and arrows in hand, as nervous clerks distributed goods. Ute hostility faded in the next three years as more traders came to them, and by 1843 Frémont's party found them to be "great friends to the whites." [10]

Then Governor Martínez killed Chief Panasiyave at Santa Fe in September, 1844, and Ute–Spanish–American relations entered a new phase. Within a month the Utes attacked Fort Uncompahgre and the villages of Abiquiu and Río Colorado, killing herders and stealing stock. Early in 1845 they attacked Ojo Caliente, Río Colorado and the Pueblo of Taos. An expedition of sixty Mexicans from Taos and vicinity, ordered out against the marauders, was badly mounted and armed and no match for the volatile Utes on their superb ponies, who slipped away without a battle.[11]

While the Mexicans were making pitiful attempts to protect their frontier settlements from Utes, they learned that Americans at Pueblo and Hardscrabble were trading the Indians guns and ammunition for horses and mules stolen from the Mexicans. Padre Antonio José Martínez, who had lost 8,000 sheep and 400 head of cattle to the Utes, accused his great enemy Charles Bent of complicity with the Indians or with those who supplied them with guns at Pueblo and Hardscrabble. Stung, Bent replied,

The Priest expectes to impress it on the mindes of theas authoritys, that I have contrall over the Publo or fort Spalding at the mouth of the fontane que Bouille. And hard scrable, at the *Piedra Amarillio* at neather of theas places have we any person imployed or any ways connected with uss, farther than some of them owe uss money, which they got several yeares passed when in our service.[12]

Bent's defense was an honest one; certainly he had no connection whatever with Pueblo and Hardscrabble. Padre Martínez's accusation that the traders of those settlements did business with Utes was also perfectly true. In the fall of 1844 Alexander Barclay had brought goods from St. Louis meaning to trade with Utes on the western slope of the mountains, only to learn when he arrived at Pueblo that the Utes had declared war.[13] Not until the fall of 1845 did American traders finally discover that the Utes were at war only with the Mexicans. Earlier that year a party of Mexican traders on the Santa Fe trail met two hundred Utes at Wagon Mound and were saved from massacre by speaking English well enough to convince the Indians that they were Americans. Charles Town and two others traveling from Pueblo to Taos had their horses stolen on the Culebra, but on following the Ute thieves and identifying themselves as Americans, their horses were returned to them. Incidents such as these alerted American traders that it was safe to trade with the Utes.[14]

Alexander Barclay and Dick Wootton were among the first Americans to test Ute friendship. In October, 1845 they packed mules with goods to take to the Ute camps on the Rio Grande del Norte, returning in November. For a year afterwards, the Utes and the Arkansas Valley traders carried on a vigorous trade, visiting each other frequently and in perfect security. In March, 1846 a village of Utes was reported to be on its way to Bent's Fort to trade oxen. Four Utes passed Brown's camp on the Greenhorn, whereupon several Hardscrabble men, among them Briggs, Cosper and some Delaware hunters, hurried off to find the Indians. They apparently found them, for they returned at the end of March with six yoke of oxen doubtless stolen by Utes from Mexican settlements. On April 16 the Utes arrived at Hardscrabble and stayed there for three days. Barclay made a good trade with them, acquiring seven mules, four cows and a bull, eighty beaver skins, three hundred castors, and a hundred twenty-one buffalo robes. By the summer of 1846 the Ute village had returned to the San Luis Valley and the region around Poncha Pass, where Gurteau and Little Beaver traded with them in June and July. In September the Utes again crossed the mountains to Hardscrabble, arriving on September 8. They left two days later after turning their horses into Barclay's cornfield and inviting their uncomplaining host to visit them in return.[15]

Barclay accepted the invitation. On October 3, he left Hardscrabble with pack mules and ascended White Oak (Hardscrabble) Creek to its head in the Wet Mountain Valley. Turning south, he followed the trail to what he called Sheep Tick Canyon Pass, which led out of the Wet Mountain Valley to the waters of the Huerfano River. Following the trail over which Antoine Robidoux had taken horse carts to his trading posts, Barclay traversed Mosca Pass into the San Luis Valley. Then he began looking for signs of Utes. On the fourth day out he turned north and reached Sawatch Creek. The next day he went over Poncha Pass to the Arkansas River where, on October 12, apparently between the present towns of Salida and Buena Vista, he found the Ute village.[16]

Barclay spent two days at the village, and his trade was probably conducted in the manner Dick Wootton describes his own trade with the Utes. On arriving at the village, the traders unpacked their goods in a lodge, where squaws prepared them supper of poor, lean dog. The next morning prices were arrived at. The traders offered for sale tobacco, hunting knives, vermilion, beads, knives, guns, and ammunition—each category represented by a stick. As an Indian offered his merchandise, including mules and ponies, buckskins, buffalo robes, and Navajo blankets, the traders laid down a stick and the haggling would begin. When agreement was reached on a price, all merchandise of that category would be traded very quickly and transferred to the traders' lodge. Wootton says, probably with his usual inaccuracy, "In this way I have traded to the amount of a thousand dollars in two and a half days." At this time the Indians traded many mules and ponies stolen from Mexicans, effacing the brands before offering them for sale. In spite of Wootton's pious statement that he did not like dealing in stolen stock, he admitted that the Indians' prices were attractively low, for he could buy a mule for ten or twelve dollars, ponies for even less.[17]

On the last day of Barclay's trade, William Guerrier arrived with goods, either in partnership or competition with Barclay. The next day Barclay left for home, but not as the crow flies. Going north up the Arkansas and into South Park, he spent the night of October 15 on Río Salado near the South Park saline where all the inhabitants of the region, white and red, obtained their salt. Barclay probably loaded some salt onto his mules, then turned south again towards the Arkansas and reached Hardscrabble on October 18.[18]

Trade with the Utes sharply declined when the entry of American troops into Santa Fe turned New Mexicans into Americans. The change of allegiance must have been confusing to the Utes who had carefully differentiated between their American customers and Mexican victims for the past two years. In October, 1846 the Utes made a treaty with Colonel Doniphan, promising to stop stealing Mexican stock. After that, the trade in stolen horses and mules tapered off.[19]

Trade with the Utes was henceforth in tanned deerskins. One trading party to a Ute village in September, 1847 was headed by Joe Doyle and Jim Waters. The traders offered the usual invitation for the Utes to return the visit. Accordingly, in October, 1847 a party of Utes arrived at Hardscrabble ready to trade. There they met a party of Arapahos probably on the same errand. Ancient and implacable enemies, the Arapahos and Utes had a ground-shaking battle just above Kinkead's house on the Hardscrabble. Luz Metcalf was staying at Hardscrabble then, as were Cruz Doyle, Juana Simpson, and Teresita and Alexander Barclay. Luz remembered standing in the Hardscrabble plaza with the other women listening to the sounds of guns six miles away. The Mexicans of Hardscrabble had gone out to aid the Arapahos in the fight, but the Utes won. The Arapahos fled down the river past the plaza towards Pueblo and the plains. The Utes came to Hardscrabble and forced the inhabitants to make them a great feast of bread and buffalo meat boiled with corn, which they ate seated cross-legged on the ground in the plaza. After that the

Utes came no more to trade at the Arkansas Valley settlements although they still welcomed traders at their mountain camps.[20]

Trading with emigrants on the Oregon Trail was easier than trading with Indians. Emigrants spoke the traders' language and traded more quickly, without elaborate haggling over price, and they were more easily bilked because they lacked the Indians' experience. So it was when traders from Pueblo, Hardscrabble, and Greenhorn met some emigrants at Fort Laramie in the summer of 1846.

The traders, all masters of their skill by now, were Edmund Conn, John Brown, Antoine Cournoyer, Bill New, Antoine Laroque, and others. Preparations for the trip in the spring had been extensive. Edmund Conn spent over a month getting together his goods and equipment. He made a trip to Taos for flour, whiskey and other supplies, including pigs for Barclay and cats to keep down mice in the grain. Two days after his return from Taos, Conn left Hardscrabble with Antoine Cournoyer for John Brown's store at Greenhorn, where he borrowed a packsaddle, trail rope, two *apishamores* (tanned buffalo hides), and a bay horse.[21]

In June the traders left the Arkansas with a large herd of mules, arriving June 23 at Ford Bernard, John Richard's crude little wooden post on the North Platte eight miles below Fort Laramie. There they met Edwin Bryant, a journalist on his way to California with an emigrant train. He had come to Fort Bernard ahead of his train in order to trade off his wagons and oxen for pack mules with the "traders from Mexico." As Bryant dickered with Bill New for seven mules with packsaddles and other equipment, in trade for a wagon, three yoke of oxen, and appendages, he felt he was getting the worst of the bargain:

The mountain traders and trappers are not rich in luxuries; but whatever they possess they are ever ready to divide with their guests. In a trade, however, they are as keen as the shrewdest Yankee that ever peddled clocks or wooden nutmegs. Coffee, sugar, and tobacco, are valued here at one dollar per pound; whiskey at a dollar per pint, and flour at fifty cents per pint. The last-named article is sometimes a dollar per pint, according to the supply, payable in buffalo or deer skins, buckskin shirts and pantaloons, moccasins, etc., etc. Money is of no value among the Indians. The traders, however, who come here from New Mexico and the United States, whenever they see their advantage, extort money from the emigrants.[22]

The next morning Bryant and eight friends who had determined to pack to California were given a lesson in mule-packing by the traders' peons. After the lesson they selected articles from their baggage to take to California in the mule packs, probably rewarding the peons with discarded crockery, pots, furniture and other remnants of a secure and settled life that would be accepted ecstatically by the housewives of Hardscrabble.[23]

Two of the emigrants did not go on to California. Robert Ewing and E. Hewitt met "Mr. Conn" (who described himself as a Navajo trader) and his friends Brown and Laroque at Fort Bernard. They returned with them to Pueblo and then to Hardscrabble, "a settlement, half Indian, half white, and here a fandango was among the means of relief and recreation after a long and dangerous travel." (The fandango that was recreation to the travelers was described as a drunken brawl by Barclay.) From Hardscrabble Ewing and Hewitt returned to the United States.[24]

Edwin Bryant and his fellow mule-packers left Fort Bernard for California, arriving at Fort Bridger two and a half weeks later. At Fort Bridger they met Tim Goodale and other Arkansas Valley traders, trading their dressed buckskins, buckskin shirts, pantaloons and moccasins with "a cool, cautious, but determined intrepidity." Bryant concluded that this trade was a very important business to them. The traders had probably obtained the buckskin clothing from the Utes, and would trade off the emigrants' livestock and provisions to Hardscrabble farmers and Pueblo storekeepers, each transaction netting a profit.[25]

A very important business, indeed!

16
Gentleman Farmer
of Hardscrabble
1845–46

BETWEEN HIS TRADING TRIP to the Utes in November and his trading trip to the Platte in January, Alexander Barclay spent the month of December, 1845 at Hardscrabble, and he found it pleasant enough. This December's work was not the cold and danger involved in the Indian trade, nor the labor and frustration of farming. This December's work was hunting, which for Barclay fell somewhere between necessity and the purest of pleasures. Another piece of work was arranging trade goods and storing buffalo robes in his "stores," one at Hardscrabble, the other at Pueblo in charge of his partner, Joe Doyle. In December Barclay did little things around the place—he made a *capot* (hooded cape) for Teresita's son, Tom Suaso; constructed five packsaddles; cut out and sewed up a hunting shirt for Doyle; fixed a crib to hold meat; and helped two of Teresita's cows to deliver their calves. And he wrote his brother George in England a long, thoughtful and somewhat deceitful letter about life on the Arkansas.[1]

He noted the decrease in buffalo and the lessening importance of the buffalo robe trade. Goods he brought from the States, he wrote, now consisted more of agricultural implements than trinkets for the Indian trade. The twenty or thirty white men who lived at Hardscrabble kept hundreds of head of cattle, raised hogs and chickens, grew corn and hunted deer, antelope, bear and elk. Their needs were modest and their envy of neighbors was negligible, for nobody owned much for others to covet. Health was perhaps the greatest blessing of the region, but freedom and the exercise of free will was another. The men of the settlement had been so deeply altered by the dangers, independence and exhilaration—the "free will, free trade and free thinking"—of frontier life that they no longer could return successfully to civilization. Nor did they want to, for they could live contented here if they were capable of contentment. So wrote Barclay to his brother George, picturing a kind of

isolated, all–male compound dedicated to the exercise of modera-
tion and, judging by lack of reference to women, of celibacy. In
truth, Hardscrabble was neither isolated nor monastic.[2]

The Arkansas Valley settlements were isolated from the United
States but by no means from one another or from New Mexico.
Barclay's diary of December, 1845 records an astonishing amount of
travel—wagons to and from Pueblo with corn or goods; men driving
horses and oxen between Hardscrabble and the St. Charles horse
camp; whole families paying visits from five, thirty, eighty, two
hundred miles distant; people going to Taos or arriving from Mora;
men hunting buffalo on the plains or deer and elk in the mountain
valleys or "goats" in the foothills. Not even the cold and snow of
December served to keep the restless populace of the settlements at
home.[3]

Much of the traveling recorded for December was on account of
those women Barclay could not bring himself to mention to his
brother. When Barclay and Teresita went to Pueblo for five days at
the end of November, it was for the purpose not only of picking up
his horses at the horse camp and a wagon load of goods at Pueblo, but
also of allowing Teresita a visit with her daughter, Cruz Doyle. At
Pueblo there was probably a fandango for the visitors or a poker or
euchre game; it was not all work. The visit was repaid early in
December when Joe Doyle brought Cruz from Pueblo and Juana
Simpson came from above (Kinkead's) to join the family. Barclay was
ill during their visit, as a quiet man might well be with a houseful of
guests. On New Year's Eve Teresita's brother and mother arrived
from Mora, and the next day the whole Hardscrabble contingent
went to a New Year's feast at Maurice LeDuc's "Buzzards' Roost,"
the old trappers' fort a few miles away on Adobe Creek.[4]

The peace was shattered this December by a case of murder and
mayhem, an example of free will that Barclay did not cite in his letter
to his brother George. On Saturday, December 20 a hired hand of
Mathew Kinkead named Wells became wildly jealous of Candelaria
Sena, a dark, half-Indian girl with whom he lived in a jacal cabin
halfway between Hardscrabble and Kinkead's. After murdering
Candelaria and her suspected lover, LaFontaine, he dismembered
the girl and fled to Pueblo. Next day the men of Hardscrabble had a
meeting to consider the Wells case, and decided that Wells'
punishment was expulsion from the valley. For four months to
come, Wells and his friends Metcalf, Brown, Wootton, Mitchell,
Burroughs and Gurteau made journeys to Kinkead's ranch to collect

Wells' corn, pigs, cattle and mules. Then Wells moved away to the Platte, or to New Mexico.[5]

By the standards of the United States Mr. Wells was not severely punished for his crime. But in New Mexico the usual punishment for murder was banishment, and Wells' peers at Hardscrabble accepted this as sufficient public vengeance in the absence of any authority in the Arkansas Valley to pronounce a harsher sentence.

Charles Bent was well aware of the lack of judicial authority on the Arkansas. Three days after his own appointment as Governor of New Mexico in September, 1846 he appointed an alcalde for the town of Peñasco Amarillo (Hardscrabble) and for any adjacent settlements. An alcalde was a citizen not necessarily or usually trained in law who settled disputes in the most elementary way by hearing arguments of plaintiff and defendant and making his decision on the spot. An alcalde also served as mayor and president of the town council, but there is no evidence of a regular town council on the Arkansas. Alexander Barclay was appointed alcalde on September 26, 1846 to serve a triangular area bounded by the Arkansas River between the mouth of the Huerfano and the foot of its canyon (Royal Gorge), the Huerfano River from source to mouth, and the dividing ridge between the heads of the Huerfano and Arkansas. If Barclay ever exercised his powers as alcalde, his official actions were outside the law, for by the time he received his appointment he had left Hardscrabble and crossed to the north side of the Arkansas into United States Indian Lands, where alcaldes held no sway.[6]

In the middle of March, 1846 Barclay began preparing for a summer of farming on the Hardscrabble. Farming was a good speculation this summer because of the shortage of corn. The disappearance of buffalo meant that Indians were increasingly dependent upon corn for their subsistence and would trade for little else. Indians on the Upper Missouri who had provided corn for many other tribes were leaving their farms and taking up the hunt. Even in New Mexico the shortage of corn was acute because fields of Pueblo Indians and Mexican farmers in the Taos Valley were being regularly plundered by the Utes.

The shortage of corn had become severe as early as 1844. Lancaster Lupton had a cornfield at Fort Lancaster that year, but it had been washed out by a flood. Fort Laramie and Fort Pierre both had cornfields in 1845, but drought destroyed them. In the spring of 1846 the bourgeois of Fort Pierre wrote that he would have to get

400 to 500 bushels of corn to oppose "the Taos Pedlers who are a great annoyance and get many robes with that article." So by 1846 it was not whiskey but corn that induced Indians to part with their robes, and Alexander Barclay broke his promise to himself that he would never again be a farmer.[7]

Obviously Barclay had not farmed at Hardscrabble before. He was surprised by killing frosts of late spring and early fall, by floods that turned dry creek beds into rivers, and droughts that turned rivers into dry creek beds. Others with experience must have helped him. Rube Herring had farmed on the Hardscrabble the summer before, perhaps even earlier. So had John Burroughs. So, probably, had Barclay's peons, Jesús, Antonio and Charno, who had farmed all their lives under similar conditions in New Mexico. Nor did Barclay have to start from scratch. The acequia madre or public irrigating ditch had already been taken out from the Hardscrabble above the fields, circling around the edge of the river bluff and returning to the river at the lowest part of the fields. Probably the lateral ditches carrying water from the acequia madre to the fields Barclay would use had already been dug. Even with all these advantages Barclay's summer on the Hardscrabble was one frustration after another.

On April 3, 1846, a cold, windy, snowy day, Barclay planted peach and cherry trees. It was his last agricultural effort until April 28, when he cut a grindstone for sharpening tools and had Teresita shut up the chickens in the henhouse for the summer to keep them out of the seed. Then he began to plow and plant—he planted yellow corn, early corn, melons, pumpkins, scarlet beans, radishes, black-eyed peas and onions. When he was not plowing and planting he was making a stand for the grindstone, plaiting a lash rope, putting handles on augers and axes, making oxbows and mule harness and a door for the henhouse, fixing his rifle, and coopering kegs. On Sunday, May 10 he plowed the acequia and on the 13th he let water into it, even though it was then raining and had rained the day before—for rain, as Hardscrabble farmers had already learned, did not soak the arid earth as ground water did. So far so good.

The first of Barclay's many miseries occurred on May 15, when the ox-drawn plow broke. He spent the rest of that day hauling logs for a horse corral and for a plow beam, and the next two days mending the plow. During the two weeks following the plow broke four times, and each time Barclay spent a day or two on "Shepherd's Fork" finding a suitable piece of wood for a new beam or stock. In the meantime he irrigated and watched his seedlings burst through the soaked earth of the furrows.

On the early morning of June 1 a crisp silver frost lay on the ground; so did Barclay's little limp seedlings. Barclay wrote that Rube Herring was half crazy at the destruction of the crop, but about his own lost month's work Barclay's diary kept a spartan silence.

For five days Barclay stayed away from his fields. He busied himself making and hanging a gate to the *cerca* (fenced garden) and repairing the horse corral. Then he began to plow again and to plant beans and corn again, to cut stakes and forks to make a fence along the road, to irrigate the corn, hoe the corn, plow the corn (with a mule named Jack who performed so badly that Barclay beat him). The Arkansas was up very high and on the morning of Sunday, June 14 Barclay and Teresita walked down to see the river. On June 24, Barclay noted it was San Juan's Day but he did not stop to celebrate it, for he was busy putting out the bull herd to pasture under the guardianship of Jesús and Montoya, and planting the last of the corn in a corner of the field, with beans and green onions below it. As June wore on he sharpened his hoes, mattocks and axes on the grindstone, irrigated his cornfields, cut out a calico shirt and talked to visitors. From Bent's Fort came St. Vrain (probably Marcellin), Longlade and the Delaware Indians Jim Dickey and Big Nigger. From Kinkead's ranch came Andrés to see his mother, Teresita.

On July 2, Barclay started out for Bent's Fort to get his wagon repaired. On the first night he slept at "Kinkead's Ranch," the abandoned buffalo farm a few miles above Pueblo. He nooned the next day at Pueblo, slept at Gantt's Fort and continued down the river. Arriving at Bent's Fort on July 6, he found it full of people and jumping with excitement.

The United States had declared war on Mexico on May 13. The news did not reach Bent's Fort or other Arkansas Valley settlements until brought by Major George T. Howard about the middle of June. When Barclay arrived at the fort in July he found a number of Americans there just arrived from Taos and Santa Fe, including George Bent, Tom Boggs, F. P. Blair, John Hatcher, Bob Fisher and Asa Estes.[8] William Bent, Marcellin St. Vrain, Blair, Boggs and others were about to leave for the Purgatory as a spy company to prevent the surprise capture of Bent's Fort by the Mexicans. Although Barclay (still a British citizen) had no taste for this kind of adventure, he and Fisher did try to catch up with Major Howard's party returning east, for what purpose Barclay's diary does not explain. But Fisher's mules got away the first day, and they were forced to return to the fort. Barclay spent four days watching the blacksmith make new wheels and iron tires for his wagon, and then he returned to Hardscrabble, his war experience over.

Back to hoeing, watering, plowing. On July 20, he wrote that Antonio had spent the afternoon shucking corn, a casual announcement that Barclay's field had been delivered of a crop. He spent the next two days at Shepherd's Fork cutting logs to make a corn crib, and then he began to relax a little. On Sunday he went walking with Teresita, Rafaela and Tomas, Juana Simpson and her children. The next week he cut more logs on Shepherd's Fork, made a milk house, and went to the upper St. Charles River to hunt lodge poles. He slept below the St. Charles canyon, where Mitchell came up and told him that American troops had arrived at Bent's Fort—a momentous announcement that seemed to have little interest for him compared to his private war with the elements at Hardscrabble.

On the last day of July came disaster. It was a drought year when farmers who now cultivate the land where Barclay worked his heart out expect no water to flow in the streams from July until October. Crops survive because they are irrigated by deep wells. But Hardscrabble had no deep wells, and everything dried up. For the next two weeks Barclay watered his melons with pots of water and tried to keep his mind off his parched fields by fixing the steps and portal to the milk house, by putting the hog pen and cow pen to rights, by hunting in the cool of evening, and going currant picking with Teresita.

On the 12th of August the sun's bright and burning face was finally covered with clouds. In the evening it began to rain; it drizzled all night long—and what was left of the crop was saved. Barclay gathered the first watermelon out of the field. Four days later it rained again and Barclay noted that the St. Louis and California pumpkins were putting out as large as hen's eggs, and the watermelons were full size. He buried some of the watermelons for seed and propped up corn stalks which had been laid flat by the rain. For two more days the blessed rain came down and Barclay cheerfully stayed inside cutting out buckskin pants and entertaining visitors, who told him about the five hundred Mormon wagons rumored to be coming up the Arkansas and the American volunteers at Bent's Fort. When the sun came out again the corn began ripening, and Barclay began making another corn crib in an excess of optimism.

Other creatures besides Barclay could see the corn ripening. First came wild turkeys at the end of August, feasting in the cornfields. Barclay shot one but it got away, to come again another day. As Barclay laid the foundations of the corn crib, all of Rube's cows and Noverto's horses got into the cornfields. On the day Barclay cut a door into the corn crib the Utes arrived at Hardscrabble to trade, turning their horses into the cornfields as they departed. As Barclay put the last logs up on the corn crib, he noted that the pastures were low around Hardscrabble, and that Poisal's and Burroughs' horses were grazing in his cornfields. By September 11 the corn crib was finished, ready for whatever corn was left after the turkeys, Indians and livestock had their fill.

Until the end of August Barclay probably had not considered leaving Hardscrabble. Teresita spent a day whitewashing the outside of the house, and Barclay spent another putting his store in order in expectation of Joe Doyle and William Guerrier from St. Louis with six wagons of goods. Doyle arrived at Pueblo on September 8. Leaving his wagons, he hurried ahead to Hardscrabble, where he had a talk with Barclay about Hardscrabble's future, or lack of it.[9]

They made the decision to leave. On September 12 Doyle and Barclay went to Pueblo and unloaded their wagons, putting the goods in their Pueblo storehouse. Then Barclay set off for a trading trip to the Utes while Doyle coped with the farm on the Hardscrabble. When Barclay returned in two weeks he found the crop harvested, all there was of it, that is, for it took Barclay less than a day to put the corn in the crib. Then he went to Pueblo with his little wagon, hired two "hands" at $8 a month each, and set them to making adobe molds and putting handles on axes and other tools. The next morning he left Pueblo with a wagon and camped that night at his new location which was on the north side of the Arkansas two miles west of Pueblo. After another Ute trading trip, he returned to Hardscrabble, packed up his goods and his family, and on October 19, 1846 he left Hardscrabble for good.[10]

17
Parkman and
the Mormons
1846–47

AMONG THE EMIGRANTS CROWDING Independence, Missouri in the spring of 1846 was a young man from Boston named Francis Parkman. His trip west that summer would result in a popular book, *The Oregon Trail*, which presents a charming picture of Pueblo and of the Mormons who were just beginning to make their wintering place half a mile away.

Parkman and his friend Quincy Shaw reached John Richard's log trading post on the North Platte River eight miles below Fort Laramie on June 15. They were greeted by Richard himself, "a little, swarthy, black-eyed Frenchman . . . in the highest degree athletic and vigorous," with black curling shoulder-length hair, dressed in a tight coat of deerskin embroidered with dyed porcupine quills, fringed and embroidered leggings and moccasins.[1]

After a month on the North Platte, Parkman and Shaw set off for the Arkansas in the first hot weeks of August. Traveling south along the foot of the Rocky Mountains over the dry, smoky plains, they traversed Goshen's Hole and camped a few days on Horse Creek. On the South Platte they passed the abandoned site of a large Arapaho village, and ate their lunch in the shade of the dilapidated walls of deserted Fort St. Vrain. At the mouth of Cherry Creek they saw the remains of an old camp of the Mormons who had passed this way with John Richard a few weeks earlier. Within six or eight miles of Pueblo they stopped to eat lunch. When they started up again they found fresh tracks of a horseman who had galloped around them and returned full speed to Pueblo. "What made him so shy of us we could not conceive," wrote Parkman, unaware of how much he and Shaw looked like government agents to the guilty smugglers of Pueblo.[2]

An hour later, Parkman stood on the bluff above the Arkansas River which "ran along the valley below, among woods and groves, and closely nestled in the midst of wide cornfields and green meadows, where cattle were grazing, rose the low mud walls of the Pueblo."³ Pueblo's site, said Parkman, was in a beautiful bottom, but the post itself impressed him as "a wretched species of fort, of most primitive construction, being nothing more than a large square inclosure, surrounded by a wall of mud, miserably cracked and dilapidated. The slender pickets that surmounted it were half broken down, and the gate dangled on its wooden hinges so loosely, that to open or shut it seemed likely to fling it down altogether."⁴ So had time and neglect dealt with Pueblo, described only four years earlier as having the appearance of neatness and comfort.⁵

As Parkman and Shaw rode up to the gate, two or three bearded Mexicans in broadbrimmed hats, lounging on the river bank, arose and disappeared. From the fort John Richard came out and shook hands warmly. He had come from Fort Laramie for the purpose of making a trading expedition to Taos, but the threat of war in New Mexico had forced him to stop at Pueblo. In the plaza stood his large Santa Fe wagons. A few squaws and Spanish women and a few Mexicans "as mean and miserable as the place itself" sauntered about. Richard led Parkman and Shaw into the fort's "state apartment," a small, neatly finished room garnished with a crucifix, a looking glass, a picture of the Virgin, and a rusty horse pistol. Instead of chairs, a number of chests and boxes ranged about the room. In another room beyond were three or four Spanish girls, one of them very pretty, who were baking cakes at a mud fireplace in the corner. They spread a poncho on the floor for a tablecloth and folded buffalo robes around it as seats, and then they laid out a supper which seemed luxurious to Parkman.⁶

Parkman and Shaw sat cross-legged on the floor among the two or three Americans present, and began to ask the news. Richard told them of Kearny's approach to Santa Fe, and one of the Americans produced a dingy newspaper describing the battles of Palo Alto and Resaca de la Palma. While they talked a large shambling man in shrunken brown homespun trousers with a pistol and bowie knife stuck in his belt slouched in. His head was swathed in a linen bandage, the result of an encounter with a grizzly bear as they learned later. He was followed by eight or ten men of the same stamp who arranged themselves about the room staring at the visitors. They were part of the Mormon company that Richard had conducted to Pueblo, and they began at once to catechize the gentiles. Parkman found them appalling, a "glitter of the eye, and a

Francis Parkman at twenty. From C. H. Farnham, *A Life of Francis Parkman* (Boston, 1900).

compression of the lips" testifying to their "true fanatic spirit—ripe for anything—a very dangerous body of men."[7]

Near sunset Parkman left the fort. He was struck by the beauty of the landscape—tall woods lining the river with green meadows on either bank; high bluffs basking in the sunlight; a Mexican driving a herd of cattle towards the gate; and Parkman's own little white tent pitched under a tree in the meadow. In the tent Richard had put a supply of green corn and vegetables, and he invited the visitors to take whatever else they wanted from the fields around the fort. This invitation, he told Parkman, was also extended yearly to several thousand Arapahos who camped around the post, helping themselves to corn and turning their horses into the fields, leaving just enough corn to encourage the inhabitants to plant again.[8]

The next morning in a drizzling rain Parkman and Shaw visited the Mormon camp across the Arkansas and about half a mile downstream from Pueblo. As they crossed the river, they passed several woebegone mountain men on horseback in rain-soaked and clammy buckskins. The white wagons of the Mormons were drawn up in the woods, and the men were out in the rain chopping down trees and making cabins along the edge of the woods and in the meadow. As Parkman and Shaw came up, the Mormons stopped work to discuss points of theology and to complain of their ill-use at the hands of the gentiles. Afterward Parkman concluded that the United States was fortunate to have been delivered of such "blind and desperate fanatics." The following day, August 22, the young men from Boston went on toward Bent's Fort and home.[9]

Parkman's harsh judgement of the Mormons was no more than an echo of the national sentiment. Feared for their unorthodox religious beliefs and practices, despised for their smug certainty that they were the Chosen People, and envied for their success in acquiring property, the Mormons had been forced by their gentile neighbors to quit every settlement they had established. As a result they had developed a group habit of self-pity and complaint which in turn increased the hostility shown them. In 1845 after they had abandoned Nauvoo, their handsome city in Illinois, they meant to escape persecution altogether by migrating westward. Some thought their destination was California, but their leader, Brigham Young, already had his eyes fixed upon the grassy plains from which the Great Salt Lake had retreated in eons past. From Brigham Young the order went out in the winter of 1846 for all Mormons to

"A Mormon Family." From William A. Bell, *New Tracks in North America* (1869). Prim and tidy in their log cabin with their pet deer, these people might have been living at Mormon Town near Pueblo when this sketch was made, except that the large glass-paned window was a luxury unknown on the Arkansas. Courtesy of Denver Public Library Western Collection.

meet the refugees from Nauvoo on the Oregon Trail. Together they would march to the Promised Land.[10]

When the order reached Monroe County, Mississippi in the spring of 1846, forty-three "Mississippi Saints," as they became known, set out in nineteen wagons for the emigrant trail. On the North Platte they met John Richard, who advised them to go no further west but to winter at the head of the Arkansas, where corn

179

was grown and supplies could be brought in from the Spanish country. When the trader offered to guide them to Pueblo they gratefully accepted. They arrived on August 7 and were welcomed and treated with kindness by the "six or eight Mountaineers in the fort with their families." Across the river and half a mile east of Pueblo they began building their cabins, at which Parkman found them hard at work on the rainy morning of August 21, 1846.[11]

The Mississippi Saints were the first of four groups to populate "Mormon Town" between August and December, 1846. The others were all detachments of the Mormon Battalion, enlisted near Council Bluffs to march to California behind General Kearny's Army of the West, thus getting free transportation on government rations. One group consisted of seventy-seven men, eight women and an unknown number of children who were detached at the crossing of the Arkansas because their women and children slowed the march. They were sent west along the Arkansas under Captain Nelson Higgins in September, arriving at Pueblo sometime in October. Immediately they set to work building more houses in Mormon Town, bringing the total number of houses to twenty.[12]

A third group of Mormons were detached at Santa Fe and consisted of twenty-seven men who were actually sick, eighty-seven more who were worn and weary, twenty women and a number of children. They were sent to Pueblo under Captain James Brown via Raton Pass and Bent's Fort, where they drew sixty days' rations. They reached Pueblo on November 17, only six of them still sick. At Mormon Town they built eighteen more log houses and a log tabernacle. They also built a blacksmith shop and a large corral for horses traded from the Indians during the first week after their arrival.[13]

The fourth group was detached at Socorro, New Mexico, for lack of rations and mules. Fifty-five of them under Lieutenant W. W. Willis went by Taos and the Sangre de Cristo Pass to Pueblo. Some of Lieutenant Willis' command had been left at Simeon Turley's ranch at Arroyo Hondo to convalesce, and these did not arrive at Mormon Town until about the middle of January.[14]

By February, 1847 Mormon Town had a population of well over three hundred souls, forty-seven of them women and an unknown number of children. Their town was in a broad and well-timbered bottom of the Arkansas. A single long street was lined with fifty-odd houses, each about fourteen feet square, built of cottonwood logs laid horizontally and chinked with mud. At the end of the street was the temple, twenty by thirty feet, built of huge logs, where prayer meetings and dances were held.[15]

As soon as they arrived at Pueblo in August, 1846, the Mississippi Saints cleared the land, planted turnips, corn, melons and pumpkins and prepared the soil for spring crops of wheat. By the middle of August their turnip patches made gay green stripes in the black bottom lands. Carefully tended, their little farm thrived. In September some Mormons showed up at Bent's Fort with green pumpkins and corn to sell. In October Captain Brown and others took nine or ten wagons to Bent's Fort to collect government rations and supplies for sixty days. Most of these supplies were not needed, and were traded off to Pueblo men. The Mormons had more than plenty to eat. Besides government rations and produce from their fields, their hunters brought back wagons heaped with carcasses of buffalo, deer and elk. Their stock of domestic cattle expanded to a considerable herd by shrewd trading and not-too-scrupulous acquisition of strayed animals.[16]

Nevertheless, it is typical of the Mormons that accounts of their winter on the Arkansas are replete with the "unhealthfulness" of the place and the "suffering and exposure" occasioned by "insufficient food and clothing." They complained of a "great number of deaths"; one Saint wrote that "the number of graves in the little cemetery gradually increased as the population of the place decreased." It was a woeful image which the Mormons cherished and nourished for years afterwards, until the legend of their stay on the Arkansas became as grim as an account of the plague. It was a fact that nine deaths, two of them newborn infants, occurred in Mormon Town that winter. Considering that most of the men were sent to Pueblo because they were too sick to make the march to California, the death rate was not higher than could have been expected.[17]

On the whole, the winter at Pueblo was a good one for the Mormons as the more honest and cheerful would admit. Relations between Pueblo and Mormon Town were cordial, a pleasant change from the hostility Mormons were accustomed to. Manomas Gibson Andrus remembered that the Spanish wives of Pueblo men "were so nice to us. If they had not been so nice when my father was so sick during the winter we would have starved to death."[18] Communication and commerce between the two settlements began immediately upon arrival of the Mississippi Saints, who traded their labor for provisions from Pueblo. Mormon turnips and corn probably benefitted from Pueblo tools and advice on such local techniques as irrigation. Mormons whose hickory shirts and drill pants had worn out over the summer traded items from their government issue at Pueblo to buy deerskins for making shirts and trousers. There were also borrowings later in the Mormon stay when good faith was firmly established: Barclay loaned his mule Kate to a Saint, and in turn borrowed several Saintly ox yokes.[19]

Social intercourse between the settlements was frequent, although the half-mile distance that separated them was far less than the wide divergence in motives, beliefs and experience. But, strange as the Mormons must have seemed to the mountain men, they were made welcome at Pueblo. Besides, the male part of the trading settlements was properly impressed by Mormon women. Dick Wootton mentioned the "several rather attractive young women," and acknowledged that the mountain men found "inexpressible enjoyment in flirting with the Mormon girls, the first females of their race many of them had beheld since they left civilization." According to George Ruxton, there were "many really beautiful Missourian girls who sported their tall graceful figures at the frequent fandangos."[20]

Dances were given two or three times a week at Mormon Town with a couple of fiddles providing music. Occasionally men from Pueblo would attend these functions. One time a party of mountaineers, bringing buffalo meat and dressed deerskins to trade, were invited to stay for a dance. The men were delighted to accept the invitation until they discovered that first they had to listen to a sermon by Captain Brown, a "hard-featured, black-coated man of five-and-forty, correctly got up in black continuations, and a white handkerchief round his neck, a costume seldom seen at the foot of the Rocky Mountains." Barclay records another fandango at Mormon Town on September 13, 1846 attended by Hardscrabble and Pueblo people at which Metcalf was the soul of fun.[21]

According to Manomas Gibson Andrus, who was only four at the time, all was not "fun." She recalls that the traders and trappers at Pueblo "did a good bit of drinking and gambling." One night at Mormon Town the Pueblo men were playing cards when an argument arose. A man was shot dead and his murderer was pursued, shot, and brought back to camp for burial. Her father, a carpenter, built the coffins. The story is doubtful, for diaries of Mormons at Pueblo do not mention it.[22]

Two marriages were performed at Mormon Town, and there were several romances resulting in marriage elsewhere. One Mormon couple was married at Independence Rock in Wyoming on their way from Pueblo to Salt Lake in 1847. Another, according to a romantic story told by George F. Ruxton in his *Life in the Far West*, was married in the States. Ruxton's tale, which he insists is true, concerns a family of half-hearted Mormons from Tennessee named Chase (Brand in later editions) who left Mormon Town early in the spring of 1847 to go to California. The daughter of the family, Mary, was thirty but still single because of a youthful love affair with a man named Labonté who had left her to go off to the mountains as a trapper fifteen years earlier. As the Mormon family traversed the country between the Arkansas and Platte rivers, their wagon was attacked by Arapahos who killed Mary's father and two of her brothers. Mary would have been next, but she was rescued in the nick of time by Labonté who galloped madly down the bluff, killed all the Indians, drew his beloved into his arms—and so forth. The intriguing thing about this stylized romance is that there actually was a Chase family at Pueblo but no Mary Chase, and the family was from Vermont instead of Tennessee. There was also a Labonté or several of them among the mountain men.[23]

Another romance, probably the source of Ruxton's story, was that of mountain man Bill New and Mary Gibson, daughter of George W. Gibson of South Carolina. After the Gibsons left Pueblo and settled in the Great Salt Lake Valley, Bill New followed them there and brought back twenty-three-year-old Mary to Pueblo as his bride and as mother to his half-Indian children, Nancy and Jane. Bill and Mary were living at Greenhorn in the summer in 1848; she was surely the first white American woman to hang her stays in that primitive place. There Mary gave birth to a child named Gethro. The family moved to Lucien Maxwell's settlement at Rayado where, late in 1850, Bill New was killed by Indians.[24]

There was a measure of proselytizing extended to the Pueblo community. The Mormon John Steele mentioned in his diary in March, 1847 that "there are preaching now prety large in Pueblo." Steele thoroughly disapproved. As he explained, the preachers were revealing the secret doctrines to "six or eight jentiles there from Missoury they know all about it now and for oughts I know all other mistreys are revealed. . . ."[25]

Of all the old Pueblo and Hardscrabble crowd, none was more taken with the Mormons than Valentine J. ("Rube") Herring. He had come West with John Gantt in 1831, trapped for Wyeth in 1835 and was a free trapper later. In recent years he had farmed on the Hardscrabble with his woman, Nicolasa. He was one of the eccentrics of the trapping clan, handsome but unsmiling, sulky and silent and superstitious as an Indian. Of great height (Ruxton says he was six and a half feet tall), spare and bony, his huge hands dangled at the ends of his long arms, and his straight black hair hung to his shoulders. Rube first put on his Mormonism by wearing the cast-off brown dress coat of a Mormon who was strangely different in shape. The skirts of the ill-fitting coat reached his ankles and completely covered his buckskin breeches, which had shrunk up to his calves. Then Rube got his hands on a *Book of Mormon* which he read out loud in his sonorous voice day and night. He suffered the badgering of the Pueblo folk with great good humor and steadfast faith, maintaining that the Mormons were the "biggest kind of prophets." One day he announced to his friends that the Mormons would hire him as guide to their next destination. Later, when they altered their destination and no longer needed his services, "a wonderful change came over his mind. He was, as usual, book of Mormon in hand, when Brother Brown announced the change in their plans; at which the book was cast into the Arkansas . . . turning away, old Rube spat out a quid of tobacco and his Mormonism together."[26]

The most unpleasant part of the Pueblo sojourn for some of the Mormons was the military discipline, for Mormon Town was not merely a settlement but a camp of United States soldiers commanded by Captain James Brown, the hard-featured preacher of Ruxton's description. As soon as the houses were built and the families made comfortable, the officers began drilling the men constantly in squads until they became highly proficient. Every morning and evening there were regular roll calls and the sound of the bugle must have drifted across the Arkansas on clear days and startled the lazy folk of Pueblo. Three times a day the soldiers paraded, and mounted guards were posted near the town at all times. On one occasion, Ebenezer Hanks was sent out on picket duty and left there for two weeks without relief—or so he recalled some years later. No doubt this excessive military zeal kept the men from boredom, but the soldiers came to hate their officers and to accuse them of great harshness.[27]

On January 11 there was a call for volunteers to build a "house to preach in," and nearly all the men turned out. When the "house to preach in" turned out to be a guardhouse, only a handful of volunteers showed up to finish it. In retaliation the officers announced that there would henceforth be no card-playing or dancing. On January 19 almost all the boys were out hunting instead of parading, which so angered Captain Brown that he put those who stayed home on guard duty. This punishment of the innocent led John Steele to confide to his diary, "I think he is very much troubled with the Big Head." On another occasion the men were marched to the parade ground, lined up and berated by each officer in turn—and all because someone had discovered a comic poem containing a slur upon an officer. The poet, George D. Wilson, was threatened with death by the officers and fled to the mountains. After his return, he and others considered going to Bent's Fort and claiming protection under the laws of the United States, but nothing ever came of it. [28]

The officers did not feel much esprit de corps, nor did they seem to have the best interests of their men at heart. In March, Captain Higgins and Lieutenant Luddington went to Santa Fe, returning in April with some barrels of whiskey for which they had paid $2.50 per gallon. They watered the whiskey down and sold it to the boys for $8.00 per gallon, and when the boys proceeded to get "drunk as fools" on it, the officers punished them. Later in the spring Captain Brown and Captain Higgins went to Santa Fe with ten men and thirteen pack mules to collect the salaries of their men. When they returned with about $8,000, they charged each man 2½% of his salary for a collection fee, justifying it by the cost of the mules ($130). [29]

In March, 1847 Captain Brown's party brought back from Santa Fe the message that the Pueblo Mormons were to start for Fort Laramie to meet the "Pioneer Company" sent ahead under Brigham Young to find a home for the Saints. On the first of May, part of the original company of Mississippi Saints crossed the Arkansas on its way to Fort Laramie. On May 24 the rest of the population of Mormon Town crossed the river on their way north. They traveled by way of Fort Laramie, South Pass and Fort Bridger. As they came down Emigration Canyon just east of present Salt Lake City on July 29, Brigham Young himself welcomed them to their Promised Land.

Two Mormon families stayed on the Arkansas through the summer of 1847, putting in a crop of corn in case the Promised Land could not produce enough to feed the Chosen People. One family, named Gibson, was still living in Mormon Town in February, 1848 when Alexander Barclay bought corn from them. By the fall of 1848 all the Mormons were gone, leaving their houses standing and empty. In November Frémont's men found "a lot of rude log houses" at Mormon Town, but six months later only three houses still stood, the others probably consumed in campfires of 1849 emigrant parties passing Pueblo.[31]

The Pueblo Saints did not come empty handed to the great colony they were to build at Salt Lake, for their stay at Pueblo had been highly profitable. By terms of their enlistment they were allowed to keep guns, tents and camp equipage issued to them, and they managed to appropriate other United States property besides what they were entitled to, including fourteen government wagons that had been sent to them with rations and not returned. As far as records show, on arrival at Pueblo none of the Mormons had cattle, and none except the Mississippi Saints had horses. On their departure they had a hundred horses owned by more than fifty men, as well as three hundred head of cattle acquired by trade with Indians or traders or picked up as stray stock.[32]

It was not only material goods which the Mormons brought from Pueblo but certain ideas and skills. Irrigation and common ownership of irrigation systems first came into the Salt Lake Valley via the Pueblo Mormons. The fort that Brigham Young built at Salt Lake was made of adobes, and Pueblo Mormons were the ones who built it. John Steele was one of three men who brought in his knapsack "the white Taos wheat," which thrived at high altitudes and low humidity and was the principal seed wheat in Utah for years afterwards.[33]

Who knows what else the Pueblo Mormons gained during their winter on the Arkansas? Perhaps because of the hospitality of the Pueblo traders, these persecuted people overcame a fear that they actually were "blind and desperate fanatics." Perhaps from the Pueblo people they learned the generosity to travelers that ever after distinguished them.

18
The Bad Winter of
1846–47

IN THE FALL OF 1846 while the Mormons were settling down in their log town for the winter, Alexander Barclay was putting his summer's crop of corn in the crib at Hardscrabble and making up his mind to move away. As a farm Hardscrabble was all too correctly named. As a trading post it was of little use, being situated in the middle of a traditional Ute and Arapaho battleground where neither tribe would dare venture. Grass at Hardscrabble was badly depleted, and the cattle of the settlement had to be pastured elsewhere. So Barclay decided to move back to the mouth of the Fountain, where his partner Joe Doyle had lived with his family for the past two years.

Barclay did not move into the Pueblo, probably because he had decided to become a full-scale cattle rancher, and Pueblo, like Hardscrabble, had little grass. He picked out a site two miles west of Pueblo where the Arkansas bottom broadened out to about half a mile wide. There was probably a fine stand of grass in the bottomland, and there were cottonwoods along the river banks to be used for lumber, firewood and shelter for the stock. On September 30, 1846 Barclay and Doyle left Pueblo with a wagonload of building implements—adobe molds, axes, spades, stakes—and started building "the Houses," as Barclay always called them.[1]

The Houses made three sides of a hollow square, and were finished in October. They consisted of a number of adobe and chinked-log rooms for dwellings, a log "lumber house," an adobe store and a corral. A stockade wall with a gate closing the square was completed many months later, as was a cattle press. The buildings had sod roofs; one rainy day in April the roofs began to leak and people were in an uproar, moving things away from mud-dripping ceilings. The next day Barclay put his sodden buffalo robes out to dry in the sun while he hauled dirt to repair the roofs. Teresita spread whitewash over the walls of the rooms to hide the ugly streaks of mud.[2]

At the Houses, Barclay was giving the Arkansas Valley one more chance to make him a man of property, and his choice of livelihood was a natural one for the region. In 1874, cattleman Joseph McCoy wrote of the Upper Arkansas Valley:

That portion of country south of the [Platte-Arkansas] Divide . . . is one of the finest, if not the finest, live stock country on the continent. The winters are very mild, the air pure, the climate healthy, the grass fine—in short, nature seems to have exhausted herself in favorable combinations in its make-up. [3]

When Joseph McCoy wrote his praise of the short-grass country of Colorado, cattle ranches were far removed from settlements, and ranchers had enough land to allow a square mile of pasture for the support of every fifteen head of cattle. Barclay lacked these ideal conditions. Grass that had looked thick and lush when the Pueblo and Hardscrabble were founded was all but destroyed by 1846 for miles around each settlement. And no wonder—every settler had his riding horse and pack horses for bringing back game; every trader had his string of pack mules and several yokes of oxen to draw wagons; every lady had her milk cow; and now Barclay had his cattle herd.

How many head of cattle Barclay had in the beginning is undetermined. By the time he left the Arkansas in 1848, he and his companions had a hundred twenty head of cows, calves, yearlings, bulls and steers. Judging by Barclay's descriptive list, they were a motley collection—strawberry speckled; black-spotted brown with white face; white-face brindle; brindle-face white; black "Spanish"; red musky with white spots around the forehead. The animals were bred regularly but not with any idea of preserving desirable traits. Such selective breeding would have been impossible, for Barclay's cattle were an all-purpose variety, used for milk, for drawing wagons and plows, and for beef, each function requiring different characteristics. The herd increased yearly; there is frequent mention in Barclay's diary of steering young bulls, and when Barclay became too ill to hunt, of slaughtering cattle for meat. [4]

The pasturing of these animals had been a major problem at the Arkansas Valley settlements long before Barclay became a cattle rancher. As early as November, 1845 Hardscrabble's grass was in grave decline. When Barclay and Wootton returned from a trading trip to the Utes that month they arrived at night with horses traded from the Indians. So difficult it was to feed these extra animals that before daybreak Barclay and Wootton set off with their horses to greener pastures. At the Taos trail crossing of the St. Charles River about nine miles south of Pueblo, John Poisal, John Burroughs, Calvin Briggs, and perhaps John Brown, were conducting a winter horse camp. Here the little St. Charles swells out into a grassy valley lined with layered limestone bluffs, providing a natural corral where a few men could control a large number of animals. It took Barclay and Wootton five days to reach the winter horse camp because their horses strayed, searching continually for grass on the overgrazed land beside the trail.[5]

In the winter of 1846–47, the depletion of grass had not improved with the advent of three hundred Mormons and their ever-increasing herd of animals, as well as the constant movement of men, wagons and oxen between Pueblo and Bent's Fort. The miseries of straying stock were never better described than by George F. Ruxton, a young British adventurer who had ridden north through Mexico in the summer and fall of 1846. He arrived at Pueblo in January, 1847 to find the surroundings entirely bare of grass. Ruxton's five pack mules and a riding horse named Panchito strayed to a small valley up a dry creek bed three or four miles from Pueblo. When Ruxton broke a hole in the ice on the Arkansas the animals came from their valley to the water hole every morning and evening, the mules following Panchito single file along a trail they had made in the snow. Their appearance at the water hole was as regular as sunrise, and Ruxton learned exactly when to catch them. After they had eaten all the grass in their valley, they moved farther away. For fifteen days Ruxton lost them completely, then found them at the foot of the mountains in a patch of grass where there was a pool of water. Now it was a day's work for Ruxton to catch his animals. Not only did he have to travel the considerable distance to their grazing ground, but also chase them on horseback when he got there, for they had become wild and independent. Once he had lassoed Panchito, the others followed obediently, single file, back to the Pueblo.[6]

At Pueblo Ruxton was entertained at the lodge of John Hawkins, "an ex-trapper and well-known mountaineer," about whose Mexican wife and daughter Ruxton told a peculiar tale. Mrs. Hawkins formerly lived in Durango as the wife of a Mexican. She was captured by Comanches and brought to Bent's Fort where Hawkins paid her ransom to the Indians. After she had borne Hawkins a daughter, her Mexican husband heard that she had been freed from Indian captivity. Trudging fifteen hundred miles from Durango to the Arkansas, he arrived at Pueblo to claim his wife and take her home. She refused to accompany him without her daughter by Hawkins, and the Mexican trudged back to Durango without her.[7]

Ruxton describes Pueblo as a small square fort of adobe with circular bastions at the corners, with walls no more than eight feet high in any part. Around the inside of the yard or corral were half a dozen little rooms occupied by half a dozen Indian traders and mountain men. Their three or four Taos women, and as many Indian women of various tribes, gave good promise of "peopling the river with a sturdy race of half breeds, if all the little dusky buffalo-fed urchins who played about the corral of the fort arrived scatheless at maturity."[8] They lived entirely on game and without bread most of the year, since they grew little corn. When their meat supply was exhausted, they went to the mountains with two or three pack animals which they brought back loaded with buffalo or venison. Game was scarce near the fort, and buffalo had disappeared from the nearby prairies. But game could always be found in the mountain valleys, particularly in one called *Bayou Salado* (South Park).[9]

Ruxton left the Pueblo for a buffalo-hunting trip to South Park with three pack mules and a man named Morgan, probably one of two tubercular Americans cured of their disease by a winter of camping in the mountains near Pueblo. Starting off up the Fountain to the foot of the mountains at present-day Manitou, Colorado, they camped on a small tributary since known as Ruxton Creek. At this spot deer were so abundant that the men decided to give up the buffalo hunt and go after deer instead. The next day as Ruxton was returning with some freshly butchered venison on his back, he met an Arapaho. Ruxton would have shot the Indian, had it not flashed through his mind that two Arapaho brothers were among the hunters on the Arkansas and their sister was married to a white hunter there. In wary friendship Ruxton clasped the Indian's hand. Subsequently, the white men were not molested by the Arapaho war party in the vicinity. Ruxton considered the Arapahos hostile, and wrote that it was "almost a miracle" that they did not discover his presence there and relieve him of his animals and his scalp. Miracle it would have been had the Arapahos not known full well that the young Englishman was there, basking in his delusions of high and heady danger![10]

George Frederick Ruxton. The anonymous artist did his research well: the face and form of the dapper little Englishman correspond to what we know of him, and the scene is his camp in Ute Pass where he met the Arapaho and nearly made the mistake of shooting him. Lithograph from *Early Days: Noted Occurrences on the Line of the Midland Railroad* (Promotional Pamphlet, c. 1890). Courtesy of Denver Public Library Western Collection.

After Ruxton's return to Pueblo two or three days later, he met the same Arapaho war party—twenty-one tall and handsome young men under a chief called Coxo ("the game-leg") loping along the trail on foot, single file. Each was naked to the waist, his body carefully painted and his scalp lock braided and adorned with a ribbon or eagle feather. A buffalo robe was thrown over his shoulders and he was armed for war. The Indians were returning from an expedition against the Utes in South Park, and they carried lariats or hide ropes to secure the horses they expected to steal. Failing to find the Utes, they came to Pueblo. On their approach the inhabitants corralled all the horses and mules, but the Indians were friendly and only wanted to trade for meat. After exclaiming over Ruxton's high Chippewa moccasins (Arapahos wore low shoe moccasins), they left as they had come, on foot.[11]

The winter of 1846–47 was very severe on the Arkansas with high winds, freezing cold, snow that stayed on the ground covering the grass, and ice that stayed on the river covering the water. The winter was a nightmare of strayed stock seeking grass and water. Barclay's diary is full of references not only to sending men out to hunt up cattle, but to sending men out to hunt up the men hunting up the cattle. One very cold day in February, fourteen-year-old Tom Suaso was sent out after cattle, and Teresita spent the day in tears, afraid he would freeze to death. Just as Barclay was about to go out after him, Tom came in. For three days in April all Pueblo's horses strayed, and all Pueblo's men were out looking for them. William Guerrier found the animals, probably in some remote mountain pasture such as Ruxton describes.[12]

One incident of straying stock almost provided Barclay and Doyle with a new kind of speculation. Late in November, 1846 the twenty-eight-wagon train of Bullard, Hook & Co. carrying merchandise to Santa Fe, crossed the Arkansas at Cimarron Crossing and camped in the sand hills on the south side of the river. During the night a blizzard blew in from the northwest so quickly and violently that the oxen panicked, broke through the guard and scattered out in the darkness over snowy, wind-swept plains. Three mules died, and twenty oxen disappeared in the storm. The teamsters cached their goods, abandoned half their wagons and made for Bent's Fort, 150 miles west, with the goods they could carry in the thirteen wagons for which they had oxen.[13]

At Big Timber the wagons made camp. The wagonmaster, James H. Bullard, talked to Joe Doyle who promised him oxen enough to rescue his stalled wagons. Doyle hurried back to Pueblo and began to gather up animals—his own and Barclay's at the Houses, ten yoke from George Simpson at Greenhorn, eleven yoke from Kinkead and Burroughs at Hardscrabble. Barclay and Doyle also rented yokes and harness from John Brown at Greenhorn and from Robert Crow and Dimick Huntington at Mormon Town. With his oxen and equipment, Barclay went to Big Timber where he borrowed more oxen from William Guerrier and spent the night in his lodge. Some of Bullard's men left for the crossing of the Arkansas with Barclay's oxen; others moved the wagons from Big Timber to Bent's Fort, where they camped for the winter.[14]

By the end of February, boredom had set in at Bullard's camp near Bent's Fort. Bullard's partner, Isaac McCarty, with William Guerrier and a man named Clay, showed up at Pueblo for a little fun and relaxation. There they found George Simpson, a willing participant in any binge. On February 27, when Barclay returned from hunting, he found them all in Simpson's room at the Houses, drinking and playing cards. The next day they moved the party to Pueblo where Barclay joined them. The frolic went on for a couple of days, until on March 2 Barclay was so drunk he had to be taken back to his Houses in a wagon. His monstrous hangover turned into something worse, and he spent two days in bed with a high fever, spitting blood.[15]

Barclay and Doyle had expected a contract to haul Bullard & Hook's train to Santa Fe, but in the spring when they arrived at Bullard's camp with oxen they found he had made other arrangements. After watching Bullard's wagons move up the Timpas towards Raton Pass, they went home and returned the oxen and yokes they had borrowed, resigned by now to the many disappointments that had to be borne by speculators on the Arkansas.[16]

Late in the afternoon of January 23, 1847 a Mormon out hunting south of Greenhorn saw, coming toward him in the dusk, something that looked half man, half deer. The Mormon stood up in his stirrups to get a better look, and the thing beckoned to him. Terrified, the hunter wheeled his mule and made off for Mormon Town at a gallop. The man in the deerskin was an exhausted little fellow named John Albert. He staggered on to Greenhorn, where Blackhawk met him and carried him into the post. It took him a day to gain strength to go on. Then he set out again and arrived at Mormon Town just at supper time. Albert told the following story at Mormon Town and then told it again at Pueblo.[17]

He and eight or ten other Americans had been employed by Simeon Turley at the mill and distillery on Rio Hondo twelve miles north of Taos. On January 19, 1847 Charles Town arrived at Turley's from Taos and hastily informed Turley that the Taos Indians, joined

193

with Mexicans, had risen in a mob at Taos and killed Governor Charles Bent and every American they could lay hands on. After Charles Town had left for Santa Fe, the mob appeared at sunrise at Turley's gate with a flag of truce. Turley indignantly refused to surrender, and the mob opened fire, keeping up a rain of bullets which shattered every window and rattled against the thick mud walls like hail. As night fell, the mob set fire to the mill. John Albert and a companion opened the back door leading to a fenced garden and dashed out, firing wildly into the crowd. Albert's friend was killed, but Albert reached the log fence and lay concealed underneath it as the mob rushed into the burning buildings and killed the remaining defenders. Turley, William LeBlanc and Tom Autobees had escaped into the night by digging a hole through the back adobe wall. Tom made it to Santa Fe and LeBlanc to Greenhorn, but Turley, who was lame, was caught and killed.[18]

Under cover of darkness John Albert crept off into the piñon-covered hills behind Turley's house, headed for the Sangre de Cristo Pass. On the eastern side of the pass he shot a deer and wrapped its skin around him, which kept him from freezing until he reached Greenhorn.[19]

After John Albert told his story at Mormon Town on January 25, 1847, the excitement was so intense that for a fortnight the Saints expended most of their energies "generally getting ready for to receive the Spaniards," in John Steele's words. Preparing themselves either to fight or flee, they kept horses nearby and brought in families whose houses were considered outside safe limits. Two Mexicans in the settlement were immediately taken prisoner. One got away the same night and the other escaped two or three days later with three Mormon mules. All the cattle were gathered in from grazing grounds miles away and sent to a safe place with twelve men to guard them. Captain Brown sent a man on a fast horse to Bent's Fort offering the services of his well-drilled company against the rebels. Captain Jackson at the fort refused the offer, saying he could not act without orders from Colonel Sterling Price at Santa Fe. Expecting the fall of Santa Fe and a subsequent scarcity of food, Lieutenants Luddington and Willis, guarded by sixty Mormons, went to Bent's Fort with wagons and teams and drew four months' provisions. While they were gone, word reached Mormon Town that the Taos rebels had been routed by Colonel Price. It was March 1 before John Steele reported that "the grait Excitement is a getting over about the Spaniards."[20]

John Albert's news was greeted by the mountain men at Pueblo with "perfect frenzy." In the first excitement, fifteen Mexican employees were seized and imprisoned in one of the rooms, while a council of war was held. In his dotage, John Albert claimed that the mountaineers lined up the prisoners and would have shot them had he not intervened in their favor, but no other source confirms this.[21] As at Mormon Town, people gathered in from the edges of settlements. George Simpson, Maurice LeDuc, Garnier, John Brown, Blackhawk and others moved their families from Greenhorn to Pueblo, along with wagonloads of household goods. From the canyon of the St. Charles, the Delawares, Jim Swanock and Little Beaver, came to the Arkansas and pitched their lodges opposite Mormon Town.[22]

On February 12 came news that five hundred Spaniards were camped on the St. Charles. In great haste the men at Barclay's Houses gathered their families and as much of their possessions as they could cram onto a wagon and moved them into Pueblo. The move took all night. During the next day the report was discredited, and everything was moved back to the Houses. Two days after this scare, Barclay spent a day splitting logs and standing them on end to make a stockade around his Houses. When Cosper brought news from Taos on February 23 that the Pueblo Indians had been defeated, Barclay's ardor for self-defense waned, and it was the middle of April before he finally put a gate on his stockade to make his Houses a defensible compound.[23]

A number of men from the Upper Arkansas—including Metcalf, Charles and Tom Autobees, Antoine Cournoyer, Baptiste Charlefou, Baptiste Sabowrain and Charles Town—fought as privates in the volunteer company which Ceran St. Vrain organized at Santa Fe to put down the rebellion. One Pueblo denizen, the Delaware Indian Big Nigger, fought on the other side, having been visiting his wife at the Taos Pueblo when the Americans attacked it. It was said that the deaths of mountain men killed in the battle were attributable to Big Nigger, for he called to his friends by name, luring them within range of his rifle. After the battle Big Nigger escaped to the Arkansas and was hidden by his Delaware compatriots, apparently at the canyon of the St. Charles. Later he returned to his tribal village above the mouth of the Kansas River, protesting his innocence. He was seen no more on the Arkansas.[24]

Leaders of the insurrection were tried at Taos in April, 1847. Many of the jurors were sometime residents of the Arkansas Valley, including Lucien Maxwell, Charles Town, Jean-Baptiste Charlefou, Robert Fisher, Charles Autobees, John L. Hatcher and Asa Estes. Archibald Charles Metcalf was appointed sheriff of Taos on March 1, 1847 with the duty of hanging those sentenced to death, which he proceeded to do with noticeable relish. Afterwards he went off to Asa Estes' tavern, where the Americans drank eggnog until they all got drunk. Metcalf threw up his job of sheriff shortly afterwards and bought trade goods from Simeon Turley's estate to trade with the Utes.[25]

Two months after the massacre, the men of the Arkansas Valley heard that two of its traders, Mark Head and William Harwood, had been shot as they approached the town of Río Colorado with mules packed with goods they intended to trade at Taos for whiskey and flour. François Laforet, a former trapper who had become the principal man of Río Colorado, was accused of having the murdered traders' goods and of instigating their murder. When the story reached Pueblo, the traders' friends were infuriated at Laforet, swearing to "have his hair" and talking of sending a war party to Río Colorado—but it was just talk.[26]

On the Arkansas the winter of 1846–47 was a bad one in more than its cold weather, and spring was more than usually welcome. With his careful eye, George F. Ruxton watched as spring made tentative approaches in the Arkansas Valley. The river, he wrote, was frozen solid until March 17 when the ice began to move, but another cold spell froze it solid again until March 24. On that day the ice broke up and floated down the river. Thereafter only the edges of the water were frozen in the early morning. Soon geese appeared, honking overhead, easy targets for the expert marksmen and a welcome change from the perpetual venison and elk meat that fed the settlements. Bluebirds followed the geese. When a robin made its first appearance, the mountain men proclaimed winter at an end. In the fresh spring mornings the hunters laid aside their guns and went to the river with rods and hooks. There were other signs of spring: bunch grass turning green at the roots, absinthe and greasewood throwing out their buds long before cottonwoods, currants or chokecherries showed sign of leaf. Thickets were filled now with singing birds, and prairie dogs barked at Ruxton as he rode through their humped-earth villages. Turkeys called in the timber and prairie hens (grouse) sent up their loud harsh cries at sunrise and sunset. When the snow had disappeared everywhere except on the very pinnacle of Pikes Peak, Ruxton was off again for the mountains around South Park where he spent some weeks alone, enchanted by the beauty and peace he found there. At the end of April the mischievous Arapahos set fire to his campsite and sent him scurrying back to Pueblo to escape a holocaust that spread from mountain to plains, sending up glare and smoke visible for two weeks on the Arkansas, fifty miles away.[27]

When Ruxton returned to the Arkansas, he decided to join his two tubercular friends and others who were making preparations to go to the States on May 1, when there would be sufficient grass for their animals. In the meantime he hunted in the Wet Mountains and at Fisher's Hole at the head of the St. Charles, so called because it was Robert Fisher's favorite spot. Then they began making preparations for the trip east. They "made meat," drying strips of it sufficient to last until the buffalo range was reached. They greased lariats and lassoes. They collected animals from feeding grounds and shoed their forefeet. They repaired packsaddles; fashioned apishamores for saddle blankets; put rifles in order and molded rifle balls; made hobbles to picket the horses; cobbled moccasins; patched deerskin hunting shirts and pantaloons.[28]

On May 2 Ruxton left for Bent's Fort where he joined a government train under Captain E. W. Enos, quartermaster stationed at the fort since August, 1846. From Bent's Fort he went to St. Louis, New York and Liverpool. In the summer of 1848 he returned for another fling at the West. This time he never got closer than St. Louis. There he died in August, 1848 of epidemic dysentery, leaving a priceless legacy of two slender volumes of prose containing a description of the Rocky Mountain West that can never be surpassed.[29]

19
The Beginning
of the End
1847–48

THE BAD WINTER OF 1846–47 was not without its profound consequences in the Arkansas Valley. Depletion of pasture caused by overgrazing of domestic animals meant that the settlers had to grow corn to feed those animals. The growing of corn was a source of irritation to the Indians. Hostility of Indians from that cause and others prompted a determination to place a military post on the Arkansas. Even the threat of a military post was enough to end the Arkansas Valley settlements, which were outside the law by nearly every provision of the Trade and Intercourse Act of 1834. So, that bad winter was really the beginning of the end for many of the Arkansas Valley settlements.

Grow corn! That was the message the winter of 1846–47 communicated to the Arkansas Valley settlers. While George F. Ruxton was preparing for his journey east, farmers on the Arkansas were preparing for the biggest season of farming in the history of the valley. George Simpson spent the summer farming at Hardscrabble; the man named Gibson put in a crop at Mormon Town; Pueblo grew wheat, beans, pumpkins and other vegetables, but most importantly corn; Greenhorn had ample crops of corn and pumpkins as well as its specialty, wheat. On the St. Charles River at the trail crossing nine miles south of Pueblo, Charles Autobees, Tom Autobees (Tobin), Blackhawk, Labonte and Levin Mitchell grew corn and pumpkins.[1]

There was no farm at Barclay's Houses, and he had to send his wagons to bring back corn from the other settlements. But corn did not solve his problem of straying stock. On a windy, cold day in the middle of November, 1847, Barclay's horses ran off, and José Dolores spent a week looking for them. To prevent this incessant straying, Barclay decided to send his cattle off to some protected valley where there was ample grass and water, and keep them there for the winter. Four peons were sent to find the animals, which took two weeks, and on December 1 Noverto marched the herd off to a distant pasture. He kept the cattle there until spring, but horses and oxen still strayed from the Houses all winter long.[2]

Bent's Fort had no cornfield nearby, but the Bents meant to have one seventy miles southwest. In the spring of 1847 John Hatcher left the fort with three wagons, fifteen yoke of oxen and twelve or fifteen men to make a farm on the Purgatory eighteen miles east of present Trinidad. They built some log houses, dug a ditch a mile and a half long and planted sixty acres to corn. In July when the crop was almost full grown, the Utes stole all the horses and mules and told Hatcher to get off the land. Hatcher refused. When the Indians came again, they killed nearly all his cattle and destroyed his wagons, saying that they would kill him if he did not leave, for the country was theirs and nobody else should settle it. Hatcher dragged back to Bent's Fort with one steer, one mule and a cart made of bits and pieces saved from his wrecked wagons.[3]

From that time on, William Bent bought his corn from the settlements up the Arkansas. On several occasions, Barclay's diary mentions Bent wagons passing his Houses on their way to Hardscrabble for corn. Bent's Fort was also dependent on the settlements for provisions. After Kearny's invasion of New Mexico, Bent's Fort was the commissary for troops stationed at Santa Fe. About 140 tons of provisions were stored in the fort and sent to Santa Fe throughout the winter and spring of 1847 at the rate of thirty wagonloads a week. The Mormons at Pueblo also drew rations, and by the fall of 1847 Bent's Fort had no more provisions. Colonel Gilpin's command, wintering on the Arkansas six miles below Bent's Fort, was advised to get supplies at "Paublo" or at Santa Fe. So Pueblo and Hardscrabble did a good business that winter in corn and provisions.[4]

The hostility shown John Hatcher at the Bent's Fort cornfield was the first indication on the Arkansas of the new mood of the Indians. Although the farms at Pueblo, Greenhorn, Hardscrabble and the St. Charles had not yet been singled out for destruction, the warning was plain and alarming. Far more chilling was the death of William Tharp, one of the more respectable traders on the Arkansas, who was killed by Indians as he was taking his robes and mules to market. Tharp had come west in about 1841 as a trader at Bent's Fort. By 1844 he had quit the Bents and become an independent trader at Pueblo. There he lived with Antonia Luna and their two children, Mary and James. On July 18, 1846 Tharp obtained his first and last trading license at St. Louis. That winter he traded with the Cheyennes at Big Timber, living with his family in an Indian lodge. It was a fine year for trade; Tharp was thought to have cleared a profit of $5,000 in buffalo robes and mules.[5]

In the spring of 1847 Tharp took down his Indian lodge, piled his robes in his wagons and went to Pueblo. With him and his family were two captives, a Mexican and a negro purchased from the Kiowas during the winter. And an exotic pair they were! The Mexican had been carried off by Comanches from his home in Durango when seven years old, and sold to the Kiowas. He was now a wrinkled and haggard twenty-five years old, speaking just enough Spanish to lament continually for his lost mother. He skulked about Pueblo wrapped in a dirty blanket with his long hair streaming over his shoulders, pressing his face to the cracks in the doors of the rooms and gazing miserably at the comforts within. The negro, formerly a slave among the civilized Cherokees, had been captured by Comanches, but his happy disposition never left him. Day and night he played a weather-beaten fiddle he found at Pueblo, scraping out the favorite tunes of the day—"Lucy Neal," "Old Dan Tucker," "Buffalo Gals"—with or without the justification of a fandango.[6]

With a large herd of mules traded from the Indians and wagons loaded with buffalo robes, William Tharp left Pueblo for the east on May 5, 1847. On the road he caught up with the Bent, St. Vrain & Co. wagons in the charge of George Bent and Ceran St. Vrain, and they all traveled together to Fort Mann, a little government wagon-repair station at the trail crossing of the Arkansas just west of present Dodge City, Kansas. Three days later the train camped at Walnut Creek with its wagons drawn up in a defensive circle. In the morning large numbers of buffalo surrounded the wagons and Tharp and Frank DeLisle went out early to hunt. Before they were three hundred yards from the wagons, mounted Indians appeared from every side, shooting at the men, cattle and wagons. DeLisle kept the Indians at bay until companions came to his rescue, but Tharp was killed, scalped and mangled, and sixty of his mules, worth about half his earnings, were stolen.[7]

Hostility of Indians was a new fact to be faced on the trail, for until the summer of 1846 it was a rare train of traders' wagons that was molested. Then came the soldiers and teamsters, raw recruits who could not distinguish a friendly from a hostile Indian, nor an Eskimo from an Aztec, and who shot at shadows if there was nothing else to shoot. There is no record of how many Indians were killed, but twenty-seven white men on the Santa Fe trail paid with their lives in the summer of 1847 for the careless or cowardly shooting of an Indian by a man in the train ahead.[8]

William Tharp was probably the victim of just such a circumstance, and Alexander Barclay would see another example on his way east with robes in the summer of 1847. Barclay left Pueblo on May 15. Below "Pretty Encampment" he found a village of Cheyennes and Arapahos in deep distress. Just that day a teamster with a government train had shot Cinemo (Tobacco), a wise old Cheyenne chief who had always been friends with the white men. On seeing the train approach, Cinemo had gone out to meet it and to warn of hostile Comanches ahead. The officer in command of the train ordered the teamsters not to allow any Indians to approach. As Cinemo came closer, unarmed, a teamster motioned him to go back. To the Indian the motion meant "come forward"; Cinemo continued to approach and was shot down. He lived for five days, imploring his relatives not to take revenge for his death.[9]

Leaving the mourning Cheyenne village, Barclay hurried on to Fort Mann to catch up with the government train under Captain Fowler, one of whose men had shot Cinemo. The train was camped next to an Arapaho village under Chief Warratoria. The chief was friendly to the whites even though some of his braves had joined the hostile Comanches and Pawnees in attacking every vulnerable train. Past Mann's Fort, Captain Fowler's train was overtaken by Ceran St. Vrain in his dearborn, with some traders from Santa Fe who joined the government train for safety. At Pawnee Fork St. Vrain's party left the government train and went ahead. Hardly had the party split, at Ash Creek, when two men of the government train were attacked and scalped. One, an American named McGuire, was killed outright; the other, a Mexican boy of sixteen, lived without the top of his head for a month afterwards. The train hurried on to Walnut Creek, where it stopped to bury McGuire beside the grave of William Tharp. From there it proceeded to Westport with one more story of Indian hostility on the trail.[10]

By the time Barclay arrived at St. Louis, he was not only considerably shaken by the violent deaths he had witnessed on the trail, but he was ill with that most painful ailment, gout. From St. Louis he wrote a relative that he intended to get out of his business into something more civilized if the winter's trade was good enough to provide him with the necessary capital. What that civilized occupa-

Thomas Fitzpatrick. From a painting by C. Waldo Love. Courtesy of the State Historical Society of Colorado Library, Denver.

tion would be Barclay himself did not yet know. He made the journey west with Ceran St. Vrain in the dearborn, arriving at Bent's Fort on September 20, three days ahead of the wagons. Barclay remained at Bent's Fort until his wagons arrived, perhaps because Thomas Fitzpatrick, Indian Agent, was staying at the fort. Barclay may have had liquor in his wagons and judged that his presence might deter Fitzpatrick from searching them. The two educated Britishers appear to have spent three days together at Bent's Fort in congenial conversation. Out of their talks came a clear direction for Barclay's future.[11]

Thomas Fitzpatrick was a sober, unsmiling Irishman whose harrowing experiences as a trapper had turned his hair white, mangled one of his hands, and left him mirthless but infinitely wise in the ways of Indians and grizzly bears. He had been appointed Upper Platte and Arkansas Agent on August 6, 1846, but his service as guide and dispatch-bearer during the Mexican War prevented him from reaching his agency headquarters at Bent's Fort until a year later.[12]

Two days before Barclay arrived, Fitzpatrick wrote a report dated Bent's Fort, September 18, 1847. In it he announced his intention of leaving in a short time to visit John Richard who had been selling liquor to Indians on the North Platte. He did not believe, he wrote, that traders of capital such as Pierre Chouteau Jr. & Co. or Bent, St. Vrain & Co. used liquor, but that numerous small traders, whose whole stock in trade amounted to only a few trinkets or three or four hundred gallons of liquor, were causing mischief among the Indians—for instance, the traders of Pueblo and Hardscrabble:

About seventy-five miles above this place, and immediately on the Arkansas river, there is a small settlement, the principal part of which is composed of old trappers and hunters; the male part of it are mostly Americans, Missouri French, Canadians, and Mexicans. They have a tolerable supply of cattle, horses, mules, &c.; and I am informed that this year they have raised a good crop of wheat, corn, beans, pumpkins, and other vegetables. They number about 150 souls, and of this number there are about 60 men, nearly all having wives, and some having two. These wives are of various Indian tribes, as follows, viz: Blackfoot, Assineboines, Arikeras, Sioux, Aripohoes, Cheyennes, Pawnees, Snake, Sinpach, (from west of the Great Lake, Chinock, (from the mouth of Columbia,) Mexicans, and Americans. The American women are Mormons; a party of Mormons having wintered there, and on their departure for California, left behind two families. These people are living in two separate establishments near each other; one called "Punble," and the other "Hard-scrabble"; both villages are fortified by a wall 12 feet high, composed of *adobe* (sun-dried brick.) Those villages are becoming the resort of all idlers and loafers. They are also becoming depots for the smugglers of liquor from New Mexico into this country; therefore they must be watched.[13]

And they *would* be watched, Fitzpatrick doubtless assured Barclay, for the necessity of military posts on the Santa Fe trail was becoming ever more obvious. One of these posts, if Fitzpatrick had his way, would be on the Mora River. As he had written Colonel J. J. Abert of the Topographical Engineers the previous May, a fort on the Mora "might induce a settlement in one of the finest grazing countries in all that region."[14]

When Barclay returned to the Houses, he helped Doyle and Guerrier put up their equipment for a trading trip to the Platte. The last wagon left Pueblo on November 1, 1847, and shortly afterwards Barclay fell ill again with gout in one shoulder and a foot. On November 11, he wrote that his gout was intolerably painful, and that he had concluded to quit the Indian trade and its life of exposure. The very next day he sold his store and business at Pueblo to Metcalf. For the rest of the winter he stayed at his Houses, sometimes hunting and attending to his livestock, sometimes confined to the house with severe attacks of gout.[15]

On November 21, 1847 Col. William Gilpin arrived at Bent's Fort with two companies of mounted men, and camped six miles below the fort. Within two weeks Barclay became aware of the presence of these troops, and on December 10, 1847 he wrote Fitzpatrick asking what they were doing there. Fitzpatrick answered that the troops were to control Indians and protect travelers and settlers, and he added that of all the military posts to be built in the Indian country, the one on the Arkansas would be the most conspicuous.[16] To the Arkansas Valley trading posts a military post on the Arkansas meant the end. If there was any doubt in Barclay's mind that the Indian trade was doomed, this letter of Fitzpatrick's would have dispelled it. But if Fitzpatrick's information had shut the door on one speculation, it opened up another—a fine large fort on the Mora River built by Barclay to sell at a stunning profit to the government.

Not all the violence of this violent time occurred on the Santa Fe trail. On Wednesday, February 2, 1848, Ed Tharp and Jim Waters got into an argument at Louis Tharp's houses at Pueblo, and Waters killed Tharp. The next day Barclay helped bury young Ed, just two months short of his twenty-fourth birthday, on the west slope of Tenderfoot Hill in the angle of the junction of the Fountain and Arkansas (a paling around the grave was still standing in 1863). The fight was over Jim's woman, Candelaria, and it was generally considered to be Jim's fault. Ed's brother Louis reported to a Missouri newspaper that the cause of the fight was a "trifling difficulty," and that Ed was "off his guard when shot."[17]

Jim Waters hid out on the Fountain for a few days while someone from Pueblo brought him meat, coffee and bread in the mornings and evenings. Then he went to Greenhorn and hired a wagon and team to fetch his belongings at Pueblo. He remained at Greenhorn, grinding corn and herding cattle for John Brown, during the rest of his stay on the Arkansas.[18]

Thomas Fitzpatrick was at Bent's Fort when he heard of the murder. On February 13 he wrote Colonel Gilpin requesting a detachment of ten men to go to the Platte in pursuit of two men, a liquor trader from Taos and a murderer from Pueblo. Fitzpatrick's request was refused. As a result he did not reach Pueblo until February 27, and he stayed there until April 18. In the meantime Jim Waters rested in safety twenty miles south under the sheltering wing of John Brown. Murderer though he was, no one at either Pueblo or Greenhorn meant to give him up to harsh American justice when banishment was the accepted punishment in these settlements.[19]

Louis Tharp's winter had been a complete disaster. He brought William Tharp's seven wagons west to Santa Fe in the fall of 1847 and began to trade at Pueblo shortly afterward. During the winter he had been robbed of merchandise and three of his men killed by Jicarilla Apaches within fifty miles of Taos. On February 25, 1848, having buried his younger brother Edward, he left Pueblo with eight men and thirteen pack mules and arrived safely at Westport. But the tragedies that struck relentlessly at the Tharp family were not quite over.[20]

On February 12, 1848 Doyle and Metcalf arrived from the Platte. Barclay and Doyle must have talked it over and decided to move to the junction of the Mora and Sapello rivers in northeastern New Mexico, where they would build a fort and sell it to the government. On March 5 Barclay left for Santa Fe. When he returned to the Arkansas on April 14, he had been to the Mora River, decided where the fort was to be built and bought the land.[21]

On the Arkansas, Doyle, Fitzpatrick, Jim Cowie and Guerrier had waited anxiously for Barclay's return from New Mexico. After his arrival they left for the United States by way of the South Platte to avoid the hostile Pawnees on the Santa Fe trail. A few days later, Barclay, Simpson and others gathered together their families, cattle and possessions in a long, clumsy caravan, and left the Arkansas to begin a new life on the Mora River.[22]

20
Barclay's Fort

ON SUNDAY, APRIL 23, 1848, one of the largest wagon trains ever to pass between Pueblo and Raton Pass left the Arkansas in a cacophony of groaning wheels, shouting teamsters, braying mules, barking dogs, squealing pigs and howling children. There were eighteen armed men including Barclay, Simpson, William Adamson, Maurice LeDuc, Tom Suaso and George Lewis, with their families and hired hands. The wagons were heavily loaded with household goods, corn, Indian goods left on hand, cats, chickens and an old six-pound mountain howitzer bought from William Bent and filled with cannister.[1]

The caravan made seven to ten miles a day and arrived at the foot of Raton Pass on May 1. The rocky road up the pass had been much improved since Kearny's army stumbled over it in 1846. But there were signs of Indians. Halfway through the pass they met eight men on foot, teamsters from Patrick Mundy's wagon train, who had a strange story to tell. After crossing Raton Pass Mundy's train of nine wagons was surrounded by a band of Ute Indians on Red (Canadian) River just south of the present city of Raton, New Mexico, and conducted to a Ute camp on Crow Creek. The Indians said they were friends of the white men and were holding the train to protect it from Jicarilla Apaches. In the night Mr. Mundy's teamsters crept away from the camp without arms or provisions and started back up Raton Pass, where they met Barclay's train.

With Mr. Mundy's deserters aboard, Barclay's wagons descended to the plains and camped near Crow Creek, where they encountered the Ute camp and its captive train. With his men armed and the howitzer in position Barclay confronted ten or twelve Ute leaders, who insisted they were protecting the trader Mundy from the Jicarilla Apaches. Before their friendly intentions could be tested, thirty-one men from Taos galloped up, including Apache-killer James Kirker and a military escort. They had been summoned by a half-blood Ute who told them the Utes were plotting with the Jicarillas to rob the trader, share the spoils and blame it on the Jicarillas, thus preserving the Utes' reputation for peace. The Utes released Mr. Mundy and dispersed; Mundy and his wagons joined Barclay's train and they all passed on to Mora without further incident.[2]

The Utes were probably telling the truth, otherwise they would have robbed Mr. Mundy before Barclay's train arrived on the scene. At any rate, they were telling the truth about Apache hostility. In 1839 the Mexican government, tired of Apache depredations, hired the American James Kirker and his gang of Americans, Delawares and Shawnees to kill Apaches. Kirker and his savage crew operated mostly against southern Apaches in Chihuahua, but their very first encounter was in September, 1839 at Ranchos de Taos in northern New Mexico, where they attacked a Jicarilla Apache band and killed forty Indians. Kirker took his last Apache scalp in 1846 and joined American troops in New Mexico, but the Apaches, weary and vindictive, had not forgotten. In March, 1846, the Jicarillas murdered an American named Crombeck near Embudo, slitting his belly and crushing his skull. When the American army was advancing toward Santa Fe in the summer of 1846, some Apaches offered Governor Armijo their services in fighting the invaders. In October, 1847, at the Poñil River in eastern New Mexico, Jicarillas attacked Louis Tharp's traders and made off with some of Beaubien's and Maxwell's cattle from their ranch. And they were not through with the Americans yet.[3]

On June 6, John Brown conducted a half-price sale of pants at his Greenhorn store, settled his accounts and closed his books. Then he started south with his wife Luisa, who was carrying their four-month-old son John Jr. in her arms. With them were Archibald Metcalf and Blackhawk, who were leading sixty horses and mules packed with deerskins traded from the Utes in the Wet Mountain Valley. Lucien Maxwell, his servant Indian George, and Charles Town, just arrived from the crossing of the Arkansas, joined them. Six or seven miles south of Greenhorn on Apache Creek the train was attacked by Jicarilla Apaches who drove off all the pack animals and their valuable burden. Some of the Indians took after Luisa Brown, who wheeled her horse, fastened her arm tightly about her baby's neck and dashed off toward Greenhorn. The men shouted at her to throw away the baby. Instead, with the Indians close behind her, she forced her horse to jump a deep arroyo and arrived at Greenhorn in safety. In this harrowing chase she wrenched young John's neck so that ever afterward he carried his head bent forward. [4]

From Greenhorn Maxwell sent a letter to his father-in-law in Taos, Charles Beaubien, by a courier who took to the mountain peaks to avoid Indians. Immediately on the courier's arrival at Taos, Captain S. A. Boake of the Missouri Mounted Volunteers left Taos with fifty men to find the Jicarilla village. They surprised and attacked it. The soldiers captured thirty horses as the Indians fled, but instead of pursuing, the Captain pleaded illness and the soldiers returned to Taos, having done little but enrage the Indians. [5]

Had Maxwell and his friends known of the soldiers' clumsy attack on the Jicarilla village, they might have decided the trip was too risky, but they were unaware of it. To avoid the Jicarillas they went north to Pueblo where they were joined by Little Beaver, a man named Piles, and Mary and James Tharp, aged six and four respectively, who were probably being returned to their grandparents at Taos after their father's death. From Pueblo the party went east to Bent's Fort, where they were joined by Elliott Lee of St. Louis and Peter Joseph of Taos. They all started up the old road toward Raton but instead of crossing Raton Pass, where they supposed the Apaches were lying in wait for them, they veered east and took a road over Manco Burro Pass.

At noon of June 19 they reached the top of Manco Burro Pass, a narrow valley between steep walls. There they rested and ate their lunch, letting their horses graze a short distance away. Suddenly they were surrounded by a hundred Apaches who fired on them, rolled stones down on them from the top of the canyon walls, ran off their horses and set fire to the grass around them. For four hours they defended their baggage and their lives, firing at every opportunity. Charles Town, Blackhawk, José Cortéz and José Carmel were killed, and the Tharp children captured. The survivors— eleven men, eight of them wounded—crept off into the timber, hiding during the day and traveling at night until they reached the plains, whence they made their separate, painful ways to Taos. Some were escorted on the last lap of their journey by Major Reynolds and forty men from Taos, with Dick Wootton as guide. Three months later the Tharp children were ransomed by American merchants at Taos for the sum of $160. The little girl died shortly afterwards, but her brother lived at Cimarron until his death in about 1902, having surmounted the misfortunes of this star-crossed family.[6]

Alexander Barclay and his friends from Pueblo moved to the junction of the Mora and Sapello rivers, known as "La Junta de los Ríos." On the south side of the Mora River in the middle of May, 1848, they began to build Fort Barclay, a building so huge that the fort at Pueblo could have fit into a corner of it. The structure covered an acre of ground, with walls sixteen feet high, thirty-three inches thick. At opposite corners were two great portholed bastions, each containing a six-pound howitzer and other armament. Inside the walls were forty rooms and offices, a well, bake-ovens and stables. Outside were two hundred acres of cultivated land irrigated by two main ditches, and an acre-and-a-half vegetable garden, entirely fenced.[7]

Barclay was in high spirits, with high hopes. The first summer of frantic activity passed quickly. As winter set in, so did frustration and illness, and losses from rain, snow and wind. Spring came as usual, and as usual Barclay took heart. As the ground softened, he began planting everything under the sun and every variety he could lay hands on, determined to learn what would thrive in this soil and climate. There were disasters—hard frosts killed the early corn, beans and pumpkins; pigs ate the peas; Indians ran off the cattle; the dam broke. But on the whole it was a good summer.

The winter of 1849–50 was less hopeful. Snowstorms of savage intensity lasted for days on end, during which cattle had to be fed in the corral. Illness was so prevalent that in December Teresita and Barclay went to Mora for a fandango only to find that it had been cancelled because everyone was sick. Hunting was fruitless; the fort hunter was able to get no more than two deer or antelope a week, and all winter long meat had to be bought at Mora. Spring came again, and with it a cold, steady, whining wind.[8]

By now it was apparent to Barclay and Doyle that winters on the Mora were colder than those on the Arkansas, that the winds blew harder and more constantly, that the other conditions of farming and stock-raising were no better than in the Arkansas Valley. And it was never far from their minds that the purpose of building Fort Barclay, after all, had been to sell it to the government.[9]

In the fall of 1850, Barclay offered the fort to the Army for $20,000 or $2,000 annual rent, but the Army turned it down. All hope of selling the big post to the United States government died in July,

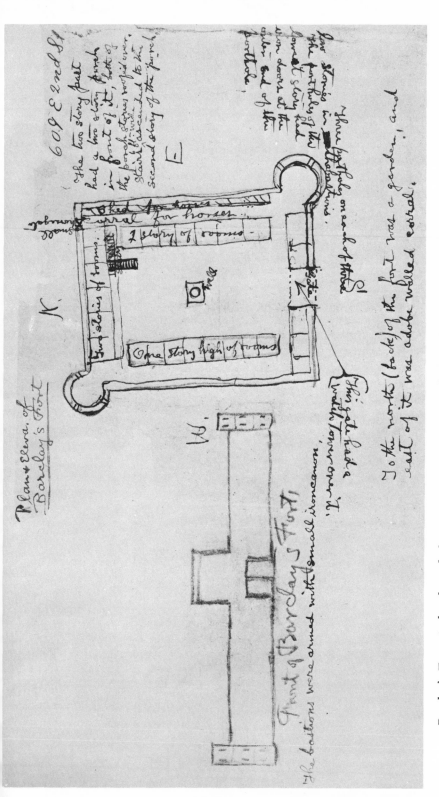

Barclay's Fort. A sketch made by F. W. Cragin in 1904 with the supervision and annotations of two of George Simpson's children and of Jake Beard. Courtesy of Denver Public Library Western Collection.

1851, when Colonel Edwin V. Sumner, new military commander of New Mexico, peremptorily ordered Barclay off the land, saying he meant to build a military post here. Barclay objected that the land was his, but the fierce and loudmouthed officer prevailed and Barclay retreated.[10]

After Sumner began construction of Fort Union on Barclay's land in 1851, the future of Barclay's Fort was dim indeed. In letters to his brother Barclay outlined the hopelessness of his financial situation: his $5,000 debt, the constant depletion of his cattle herd through Indian depredation, the huge cost of feeding his household and help. In the summer of 1851 Barclay and Doyle made other speculations in goods for the Santa Fe market and in freight contracts, but the fort was an acknowledged failure. Early in 1853, Barclay and Doyle offered it for sale and in the meantime they returned to the Indian trade.[11]

On November 2, 1852 Barclay and Doyle were issued a license to trade with Indians. Late in November Barclay went to Fort Laramie on a calamitous trading expedition. The Indians to whom he meant to trade a supply of Navajo blankets had moved away; the horses and mules he had bought to sell to emigrants were not in demand; and a toll bridge he had invested in on the emigrant trail was washed out in a flood. Utterly discouraged, he returned to his big, useless fort in October, 1853 to find his partner Doyle determined to move back to the Arkansas.[12]

Doyle's powerful urge to leave Barclay's Fort was caused in some part by the gradual disintegration of strong ties that bound him to Barclay and Simpson and to his mother-in-law, Teresita. But above all it was the imminent and painful separation of Teresita and Barclay that threw them all into a state of embarrassment and confusion. At the center of the trouble was Teresita, whom both Barclay and Doyle had come to call "the old woman." Now in her early forties, she had turned captious and quarrelsome, jealous and demanding. When Barclay was in St. Louis in the summer of 1852, Teresita moved to Mora, and when Barclay returned that fall they were separated. Later in the fall Barclay moved to Mora to be with her, but their reconciliation did not last.[13]

No less a problem was George Simpson with his excessive drinking and irresponsible capers. In the fall of 1848 he absconded with funds belonging to Barclay and Doyle, then went to St. Louis and refused to go back to his family in New Mexico until his mother and

Site of Barclay's Fort, one half mile west of Watrous, New Mexico. Courtesy of James W. Arrott, Sapello, New Mexico.

Barclay forced him to return. In 1850 he went to California with Robert Fisher and stayed there two years, leaving Juana and the children to fend for themselves.[14]

During his absence his friends and parents supported Juana, and Juana took steps to become self-supporting. When she married George she was probably illiterate, as were almost all the women of New Mexico. By the time Simpson returned from California by the Isthmus in 1852, Juana had not only learned to read and write, but to teach. Said Jesse Nelson, "the way Mrs. Geo. Simpson earned money by teaching is a wonder." In September, 1853 Governor Lane visited the Simpson family at Mora, noting that they had four children and "bright prospects" for another. "His wife," wrote Governor Lane, "has a fine face & was engaged in Teaching a class of little girls."[15]

As Juana became ever more admirable, George did not. One day in a drunken rage he beat Juana and the children. Teresita, who was then living with the Simpsons at Mora, brought suit against George in the alcalde court. In retaliation, George presented to the court a forged account purporting to be an unjust claim of Barclay against Teresita. The hoax was not uncovered until after Teresita and Doyle left for the Arkansas, bearing resentment against Barclay. Three weeks after Doyle had left for the Arkansas, Juana Simpson gave birth to a son who was named Alexander Barclay Simpson. Despite this apology, the damage had been done.[16]

Fort Barclay was a graveyard of shattered relationships, but none were so poignantly parted as Barclay and Teresita. When Barclay returned from his unfortunate Laramie expedition in October, 1853, he found Teresita's jealousy and rancor unbearable, and he proposed that she accompany Doyle and others to the Arkansas. Teresita was furious that Barclay should be willing to send her away, and off she went to spite him, leaving him restless and miserable. He fretted through the lonely days, drew a little sketch of Teresita as he first saw her, and wondered if he had acted wisely in discarding her or if Teresita's complaints against him were better founded than he had thought. Alone in the big fort, commissioned to sell it at ever half what they had invested in it, his depression became disabling.[17]

After Thomas Fitzpatrick's death early in 1854 Barclay made some attempt to obtain the appointment of Upper Arkansas Indian Agent but nothing came of it. When he returned to St. Louis in the summer of 1855 he looked very much worn to Robert Betts, his St

214

Louis agent. Barclay, in turn, thought Betts was unaccountably cool to him, perhaps because Barclay had turned Roman Catholic.[18]

Depressed and ill as he was, he never lost his wry humor. An incident that may have happened during his last journey to St. Louis in 1855 makes a cheerful note on which to take leave of him. A columnist of 1888 tells the story:

Barclay was English with a thorough education and possessed much eccentric humor. Once after making an annual trip across the wide plains to Westport, Missouri—then the nearest shipping point, he stopped (as all western men did on their arrival at that frontier town) in old Harris' hotel. At rather a late hour he went to his room and was surprised to find his bed occupied by a man who started up, saying "How dare you come into my room? My name is Jones and in the morning I shall demand satisfaction for this coarse rudeness." Then a little wizzen-faced woman also popped up beside the man where she had been hidden under the blankets. Barclay, who was the very model of a gentleman, although a mountaineer and somewhat uncouth in his personal appearance, caught sight of this unexpected apparition, doffed his hat at once, and bowing, pointed at the alarmed old lady as he backed out of the room cooly remarked with natural politeness, "Mrs. Jones, I presume."[19]

Barclay died at his fort in December, 1855. A few months later George Barclay sent a representative named Herbert Yatman to New Mexico to investigate his brother's estate. The lawyer, if such he was, nosed around Fort Barclay until he discovered a number of things that were not so: that Doyle had swindled the estate of Barclay's share of the fort; that if Barclay left a will, his greedy associates had destroyed it; that there was a fortune at hand, for Barclay and Doyle had been doing splendidly at the time of Barclay's death. Mr. Yatman also discovered Teresita, although not in person, for he described her as an elderly Spanish woman who appeared to be no more than a housekeeper to Barclay, a dismal little ending to the story of that passionate attachment.[20]

21
The Tide
of Fortune Wanes
1848–53

THE YEAR 1848 SHOULD have dawned brilliantly over the Arkansas Valley settlements. At the sources of the Platte and Arkansas beaver were again abundant, and the pelts commanded a price in St. Louis that made the little animals worth trapping. Buffalo robes too were in great demand in the East; an agent in New York wired London to send back robes that had been gathering dust there since the big slump of 1845 for now they would sell in the United States.[1]

The Indian trade was safer and pleasanter than it had been for years. Whiskey was almost outmoded; most of the Indians were content to trade for corn, flour, sugar and coffee. Thomas Fitzpatrick wrote in February, 1848 that he knew of only one trader from Taos who had gone to the Platte with liquor since August, 1847. Competition was curtailed; the four South Platte forts stood empty, and other little forts on the Arkansas had been abandoned. The Indians were eager for business. Sioux villages spread along the South Platte for eighty miles. Cheyennes and Arapahos camped in Big Timber were making many robes, even though they had to hunt buffalo hundreds of miles farther east than in years past. The Sioux, Cheyennes, Arapahos and Kiowas had never been more peaceful than in the spring of 1848, or more afraid of being drawn into war with the white men. The Utes professed friendship and welcomed white traders. The Santa Fe trail, terrorized the previous summer by Comanches, was relatively safe, for Lieutenant Colonel William Gilpin and five companies of the Santa Fe Battalion were camped on the trail to keep peace. One fight with an American lieutenant and his men near Fort Mann was all the excitement the Comanches offered in the summer of 1848. Only the Jicarilla Apaches in northern New Mexico were hostile.[2]

The year before Pueblo trappers and Indian traders would have been putting their equipment together and packing their mules and wagons to take advantage of the fine prospects. This year they were packing up their household goods and moving away, because better opportunities for speculation lay elsewhere. To the north emigrants continued to flow west over the Oregon Trail; to the east and south wagons supplying Santa Fe made a continuous caravan; to the west the Mormons had started their new city near Great Salt Lake and were eager for trade. Pueblo was left as high and dry as a boulder in a swift stream. In June, 1848, a traveler found at the mouth of the Fountain "absolutely nobody living—only the empty Fort Pueblo and the deserted log houses of the Mormons."[3] The fort would stand and be occupied off and on for another six years, as long as it had already stood and been occupied—but its trade would consist of grasping little bargains with gullible emigrants, and with John C. Frémont on his catastrophic fourth expedition.

The traveler who had found absolutely nobody at Pueblo was Jesse Hodges Nelson. He, Kit Carson and ten others left Taos on June 25, 1848 on their way to the States. They went by way of the South Platte to avoid the Apaches. As far as Greenhorn they had an escort of trigger-happy soldiers, "more dangerous than Indians," said Nelson. At Greenhorn they found only Bill New, Calvin Jones and some Mexican hired hands, and there they left Ben Ryder, who was suffering from rheumatism. They proceeded to the trail crossing of the St. Charles where there were a few farmers—John Brown and his family, Charles White, probably Jim Waters, Rube Herring and others, occupying old houses in various stages of repair and using old fields and irrigating ditches.[4]

Jesse Nelson and Kit Carson did not pass Hardscrabble in the summer of 1848, but they would not have found it empty. Calvin Briggs and John Burroughs were busy growing the Hardscrabble settlement's last crop of corn, and Lancaster Lupton was running its last store. From Lupton's account book we can tell who some of the people were at Hardscrabble in its final days. Marcelino Baca paid for staples and goods bought by himself and his Pawnee wife with "sundry Services hunting &c." and with hogs and beaver skins. Lupton also did business with "Mrs. New," George Simpson, V. J. Herring, Noverto, Briggs, Burroughs, Kinkead, Conn and a number of hired hands. The account book ends with a scrawled quotation from Shakespeare, "there is in the affairs of men a tide which taken at the flood leads on to fortune"—a text of bitter irony not only for Lancaster Lupton but for all the men who threw in their lot with the Arkansas Valley in these declining years when the tide of fortune was ever on the wane.[5]

By November, 1848 Pueblo was populated again. Accounts of Frémont's fourth expedition mention "many old mountain–men," two little boys, and the usual crowd of hired hands, horses, mules, dogs and chickens reminiscent of the good old days. But the good old days were over, for Frémont as well as for the Pueblo. At this time Frémont was grimly trying to recoup his reputation lost in his arrest in California in 1846, his subsequent court-martial and resignation from the Army. There were no shooting matches at Pueblo, no jolly jokes about the Frenchman shrieking "Indians!" when his powder horn blew up, no description of Pueblo as "in thriving condition." Nor could Frémont boast that he could ride to California in thirty-five days. Few men at Pueblo thought he would reach California at all. It was the worst winter in memory. Already snow was two or three feet deep on the sides of the mountains, and much deeper in the passes where Frémont intended to go.

Frémont's fourth expedition was privately financed through the efforts of his father-in-law, Senator Thomas H. Benton, to prove the feasibility of a central railroad route through the Rocky Mountains in winter. With thirty-odd men and a hundred mules and horses Frémont arrived at Mormon Town, "a lot of rude log houses," at noon on November 21, 1848. The party camped among the large cottonwoods to the east, where a little snow lay in patches. During the afternoon there was visiting back and forth between Frémont's camp and the Pueblo. Benjamin Kern wrote in his diary that he was much pleased to see some cattle attended by two small boys and to have boiled milk and rice for supper. His brother Richard was less enchanted: "there is a fort built of Adobes," he wrote, "a miserable looking place, the inside resembling a menagerie—a compound of Spaniards, Horses mules dogs chickens and bad stench."[6]

During the afternoon Bill Williams, who happened to be visiting at Pueblo, came to Frémont's camp and was hired as guide. There has been controversy ever since as to whether the disaster to come was Frémont's or Williams' fault. During the night that followed mountain men of Pueblo, including John Brown and John L. Hatcher, had a hot argument over the advisability of trying to cross the mountains in this awful winter. The mountain men agreed in hindsight that Frémont would come to grief, but at the time there was more diversity of opinion than they remembered. Lancaster Lupton, for instance, wrote Senator Benton from Pueblo on November 28 that "the snow is unusually deep in the mountains, and many old mountainmen here have expressed a doubt whether he can get over with so large a cavalcade—about one hundred horses and mules and thirty-odd men," but, added Lupton tactfully, "I think he will do it. . . ."[7]

Frémont had no doubt he would do it. At Pueblo he bought some provisions and fresh horses and went upriver to Hardscrabble, "White Oak Creek." Richard Kern described it as "a miserable place containing about a dozen houses Corn Cribs and Corrals. It is the summer resort of the hunters—the houses are built of Adobes, and are very comfortable—they seemed like palaces to us, as we enjoyed the luxuries of a table & stools."[8]

At Hardscrabble Frémont was furnished 130 bushels of shelled corn by Burroughs and Briggs, who had raised a crop the previous summer and were still living there with their Shoshone wives and families. Frémont's men sacked the corn on Friday, November 24, and that night they feasted on chicken and baked pumpkin provided by the ladies of Hardscrabble. The next day they packed their riding horses with corn and the mules with baggage, and set off up the Hardscrabble on foot. They went across the Wet Mountain Valley towards the peaks of the Sangre de Cristo range and across the San Luis Valley towards the San Juan Mountains, blue-white and menacing. In the La Garita hills the expedition foundered in deep snow and disintegrated, ten men dying, the survivors staggering into Taos in blighted little groups.[9]

After Frémont left, the rest of the winter of 1848–49 on the Arkansas was unrecorded, but we may be sure that ferment of the gold excitement in California was bubbling up on the Arkansas as it was everywhere else. News of California gold discoveries began to be reported in St. Louis newspapers in October, 1848. In February, 1849 emigrant companies for California were being organized in St. Louis, Independence and Westport. Some of these emigrant companies passed Pueblo in the early summer, but by that time Pueblo men had already left for California and would precede most of the emigrants to the gold regions by several months.

In the spring of 1849 it was "California Ho!" for the people of the Arkansas Valley. About the first of June a wagon train left the Arkansas with John and Luisa Brown and their three children, John Burroughs and Calvin Briggs with their Shoshone wives and numerous offspring, Lancaster Lupton with his Cheyenne wife and four children, Valentine J. Herring apparently without his Nicolasa, Charles White, Alexis Godey, Jim Waters and Candelaria. They

"View of Sangre de Cristo Pass." Sketched by Richard Kern in 1853 for E. G. Beckwith's Pacific Railway Survey *Report*. Courtesy of Denver Public Library Western Collection.

were said to have joined an emigrant train as far as Salt Lake City, where they spent the Fourth of July. They arrived at Sutter's Fort on September 1, 1849.[10]

Most of the California contingent of Arkansas Valley settlers became successful citizens, abandoning the crudities and wild independence of life on the Arkansas and adapting smoothly to the genteel standards of middle-class California towns. Brown, Waters, Godey and Herring finally settled in San Bernardino, where Brown and Waters, friends to the end of their long lives, became wealthy and respected. Rube Herring, whose twenty years as a trapper afforded him little intellectual stimulus beyond his brush with the

Book of Mormon, became, of all things, Superintendent of Schools. A more modest success was enjoyed by Calvin Briggs and John Burroughs, who settled at Sacramento. Briggs later became a rancher in Tulare County and died in 1868; his son Thomas, born on the South Platte of a trapper father and Shoshone mother, became a successful rancher, meatpacker and good citizen of Bakersfield. Burroughs returned with his large family to his native state of Kentucky, to provide his children with a better education. Lancaster Lupton moved with his Cheyenne wife and eight children to Arcata, California, where he died in 1885.[11]

Mathew Kinkead also left the Arkansas, perhaps earlier than the others. In the summer of 1848 he was seen on the Big Sandy west of South Pass by an emigrant who wrote:

a Mr. Kincaid is now in camp trading with our men, he having some 200 head of cattle which we need in some measure. This gentlemen (Kincaid) removed to these mountains from Boone County, Missouri in the year 1824. He is quite an old man, yet active, although he has been injured in time passed by being lame.[12]

This "old man" was only fifty–three when the emigrant saw him, and he had a lot of life in him yet. Kinkead's granddaughter tells us that he and his son Andrés lived in Sacramento, where he became very wealthy and owned ships and haciendas. By 1891 he had died and Andrés, known now as Andrew J. Kinkead, rancher of Tulare County, California, returned to New Mexico to sell his father's interest in the Mora Grant, in some lots at Taos and in some property in Salt Lake City. At that time Andrés visited his mother, Teresita Suaso, ninety-one years old, at the late Joseph B. Doyle's ranch at Undercliffe, Colorado, three years before she died. Andrés died at Santa Fe July 7, 1908, leaving a son and five daughters at Pottersfield, California.[13]

The great emigration to California in 1849 was sucking men and their capital westward from the Arkansas Valley. One by one in the years to come the settlements on the Arkansas were abandoned, among them Bent's Fort. The fortunes of that great emporium had been declining since the Mexican War, when its trade was disrupted, its rooms commandeered for sick soldiers, its offices occupied by resident quartermasters, its storerooms filled with army provisions and its corrals with army mules. Ceran St. Vrain offered

Former Arkansas Valley settler James W. Waters in 1874 as Supervisor of San Bernardino County, California. From *L. A. Ingersoll's century annals of San Bernardino County* (Los Angeles, 1904). Courtesy of Bancroft Library, Berkeley.

the post to the government in 1847, but the government refused to buy it. In 1848 the firm of Bent, St. Vrain & Co. came to an end, deeply in debt to P. Chouteau Jr. & Co., its St. Louis agent. In 1849 William Bent closed the gates of his fort and set fire to the magazine, which blew up with a loud report although no serious damage was done to the rest of the building. Then Bent went to Big Timber and traded with the Cheyennes and Arapahos. The old post served for decades as stage station, corral, and playground for pothunters. In 1976 the National Park Service rebuilt it as a Bicentennial project, a reconstruction so true in spirit that ghosts must walk there at night when the crowds are gone.[14]

In the summer of 1849 there were still a few men at Pueblo and

Greenhorn—Seth Ward, William Guerrier, Charles Kinney, Dick Owens, the Delawares Jim Dickey and Jim Swanock, Archibald Metcalf, Joe Dennis, the half-Cheyenne Tesson, Marcelino Baca and his friend Montoya, and probably John Poisal. None of these men left letters, business records or diaries that have come to light. From 1849 until the Arkansas Valley was populated again in 1853 its history was written by passersby.[15]

Most of the people who passed by Pueblo and Greenhorn in the summer of 1849 were gold seekers on their way to California. There were three large parties of them. Two parties came up the Arkansas to avoid the crowds on the Overland Trail, where hundreds of wagons were digging new ruts in the Platte Valley, thousands of animals were eating up every blade of grass, and an epidemic of cholera was filling trailside graves from Independence to Laramie. The third party was bent upon examining the "Taos mines" at the headwaters of the Arkansas, which were understood to be close to Taos.

The first emigrants at Pueblo in 1849 were a party under Captain Lewis Evans from Arkansas consisting of 126 men, forty wagons, fifteen Cherokee Indians, five Negro slaves and two young unmarried women who were "seeking their fortunes in the West." The Evans party had meant to follow the old Oregon Trail up the Platte, but in east-central Kansas they began finding the tragic flotsam of the great emigration—graves, carcasses of cattle, scattered pieces of iron from hundreds of wagons abandoned and burned in campfires—grim evidence of cholera and scarcity of grass. They decided to avoid the main road and ascend the Arkansas. On May 29 at abandoned Fort Mann they met the eastbound wagons of Seth E. Ward and William Guerrier, packed to the bows with 6,000 buffalo robes. Ward and Guerrier probably assured the emigrants they could obtain provisions and guides at Pueblo.[16]

Captain Evans' party arrived at Pueblo a week or two after John Brown and his friends had left for California. Pueblo was not without residents ("trappers" the emigrants called them, and this time the term may have been entirely accurate) who warned them that they could not cross the mountains with wagons. Surprised and dismayed, the party broke up. Four wagons returned to Arkansas. Thirty men hired a part-Osage guide to take them to Salt Lake City. Thirty more men on the mountaineers' advice went to Greenhorn and traded their wagons and teams at a pittance for mules and packsaddles at a premium. They hired Dick Owens to take them to the California diggings in sixty days for a wage of $7 per day. Off they went, arriving at Salt Lake City a month later. [17]

On June 23, after most of Captain Evans' party had left Pueblo, two more emigrant parties showed up. One, guided by James Kirker, came in wagons to the mouth of the Fountain with the intention of examining the "Taos mines" before committing themselves to go all the way to California. The other company, from Ithaca, New York, had pack mules and came to Pueblo to await the arrival of the now-famous Kit Carson, whom they meant to hire as guide. The "wagon men" and the "mule men" reached the mouth of the Fountain at about the same time and camped together for about ten days on the north side of the Arkansas. Their first business was the funeral of a man who had shot himself by mistake, a Mexican War veteran whom they buried with honors, firing a military salute and planting a small American flag over his grave. Then blacksmiths set up a forge and charcoal kiln and began to repair shrunken wheels and loose iron tires. Other men cut timber and made rafts on which to carry wagons across the river. During their second night the cattle took fright and dashed through camp, smashing wagons, upsetting tents and breaking cooking utensils, before disappearing into the darkness. The next day most of the animals were found thirty miles away by a party of horsemen led by James Kirker, who, despite his age, followed the trail of the lost cattle at a gallop. Several parties hunted grouse and deer, and one group of young men made the classic mistake of setting out to conquer a mountain in a day only to spend an uncomfortable night on the mountainside. Not one of the emigrants' accounts mentions the old Pueblo or the "trappers" encountered there by Captain Evans' party. The only buildings noted were those of Mormon Town, described as three deserted log cabins. [18]

The "wagon men" prospected in nearby gulches but found only about three dollars' worth of gold. Discouraged, eight of them started home. The rest went to Greenhorn, "a Trading Post occupied by several white Hunters and a number of Indians of various Tribes, many of whom had Huts outside the post. The Fort was packed with valuable furs, which the Hunters carried on Pack Mules and sold to the Santa Fe Traders." [19] A delegation of about fifty men left Greenhorn to explore for gold on the western slope of the Sangre de Cristo Pass, but not enough "color" was found to justify further exploration, so they set off for New Mexico with their guide, James Kirker. Six others with tragic destiny stayed at Greenhorn to sell their wagons. They spent two days unloading wagons and making up packs, and the ladies at Greenhorn fell heir to their food and "comforts." A Delaware guide whom they hired for fifty dollars and a good horse led them to Salt Lake City without loss but deserted them later in the desert. They drifted far to the south and most of them had not been heard from two years later.[20]

In the meantime, mountain man Charles Kinney had been fetched instead of Kit Carson as guide for the "mule men". Kinney had been living at Greenhorn "among the Indians, with a very ladylike little white woman for a wife, fair-complexioned and modest in her appearance."[21] Kinney charged the mule men $700 and the choice of three mules and two wagons, and he got them safely to Salt Lake. There they hired half-Cherokee Charley McIntosh to take them to California.[22]

If there were still white men at Pueblo in the summer of 1850, the accounts of three different parties of emigrants do not mention them. On June 13, 1850 a party of a hundred-odd Cherokees on their way to California with thirty-four wagons arrived at "Peueblo" where they exchanged packs and mules for wagons and oxen with a company already camped there. Then another ox train of thirty-three wagons arrived, and the three parties joined for a big dance. The Cherokees left on June 15 for Salt Lake City, and the packers who had arrived just ahead of them went on to Greenhorn, intending to pack through the mountains to California.[23]

Pueblo was probably occupied off and on after 1850, but there is scant record of it. Travelers of 1853 describe the old fort as a well-preserved derelict: "Pueblo a collection of deserted adobe huts at the mouth of the Boiling Spring river," writes one traveler,[24] and another says, "the building was there yet in a very good state of preservation."[25]

Greenhorn was occupied continuously until the fall of 1853. Its prosperity in the summer of 1849 attracted the attention of the Indians, presumably Arapahos, who announced at Bent's Fort that "they intended to go over to the settlement of thirty whites, southwest of the Arkansas, in the direction of Taos, and take all their corn, of which they have an abundance. If they raised any objection, they would then take their cattle; and if they still objected, they would make way with the men."[26]

There is no record of Indians carrying out their threat against Greenhorn in 1849, but in the summer of 1850 Apaches were posted south of Greenhorn lying in wait for travelers, one of whom was Kit Carson. Carson, George Simpson and Tim Goodale had spent the month of June at Fort Laramie with forty or fifty mules and horses to trade with emigrants (they were not the only ones—the sutler at Fort Laramie wrote that "all the Arkansas men were here, scattered from Ash Hollow to North Fork ford").[27] On the first of July, Goodale and Simpson set out for California and Carson for his home at Rayado, New Mexico. When Carson arrived on the Greenhorn with one Mexican boy, he learned that Apaches were ahead of him on the road with murderous intent. He could persuade only one man, Charles Kinney, to accompany him to New Mexico. Carson and Kinney got through safely to Rayado, only to find that Apaches had run off every animal there.[28]

By the summer of 1851 the Indians were thoroughly provoked against Greenhorn, where they killed a man, and against a settlement on the St. Charles where they carried off provisions, animals, money and one captive. The next summer a party of Navajos, Jicarilla Apaches and Utes on their way to attack Kiowas and Arapahos stole horses and killed cattle at Greenhorn.[29] If the settlement on the St. Charles was still occupied after the summer of 1852, by 1853 it had been abandoned, leaving in the Arkansas Valley only a handful of traders and farmers who were still blind and deaf to the warnings of the Indians. By summer the Indians and their threats were forgotten in a surge of resettlement, encouraged by the prospect of riches following in the wake of a steam engine.

22
The Railroad
is Coming!
1853–54

By the beginning of 1853 a stillness had settled over the upper Arkansas Valley, broken only by the lonely songs of winter birds, the purling of rivers under the ice and the sounds of infrequent travel. Most of the Arkansas Valley settlements were tranquilly decaying, their gates ajar and whining in the wind, their rooms the nesting places of wild creatures, their courtyards filled with tumbleweeds and their roofs a jumble of fallen timbers. Pueblo was still standing and sturdy but nothing was left of the log houses at Mormon Town. A couple of shanties remained on the St. Charles. Travelers who took shelter in them heard early in the morning the ghostly crowing of domestic cocks, now as wild as the prairie fowl that started up from the stubble of old cornfields. Only two settlements were occupied—William Bent's log trading houses in Big Timber at the Cheyenne and Arapaho winter camps, and Greenhorn where Marcelino Baca and his friend Montoya lived with their Indian wives and families.[1]

Then, in the summer of 1853, the settlers returned. Again there were cattle grazing on the uplands, plows turning over the bottom lands, traders hauling wagonloads of corn to Indian villages and noisy drunken fandangos lasting far into the night. Again there was hope that man could finally settle this difficult, beautiful valley.

For the railroad was coming! In March, 1853 Congress approved a bill for the survey of a proposed central route to the Pacific up the Arkansas and Huerfano rivers and over the Sangre de Cristo Pass. That summer a party under Captain J. W. Gunnison made the survey—but by this time scores of settlers from New Mexico had already moved to the Arkansas.[2]

Congressional debates over the route of the railroad were known to leading businessmen of New Mexico. One of these citizens was Ceran St. Vrain, surviving partner in the Vigil and St. Vrain Grant, which encompassed the valleys of the Purgatory, Huerfano,

Charles Autobees, 1864. Photograph by S. S. Smith, Pueblo's first photographer. Courtesy of Pioneers' Museum, Colorado Springs.

Apishapa and Cucharas rivers south of the Arkansas through which the railroad would pass. The condition upon which the Vigil and St. Vrain Grant had been made by Governor Armijo in 1843 was that the grantees establish a colony there the following spring. No colony was established that spring or any other. The various settlements that had been started (the St. Charles farm; the Bents' stock farm south of their fort; John Hatcher's Purgatory farm) had all failed. Aware that his grant would soon come under the scrutiny of a United States agent examining the validity of Mexican land grants, St. Vrain hastened to get it settled in the spring of 1853.[3]

St. Vrain persuaded Charles Autobees, a tough Missourian of proven honesty, courage and intelligence, to collect some settlers and establish a permanent colony on the grant. Autobees had been living in Río Colorado, a village north of Taos, ever since his job at

Turley's Mill had gone up in smoke in January, 1847. Around the first of February, 1853 Autobees left Río Colorado with a train of sixty pack mules and twenty-five men. Some were traders—William Kroenig, William LeBlanc, Marcelino Baca (returning to Greenhorn), J. B. Beaubien, nephew of the Taos storekeeper—on their way to the Arapahos at Big Timber with provisions, for the winter had been a cold one and the Indians were hungry. The snow was so deep on the west side of the Sangre de Cristo Pass that the party traveled only ten miles in eight days. At the top they spent another day stamping a path through a mammoth drift that lay across the trail. But on the eastern side of the pass, at the headwaters of the Huerfano, the climate changed to spring and the snow disappeared.[4]

Autobees and his settlers arrived on the Huerfano on February 20, 1853 and began a settlement which satisfied the conditions of the grant by existing "continually without interruption" for the next twenty years. This first and lasting settlement on the Huerfano was not at its mouth but two miles upstream, in a mile-wide bottom on the west side of the river, where the banks were thickly wooded with willows and cottonwoods and the river bottom was covered with soft grass and wild flowers. Here Autobees built his ranch headquarters and made his home until he died thirty years later.[5]

In the meantime the traders from Río Colorado had proceeded to Big Timber and traded off their provisions to the Cheyennes and Arapahos. On their return they stopped at Greenhorn. Baca and Montoya urged them to spend the summer and put in a crop of corn. Kroenig and LeBlanc accepted the invitation, for the land was level, ditches dug, houses and corrals in good repair. Later that spring LeBlanc left for Río Colorado and Kroenig continued to farm by himself. By May 20 Kroenig and his six peons had planted corn, beans, wheat and vegetables, Montoya supplying them with venison and antelope at a dollar per carcass.[6]

William Kroenig was twenty-six when he first came to the Arkansas Valley in 1853. He was a kindly, honest German from Westphalia, educated by Jesuits and trained as a merchant. After his arrival in New Mexico he ran a store at Río Colorado for the Taos firm of Maxwell and Quinn. Business was slow until one day in 1849 a band of Utes marched into town and cleaned his shelves of every bit of merchandise, paying good money for it. The young storekeeper decided to become an Indian trader.[7]

Kroenig's summer of farming at Greenhorn was to provide corn and beans for the Indian trade. After the harvest, Kroenig took his share of the crop to Fort Laramie. The Indians around the fort were selling not only buckskins and buffalo robes, but also sheep and cattle obtained from the emigrants, and for cheap prices. Kroenig could buy a full-grown cow for a dollar and sometimes have her calf thrown in. In this manner Kroenig collected ninety-four head of cattle and two hundred sheep which he drove to La Junta de los Ríos near Fort Barclay.[8]

While Kroenig was driving his cattle and sheep to New Mexico in the first week of August, Captain Gunnison and his party of United States topographical engineers were ascending the Huerfano River as part of a survey for the railroad route to the Pacific. As the command toiled up the rocky canyons, it became apparent that they were not on the Huerfano but on the Apishapa. Lieutenant Beckwith and a detachment of five men were sent to find the Greenhorn settlement and procure a guide there to take them over the mountains.[9]

At Greenhorn Lieutenant Beckwith found six New Mexican families living in a compound of low adobe houses. In front of each house was a yard sixty feet wide enclosed by poles planted in the earth and lashed to horizontal strips of wood by rawhide thongs. Behind each house was a corral made the same way. Both enclosures were intended as a protection against the Utes, who the year before had killed cattle, destroyed grain and stolen horses. The little farm grew two hundred *fanegas* of wheat, fifty of corn, some beans and watermelons, and it supported a few cattle and some poor, thin horses.[10]

As the Lieutenant and his men approached, the people of the settlement assembled on the roofs of the houses. When the strangers were established as friends, they were invited inside and offered a seat on the only article of furniture in the room, a bench against the wall. The Lieutenant was soon introduced to Marcelino Baca, whom he hired as guide to lead the command to Fort Massachusetts, a new military post on the eastern edge of the San Luis Valley at the foot of the Sangre de Cristo Pass. Beckwith wrote in his report that Baca had lived with his Pawnee wife at Greenhorn, but his losses to the Utes were considerable, and he had moved to Pueblo. In the spring of 1853 he was sole occupant of Pueblo and he planted a little corn there. Before summer his crop was flooded out and he returned to Greenhorn.[11]

Marcelino's wife, a courteous lady of "matronly grace and dig-

William Kroenig photographed in the late 1890's by Furlong. Courtesy of Denver Public Library Western Collection.

nity," spread Beckwith's pallet and blankets outdoors in the front yard where the family slept on summer nights. In the morning the Lieutenant and Marcelino returned to Captain Gunnison's camp, and the party started over the Sangre de Cristo Pass. At Fort Massachusetts Marcelino left to return to Greenhorn.[12]

After the last of the wheat and corn crop was harvested in the fall of 1853, Baca moved to the east side of the mouth of the Fountain a mile below Pueblo on the north side of the Arkansas, where he built a log house for his family, thirteen jacal and log houses for his help, and a big corral for his stock. In the angle made by the junction of the rivers he dug a long irrigating ditch and plowed a large cornfield to grow fodder for his enormous herd of animals—500 head of cattle and fifty horses.[13] Marcelino Baca was a wealthy man now, but he would discover that the Indians who had made him rich as a trader would not allow him to stay rich as a farmer.

In New Mexico Ceran St. Vrain continued recruiting settlers for his grant to bolster the original settlement made by Charles Autobees. St. Vrain's prize recruit was Dick Wootton, whose many business failures had finally ended in a successful speculation. Wootton had left the Arkansas in the summer of 1847 to become sutler for troops stationed at Taos. There he began wooing Dolores, the beautiful daughter of ex-trapper Manuel LeFevre and his Mexican wife. Family legend says that LeFevre kept his prospective son-in-law doing chores around the house for a year before he would allow him to marry Dolores. They were married on March 6, 1848 on the same day that Dick was appointed sheriff of Taos. He resigned as sheriff a year later and continued to live in Taos as merchant and sutler in partnership with Charles Williams, a soldier with Kearny's army who had married Dolores Wootton's sister. Wootton and Williams had a large store on the south side of the Taos plaza, but a big part of their business was furnishing beef for soldiers in New Mexico. They kept their large herd of cattle pastured 200 miles to the north at the mouth of the Huerfano. In 1849 the Utes stole a hundred head of fine beef cattle south of Raton Pass as the animals were being driven from the Arkansas River to Taos, leaving Wootton poorer by $5,000.[14]

In 1851, Colonel E. V. Sumner cancelled civilian contracts with the Army and removed the soldiers from Taos and Santa Fe to military posts far from the corrupting influence of the towns. Colonel Sumner's act was devastating to New Mexico's economy; like all the other New Mexico merchants, Wootton and Williams suffered. To recoup they made a brilliant and much-imitated speculation. In June, 1852 they borrowed capital and bought fourteen thousand sheep which they fattened near Fort Barclay. In the fall Wootton and thirty-one men drove the flock to California and sold it for very high prices. Wootton arrived back at Taos in January, 1853 with a profit of $40,000.[15]

With this fortune Wootton and his friend Levin Mitchell moved to the Arkansas in 1853. Mitchell, the big, red-haired ex-trapper, had moved with Wootton in 1847 from Pueblo to Taos, where he was appointed deputy sheriff but did not serve long if at all. By April, 1849 he had started a ranch at La Cueva on the Mora River near Fort Barclay and another on the Cimarron, where he remained until he returned to the Arkansas.[16]

In August or September, 1853 Wootton and Mitchell joined Charles Autobees and William Kroenig in building the Huerfano village on the south side of the Arkansas a mile west of the mouth of the Huerfano. Financed by the proceeds of Wootton's sheep speculation, Kroenig's trade profits and whatever Ceran St. Vrain would have furnished in men, equipment or cash, the village was intended to be a permanent settlement—a stop on the transcontinental railroad.[17]

While the Huerfano village was struggling into existence, another group of refugees arrived on the Arkansas, impelled not by promises of free land on the Vigil and St. Vrain Grant, but by the economic depression in New Mexico and the family troubles at Fort Barclay. Joseph Doyle had suffered considerable loss in the failure to sell Fort Barclay to the government, but, unlike Barclay, he had not broken under the weight of it. In 1852 Doyle hired Calvin Jones and others to trade during the winter with Indians for two successive years, and in the summer to drive an ox train east with the robes. His ventures must have met with some success, for by the fall of 1853 he could afford a good-sized outfit to take to the Arkansas.[18]

Doyle left Fort Barclay on October 15, 1853 with his wife Cruz and their children James and Fannie; with George Simpson but not his family (Juana gave birth three weeks later at Mora); with Teresita and her son Tom Suaso; with Maurice LeDuc, his wife Elena Mendoza and their sons Amado and Augustin; with Bob Rice, a boy of about fourteen whom Doyle had found living with White Antelope's Cheyennes two years earlier and had taken into his household; with Ben Ryder and his wife Josie, former carpenter and housekeeper respectively at Bent's Fort, and their children; with Charley McIntosh, half-Cherokee mountain man and his wife Anicata and daughter Mary; with Charles Pray and wife Lina Goméz; with Teresita's brother Benito Sandoval, his wife María Espinosa and their four sons; and with Juan Ignacio Valencia and Tanislado de Luna and his family from El Paso.[19]

All these people moved into the Pueblo. Benito Sandoval and his hands spent the autumn putting new roofs on the rooms and whitewashing the inside walls. A few months later Joe Doyle and others decided to move to the mouth of the St. Charles. For the rest of the winter Benito fetched timber and made planks for Doyle's new house on the south side of the Arkansas six miles east of Pueblo. In the spring of 1854 the Doyles moved into their new log *placita* consisting of a large number of rooms enclosing an open square like a Mexican country house. By the fall of 1854 Doyle had become dissatisfied with his new house. The mouth of the St. Charles was exposed to too many floods, and he decided to move once more, this time to the village at the mouth of the Huerfano. Into Doyle's abandoned St. Charles *placita* moved another group of settlers—Levin Mitchell and his wife Luz Argüello; Samuel Harrison, whose assets were $40,000 according to the 1850 census, but whose character was "bad"; Charley Carson, cousin or nephew of the famous Kit; John Jurnegan; George McDougal, dissipated brother of a later Senator from California; Tom Suaso; Francis Yara; Allen P. Tibbetts, a huge American hunter; his partner, Jonathan W. Atwood; and two obscure men named Steel and Totes and their Indian wives.[20]

The Huerfano village, twenty miles below Pueblo, became one of the largest settlements the Arkansas Valley had yet seen. Its houses, widely varied in construction and design, were organized quite differently from those in former settlements, partly because in their advanced knowledge of Indians, defense against siege was no longer judged necessary, partly because of the terrain. The Arkansas bottom west of the mouth of the Huerfano was of rich black soil thickly covered with grass, and the banks of the river were densely lined with cottonwoods. The bottom varied from half a mile to a mile in width and was defined on the south by steep, thirty-foot bluffs of a gravelly loam. In this wooded, protected place the houses were not concentrated around a central plaza but strung randomly along the river bottom. There were five *placitas* belonging to Doyle, Wootton, Autobees, Kroenig and Juan ("Guero") Pais. South of the *placitas*, backed up against the bluffs, were jacal cabins where the hired hands lived. Down by the river were "dug-outs" excavated from the soft banks where other French and Mexican laborers lived, among them Jean-Baptiste Charlefou and John Smith with his Cheyenne wife. At one end of the village were a few Indian sweathouses made of wooden frames covered with tanned buffalo hides (apishamores) inside which steam was captured by pouring water over red-hot stones. Halfway between the *placitas* of Doyle and Wootton was the hewed log cabin of Tom Whittlesey or Whittle and his wife María; he was "a bad man, a murderer," nicknamed "Tomas el matador."[21]

Each of the *placitas* was a small and rather elaborate fort. Doyle's was the largest, measuring about 75 by 60 feet and constructed of jacal to resemble an adobe wall. It had rooms for Doyle's and Simpson's families as well as a dining room, kitchen, blacksmith shop, storage rooms and a trade room (patronized not by Indians but by Doyle's employees, for Doyle did his trading at the Indian villages). Wootton's *placita* was of horizontal logs surrounded by a log stockade with sharp–pointed pickets and bulletproof bastions at opposite corners; Wootton described it as "a substantial fortress." Besides living quarters for the Wootton and Ryder families and their employees, the *placita* had a trade room and an open shed with puncheon (split logs flat-side-up) floor for storing wagons and heavy implements, and for husking and storing corn. The roof of the shed was covered with a few inches of soil and used by the women for farming. Wootton's *placita* had a blacksmith shop containing a forge and bellows, a yard with a big Mexican bake–oven, and a corral. At the east end of the village was a ferry over the Arkansas to a grove of cottonwoods on the opposite side of the river where emigrants often camped. Thirty feet above the ferry was a ford.[22]

The new settlers on the Arkansas intended to stay here. The West was a different place than in the 1840's when their settlements were tentative and purely speculative in purpose. New Mexico and California now belonged to the United States. There was a Mormon colony in Utah, and Great Britain had given up its claim to the Oregon country. To all these places there would be great and small migrations of Americans until the country from the Atlantic to the Pacific would be solidly populated. On this assumption the Pacific Railroad was promulgated. The central route up the Arkansas was thought to be the most direct, the shortest and, according to Senator Benton, the easiest. Could there be any doubt that settlement on the Arkansas River was destined to be permanent?

The leaders of the Arkansas Valley settlements believed in it, and they bet their money on it. Means of making a living on the Arkansas was, for the time being, the same as before. Doyle was the Indian trader and his trade was profitable, for if buffalo had decreased in number, so had Indian traders. Wootton was the stockraiser, as he had been since the needs of the Army of the West had drawn him to New Mexico in 1847. Cattle, mules and horses were still needed in New Mexico, and Wootton had discovered that the best place to pasture them was on the Arkansas. Baca was also a stockraiser, and a farmer too. So were Autobees and Kroenig, for as long as there were cattle and people on the Arkansas there was need for corn and other vegetables. These men were no longer experimenting. They had already learned how to farm in the Arkansas Valley, how to trade with Indians and how to raise livestock. When the railroad came through they would become merchants, for they were all past masters of commerce. They would be—indeed, they already were— men of property. The Arkansas Valley was finally going to make them rich.[23]

Principal man at Pueblo ("*commandante del fuerte*") was Benito Sandoval, and he too was a man of property. In 1854 Benito was forty years old, two years younger than his sister Teresita. He had spent most of his life working for others—for José Pley at Coyote, New Mexico and for Barclay and Doyle at Barclay's Fort, where he was trusted and esteemed. His hard work had paid off—at last he owned a herd of about fifty cattle. In the spring of 1854 he moved to a log cabin on Baca's ranch at the mouth of the Fountain and helped Baca farm the cornfield. By fall Benito owned ninety bushels of corn. After the corn was sold, Benito's wife and youngest son, Juan Andrés, returned to Mora for a visit to his daughter Cecilia, wife of William Adamson. Benito and his three other sons moved into the Pueblo for the winter. After Christmas Benito's wife would return, and the whole family would move to the Huerfano village.[24]

But for Benito Sandoval Christmas never came. In December the Utes took one last swipe at the Arkansas Valley settlements, and this time their hostility, which had so long confined itself to hints and warnings, bore bloody fruit.

23
An Apology
for the Utes

EARLY IN THE MORNING of December 24, 1854 a band of Chief Blanco's Muache Utes with a few Jicarilla allies entered the gates of the Pueblo and murdered all but four of its inmates. There is no reason to think that any of these Indians had a particular grudge against any of their victims. To the white men it was a brutal, savage, meaningless attack and there was no excuse for it. To the Indians, however, the massacre was a culmination of eight years of frustration and misunderstanding in their dealings with the United States government and its contradictory agents, and disappointment in its dishonored treaties and broken promises. Before the massacre at Pueblo can be understood, the Indians must be granted their side of the story.

After the American conquest of New Mexico the Utes behaved well. A month after General Kearny took over Santa Fe he talked to a delegation of fifty or sixty Utes to whom he gave some blankets, some calico, and some stern advice—to be peaceable or he would send his soldiers after them. Kearny made no promises that if they heeded this advice they would be given presents. It was the first "treaty" the Utes had ever made with the Americans and they were too intimidated to demand that their good behavior be rewarded. Three weeks later fifty more Utes came in and had a talk with Colonel Doniphan, who gave them the same threats mixed with a few trinkets and proclaimed that he had made a "permanent treaty." Surprisingly, Doniphan's informal treaty turned out to be as "permanent" as later ones properly drawn up by authorized representatives, for at this time the Utes were generally friendly towards the Americans and loyal to their commitments.[1]

The Utes that Kearny and Doniphan talked to were Muache Utes, the most easterly ranging of six bands forming the Ute nation of six or seven thousand souls. The Muaches, numbering about a thousand souls, claimed the San Luis Valley and the mountains bordering it on the east, especially the Wet Mountain Valley where they had summer camps, and the plains of northeastern New Mexico and southeastern Colorado, where they hunted buffalo and Arapaho scalps. This was their land. If they exacted tribute of travelers passing through the San Luis Valley or packed their saddlebags with Hardscrabble corn or stole horses from Greenhorn or drove John Hatcher off his Purgatory farm, it was their right to do so for the white man was trespassing.[2]

Aside from these demonstrations of ownership, the Utes were peaceful in 1846 and 1847 at a time when the Comanches, Kiowas and Arapahos were making a shooting gallery of the Santa Fe trail. The Apaches and Navajos had killed over fifty citizens and stolen some 60,000 head of stock from the Rio Grande valley below Santa Fe in the year 1847, but the Utes stayed out of the fight and disdained to enrich themselves in this manner. In 1848 the Utes got little credit for taking the trader Mundy into "protective custody." Some accounts (none eyewitness) later linked the Utes with the Jicarilla Apaches who attacked the travelers at Manco Burro Pass. But if any Utes were present, they were too few to destroy the tribe's reputation for peace.[3]

In the early months of 1849 the Utes had a devastating battle with the Arapahos on the plains and were defeated badly, losing most of their stock. In starving condition, they began stealing stock from Río Colorado. They intended, as the chiefs told their traders, to make reparation later. But they had no time to do so, for in March, 1849 Lieutenant J. H. Whittlesey was sent out with fifty-seven soldiers to "chastise" the Utes, using Charles Autobees, Asa Estes, Bill Williams and others as guides and spies. The soldiers surprised a village, killed ten braves, captured two squaws and a chief's son, and destroyed fifty lodges with all the provisions and camp equipage. To balance the account, in the spring of 1849 the Utes killed Bill Williams and Benjamin Kern who had returned to the scene of Frémont's disaster of November, 1848 to raise a cache of instruments and papers.[4]

In June, 1849 the Utes notified white authorities that they were willing to surrender perpetrators of the murders and to restore stolen property. Accordingly, James S. Calhoun, who had been sent out in July as Superintendent of Indian Affairs for New Mexico, signed a treaty with them on December 30, 1849. The treaty provided for cessation of hostilities, restoration of captives and stolen property, extension of the Intercourse Act of 1834 to the tribe, annexation of their lands to New Mexico and free passage for white men through their territory. The Utes were to live within prescribed limits and to cultivate the soil. The United States on its part agreed to establish military posts in the Ute territory and to "grant to said Indians such donations, presents and implements, and adopt such other liberal and humane measures, as said Government may deem meet and proper." The treaty was ratified by Congress the following September.[5]

For over four years the Utes kept their side of the bargain. There were, to be sure, several thefts of stock, restored in part when the matter was laid before the chiefs; there were also a few murders, which were usually found upon investigation to be as much the fault of the victims as the Indians. For four years Superintendent Calhoun described the Utes as "perfectly quiet," "submissive," "peaceable and kindly disposed towards our citizens, receiving travelers with hospitality." They were "the easiest managed of any Indians in the territory and with good treatment can always be relied on."[6]

The Utes' peace with the white man was bought at great cost to themselves. As the hostile Indians of New Mexico made off with cattle, sheep, horses, guns and clothing, goods and captives, the Utes grew poorer and poorer, lacking even guns and ammunition to kill game. Not a penny of the "donations and presents" promised them in the treaty of 1849 had been distributed as late as August, 1852. No Indian agent had been stationed among them, nor had implements for farming been provided them, nor teachers to show them how to farm. In June, 1852 a military post called Fort Massachusetts was established at the eastern edge of the San Luis Valley, but it was located in the wrong place either for defense of its own garrison or for defense of the Utes against the Plains Indians, which was its stated purpose.[7]

Worst of all, the frequent forays of the Arapahos, Cheyennes and Kiowas into the San Luis Valley to rob and kill Utes were all but subsidized by the United States Government. By terms of two treaties made by Thomas Fitzpatrick in 1851 and 1853 with the Arapahos, Cheyennes, Kiowas, Comanches and Kiowa-Apaches, the United States guaranteed these Plains tribes a specified annuity and provided them with guns and ammunition. But no annuity was provided for the Utes, and their traders were specifically forbidden to sell them guns and ammunition.[8]

In November, 1852 the United States agent finally gathered some

Utes together at Abiquiu. They were given a feast of mutton and beef and $3,000 worth of flour and trinkets to be distributed among four hundred warriors and one hundred women and children. It was a happy occasion, the white men reported: The Utes, they said, were "highly pleased at the reception they had met." But Chief Coniache made a speech that the white men should have listened to with great care. In beautiful and simple language the chief described how his people had always lived by the hunt and did not know how to live in houses or to farm. He begged for powder and lead to kill game. He said that "the prairie Indians have committed many depredations upon our people, and we are told we must not make war. We do not wish to have our hands bound together, when our enemies are permitted to steal our stock and murder our wives and children. If we are not to make war, we shall expect the Americans at the fort [Massachusetts] to protect us and our property." Coniache spoke quietly and without threats and he asked for precious little: powder and lead and protection from the Plains Indians. But that little was not forthcoming.[9]

Still the Utes remained at peace. In February, 1853 forty Ute families were found in starving condition on the Costilla and Culebra rivers, many of their people killed and most of their horses stolen by Arapahos and Cheyennes. Governor William Carr Lane, who was now beginning to understand the problem, suggested that the Utes be removed west of the Rio Grande and that Plains Indians be forbidden to enter Ute territory. Before his policy could be examined, Governor Lane was succeeded by David Meriwether with far different ideas. At the same time the Ute agent, Dr. Michael Steck, who was just beginning to be of use to his Indians, was replaced by Meriwether's son–in–law, a Kentucky lawyer who had never laid eyes on a Ute.[10]

In September, 1853 Chico Velasquez, a Muache chief, came to see Governor Meriwether. Chico Velasquez was said to have sworn eternal enmity for the white man. His proudest possession was a pair of leggings artistically decorated with clusters of fingernails, some American, some Mexican, some Negro. Governor Meriwether, therefore, put his hands behind his back when the Indian offered to shake hands. But Chico Velasquez promised to comply with the Governor's wishes and to see that all stolen stock was returned, and he was as good as his word. To Meriwether's surprise, the chief made his people give up some government horses they had stolen from the Arapahos. He also refused to participate in a war of the

Chief Coniache of the Utes. He is dressed in a fancy military coat similar to those given by Governor Meriwether to Chico Velasquez and his friends. From H. L. Conard, *"Uncle Dick" Wootton* (1890). Courtesy of Denver Public Library Western Collection.

Timpanagos Utes against Mormons in Utah, and he continued to keep his hungry people quiet.[11]

Not so peaceful were the Utes' allies, the Jicarilla Apaches, numbering two or three hundred souls who lived in the plains and foothills of northeastern New Mexico and along the Rio Grande north of Taos. On July 1, 1852 Governor Lane made a treaty at Santa Fe with the Jicarillas which was nearly identical to the Ute treaty of December, 1849. Still the Congress of the United States failed to appropriate any money for its Indian wards in New Mexico. A large part of the Jicarillas were now settled on two farms near Abiquiu and Fort Webster and fed out of funds appropriated not for their own use but for contingent expenses of the New Mexico Superintendency. In August, 1853 Governor Meriwether told the Indians that his predecessor, Governor Lane, had exceeded his authority in feeding them and that no more food would be forthcoming for lack of funds. For the Jicarillas it was either starvation or depredation; they left their farms and began to steal. By February, 1854 their thefts had cost the people of the Territory between fifty and a hundred thousand dollars according to Governor Meriwether, who pointed out that feeding them would have cost between fifteen and twenty thousand dollars.[12]

In March, 1854 soldiers sent out to pursue the Jicarilla marauders were badly defeated in a battle, only eight out of sixty escaping unhurt. In retaliation all available forces were gathered to fight the Indians. Near Fisher's Peak (now Trinidad, Colorado) the soldiers attacked a Jicarilla village, killing a few Indians, capturing thirty-eight horses and destroying all the lodges.[13]

It was suspected that there had been Utes among the Jicarilla enemy. On their way home the soldiers passed an old site of a Ute village at a source of the Canadian River, but the report of the campaign showed no other indication that the Utes had been anywhere near. In fact, at that time Chico Velasquez's band was engaged in protecting a herd of government animals grazing near Fort Union from Jicarilla depredation, and Chico Velasquez himself had been hired to recover cattle already stolen. Among the whites there was conjecture that the Ute chief had been in league with the Jicarillas all along. Even if this were true, it was undeniable, as Muache agent Kit Carson wrote, that "the Utahs as a nation profess friendship and appear peaceable and friendly disposed . . . and it is only a few bad men who have been committing depredations." Notwithstanding, Carson urged that "before the Utahs can be made to respect treaties, citizens and their property, they should be severely *chastised* and *punished* and be made to *know* and *feel* the power of the government.[14]

Agent Carson to the contrary, it might have been interesting to see how the Utes would have reacted to some of those presents and tools, teachers and donations and protection from the Plains Indians that the government had promised them. For five years while the Utes maintained peace under the most difficult circumstances, the United States did nothing for them except build a military post in the wrong place, distribute some flour, meat and trinkets on a single occasion, and for a brief period prevent settlement on Ute lands in the San Luis Valley.

In the summer of 1851 a group of Mexicans came to the Conejos and built three leagues of irrigating ditches before the Utes drove them away. In October the Mexicans offered the Utes ten horses, ten oxen, ten rifles, ten silver-ornamented bridles, ten blankets and ten of any other article they could name for the privilege of settling on the Conejos. The Indians accepted the offer, but the Mexicans never paid up. In the spring of 1852, 147 settlers signed a document agreeing to settle on the Conejos in defiance of the Utes. Foreseeing trouble, Agent John Greiner summoned twenty Ute chiefs to discuss the problem. After hearing the Indians' side of it Greiner agreed with them and wrote the settlers that the laws of the United States would not permit them to settle there—and that year they did not. Nor did white men make a new settlement anywhere on Ute lands that year, if we may assume that John Greiner and the Utes would have paid close attention to it. But John Greiner, whom Governor Lane described as "one of the few, very few agents, in this Ter., who has done his duty & his whole duty," was not to be agent much longer. By 1854 Greiner was gone, and there were white settlements on the Culebra, Costilla and Conejos. If the Utes complained, their complaints were not recorded.[15]

New Mexican authorities had done little to investigate reports that Utes had attacked settlements on the Greenhorn and St. Charles, probably for the same reason that Greiner discouraged settlement on the Conejos—settlers had no business there in the first place. By terms of the 1849 treaty which Superintendent James Calhoun had carefully explained to the Utes, the laws regulating trade and intercourse with the Indians were to apply to them, which meant that they were to be protected from unlicensed traders and from white settlers on their lands.[16]

Consequently, the Utes began a series of warnings to settlers south of the Arkansas. One day near the Huerfano village, María Whittlesey, riding horseback with her two children, was surprised by Utes. Tying her baby to her with a reboso, her older child behind her, she dashed for home with the Utes in hot pursuit. A second warning came on October 16, 1854 when Charles Autobees with four men and some Arapaho women and children started out from the Huerfano village with a wagonload of flour and corn to trade to the Arapahos on the Platte-Arkansas divide. At Chico Creek, five miles east of Pueblo, Autobees was accosted by Coniache and twenty-seven Utes who said they would not harm Autobees if he handed over the Arapahos. Autobees refused; the Utes attacked. In a fight lasting two and a half hours Autobees was wounded and four of his animals stolen.[17]

There was a third warning which the records say little about. In the fall of 1854 a Mexican trader from Culebra (as the village of San Luis, Colorado was then called) was killed by Utes on Apache Creek near Greenhorn. News of the trader's death apparently had not reached Governor Meriwether's ears by October 29, 1854, when he wrote that "the Utahs have been quiet for about a year past and have committed no depredations since my interview with them last fall."[18]

At that time the governor was trying to pacify the Utes, who were greatly excited because a Mexican had murdered a Ute in cold blood. The governor offered $100 for the murderer, who was promptly delivered up. In a conference with Chico Velasquez and another chief the governor promised that he personally would take the murderer to Santa Fe to stand trial, and that the Utes should be present to see him "hung up to a tree like a dog." Then he gave the chiefs each a gray cloth coat made especially for them, decorated with red and yellow braid, brass buttons down the front and a rosette on each shoulder. "These were the first coats that either had ever had on his back," wrote Meriwether, "and pleased them very much."[19]

Governor Meriwether's interview with the Ute chiefs was a catastrophe—the last straw for the embittered Indians. The Mexican who had murdered the Ute was taken to Taos and put in jail, from which he escaped and was never found again. Thus the Utes were cheated of their first intense look at United States justice. Far more serious, the chiefs who had donned Governor Meriwether's gift coats contracted smallpox on their way back to their people, and they died. On his deathbed Chico Velasquez expressed a desire to see the governor once more, but a part of his people believed that the governor had purposely infected the coats with the deadly pox. After their leader's death they went on the warpath.[20]

Their new leader was Coniache, a "mild, well-disposed Indian" whom Governor Meriwether doubted could control his band as well as Chico Velasquez had. Under him was Tierra Blanca, whom Meriwether described as "one of the most forbidding looking beings I ever saw in all my life. He had but one eye, and his face was scarred with smallpox in a most terrible manner, but I soon discovered him to be a shrewd, cunning rascal.[21]

Blanco, as he was called, was distinguished by his red woolen shirt. It was also his distinction to be the leader of the party of Utes that wiped out Pueblo in 1854 in a violent reaction against the white men who had failed their Ute brothers in nearly every particular.

24
Massacre, 1854

DURING THE WEEK BEFORE CHRISTMAS, 1854 all was quiet on the Arkansas. Joe Doyle and Bob Rice had taken two cartloads of goods to trade with the Arapahos at Bijou Basin on the Platte-Arkansas divide. Benito Sandoval's sixteen-year-old son Pedro had taken two wagons from Pueblo down the Arkansas, one loaded with corn for Levin Mitchell at the St. Charles, the other with Benito's furniture and household goods bound for the Huerfano village.[1]

Dick Wootton, George McDougal and three others from the Huerfano village and the settlement at the mouth of the St. Charles had gone hunting up the Arkansas. They had meant to be gone several days, but on Coal Creek Wootton saw two things that bothered him—a glimpse of an Indian and fresh pony tracks. Wootton persuaded his companions to head for home. At Pueblo an old man came running out to tell them that he had seen tracks of a big band of horses which had crossed the river the night before. Wootton said that Utes were probably on those horses waiting for a chance to attack. He warned the old man not to let any Indians inside the fort, and then he and his friends returned to the Huerfano village.[2]

On the eve of the Christmas holiday, which Mexicans celebrate on December 24, there was an all-night card game at the fort. Three men from Baca's attended—José Ignacio Valencia, Tanislado de Luna and Rumaldo Córdova. The only woman at the fort that night was Chepita Miera, wife of Juan Blas Martín. Chepita was preparing to move out of the fort in the morning and she had her things already packed onto Rumaldo's wagon, which stood outside the gate. The party did not break up until just before daybreak. José Ignacio Valencia stumbled out of the fort into the chill winter dawn to return to his cabin at Baca's. When he got home he remembered that he had left his knife at the Pueblo, so he started back to the fort.[3]

Before dawn, young Benito (Guero) Pais left the fort on horseback to fetch some milk at Baca's. Just beyond the gravel ford of the

Fountain, the boy heard a whistle. He looked up towards the loma or bluff north of Baca's house and there, outlined against the yellow sky of daybreak, were Indians on horseback. Guero galloped on to Baca's and gave the alarm.[4]

As Guero Pais was leaving the Pueblo and José Ignacio Valencia was returning to it for his knife, Felipe Cisneros went out to get the horses in. The cattle, which should have been put in the corral the night before by the cattle-herder, were also out. Felipe Cisneros climbed to the top of the loma and saw no horses or cattle. Alarmed, the boy ran back down to Baca's. As he got to the foot of the hill he saw an Indian riding up to the house. Ducking into a ravine, Felipe ran down the length of it to the timber on the banks of the Arkansas and there he hid.[5]

After Guero Pais gave the alarm, Marcelino Baca ran to the jacal cabins behind his house and woke up the wives of José Ignacio Valencia, Tanislado de Luna and Rumaldo Córdova. The women returned with him to his house. Baca also saw the Indians on the loma. He thought perhaps they were friendly as did others in his house. But José Barela, the wise old man, remembered that a trader had been killed at Apache Creek a short time ago by Blanco's band of Utes. He said, "No, don't make friends with the Indians or they'll kill us!" So Baca ordered the house closed up tight and told the men to get their guns.[6]

Chief Blanco rode up to the house on Baca's best white mare with a hundred Utes and a few Apaches behind him. Baca and Barela went out to meet him, one to the east of the house and the other to the west, with their rifles aimed at Blanco's head.

"*Amigo,*" said Blanco in a friendly voice, but Baca warned the Indian that if he came a step nearer his head would be blown off.

Suddenly from inside the house where the women were wailing in terror little Elena Baca ran out to her father, then crossed the perilous distance to old Barela, who sent her back into the house. Elena's Pawnee mother whipped her soundly for her recklessness, saying that she would kill Elena before she would let the Utes capture her. Fifty years later Elena remembered these terrible words.[7]

The Indians rode away without any demands or threats, without robbing Baca of his corn or of the cows and calf in the corral behind his house. But they had already stolen every animal they had found on the loma before dawn, leaving Baca a poor man.[8]

The people at Baca's watched the Indians going off towards the

Fountain and Pueblo. They knew there was no way to warn the men at the fort. But Blanco would surely try to raid the American settlements down the Arkansas, so old Barela saddled his horse and set off to warn them. Before he had gotten more than a few hundred yards from Baca's house, he was hailed by the frightened voice of Felipe Cisneros from the cottonwoods close to the Arkansas. Barela told the boy to stay there, hidden, until his return.[9]

Half an hour after the Utes left Baca's, at seven or eight in the morning, Cisneros and the people at Baca's heard "shooting and crying and shouting" coming from the direction of the fort and then—silence.[10]

It was five hours before old Barela returned from warning the villages down the Arkansas. Not until then did Barela, Baca and Cisneros decide that it was safe to go to the fort and see what had happened. Before they had gone a quarter of a mile, they found the body of José Ignacio Valencia on the east side of the Fountain at the gravel ford where the Utes had caught up with him and killed him.

They left Valencia's body and crossed the river. Staggering towards them was Juan Rafael Medina clutching a great cut in his belly through which his guts were spilling out. He was gasping for water. Cisneros ran back to the river and scooped up some cold water in his hands. Medina drank and died, but from the few words that gurgled from his lips the men understood that no one was left alive at the fort.[11]

At the gap or *Puertocito* they found the body of Guadalupe Vigil, a Navajo Indian, with an arrow in his back. He must have been running from the fort towards Baca's when he was pursued and killed. Another arrow pierced one of his fingers, as though he had tried to protect his face with his hands.[12]

Outside the fort were corpses of two or three Utes. Near the gate sat Rumaldo Córdova, bent over and covered with blood but alive and conscious. He could not answer their questions for he had been shot in the mouth, but he told them what had happened in Indian sign language. With his hands Rumaldo indicated that Chepita Miera, his sister-in-law, had been sitting in his wagon outside the gate waiting for him when the Utes came up. The Indians yanked her off the wagon and she screamed. Rumaldo ran out from the fort and tried to pull her away from the Indians. He was shot through the side of the neck with an arrow and through the mouth with a gun and left for dead. Later he managed to reach the chicken coop outside the walls, and there he hid until the Utes left. Then he crawled back as far as the gate and collapsed. That, said Rumaldo in signs, was how the massacre began.[13]

Felix Sandoval, then a lad of twelve, remembered it differently. He said an Indian came to the fort alone, asking for something to eat. He was refused admittance. A few minutes later Chief Blanco came to the gate and got off his horse. Benito Sandoval and Rumaldo opened the gate, and Benito ordered Rumaldo to shoot Blanco. Blanco turned his face towards Rumaldo, who recognized him and drew him into the fort, saying, "This is my friend!" After more Indians had pushed through the open gate into the courtyard, Blanco grabbed Rumaldo's gun out of his hands and shot him through the mouth. In the uproar that followed, an Indian caught Felix Sandoval and put him astride his horse behind the saddle. As they left, Felix looked back and saw an Indian shoot his father through the chest.[14]

The courtyard of the Pueblo was deathly still when Baca, Barela and young Cisneros entered it. On the bloodied earth lay the bodies of Francisco Mestas, Juan Blas Martín and Manuel "Trujeque" Lucero, whose fingers held the handle of a flatiron in a death grip. In the northwest bastion the body of Benito Sandoval lay crumpled at the foot of a ridgepole which bore his bloody fingermarks for years afterwards. After being shot Benito had picked up his rifle and his seven-year-old son Juan Isidro and had run into the bastion, locking himself and the boy in. The Utes tore open the roof of the room, shot the father through the top of the head and captured Juan Isidro, but not before Benito had picked off two of his murderers with his rifle.[15]

Late that afternoon a party of men came from the Huerfano and St. Charles villages to bury the victims. They found the remains of Joaquin Pacheco on the banks of the Arkansas half a mile from the fort, his body lanced through and through so savagely that the lances left holes in the ground underneath him. In front of the fort they dug a common grave in which they buried five of the victims, covering the grave with logs to keep wolves from digging it up.[16]

Then they hitched up Rumaldo Córdova's wagon still standing in front of the fort. Into it they placed the wounded Rumaldo and the bodies of the men they found on the road—Juan Rafael Medina and José Ignacio Valencia. They buried Guadalupe Vigil in the *puertocito* where he had fallen, but the others they buried near Baca's house. They left the corpses of five or six Utes for the wolves. That night there was a wake at Baca's for the souls of the dead, and prayers for those who were missing. The bodies of Juan "Shoco" Aragon and Tanislado de Luna were never found.[17]

After the massacre the Utes went up the Arkansas towards the Wet Mountains with their captives, the brothers Felix and Juan Isidro Sandoval and the woman Chepita Miera. They made camp that night on Grape Creek, happy and contented, for they had many animals from their raid on Baca's and their saddlebags were filled with Benito Sandoval's corn. In the morning their joy vanished when their camp was attacked by Arapahos. During the battle the Ute women folded up the lodges and ran into the forest with the captives. Afterwards the Ute warriors joined their families, and they traveled up the trail slowly and sadly, for they had lost men and horses. When they came to a little spring some of the Indians dismounted and drank. Chepita too was allowed to get off her horse and drink. Then she washed her face, and as she was washing an arrow flew past. She turned around and saw an Indian with bow and arrow in his hands. As she started to run away, the Indian shot another arrow which struck her in the back and came out through her breast. Seizing the head of the arrow in her hands, she fell to the ground, and the Indian children, who had been standing around watching, stoned her to death with small rocks. The Indians told Felix Sandoval that Chepita had to die because she was down-hearted and refused to be comforted.[18]

A month after the massacre, soldiers from Taos discovered Chepita Miera's scalp hanging from a tree in the Wet Mountain Valley. The scalp had long black hair with ribbons on it. One of the soldiers wrapped it in paper and took it to Chepita's brother in Taos. Felix Sandoval told the story of Chepita's death when he was delivered up to the Americans at Abiquiu eight months later. Juan Isidro Sandoval was a captive for five years and ten months. Three months after his capture the Utes traded him to the Navajos, among whom he remained a slave until he was bought by a Mexican trader, who restored him to his mother for about $300 in silver and merchandise, including a Hawken rifle.[19]

On December 27 the Utes attacked again. About two miles below Baca's house, they killed Marcelino's brother Benito and two unsuspecting Americans who had come from Bent's Fort in Big Timber to buy corn from Baca. Near the St. Charles village the Indians stole forty head of Levin Mitchell's cattle and killed a Pueblo Indian herder, shooting his Mexican companion in the back with arrows.

The Mexican played dead until the Indians left, and then managed to reach the St. Charles village with three arrows sticking in his back. Six Americans from the village pursued the Indians into a thicket beside the river and killed one. After an all-day siege of the thicket, the St. Charles men went home and the Indians escaped. A few days later J. W. Atwood, John Jurnegan and Marcelino Baca set out for the Sangre de Cristo Pass and New Mexico to summon help.[20]

On January 7, 1855 Atwood, Jurnegan and Baca arrived at Camp Burgwin near Taos and told their appalling story. Atwood was sent on to Fort Marcy, Army Headquarters at Santa Fe. His report was forwarded to the commander of Fort Union, where preparations were begun for a final, devastating campaign against the Utes and their Jicarilla Apache allies. While letters and dispatches were flying back and forth between Army Headquarters and Fort Union, the Utes once more galloped down the Arkansas.[21]

By this time no one was living at the mouth of the Fountain. All the occupants of the Pueblo had been murdered or captured, and Baca's family and employees had moved to the St. Charles village. Some of the frightened St. Charles traders were planning to move farther down the Arkansas, and they had their belongings loaded onto wagons in charge of nine Cherokee teamsters. After the teamsters had passed the Huerfano village, they were attacked and killed by Utes and their wagons burned. Then the Indians galloped back to the Huerfano village, where a man had just finished digging a grave for Rumaldo Córdova. The gravedigger dropped into the grave and the Indians passed by without seeing him.[22]

Joe Doyle was still on his trading trip to the Arapahos when the Indians attacked the Huerfano village, but his wife and children had gone to Wootton's house, as had others in the village. Wootton was prepared; around the edge of his roof he had piled sacks of corn behind which men were stationed with their rifles cocked. More men on horseback waited behind the gate of his *placita*. When the Indians dashed past, a dozen mounted men burst out the gate, and the men on the roof began firing. The startled Indians fled.[23]

Involved in this attack of January 19, 1855 were a war party of 180 Utes and Jicarillas led by Blanco and the Apache chief Guero. Official reports indicate four men killed, three of them Americans, and a hundred animals captured. The reports mention nothing about the murder of the Cherokee teamsters.[24]

By the end of February a military expedition against the Utes was organized and on the march with orders to pursue the Indians, rout them out of their mountain hideouts, meet them in pitched battles. The most effective arm of this five-hundred-man expedition was five companies of volunteers under Lieutenant Colonel Ceran St. Vrain. The campaign raged for months through the mountains and valleys, with the Indians always on the move and starving because they could not stop to hunt. By June 30 General Garland wrote that the Utes were making offers of peace, and in September a treaty was concluded with the Muache and Jicarilla chiefs at Abiquiu.[25]

Indian attacks put an end to the settlements on the Arkansas. In the spring of 1855 Joe Doyle, Ben Ryder, Levin Mitchell and others took their families back to New Mexico. Atwood and Tibbetts moved down the river to abandoned Bent's Fort, where they traded with the Cheyennes in a few rooms they had refurbished. Marcelino Baca, stripped of most of his wealth, returned to Greenhorn and then to Río Colorado. On February 21, 1862 he was killed by a shot in the forehead at the Battle of Valverde, while serving with the New Mexico volunteers against Confederate invaders.[26]

By the summer of 1855 the only men left on the Arkansas were those at the Huerfano village—Kroenig, Autobees, Wootton and their families and employees. Wootton might have moved earlier had his wife Dolores not been far along in pregnancy. The Woottons had begged Chepita Ryder to act as midwife at Dolores's confinement, but the Ryders were afraid and fled to New Mexico. On May 6, 1855, after giving birth to her fourth child, Dolores died at the Huerfano village and was buried at the base of the cobblestone-covered hill where Rumaldo Córdova had been buried in January. The bereaved Wootton took his family up the Arkansas to live for a few weeks in the bloodstained Pueblo with George Simpson and Tom Suaso. Then they all went to Greenhorn to spend the summer farming. In the fall Wootton moved to Fort Barclay, and his children were sent to their LeFevre grandparents in Taos.[27]

On the Arkansas two men and their employees remained—Charles Autobees on his ranch two miles up the Huerfano and William Bent in his stone fort at Big Timber. These two indomitable frontiersmen held the Arkansas Valley until reinforcements arrived with the 1858 migration of gold-seekers.

That was the end of the early Arkansas Valley settlements. Doubtless there were many travelers who spent the night at the Pueblo, shuddering at the brown stains of violence spattering its whitewashed walls. Dick Wootton describes camping there with a companion who had noisy nightmares about ghosts and headless Mexican women. As far as we know, the Pueblo was never again occupied. In 1858, after the gold rush to Cherry Creek had produced little gold, many emigrants spent the winter at the mouth of the Fountain. They liked it so well they decided to settle there, and so the city of Pueblo was born, its first houses made from the old adobes of the Pueblo.[28]

25
The End of the
Beginning

THERE IS NOTHING LEFT of the Arkansas Valley settlements. Everything is gone, changed, knocked down, dug up. An exceptional
effort of imagination is needed to picture what the land around the
trading posts must have looked like. Rivers have been tampered
with; the course of the Arkansas has been altered. Wild life that once
abounded has been destroyed or driven away. Grass, trees, flowers,
the very air have suffered from man's incursions. From an airplane
the outline of Hardscrabble is still visible in an alfalfa field near
Florence, Colorado; on the hillside above the site of Greenhorn old
wagon tracks still cut the prairie marking the trail south to the
Sangre de Cristo Pass and Taos. Nothing else remains.

Not a vestige of the Pueblo is left. Its site, serving alternately as a
vacant lot or a used car lot, is littered with fragments of glass and
china, beer cans and dirty newspapers—shards of an all–too–recent
occupation. It would be a miracle to find a trade bead or plow bolt
here, where floods and bulldozers have wreaked their destruction.
Even the memorials to the fort are inadequate. A monument
erected by the Daughters of the American Revolution says, "FORT
PUEBLO. Site of Indian Massacre, December 25, 1854"—but the
monument is not on the site of the fort, the date is dubious and the
massacre was only a tragic postscript to the fort's real history. In an
abandoned airport hangar south of Pueblo there is a full-scale replica
of the fort, or of a fort that might have resembled it, for nothing but
the crudest sketches remained to guide its reconstruction.

When Greenhorn was finally abandoned in 1856, it was the end of
the beginning. The era of the Arkansas valley trading posts ended
just two years before real and permanent settlement began. But
there was a continuity between the old trading posts and the new
towns. Without the assurance that man had lived here once and
could again, disappointed gold-seekers might one and all have returned to Kansas or Georgia. Or their infant settlements might have

been destroyed by Indians who still owned the land and the fruits thereof. White friends of the red men—Bent, Poisal, John Smith, Autobees—advised the Indians to remain calm, be friendly and wait; their White Father in Washington would devise something splendid for them if they would only wait. And while they waited their lands were engulfed in a tide of white men, a wave on which the Indians were finally swept off to reservations.

The continuity was in the men like Bent and Autobees who stayed in the Arkansas valley, or those who returned like Doyle and Wootton. They were the ones who had opened up the valley, pacified the Indians, plowed under the virgin turf, planted seeds and fruit trees, trusted cattle to the stunted grasses, calculated frost, measured potentialities. The Arkansas valley had almost no secrets from these frontiersmen. Hardly a buffalo trail was unfollowed, a stream unforded, a pass unexplored. Few caprices of climate could surprise them, few horrors of poisonous plants or insects could catch them unawares, and the Indians were no mystery to them. These were the skills and knowledge the old-timers taught the new settlers. Lessons learned in twenty-five years of living on the land and off it were not lost with the abandonment of Greenhorn in 1856.

Mediator and peacemaker between white and red men was William Bent, who continued to live with his Cheyenne wife and family and to trade with the Indians in his stone fort at Big Timber until 1860. Then he built a log house on his ranch at the mouth of the Purgatory where he died in 1869. Charles Autobees lived out his life at his ranch two miles up the Huerfano from its mouth with his Indian and Mexican wives and families, and his tenacity was an inspiration to new settlers.[1]

Joe Doyle was also an inspiration to new settlers and became one of their leaders. Three months after Barclay's death in December, 1855 Doyle sold Fort Barclay to William Kroenig and Morris Beilschowsky for over $7,000. Then Doyle, Kroenig, Ryder, Wootton, Simpson and their families moved into the fort, where for a few years they lived a settled life. Teresita's daughter, Rafaela Kinkead, was married to William Kroenig in 1856 at Fort Barclay, where she died two years later after the birth of her second child. She was buried near her stepfather, Alexander Barclay, in the little graveyard half a mile from the fort. At Fort Barclay there were schoolteachers and a schoolroom; at a chapel nearby Juana Simpson gave the children religious instruction.[2]

During these years Joe Doyle was a freighter, his wagons rolling along the trail between Kansas City and Santa Fe. Dick Wootton was his employee or partner on some of the trips. In 1858 Doyle and Wootton hauled some goods to a camp near Salt Lake for General A. S. Johnston's army, engaged in a little war against the Mormons. On the way back they passed the mouth of Cherry Creek on the South Platte, where they found a group of prospectors panning gold on the future site of Denver.[3]

The prospectors had been directed to Cherry Creek by none other than George Simpson. In May, 1858 Simpson was serving as a citizen teamster with Captain R. B. Marcy's command, bringing supplies to General Johnston's army. While the command was camped at Cherry Creek George idly washed out twenty-five cents' worth of gold. Later, at Sweetwater on the Oregon Trail, Simpson gave the gold to three dispatch bearers on their way to the States, carelessly telling them he had found it "near Pikes Peak." When he arrived at Westport in September he was astonished to find that his few grains of gold had sent hundreds of prospectors rushing off to "Pikes Peak."[4]

During the next three years there was a stampede to the foot of the mountains, changing the Rocky Mountain West where the trapper, trader and farmer had pursued their quiet occupations into a noisy, busy, brawling region of town-builders, miners and freighters. Some of the old-timers threw themselves energetically into the new order of things. On Christmas Eve, 1858 Richens L. Wootton arrived at Auraria (Denver) from Barclay's Fort with a wagon train of goods and whiskey. Like a jolly Santa Claus, Dick rolled out his kegs of whiskey, put tin pans and cups on top of them and invited the miners to have some Christmas cheer on him. By the following June Wootton had built a store and saloon and later a hotel, which, in his bighearted way, he filled with nonpaying guests. After the hotel failed, in the fall of 1861 he moved to a farm eight miles above Pueblo on the Fountain, leaving Denver speculations to his more competent friend Joe Doyle.[5]

Doyle's freighting had proved highly profitable. In June, 1859 he brought $30,000 worth of goods to Denver and sold them under the name of J. B. Doyle & Co., which became the largest mercantile firm in the territory. It did half a million dollars' worth of business a year and had branches at Canon City, Pueblo, Tarryall (Fairplay) and other mining camps in the mountains.[6]

In the meantime the cities of Pueblo, Canon City and Colorado

Graves of Joseph Doyle, his wife Cruz, and son Alexander, and of Thomas Suaso and his wife Clara Gutierrez, overlooking the Doyle Ranch on the Huerfano. Photograph: Myron Wood, Colorado Springs.

City were born. Members of an emigrant party from Lawrence, Kansas, joined by George McDougal from Autobees' ranch and William Kroenig from New Mexico, laid off Fountain City east of Fountain Creek above its mouth, incorporating houses that had formed Marcelino Baca's settlement of 1854. Before the winter was out they had erected thirty log, adobe and jacal cabins, most of the adobes coming from the walls of the old fort across the Fountain. Eighty lodges of Arapahos camped nearby for three months that winter, trading furs and skins. Fountain City settlers were so delighted with the dry, mild winter that when spring came they decided to settle down and farm instead of leaving to look for gold. Taking out a ditch from the Fountain or repairing Marcelino Baca's old ditch, they put in crops of corn and vegetables. About the middle of October, 1859 William Kroenig and others from Fountain City founded Canon City at the mouth of the canyon of the Arkansas (Royal Gorge). In the fall of 1859 a third village called Colorado City (near later Colorado Springs) was begun on Fountain Creek. So by 1860 the Arkansas Valley had three permanent settlements, all established with the help of the earlier settlers in the valley.[7]

Ceran St. Vrain now found little difficulty enticing settlers to his Vigil and St. Vrain Grant. In 1861 William Kroenig bought land on the Huerfano where he built a house, started a farm and made cheese to sell to the new population of Denver. In 1863 he sold his land and moved back to the vicinity of Barclay's fort, where he died in 1896.[8]

Joe Doyle also became a rich man. In November, 1859 he bought two miles of the Huerfano valley from Ceran St. Vrain. By 1863 he owned three miles of the valley planted to wheat, corn, potatoes, beans, oats, tobacco, cotton, melons and other crops that had been grown at Pueblo, Hardscrabble and Greenhorn in years past. On the uplands he ran a thousand head of cattle. He built a large flour mill and a two-story clapboard mansion made of lumber brought from the east. His house was painted white, probably in memory of the stately neoclassic houses recalled from his Virginia boyhood, but he gave it a Spanish name, "Casa Blanca." It was furnished elegantly and staffed with a proper complement of servants. On the ranch were a large store, a post office, a wagon and blacksmith shop, a schoolhouse, a flour mill and houses for the host of employees on the place.[9]

In 1864 Doyle was the richest man in Colorado Territory and one of the most politically important. On March 1, 1864, while serving as a member of the Territorial Legislature in Denver, Doyle had a heart attack and died three days later at the age of forty-six. The hearse containing his body was escorted out of Denver by a large crowd of citizens and dignitaries including Governor Evans. Doyle was buried on a point of land overlooking his house on the Huerfano. At news of his death, said a newspaper correspondent from Pueblo,

Monument over George S. Simpson's grave on top of Simpson's Rest, Trinidad, Colorado. All but the two bottom stones of the monument were destroyed by vandals according to A. R. Mitchell of Trinidad, from whose collection this photograph came.

"the countenance of every citizen of southern Colorado wears a cloudy and gloomy look," and well it might, for the whole economy of the Arkansas valley was more or less involved in his many enterprises and dependent upon his steady generosity and good sense.[10]

After Doyle's death his family disintegrated and his fortune diminished. On March 1, 1865, Cruz died leaving four minor children and a host of hangers-on eager to seize control of the huge estate. The children were taken to Mora to live with their grandmother Teresita for a year. In 1867 Teresita brought them back to live at Doyle's ranch, where they matured in an atmosphere of bitter quarreling over the administration of Doyle's estate.[11]

The death of Cruz Doyle changed the plans of Dick Wootton, who had intended to marry her. Dick suspected that she had been poisoned to keep him from getting control of the Doyle property—such was the hysteria that characterized the Doyle household at this time. In April, 1865 Wootton left his farm on the Fountain and took possession of land at the northern foot of Raton Pass, where he established a tollgate and a tollroad over the pass. He built himself a fine two-story mansion with a veranda all around it, in recollection of another Virginia boyhood, and there he lived and collected tolls for the rest of his life. In 1867 he married his fourth wife, thirteen-year-old María Paula Lujan (cousin of his first wife Dolores) and proceeded to sire ten children. Always boisterous, genial and shrewd, Dick was frequently in the newspapers, defending himself against an indictment for fornication, selling liquor without paying a tax, building a new bridge near Bent's Fort, raising the toll on the New Mexican side of his road when the county commissioners made him lower it on the Colorado side, giving his name to the Santa Fe Railroad's largest locomotive, the "Uncle Dick," getting thrown out of a saloon, and publishing his autobiography, *"Uncle Dick" Wootton*, which represents his magnificently eventful life as even more eventful than it was. He died in 1893, having survived all but three of his twenty children.[12]

George Simpson and his family settled down at Doyle's ranch in 1861, but after Cruz Doyle's death in 1865 they moved to Trinidad. George was elected County Clerk in 1867, but much of his time was spent writing articles and poems under the pseudonym of "Senex" for St. Louis, Kansas City, Denver and Trinidad newspapers. His chief income was probably the annuity he still received from his parents and the little stipend Juana made teaching the Spanish-speaking children of Trinidad. George stopped drinking before he

Juana Suaso Simpson, June 20, 1899, with her grandson, Burgess Lee Gordon, later a distinguished physician. Courtesy of A. R. Mitchell, Trinidad, Colorado.

died. In his last years he earned a certain amount of respect serving on school boards and in other civic capacities and walking around the tough frontier town clad in a Prince Albert coat and other garments of extravagant dignity. He died in 1885.[13]

As for Juana, she needed no fancy clothing to gain the love and respect of all who knew her. She was "Doña Juanita" in the town of Trinidad, the foremost lady, the ministering angel of the church, school and hospital. After George's death she lived with her daughter Isabel Simpson Beard until her own death in 1916 at Monrovia, California.[14]

The early settlements of the Arkansas Valley were founded to make money by refugees from the frivolous drawing rooms of St. Louis, the squalor of Dickensian London, the agrarian poverty of New Mexico or backwoods Canada, the decline of the trapping business. Fired with the desperate materialism of the nineteenth century, the leaders of the settlements meant to make a fortune in the wilderness and return home to spend it. "I am not going home until I make *something*," wrote young George Simpson; Alexander Barclay kept writing his relatives that he would return to England as soon as some speculation or other came ripe.

But failure clung to the settlers. Their aspirations were blighted by bad judgment, poor timing, inclement weather or hostile Indians. Alexander Barclay's summer of farming on the Hardscrabble was a catalogue of catastrophes. William Tharp's best year as an Indian trader ended in his murder by Indians just as he was about to reach the safety of civilization with his prize. Lancaster Lupton, a perennial hard-luck case, idly traced in his account book a text that for sheer irony served him and his companions very nicely: "There is a tide in the affairs of men which, taken at the flood, leads on to fortune." In the Arkansas Valley a flood inevitably led to disaster, not fortune.

Engrossed at first in furious pursuit of the main chance, these speculators slowed down as the years went by, stopping to sniff the sweet air and scan the glorious mountains around them. At some point in each of their lives they were astonished to realize how well they ate, how comfortably they slept (and seldom alone!), how sturdy and spartan were their lives and what a wild and wicked lot of fun they had. When it came time to go home they hedged and procrastinated and finally rejected their former lives altogether, settling down in the West—in the "great American desert"—and becoming its pioneers.

Appendix A
First Men at Pueblo

IN 1904 JUANA MARÍA SUASO SIMPSON, the last person then alive known to have lived at the Pueblo in the first year of its existence, said there were five builders and owners of the Pueblo: Robert Fisher, Mathew Kinkead, George Simpson, Francis (Edmond) Conn and Joseph Mantz or Mantas. She remembered three other men at the fort the first year who had no proprietary interest in it: Bill Tharp, Charles Town and Bill New.[1] The only man on the list known to have had other employment that year was Bill Tharp, who was in St. Louis with Bent, St. Vrain & Company wagons in the summer of 1842 and who drew a full year's salary from the company at St. Louis in July, 1843.[2]

George Simpson stated under oath in 1883 that he had founded the post: "I wintered in 1841 at Bent's fort and St. Vrains on the Arkansas . . . [then went] to where Pueblo is now, and established trading posts there in 1842."[3] John Brown wrote, "Up this river [Arkansas] we made our way, till a point was reached near where the old Fort Pueblo was first erected, which, in after years, I helped to build."[4] Dick Wootton, interviewed by Frank Hall about 1875, said, "The first settlement and cultivation of the soil by civilized beings took place in the spring of 1842 . . . within the present limits of the city of Pueblo . . . The first actual settlers who cultivated the soil within the present limits of Colorado were a party of men named Fisher, Sloan, Spaulding, Kinkaid, Beckwith, Slate and Simpson, first names wholly forgotten."[5] In another volume of this same work of Frank Hall, the author writes, "The Pueblo fort . . . is said to have been built about the year 1842 by George Simpson and two associates named Barclay and Doyle," an error repeated by many historians (including the present writer).[6] William Kroenig, close associate of the early men of Pueblo and husband of Rafaela Kinkead, in describing a journey made in 1853, said, "Next day we camped close to Pueblo, a fort made of adobes and built I believe by Mr. G.

Simpson."[7] Owen J. Goldrick, tutor for Joseph Doyle's children in 1858, wrote, "Here lies before us the ruins of the old *pueblo* . . . where Spaulding, Fischer, Doyle, Murray, Wootton and other pioneers . . . held their trading posts in '42 and '48 . . . ."[8] Pedro Sandoval told F. W. Cragin that, "at 'el Pueblo' . . . the first men were (as he understood) Bill Garey, Bill Tharp . . . ." Sandoval's statement was interrupted at this point and we lose the other "first men."[9] Tom Autobees told Cragin, "Some of those who owned an interest in it were: Sim Turley, Bill Garey (Wm. Guerrier), Jo Richard." Tom got this from his father, Charles Autobees, who delivered Turley's whiskey to the fort and naturally remembered only the whiskey traders.[10] Col. Henry Inman, that source of all misinformation, wrote, "The old Pueblo fort, as nearly as can be determined now, was built as early as 1840, or not later than 1842 . . . by George Simpson and his associates, Barclay and Doyle. Beckwourth claims to have been the original projector of the fort . . . in which I am inclined to believe he is correct."[11]

Joseph Mantz or Mantas takes leave of our narrative at this point, but he deserves such biography as fugitive references can afford him. A Joseph Monsa, Monse or Manso was with William Ashley in 1823;[12] with the American Fur Company at Fort Clark in 1835, and at Fontenelle's Council Bluffs post in 1836-37.[13] A "Monta" was charged with the murder of a Ree chief near Council Bluffs in June, 1837.[14] Joseph Martz ("Joe Mort") survived an attack on Fraeb's trappers by Sioux and Cheyenne on August 21, 1841 at Battle Creek, Wyoming.[15] José Manta was father of a natural son born to María de Jesús Romero at Taos in October, 1845, but even before the child was born, Manta had gone to Fort Pierre on the Missouri, where he was still, or again, working in December, 1847.[16]

Appendix B
Location of the Pueblo
and Mormon Town

NO EARLY MAPS OR PLATS of the city of Pueblo show the old fort, according to Edward F. Rizer who spent half a century in the Pueblo County Assessor's office in charge of maps. The best information is from various pioneers who lived in Pueblo when the ruins of the fort were still visible, and who were still living there years later when not a trace of the fort remained. Fortunately there were several such old–timers.

In 1907 and 1908 F. W. Cragin interviewed three old men— G. W. Bilby, James Edward Smith and John A. Thatcher—who had all lived in Pueblo since the early sixties and recalled the site of the post. Bilby was the first schoolteacher in the infant city. In 1863 and for a few years afterwards he lived in a three–room adobe house about sixty feet north of the ruins of the fort. He told Cragin that in 1863 the fort was merely an outline of an adobe wall with ruins of rooms attached to the walls on the east and north side and the opening for the gate on the east.[1]

James Edward Smith, also a Pueblo pioneer of 1863, remembered the location of the fort in relationship to the later Fariss Hotel (1882). Under Smith's direction Cragin drew a sketch map of the site of the fort, part of whose east wall was covered by the west or back wall of the hotel. Cragin included on his map Bilby's house, a slough of the river, two other houses and a well. He also added a little rectangle in front of the hotel marked "graves of five Mexicans."[2] John Thatcher recalled the location of the gravel ford at the top of the river's meander, a few feet west of the present intersection of Santa Fe Avenue and First Street.[3]

Dr. Cragin was not the only researcher to turn up "experts" on the location of the old fort. Wilbur F. Stone, an early lawyer of Pueblo, wrote in 1880 that "the quadrangular foundation of the adobe walls can still be traced near where two small adobe houses now stand on the west side of Union Avenue," which may explain the two adobe houses located on Cragin's sketch map.[4]

In later years Judge Stone interviewed Henry A. Dubbs who located the fort as follows:

"The Pueblo" was built on the north bank of the Arkansas River about 150 feet west of what is now Union Avenue and about 200 feet south of the Santa Fe Railroad Company's depot. The site can best be described for permanent record, as on the north half of Block 43 and the adjacent portion of Front (now First) street, according to the plan of Pueblo, and the Fosdick map of 1869. It did not adjoin the west line of what is now Union Avenue, as the Arkansas River in 1869, and theretofore, flowed at that place. The monument erected adjacent to the City Hall at Pueblo, commemorating the Pueblo, is not on the site itself.[5]

Elliott Coues, editor of Zebulon Pike's Journal, found another old-timer in C. H. Small, head of the Pueblo Board of Trade, "whose knowledge of real estate in that city is probably unsurpassed." Small's letter to Coues, dated Feburary 23, 1894, said:

A fort was once built on the south side of the Arkansas just north of the Farris [sic] Hotel—between this hotel and the Santa Fe R.R. tracks at Union Avenue. The channel of the river changed in the seventies to a more southerly and straighter course. The occupants of the fort were all massacred by Indians on one occasion. In laying a pipe on Union Avenue two years ago, one or more skeletons were exhumed, doubtless the remains of those massacred. This was at the depth of ten feet below the present level of the street, and directly in front of the Farris Hotel; the logs of the old fort were come upon at the same time. The grade of the street has been raised five feet, about 1885.[6]

Glenn R. Scott of the U.S. Geological Survey in Denver questioned yet another old-timer, Arthur J. McQuaid, employed as guide at Walters' Brewery, who said that the Pueblo was "at Union, Victoria and Grand Avenue up to the Santa Fe tracks," a block or so southwest of Cragin's location. Business people in this part of Pueblo believe that the site is centered beneath a garage in this area.[7]

Many of these locations for the fort mention its relationship to the Fariss Hotel, which, for a wonder, is still standing and identifiable, for the name of it is still faintly visible on the south wall of the building. Built in 1882, as its old pediment proclaims, it is now a derelict, three–story brick building occupying lots 8 and 9 of Block

58, Hobson's subdivision in downtown Pueblo. Behind it is an alley, and behind that is a wedge–shaped lot bounded on the north by First Street. Two hundred feet to the north of the old hotel are the Santa Fe railway tracks and the former location of the Santa Fe depot. The site of the Pueblo was, if Cragin's informants were correct, the alley and vacant lot behind the old hotel, and perhaps a small part of First Street, although without knowing the measurements of the fort itself or its shape or conformation to the points of the compass, any specific placement would be guesswork.

Cragin's sketch map of the river indicates a meander or loop flowing north along present Union Avenue almost to Second Street, then east to a point halfway between Main and Santa Fe Avenue before turning south to flow along the base of Tenderfoot Hill. A map traced by Cragin in the U.S. Land Office at Pueblo showed that the top of the meander in 1872 was at Santa Fe Avenue. There the river was crossed by a footbridge, located by John A. Thatcher at about a block below or east of the old ford. [8]

A drawing entitled "Bird's Eye View of Pueblo, and South and East Pueblo" in *Crofutt's Grip-Sack Guide of Colorado* (1881) shows the top of the meander at Santa Fe Avenue where the river was crossed by a bridge. It also shows the Atchison, Topeka and Santa Fe tracks and depot. By 1881 the river had made a channel to the south of the meander beside which the Pueblo was located. [9]

By the beginning of the twentieth century the loop or meander was gone, and the river flowed in a straight channel about 750 feet southwest of the fort site, where the present Missouri Pacific tracks are laid, just south of City Hall. [10] In 1921 the Arkansas flooded, covering the land on which the Pueblo once stood to a depth of five feet or more. After the flood the Arkansas was forced into a channel about four blocks farther south, where it flows today between concrete floodways, half a mile from the site of the old post. The legal description of the site of the fort as herein located would be SE ¼ of the NE ¼ of Sec. 36, Twp. 20 W. of Range 65 W.

There is much less certainty about the location of Mormon Town. Two maps drawn by F. W. Cragin show a location for it, but neither cites a source on the map itself. In Cragin's notes he tells of going to the office of Pueblo City Engineer William Peach on July 25, 1908, where he saw a sketch made by Peach with the help of James Edward Smith showing the site of the old Pueblo and that of the Mormon settlement. Peach did not allow Cragin to copy the blueprint, but Cragin made a tracing from a map of Pueblo in Peach's office. On this map Cragin superimposed a string of houses labelled "Mormons" on the south side of the Arkansas, north of the railroad tracks, half a mile west of the Pueblo. Since the time Cragin visited Peach's office in 1908, the Arkansas has changed its course again. Now the river is south of the railroad tracks and the most westerly house of the Mormons, as indicated on Peach's blueprint, would be located north of both river and tracks, about 700 feet southeast of the Fourth Street bridge or, approaching from the other direction, about 1,200 feet northwest of the present Union Railway Station.[11]

A township map in the Cragin Collection shows the Mormon houses of 1846–47 in Section 36 just northwest of Union Avenue, which would locate them approximately at the site of Union Station. Unfortunately Cragin does not say why he or William Peach thought the Mormon houses might have been in that location.[12]

A bronze tablet erected a hundred yards east of the junction of Santa Fe Avenue and U.S. 50, half a mile south and a little east of the old Pueblo, marks the site of Mormon Town. There seems to be more evidence for this location than for its location west of the Pueblo.[13] Somewhere in the great rockbound archive of the Church of the Latter Day Saints at Salt Lake there must be a description of the location of Mormon Town—may it soon come to light!

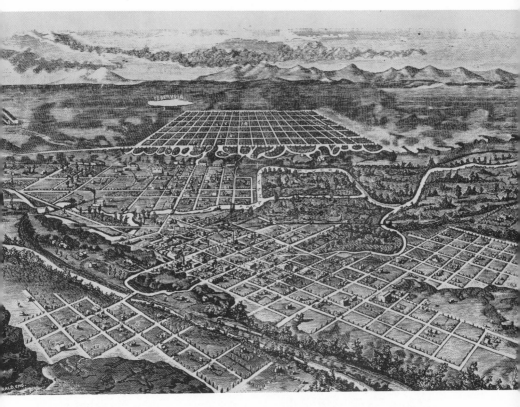

"Bird's Eye View of Pueblo, and South and East Pueblo." From *Crofutt's Grip-Sack Guide of Colorado* (Omaha, 1881). The old meander inside which Pike put his block house, and outside which George Simpson put his trading post, is left of center in this picture, just about to be cut off by a new and straighter river channel. Union Avenue is to the right of the meander. The Arkansas River now runs far to the south of the course shown here. In fact, the Union Depot (number 5 on this map) is now on the north bank of the river. Courtesy of Denver Public Library Western Collection.

Appendix C
Sources for an Account
of the Pueblo Massacre

AS IN ACCOUNTS of any historical event, the facts about the Pueblo
massacre have undergone various changes at the hands of various
writers over the years, although there is no real difference of opinion
as to the importance of the event, which was that it marked the end
of the early Arkansas Valley settlements which otherwise might have
been the first permanent settlements in the state of Colorado.

The account of the massacre presented here is based on memories
of old-timers. As any historian knows, old-timers are almost always a
poor source, especially if their memories have been tampered with
by newspaper reporters, lawyers, historians or other corrupters of
the truth. But the eyewitnesses to the Pueblo massacre seem to have
retained their pristine certainty about what they saw, what they did.
The herder Felipe Cisneros remembers well how he climbed to the
top of the loma, ran down again and hid in the brush by the river as
old José Barela started down the Arkansas to warn the other settlements. Cisneros also remembers where the bodies were and what
they looked like—how could he forget? Elena Baca, then eight or
nine years old, never forgot Blanco's visit to her father's house on
Marcelino's best white mare nor the whipping she got for her
recklessness. Felix Sandoval saw poor Chepita Miera die, and the
memory of it must have haunted him all his life.

The testimony of these old-timers hangs together remarkably
well. There are discrepancies, to be sure. Felipe Cisneros and Elena
Baca differ as to whether Juan Rafael Medina died immediately after
drinking the cold water or later that afternoon at Baca's. Others
cannot decide whether Rumaldo Córdova was shot inside or outside
the fort; whether Benito Sandoval was wounded with a lance or a
bullet; whether Chepita Miera was young and beautiful or fat and
forty; whether Guadalupe Vigil was buried at *el puertocito* where he
fell, or with Juan Rafael Medina in the river bottom near Baca's, or
on Brewery Hill as the loma behind Baca's is called today. Minor

matters, all. The story that emerges from details long remembered by those who lived through this memorable event has about it the simplicity—the horror—of truth.

Contemporary official reports were meager. The adjutant at Santa Fe wrote that "on the 25th of December last, a body of Indians, known to be Utahs and Jicarilla Apaches, numbering one hundred or more, made an attack on the settlements on the Arkansas river and killed at the Pueblo about 18 miles above the mouth of the Huerfano, 14 men, wounded two, carried off one woman and two children, all mexicans—and some two hundred head of stock."[1] On this information from Jonathan Atwood subsequent military reports were based.

Another contemporary account was that of DeWitt Peters, surgeon at Fort Massachusetts who entertained Atwood, Jurnegan and Baca in his quarters as they passed the fort on their way to report the massacre. A few days later Peters wrote his sister what they told him: a band of 150 Utes murdered seventeen Mexicans and stole about $6,000 worth of stock. The Indians had come to the fort professing friendship and asking for something to eat. The Mexicans took them into the fort and were cooking for them when the Indians seized the Mexicans' guns and began to slaughter them. The Indians also drove off all the cattle and took a woman and two boys prisoners.[2]

As the years passed, accounts of the massacre changed. The story tellers dropped extraneous, unpleasant or incomprehensible details—the flatiron in Trujeque's hand, the fiendish force of the lances that pierced Pacheco's body—and stressed or added other details that gave the story form, symmetry and meaning. George Simpson made a major change in the story with the addition of a shooting match, based perhaps on Rumaldo's account given in wordless gestures as he lay dying at Charles Autobees' *placita* on the Huerfano. Simpson eliminated the ghastly details remembered by eyewitnesses and pared the account down to a storylike structure.

On Christmas Day, 1854, Simpson wrote, seventeen persons at Fort Pueblo, including a woman and two boys, were celebrating a feast when they noticed an Indian watching them from the other side of the river. The Indian made friendly signs and was invited into the fort by Sandoval, who recognized him as Blanco, his friend. Blanco said he had come with a few braves to hunt buffalo and wondered if the Cheyennes and Arapahos were far enough away for him to bring his village down from the mountains. After being entertained in the fort for a while Blanco's eye was drawn to some guns in the corner, and he suggested a shooting match before he returned to his camp nearby. As the match progressed, more Indians appeared, shaking hands and taking part in the contest, until Blanco suggested they stop and have a friendly smoke. All went inside, and the Mexicans left their guns in a corner of the small room as the Utes crowded in. On signal, every Mexican was shot down or tomahawked, some killed with their own guns. The woman and boys were captured and the woman killed "because she grieved too much and would not be comforted," as the two captured boys said when they were freed. After the massacre the Utes proceeded to Baca's but were foiled in their murderous designs by José Barela, who told Blanco he would shoot him if the Utes made a step forward. Subsequently the Utes left the people at Baca's alone and were content to steal all the horses grazing on nearby hills.[3]

George Simpson died shortly after publishing his story of the massacre with its strong echoes of the words of Cragin's informants. (Or were their words echoes of Simpson's article?) The story passed into his family where it underwent further changes with the introduction of liquor, becoming as impersonal and moral as a traditional ballad. Now the Indians were invited into the fort after the shooting match not just for a friendly smoke but to share the Christmas feast. As the men of the fort became drunk, the Indians controlled their thirst and at a signal slaughtered their besotted hosts. Such was the story told to F. W. Cragin in 1904 by Mrs. Simpson and her son-in-law Jacob Beard, and so Cragin wrote it up as Chapter 27 of his projected "Rocky Mountain Library." Cragin altered it further, adding dramatic conflict by characterizing Blanco as a charming old politician, Sandoval as a suave and generous host, and the denouement as the inevitable result of the interaction of the characters of these two men and, of course, too bibulous a Christmas. In 1907 and 1908, long after Cragin had completed Chapter 27, he interviewed the eyewitnesses. He never worked the new material into his chapter for the "Rocky Mountain Library," a project of such scope that it was soon after abandoned.[4]

Another version of the massacre that was told simply at first and embellished later in interesting ways, was that of Charles Autobees. He also knew Rumaldo Córdova's story and he had the advantage over George Simpson of having been a member of the burial party and at the site of the massacre a few hours after it happened. Autobees' version, published in a Pueblo newspaper in 1872, included no shooting match, no feast and no drunkenness. As Autobees told it, the Indians first showed up at Marcelino Baca's house, but the quick eye of one old man at the house saw a horse of Baca's among the Indians' horses and knew they meant mischief. The house was closed up at once and the Indians rode off towards the fort. At Pueblo the Indians' pretensions of friendship were accepted as genuine and they were admitted to the fort without hesitation. Each Indian seized the hand of a white man in simulated friendship just before delivering the fatal shot or blow. The inmates of the fort were killed without warning or resistance.[5]

Like Charles Autobees himself, his story was plain and honest. But when it was copied by R. M. Stevenson for his history of Pueblo County in the *History of the Arkansas Valley, Colorado* (1881), it too became a temperance lecture. After the Indians were admitted to the fort, they and their hosts imbibed "a liberal supply of the liquid that both cheers and inebriates." The "natural result" was that the Indians attacked the whites and killed them all. Stevenson thus absolves the Utes from any premeditation of massacre, and seems to blame it all on liquor. Frank Hall, copying Stevenson's story, has the entire company "furiously drunk."[6]

How very far we have come from the simple description of death by violence told by the eyewitnesses! We must agree with the later stories that there was some drunkenness—could the all-night card party have kept afloat without booze? The actions of José Ignacio Valencia stumbling about in the cold winter dawn looking for his knife, and of Rumaldo fatuously declaring Blanco to be his friend, were probably not those of sober men. But if they were drunk, they became so before the Indians arrived, and their drunkenness was not the pivot of the massacre. Drunk or sober they were doomed. The shooting match and feast afterwards developed from heaven-knows-what intimations and were seized upon by writers to make the massacre a story, a fiction in which to submerge the grimness, the pointlessness of the disaster.

The massacre is usually said to have happened on Christmas Day. But Christmas Day for the Mexicans was December 24. Almost all the eyewitnesses make this plain. Pedro Sandoval remembered that it was December 23, the day before the massacre, that he was sent down the Arkansas with wagons. His sister, Cecilia Adamson, says, "Pedro Sandoval on Dec. 23, 1854, started from Ft. Pueblo to Huerfano (village) and got there on evng 24th & found that the news of the massacre had already reached there . . . ." Cragin's notes of an interview with Tom Autobees reads, "Massacre at Fort el Pueblo, 24th December (Mexican Christmas)." Jesús Pando of the burial party said, "The massacre at el Pueblo was December 24." Elena Baca Autobees said, "When the massacre occurred, morning of the 24th . . . ."[7]

If Cragin's informants seemed certain that the massacre occurred on the morning of the 24th, others appeared equally positive that the date was December 25, the American Christmas Day. After an interview with J. W. Atwood on January 11, 1855, Adjutant General Nichols wrote down the date of the massacre as "25th of December last," and other official reports copied his date. On January 13, 1855 Marcelino Baca appeared before the Governor and Superintendent of Indian Affairs, David Meriwether, and swore to a statement about his losses occurring "on the twenty-fifth day of December A.D. 1854."[8]

A determination of the correct date becomes a nice exercise in the evaluation of sources. Which is likely to be more accurate, accounts of eyewitnesses fifty years after the event, or contemporary accounts of non-participants? Did F. W. Cragin, fascinated to find a single witness to the fact that the massacre occurred on December 24 instead of the established date of December 25, then interpolate this date into notes of interviews with other informants? Did Adjutant Nichols and Governor Meriwether hear Atwood and Baca say "Christmas" and automatically and erroneously write down "December 25"?

Notes

CHAPTER 1

1. John Bidwell, *Echoes of the Past about California*, ed. M. M. Quaife (Chicago, 1928), 18–23; H. E. Tobie, "From the Missouri to the Columbia, 1841," *Oregon Historical Quarterly*, Vol. XXXVIII (1937), 135–49.

2. Francis W. Cragin's notes of an interview with Jacob Beard, El Paso, Texas, Oct. 30, 1904, Cragin Coll.; *Narrative of Nicholas "Cheyenne" Dawson*, ed. C. L. Camp (San Francisco, 1933); Tobie, "From the Missouri to the Columbia, 1841," *Oregon Historical Quarterly*, Vol. XXXVIII (1937), 135–49; "Letter from Senex [George Simpson]," *Trinidad* (Colo.) *Daily News*, Jan. 20, 1882, p. 1, c. 3.

3. Senex [George Simpson], "Pah-U-Tah," *Trinidad* (Colo.) *Daily News*, May 14, 1882, p. 2, c. 1–3.

4. Bidwell, *Echoes of the Past*, 38; *A Journey to California, 1841: The first emigrant party to California by wagon train: The Journal of John Bidwell* (Berkeley, 1964), 16.

5. Senex [George Simpson], "Pah-U-Tah," *Trinidad* (Colo.) *Daily News*, May 14, 1882; Alpheus H. Favour, *Old Bill Williams, Mountain Man* (Norman, 1962).

6. H. L. Conard, *"Unce Dick" Wootton*, 202; Matthew C. Field, *Prairie and Mountain Sketches* (Norman, 1957), 190–93; "Diary of Edward Kern, 1845–6, with Fremont," *Life*, Vol. XLVI (April 6, 1959), 96–97. An unpaid note, dated Fort William, March 13, 1843, for $300 and four beaver traps, was among William Bent's papers and is reproduced in Favour's *Old Bill Williams*, p. 149; another unpaid draft of Williams' is mentioned in Simeon Turley's letters of April 18, 1841 and August 3, 1841, in Janet Lecompte and Lester F. Turley, "The Turleys from Boonslick," *Missouri Historical Society Bulletin*, Vol. XXVII (1972), 192–95. See also Favour, *Old Bill Williams*, 162, 164–65, and George Frederick Ruxton, *Life in the Far West*, 123–37, 188.

7. Janet Lecompte, "Levin Mitchell," *The Mountain Men and the Fur Trade of the Far West*, ed. LeRoy R. Hafen, Vol. V (Glendale, 1968); Harvey L. Carter, "Louis Ambroise," *Mountain Men*, Vol. VIII (1971); Harvey L. Carter, "Mark Head," *Mountain Men*, Vol. I (1965). For Charley Raymond, see Francis Parkman, *The Oregon Trail*, 116, 166, 305; and U. S. Census, 1860, San Miguel County, N. M. Others Simpson met at Fort Laramie were Cutrock Brown, Jimmy Daugherty (Leonard K. Smith, "On the Old Frontier, Fragments of Forgotten History," MS loaned to me by author), Rocheile Pierre and Kit Carson (Leonard K. Smith, "George Simpson, Pioneer and Poet," *The Denver Times*, Nov. 21, 1903, magazine section, p. 4–5). Smith had access to Simpson's notebooks, now missing.

8. This picture of the trapper in decline is drawn from many sources, among them Senex, "Pah-U-Tah"; Lewis H. Garrard, *Wah-to-yah and the Taos Trail*, 190, 306–307; George F. Ruxton, *Adventures in Mexico and the Rocky Mountains*, 233; Ruxton, *Life in the Far West*, 106–107; Rufus Sage, *Scenes in the Rocky Mountains*, 17–19.

9. Diary of Manuel Alvarez, 1841, Alvarez Papers; LeRoy R. Hafen and Ann W. Hafen, *Old Spanish Trail* (Glendale, 1954), 236–39; Sage, *Scenes in the Rocky Mountains*, 27; "Diary of Edward Kern," *Life*.

10. Senex, "Pah-U-Tah."

11. Harvey L. Carter and Janet S. Lecompte, "George Semmes Simpson," *Mountain Men*, Vol. III (1966), 285. For George's annual remittance, see E. B. Sopris, "Colorado Before and During the Civil War," MS in the Colorado Historical Society Library, Denver, and S. W. DeBusk on George Simpson, DeBusk Memorial, 295–96, in the same library.

12. Senex, "Pah-U-Tah."

13. For his drinking, see Cragin's notes of an interview with Jesse Nelson, Smith's Canyon Ranch, Colo., July 9, 1908, Cragin Coll.; for his sketches, see Senex, "Pah-U-Tah," *Trinidad* (Colo.) *Daily News* for 1882, April 16, 26, May 14, 21, 30, June 18, July 15, Oct. 5, and several updated clippings in Dawson Scrapbooks, I, 409, 411, and X, 298. For evidence that he did not go trapping, see Testimony of George S. Simpson, Trinidad, Colo., Oct. 29, 1883, *Transcript of Record, U.S. v. Maxwell Land-Grant Co.*, et al, U. S. Supreme Court, Oct. term, 1886, no. 974, p. 142; Cragin's notes of an interview with Jacob Beard (Simpson's son-in-law), El Paso, Texas, Oct. 30, 1904, Cragin Coll.; Leonard K. Smith, "On the Old Frontier . . ."; and Simpson's obituary in the *New York Sunday World*, June 17, 1888, p. 22, c. 3–4.

14. Letter of Charles Bent to Manuel Alvarez, Fort William, April 30, 1841, Alvarez Papers; LeRoy R. Hafen, "Fort St. Vrain," *Colorado Magazine*, Vol. XXIX (1952); Hafen, "Fort Jackson and the Early Fur Trade on the South Platte," V (1928); Hafen, "Fort Vasquez," *Colorado Magazine*, XLI (1964).

15. Leonard K. Smith, "On the Old Frontier . . ."; Harvey L. Carter, "Jimmy Daugherty," *Mountain Men*, I (1965).

16. Robert Newell, "Memorandum," University of Oregon Library, Eugene; P. A. Sarpy to H. Fraeb, Fort John, Feb. 18, 1838, Chouteau Coll.; invoice of goods sent by James C. Robertson from Fort Jackson to Arkansas River, April 22, 1838, Chouteau Coll.; Sidney Smith Diary, *To the Rockies and Oregon, 1839–1842*, ed. LeRoy R. Hafen and Ann W. Hafen (Glendale, 1955), 72; E. Willard Smith Journal, *loc. cit.*, 165; John Brown, *Mediumistic Experiences of John Brown, the Medium of the Rockies*, 23, 34; F. W. Cragin's notes of an interview with Tom Autobees, Avondale, Colo., Nov. 9, 1907, Cragin Coll. Fleeting references to these posts are found in Alexander Barclay's diary, Barclay Papers (microfilm copy in the Colorado State Archives, Denver).

17. Janet Lecompte, "Gantt's Fort and Bent's Picket Post," *Colorado Magazine*, Vol. XLI (1964).

18. In December, 1832, Ceran St. Vrain rented mules at Taos for twelve days for the purpose of taking cargo to the north to be used in the building of a fort. José María Martínez, Alcalde of Taos, to Gov. Santiago Abreú, Dec. 24, 1832, Governor's Papers, Mexican Archives of New Mexico, State Records Center and Ar-

chives, Santa Fe; Lecompte, "Gantt's Fort and Bent's Picket Post," *Colorado Magazine*, Vol. XLI (1964).

19. Lecompte, "Gantt's Fort and Bent's Picket Post," *Colorado Magazine*, Vol. XLI (1964).

20. *Ibid.*

CHAPTER 2

1. My description of Bent's Fort and its trade is from many sources, principally the following: J. W. Abert, *Western America in 1846–47: The Original Travel Diary of Lieutenant J. W. Abert who mapped New Mexico for the United States Army*, ed. John Galvin, 17–23; Will Boggs's drawing of Bent's Fort in 1844, Cragin Coll.; George F. Ruxton, *Life in the Far West*, 189–91; "Captain Ford's Journal of an Expedition to the Rocky Mountains," ed. Louis Pelzer, *Mississippi Valley Historical Review*, Vol. XII (1926), No. 4, 566–67; William H. Emory, "Notes of a Military Reconnoissance . . . Made in 1847–7," 30th Cong. 1st Sess, *H. Exec. Doc. 41* (Ser. 517); J. W. Abert, "Journal of Lieutenant J. W. Abert, from Bent's fort to St. Louis, in 1845," 2; Thomas J. Farnham, *Travels in the Great Western Prairies . . .* [1843], Vol. XXVIII in R. G. Thwaites, *Early Western Travels, 1748–1846*, 161–173; *Matt Field on the Santa Fe Trail*, ed. John E. Sunder, 44–46, 73, 144–45, 245; George Bird Grinnell, "Bent's Old Fort and Its Builders," Kansas Historical Society *Collections*, Vol. XV (1923), and the best complete account, David Lavender, *Bent's Fort*.

2. Harold H. Dunham, "Charles Bent," *Mountain Men*, Vol. II (1965); Samuel P. Arnold, "William W. Bent," *Mountain Men*, Vol. IV (1966).

3. Harold H. Dunham, "Ceran St. Vrain," *Mountain Men*, Vol. V (1968).

4. Janet Lecompte, "Bent, St. Vrain & Co. among the Comanche and Kiowa," *Colorado Magazine*, Vol. XLIX (1972); Grinnell, "Bent's Old Fort and Its Builders," Kansas Historical Society *Collections*, Vol. XV (1923).

5. Agreement between H. Picotte acting for Pratte, Chouteau & Co., and Ceran St. Vrain acting for Bent, St. Vrain & Co., St. Louis, July 27, 1838, Chouteau Coll.; Frederick Laboue to P. D. Papin, Platte River, Dec. 15, 1838, Chouteau Coll.; John Rolette, River of Arabas, Jan. 8, 1839, Chouteau Coll.; T. D. Bonner, *Life and Adventures of James P. Beckwourth*, 290–301; Joseph Juette, Mar. 1, 1839, Chouteau Coll.

6. Janet Lecompte, "Bent, St. Vrain & Co. among the Comanche and Kiowa," *Colorado Magazine*, Vol. XLIX (1972).

7. Janet Lecompte, "Charles Autobees," *Colorado Magazine*, Vol. XXXV (1958); Ralph Carr, "The Sangre de Cristo Land Grant," *The Westerners Brand Book*, Denver Posse, 1947 (Denver, 1949); Lawrence R. Murphy, "Beaubien–Miranda Land Grant," *New Mexico Historical Review*, Vol. XLII (1967).

8. Matt Field, *Matt Field on the Santa Fe Trail*, 73, 149–153; F. A. Wislizenus, *A Journey to the Rocky Mountains in the year 1839* (St. Louis, 1912), 141; Farnham, *Travels* in Thwaites, *Early Western Travels*, XXVIII, 173–183.

9. See sources cited in note 1, this chapter.

10. Ruxton, *Life in the Far West*, 189–91; Grinnell, "Bent's Old Fort and Its Builders," Kansas Historical Society *Collections*, Vol. XV (1923).

11. Jacob Beard, Simpson's son–in–law, told F. W. Cragin sixty years later that after Simpson's arrival on the Arkansas, he "asked his father to send him a stock of Indian goods as per invoice that he sent with the request. This his father did and so

he began trading with Indians in a room rented in (Bent's?) trading fort" (Cragin's notes of an interview with Beard, El Paso, Texas, Oct. 30, 1904, Cragin Coll.) The parentheses and question mark are Cragin's, and his supposition is in error. The Bents would hardly have allowed a rival trader to use their fort as a base, nor could Simpson have ordered goods in the fall of 1841 and expected to receive them from St. Louis before the summer of 1842. The fort where Simpson began trading was the Pueblo.

12. Leonard K. Smith, "On the Old Frontier, Fragments of Forgotten History." See note 7, Chapter 1.

13. All these traders except Bill Garey have been sketched in *Mountain Men*. Garey (William LeGuerrier) was the son of Charles and Felicite (Ortes) LeGuerrier of St. Louis (F. L. Billon, *Annals of St. Louis in Its Early Days* [St. Louis, 1886], 443–44). By 1840 he was working for the Bents (Ledger CC, pp. 39, 307, 345, Chouteau Coll.). On August 9, 1845, he was Cheyenne interpreter at a council at Bent's Fort (J. W. Abert, *Through the Country of the Comanche Indians in the Fall of the Year 1845* . . . , 4); lived later at Pueblo; and in the 1850s was the trading partner of Seth E. Ward (see *Mountain Men* for sketch of Ward).

14. Harvey Lewis Carter, *'Dear Old Kit': The Historical Christopher Carson*, 79. Frederick's real name was Justin Grosclaude (Journal History, Church of Jesus Christ of the Latter Day Saints, Church Historian's Office, Salt Lake City, under date of Nov. 24, 1846). Kit says he was hired for a dollar a day, but the records of P. Chouteau & Co. show that he was paid $495.02 on May 19, 1842 at St. Louis for his winter's work (Book CC, p. 359, Chouteau Coll.). See *Montana*, XIX (1969) for a polite but stubborn epistolary argument between Dale Morgan and Harvey Carter as to the date Kit Carson came to Bent's Fort.

15. H. M. Chittenden, *The American Fur Trade of the Far West*, I, 7; David Lavender, *The Fist in the Wilderness* (N.Y., 1964), 412; "Captain Ford's Journal of an Expedition to the Rocky Mountains," ed. Louis Pelzer, *Mississippi Valley Historical Review*, Vol. XII (1926), 566–67. Tabeau, in 1804, denies that the Cheyennes or other buffalo-hunting Indians trapped (Annie Heloise Abel, *Tabeau's Narrative of Loisel's Expedition to the Upper Missouri* [Norman, 1939], 152–53), but J.-B. Truteau said, in 1796, that the Cheyennes trapped and sold their skins to the Sioux for merchandise (A. P. Nasatir, *Before Lewis and Clark* [St. Louis, 1952], II, 379). I have found no evidence that the Cheyennes or Arapahos on the Arkansas trapped or sold beaver to the white man.

16. "Abstract of Licences . . ." for 1834, 1838, 1842, in Letters Received, Office of Indian Affairs, St. Louis Superintendency, National Archives; letter of J. F. A. Sanford, June 1, 1839, to P. Chouteau Jr., Chouteau Coll.

17. Alexander Barclay to George Barclay, Westport, Jackson County, Sept. 1, 1842, Barclay Papers; J. C. Frémont, *Report of the Exploring Expedition to the Rocky Mountains in the Year 1842* . . . , 31.

18. Dorothy B. Dorsey, "The Panic and Depression of 1837–1843 in Missouri," *Missouri Historical Review*, Vol. XXX (1936); Sage, *Scenes in the Rocky Mountains*, 155; J. C. Frémont, *Report of the Exploring Expedition*, 35; Lupton Papers, Colorado State Historical Society; Robert Campbell to William L. Sublette, May 23, 1842, in "Correspondence of Robert Campbell, 1834–1845," Missouri Historical Society, St. Louis, *Glimpses of the Past*, Vol. VIII (1941), 32, 43.

19. William L. Sublette to W. D. Stewart, St. Louis, Sept., 1842, "Correspon-

dence of Robert Campbell, 1834–1845," Missouri Historical Society, St. Louis, *Glimpses of the Past*, Vol. VIII (1941), 43.

CHAPTER 3

1. Alfred Barnaby Thomas, *After Coronado*, 65–66.
2. Edwin James, *Account of an Expedition*, in R. G. Thwaites, *Early Western Travels 1748–1846*, XVI, 3–44; *The Journal of Captain John R. Bell*, in *The Far West and The Rockies Historical Series*, IV, 159–90.
3. James, *Account of an Expedition*, in Thwaites, *Early Western Travels*, XVII, 148; map, Vol. XIV.
4. For this picture of the Arkansas Valley today, I am indebted to ranchers Andrew Marshall and Jon Frost, and to County Agent M. V. Haines; for Arkansas Valley irrigation systems I have used testimony in *Transcript of Record, State of Kansas v. State of Colorado et al*, U. S. Supreme Court, Oct. term, 1905 and Oct. term, 1906. See also M. V. Haines, *Farm and Ranch Guide*, Pueblo County (Fort Collins, 1957); Walter Prescott Webb, *The Great Plains* (Boston, 1931), 28–31; Alvin T. Steinel, *History of Agriculture in Colorado* (Fort Collins, 1926), 109–10; *Pasture and Range Plants* (Phillips Petroleum Co., Bartlesville, Okla., 1963).
5. George E. Hyde, *Life of George Bent: Written from His Letters*, ed. Savoie Lottinville (Norman, 1968), 60; Frank Gilbert Roe, *The North American Buffalo* (Toronto, 1951), 521–50. Spanish visitors to the mouth of the Fountain found few buffalo (Thomas, *After Coronado*, 64–68, 73, 75, 122–26), and Pike remarked that buffalo became less numerous as he approached present Colorado by the Arkansas, but his journal shows that he continued to find some buffalo along the foot of the mountains *(The Journals of Zebulon Montgomery Pike*, ed. Donald Jackson (Norman, 1966), I, 344, 349.
6. Herbert Eugene Bolton, *Coronado, Knight of Pueblos and Plains* (New York, 1942), 291; George P. Hammond and Agapito Rey, *The Rediscovery of New Mexico, 1580–1594* (Albuquerque, 1966), 323–26; Bolton, *Spanish Exploration in the Southwest, 1542–1706*, 200–201.
7. "True account of the Expedition of Oñate Toward the East, 1601," in Bolton, ed., *Spanish Exploration in the Southwest*, 250–67; Thomas, *After Coronado*, 5–39.
8. *Bolton and the Spanish Borderlands*, ed. John Francis Bannon (Norman, 1964), 159–60; Amos Stoddard, *Sketches, Historical and descriptive, of Louisiana* (Philadelphia, 1812), 147.
9. Alfred Barnaby Thomas, *Forgotten Frontiers, 123–29*, and "San Carlos, A Comanche Pueblo on the Arkansas River, 1787," *Colorado Magazine*, Vol. VI (1929).
10. *State Papers and Correspondence Bearing upon the Purchase of the Territory of Louisiana* (Washington, D.C., 1903), 32, 234, 271; Donald Jackson, *The Journals of Zebulon Montgomery Pike*, I, 285–422. For early Santa Fe traders, see Thomas James, *Three Years Among the Indians and Mexicans*, ed. A. P. Nasatir (Philadelphia, 1962), 58–59, 84, 98–99; Frank B. Golley, "James Baird, Early Santa Fe Trader," *Missouri Historical Society Bulletin*, Vol. XV (1959); Herbert E. Bolton, "New Light on Manuel Lisa and the Spanish Fur Trade," *Southwest Historical Quarterly*, Vol. XVII (1913); Janet Lecompte, "Jules DeMun," *Moun-*

tain Men, Vol. VIII (1971); David Meriwether, *My Life in the Mountains and on the Plains*, 78–96. The Florida Convention designated the boundary as a line drawn north from the Red River of Texas at Long. 100° W. to the Arkansas and along the Arkansas to its source in Lat. 42° N., or wherever the source might be (James A. Robertson, *Louisiana under the Rule of Spain, France, and the United States, 1785–1807* [Cleveland, 1911], Vol. II, 164). For the Spanish fort, see Chauncey Thomas, "The Spanish Fort in Colorado, 1819," *Colorado Magazine*, Vol. XIX (1937).

11. "Journal of Two Expeditions from Boone's Lick to Santa Fe, by Capt. Thomas Becknell [William's brother and journalist]," in A. B. Hulburt, *Southwest on the Turquoise Trail: The First Diaries on the Road to Santa Fe* (Denver, 1933), 56–68.

12. Althea Bass, *The Arapaho Way* (New York, 1966), 2; Dale L. Morgan, *The West of William H. Ashley* (Denver, 1964), 103, 191, 316n.

CHAPTER 4

1. F. W. Cragin's notes of an interview with Jacob Beard, El Paso, Texas, Oct. 30, 1904, Cragin Coll.; Taos Matrimonial Records, 1833–1845, p. 187, State Records Center and Archives, Santa Fe. Of his trip to Taos in 1842 Simpson says, "I went down by the Sangre de Cristo route. I only went to Taos and returned" (Testimony, Oct. 29, 1883, Trinidad, Colo., *Transcript of Record, U.S. v. Maxwell Land-Grant Co.* et al.).

2. See Appendix A, "First Men at Pueblo."

3. Unless otherwise indicated, sources for material on Kinkead may be found in Janet Lecompte, "Mathew Kinkead," *Mountain Men*, Vol. II (1965)

4. Juana María Suaso was born Dec. 26, 1827; María de la Cruz, July 1, 1831; José Tomas, Dec. 21, 1833; all legitimate offspring of Manuel and María Teresa (Sandoval) Suaso of San Fernando (Taos). Their grandparents were Miguel and María Josefa (Vialpando) Suaso and Gervasio and Ramona (Barela) Sandoval (Taos Baptismal Records, Books B–47, p. 43; B–48, p. 61; B–49, p. 51). Rufina Suaso is mentioned as Teresita's daughter in the William Blackmore Papers (State Records Center and Archives, Santa Fe), and she turns up on the Arkansas (in the Barclay Diary), but I cannot locate her baptismal record. Tom Autobees said Teresita was peach-pretty, and he did not know her until she was past forty (Cragin's notes of an interview with Tom Autobees, Avondale, Colo., July 29, 1908, Cragin Coll.). Teresita's nephew, Pedro Sandoval, gave her birth date as 1811 (F. W. Cragin's notes of an interview with Pedro Sandoval, Mora River, June 12, 1908, Cragin Coll.).

5. Andreas's baptism is recorded in Taos Baptismal Records, B–49, p. 166b, State Records Center and Archives, Santa Fe; Suaso's land sale and death are in Mora County (N.M.) Records, Book III, 235–36. Rafaela married William Kroenig in 1856, and died in 1858 after the birth of her second child (F. W. Cragin's notes of an interview with Rafaela's daughter Fanny (Mrs. Frank Meredith Jones), East Las Vegas, N.M., June 26, 1908, Cragin Coll.).

6. Letter of Manuel Alvarez to Daniel Webster, Washington, D.C., Feb. 2, 1842, U.S. Diplomatic Despatches, Santa Fe, Vol. I, 26–29, RG 59, National Archives; Archive #1317, Book of Decrees of Gov. Armijo, Aug. 26, 1840—Jan. 18, 1842, Mexican Archives of New Mexico; William Binkley, "New Mexico and the

Texan Santa Fe Expedition," *Southwest Historical Quarterly*, Vol. XXI (1923).

7. Dick Wootton's testimony of 1885: "In 1841 I took a lot of sheep to Kansas City for a man named Kinkaid . . . in 1843 and 1844 I was engaged in catching buffalo calves and raising them in the summer time . . ." (Testimony of Richens L. Wootton, May 20, 1885, Las Vegas, N.M., *Transcript of Record, U.S. vs. Maxwell Land-Grant Co., et al*, U.S. Supreme Court no. 974 (Oct. term, 1886), 688). In Frank Hall, *History of the State of Colorado* (Chicago, 1890), Vol. II, 235, a Wootton interview reveals that Dick purchased "a large flock of sheep" in New Mexico, drove them to Westport, Mo., and traded them for cattle, which he drove to a camp six miles above Pueblo the next winter (1840). A third account, H. L. Conard's *"Uncle Dick" Wootton* (Chicago, 1890), 65–89, says that Dick found his twin calves in 1840, kept them at Bent's Fort until he started buffalo farming at Pueblo with about forty milk cows and forty-four buffalo calves. He kept the calves until they were three, then drove them to Kansas City like cattle, with two or three pairs "broke to work like oxen." Matt Field, who visited Bent's Fort in the summer of 1839, remembered that the domestic cattle grazed peaceably with the pair of calves until it was feeding time, when the cow had to be tied before submitting to the calves' "ungentle fashion of handling the udder" (*Matt Field on the Santa Fe Trail*, ed. John E. Sunder (Norman, 1960), 245). Dick says he caught his calves in 1840; Field saw the calves in 1839. Either they are not the same calves or Dick was, as usual, wrong about the date.

8. Frederick Webb Hodge, George P. Hammond and Agapito Rey, *Fray Alonso de Benavides' Revised Memorial of 1634* (Albuquerque, 1945), 230; Escudero, *Noticias* in H. Bailey Carroll and J. Villasana Haggard, *Three New Mexico Chronicles* (Albuquerque, 1942), 102; W. Bullock, *Sketch of a Journey through the Western States of North America* . . . [1827] ed. R. G. Thwaites, *Early Western Travels 1748–1846*, XIX, 140; Maximilian, Prince of Weid-Neuweid, *Travels in the Interior of North America* [1843] ed. R. G. Thwaites, *Early Western Travels*, XXIV, 129; Frank Gilbert Roe, *The North American Buffalo* (Toronto, 1951), 706–707.

9. The site of Kinkead's ranch on the Arkansas is verified by a reference in Barclay's diary to it (Barclay Diary, July 2, 1846). The adobe ruins of the barn were described by Stephen S. Smith to F. W. Cragin, Pueblo, July 18, 1903 (Cragin Collection). For Goodnight's Rock Creek Ranch see J. Evetts Haley, *Charles Goodnight, Cowman and Plainsman* (Norman, 1949), 260.

10. John Brown, *Mediumistic Experiences of John Brown, the Medium of the Rockies*, 23, 34, 188–89. Brown does not give a date for his winter at Lupton's post, but he describes Jimmy Daugherty's death, which occurred between the time George Simpson saw him at Fort Laramie in June, 1841 (Leonard K. Smith, "On the Old Frontier . . ." MS, loaned to me by the author) and September, 1842 when Rufus Sage reported his death (*Scenes in the Rocky Mountains*, p. 168). During that winter Brown and Jimmy had set off afoot driving two yoke of oxen from Lupton's Arkansas Fort to Fort Lancaster on the South Platte to fetch a wagonload of dried buffalo meat. Rube Herring, bourgeois of Fort Lancaster, excused Brown from returning with Daugherty, who set off for the Arkansas with a Mexican. At Jimmy's Camp, just east of present Colorado Springs, the Mexican murdered Daugherty, stole his blanket and two bolts of manta, and escaped to Taos. Barclay's diary, March 5, 1847, indicates that "Lupton's Houses" were on the Fountain near its mouth.

11. T. D. Bonner, *Life and Adventures of James P. Beckwourth*, 320. George

Simpson says that Beckwourth's mother was a servant in his uncle's household (*Trinidad* (Colo.) *Daily News*, June 18, 1882, p. 3, c. 3–4). By uncle, Simpson probably means Rufus Easton who married Brecia Simpson's sister Mary. Their daughter, Mary Smith Easton, married George C. Sibley and started Lindenwood College (Kate L. Gregg, ed., *The Road To Santa Fe; The Journal and Diaries of George Champlin Sibley* [Albuquerque, 1952], 15, 20).

12. Bonner, *James P. Beckwourth*, 320.

13. *Ibid.*, 320, 328; L. A. Ingersoll, *Ingersoll's century annals of San Bernardino county, 1769–1904* (Los Angeles, 1904), 650. Jim and Louise spent part of the summer on an island in the South Platte with Baptiste Charbonneau and his stranded bull boats (see Chapter 2) where, on July 9, 1842, J. C. Frémont met them and described Louise as "a young Spanish woman from Taos" (Brevet Captain J. C. Fremont, *Report of the Exploring Expedition to the Rocky Mountains*, 31). L. Burr Belden's sketch of John Brown in *Mountain Men*, Vol. VII (1969), 48, says that Luisa Sandoval married John Brown in Taos on May 1, 1845, but there is no record of it in Taos matrimonial records I have seen, nor does Matilda turn up in records of Greenhorn, although she is mentioned as the Brown's eldest daughter after they moved to California. California census records show that Matilda was born in 1844 in "New Mexico," which then included the Arkansas Valley (Los Angeles County, Calif., 1852 census, p. 49).

CHAPTER 5

1. F.W. Cragin's notes of interviews with Vicente Trujillo, Avondale, Colo., Nov. 9, 1907, and with Jacob Beard and Mrs. George Simpson, El Paso, Texas, Oct. 30, 1904, Cragin Coll. See Appendix B, "The Location of Pueblo and Mormon Town."

2. There are dozens of descriptions of building with adobe, none more comprehensive than the treatment in E. Boyd, *Popular Arts of Spanish New Mexico* (Santa Fe, 1974), 2–44.

3. George F. Ruxton, *Adventures in Mexico*, 218; F. W. Cragin's interview with Vicente Trujillo, cited; Francis Parkman, *The Oregon Trail*, 300. Thomas Fitzpatrick described Pueblo's walls as twelve feet high (Report, Bent's Fort, Sept. 18, 1847, 30th Cong., 1st Sess., S. *Exec. Doc. 1* (Ser. 503). For comparison, Fort Platte's walls were twenty feet high, Fort Laramie's fifteen, and Bent's Fort's fourteen (LeRoy R. Hafen and Francis Marion Young, *Fort Laramie and the Pageant of the West, 1834–1890* [Glendale, Calif., 1938], 127; Lieutenant Abert's sketch of Bent's Fort in *Western America in 1846–1847: The Original Travel Diary of Lieutenant J. W. Abert*, 19).

4. Parkman, *The Oregon Trail*, 301; Cragin's interview with Vicente Trujillo, cited.

5. Other "small" forts, perhaps about the size of Pueblo, were Fort St. Vrain (1837), 106 by 128 feet (LeRoy R. Hafen, "Fort St. Vrain," *Colorado Magazine*, Vol. XXIX [1952], 248) and Fort Vasquez (1835), 105 by 123 feet (Hafen, "Fort Vasquez," *Colorado Magazine*, Vol. XLI [1963], 211). Compare with the size of Fort Union on the Missouri, which was 220 by 240 feet (Maria E. Audubon, *Audubon and his Journals*, ed. Elliott Coues [New York, 1900], II, 181), or Bent's Fort, which was 137 by 178 feet (Herbert M. Dick, "The Excavation of Bent's Fort, Otero County, Colorado," *Colorado Magazine*, Vol. XXXIII [1956], 186). B. W. Bilby, who lived near the ruins of the Pueblo in 1863, said it was then an outline of adobe

wall perhaps 60 by 50 feet with rooms attached to walls on the east and north sides (Cragin's notes of an interview with Bilby, Oct. 15, 1907, Pueblo, Colo., Cragin Coll.), which would make the space enclosed only about 30 by 40 feet. At the other extreme is Vicente Trujillo's measurement of seventy yards square, which would make it the largest post in the west. (Cragin's interview with Trujillo, cited). Beckwourth's estimate of 60 yards square is also far too big (T. D. Bonner, *Life and Adventures of James P. Beckwourth*, 320).

6. The picture illustrates George Rex Buckman's article, "An Historical Rocky-Mountain Outpost," *Lippincott's Magazine*, Dec., 1880.

7. Ruxton said there were "half a dozen little rooms" (*Adventures in Mexico*, 218); Thomas Breckenridge, at Pueblo in 1848, remembered "half a dozen adobe houses" (LeRoy R. Hafen and Ann W. Hafen, *Frémont's Fourth Expedition* [Glendale, 1960], 176); Cragin's drawing of Vicente Trujillo recollection of the fort shows a dozen or more rooms (Cragin's interview with Trujillo, cited), as does a diagram drawn to the direction of Josiah Smith, who first saw the fort in 1858 (Cragin's notes of an interview with Smith, Pueblo, July 18, 1903, Cragin Coll.). Trujillo's fort had rooms covering all four sides of the wall except for the gate and corral; Smith's fort had rooms on the north and south sides only (most informants place the corral on the south side). Bilby says rooms were on the north and west sides only, but by the time he saw the fort (1863), most of the rooms had disappeared (Cragin's interview with Bilby, cited).

8. Janet Lecompte, "John Hawkins," *Mountain Men*, Vol. IV (1966); Jacob Beard describes a quarrel in the blacksmith shop at Pueblo during which Bill Williams jumped behind the door and pointed a hatchet at George Simpson, saying playfully, "This fellow never snaps," which ended the quarrel and, more importantly, indicated that the blacksmith shop had a door (Cragin's notes of an interview with Jacob Beard, cited). Many references in Barclay's diary of 1846, 1847, and 1848 show that Pueblo men frequently used the Bent's Fort blacksmith shop.

9. Ruxton, *Adventures in Mexico*, 272; Cragin's interview with Vicente Trujillo, cited.

10. Tom Autobees describes John Richard's store as a picket building (Cragin's notes of an interview with Tom Autobees, Avondale, Colo., July 29, 1908, Cragin Coll.); Ruxton describes the warped doors of the Pueblo and tiny windows of New Mexican houses (*Adventures in Mexico*, 272); Jackson W. Moore, Jr. found glass windows in Bent's Fort (*Bent's Old Fort: An Archeological Study* [Denver, 1973], 14–15) and E. Boyd describes typical doorways and mica windowpanes (*Popular Arts of Spanish New Mexico*, 16, 18, 21).

11. James J. Webb, *Adventures in the Santa Fe Trade, 1844–1847*, 93; Josiah Gregg, *Commerce of the Prairies*, as reprinted in R. G. Thwaites, *Early Western Travels 1748–1846*, Vol. XIX, 335. When Kinkead sold his house in Mora, the deed shows that its plank floors were sold separately, as well as the vigas, which were stored in the back yard of Kinkead's neighbor, Francisco Conn (Mora County [N.M.] Records, Book III, 235–36).

12. *Report of Lieut. J. W. Abert, of his Examination of New Mexico, in the years 1846–47*, 30th Cong., 1st Sess., *Sen. Exec. Doc. 23* (Ser. 506), 10; W. H. H. Davis, *El Gringo: or, New Mexico and her People* (New York, 1857), 177; Gregg, *Commerce of the Prairies*, Vol. XIX, 336; E. Boyd, "Fireplaces and Stoves in Colonial New Mexico," *El Palacio*, Vol. LX (1958), 222.

13. E. Boyd, *Popular Arts of Spanish New Mexico*, 7, 9; Janet Lecompte,

"Charles Autobees," *Colorado Magazine*, Vol. XXXV (1958), No. 1, 63; letter of Nathaniel P. Hill, Aug. 1, 1864, in "Nathaniel P. Hill Inspects Colorado," *Colorado Magazine*, Vol. XXXIV (1957), No. 1, 26.

14. Ruxton, *Adventures in Mexico*, 145; Parkman, *The Oregon Trail*, 301–302; Gregg, *Commerce of the Prairies*, as reprinted in R. G. Thwaites, *Early Western Travels 1748–1846*, Vol. XIX, 337.

15. Ruxton, *Adventures in Mexico*, 145; E. Boyd, *Popular Arts of Spanish New Mexico*, 209–10, 263; Lieutenant E. G. Beckwith's report in *Report of Explorations and Surveys . . . for a Railroad from the Mississippi River to the Pacific Ocean*, Vol. II, 34–35.

16. Parkman, *The Oregon Trail*, 302; George Wilkins Kendall, *Narrative of the Texan Santa Fe Expedition* (New York, 1844), Vol. II, 150–51.

17. Bainbridge Bunting, *Taos Adobes: Spanish Colonial and Territorial Architecture of the Taos Valley* (Santa Fe, New Mexico, 1964), 7.

18. Bent's Fort probably cost far less than the $21,000 or $16,000 William Bent was said to have asked for it in 1848 or 1849 (George Bird Grinnell, "Bent's Old Fort and Its Builders," Kansas Historical Society *Collections*, Vol. XV [1923], 54n). Fort Laramie, the best built of all American Fur Company posts, was said to have cost $10,000 to build in 1841, but it sold to the government in 1849 for $4,000 (Hafen and Young, *Fort Laramie*, 70, 142). Fort Barclay, biggest and most elaborate of all, cost its builders $11,000 in 1848 and sold for a little over $7,000 in 1856 (Alexander Barclay to George Barclay, Barclay's Fort, Dec. 28, 1851, Barclay Papers; Taos Company (N.M.) Records, Book A–1, 116). Congress appropriated $3,000 for each trading post to be built along the Oregon Trail in 1846 (*U.S. Statutes at Large*, Vol. IX, 13). Yet in 1855 the American Fur Company sold its Fort Pierre to the U.S. Army for $36,500 (John C. Ewers, "Folk Art in the Fur Trade," *Prologue*, Vol. IV, No. 2 [Summer, 1972]).

19. The following sources call it "Pueblo": J. C. Frémont, *Report of the Exploring Expedition*, 116, 287; Josiah Gregg's map of 1844 reproduced in Carl I. Wheat, *Mapping the Transmississippi West*, Vol. II (San Francisco, 1958), 181; *Western America in 1846–1847: The Original Travel Diary of Lieutenant J. W. Abert*, 19, 22; Parkman, *The Oregon Trail*, 301; Lewis H. Garrard, *Wah-to-yah and the Taos Trail*, 191; W. A. Nichols, A.A.G., Santa Fe, to Col. T. T. Fauntleroy, Fort Union, Jan. 11, 1855, National Archives, RG 98. For "Pueblo Almagre," see letter of Charles Bent to Manuel Alvarez, March 4, 1846, Alvarez Papers; for "the Arkansas Pueblo," see Garrard, *Wah-to-yah*, 353; for "Pueblo Colorado," see Cragin's notes of an interview with Mrs. Felipe LeDoux, Las Vegas, N.M., Feb. 13, 1908, Cragin Coll.

20. Solomon Sublette was the first to use "Fort Pueblo" in 1844 (letter of Oct. 9, 1844, Sublette Papers, Missouri Historical Society, St. Louis); Rufus Sage's map accompanying his *Scenes in the Rocky Mountains*, first published in 1846, also has "Ft. Pueblo" (LeRoy R. Hafen and Ann W. Hafen, *Rufus B. Sage, His Letters and Papers, 1836–1847* [Glendale, Calif., 1956], Vol. IV of *The Far West and Rockies Historical Series*, following p. 353); Dale L. Morgan, *Overland in 1846*, II, 652; Jacob Robinson, *A Journal of the Santa Fe Expedition under Colonel Doniphan* (Princeton, 1932), 17; letters from the *Leavenworth Times*, Jan. 1, 1859, and the *Kansas City Journal of Commerce*, Sept. 12, 1858, in Leroy R. Hafen, *Colorado Gold Rush: Contemporary Letters and Reports, 1848–1859* (Glendale, 1941), 133, 51, 255–56.

21. Names for the fort indicating private ownership will appear later in this work. "The lower Pueblo" occurs in Theodore Talbot, *Journals of Theodore Talbot 1843 and 1849–52 With the Frémont Expedition of 1843 and with the First Military Company in Oregon Territory, 1849–1852*, 23; "Pueblo de S. Carlos" appears on "Map of the Territory of New Mexico Compiled by Bvt. 2nd Lt. Jno. G. Parke . . ." and on maps copying it; "Napesta" appears in Wilbur F. Stone's article, "Pueblo," (Pueblo) *Colorado Chieftain*, June 17, 1880, p. 1, c. 4 and in R. M. Stevenson, History of Pueblo County," *History of The Arkansas Valley, Colorado* (Chicago, 1881), 765.

CHAPTER 6

1. Sage, *Scenes in the Rocky Mountains*, 172.

2. Janet Lecompte and Lester F. Turley, "The Turleys from Boonslick," Missouri Historical Society *Bulletin*, Vol. XXVIII (1972), No. 3, 194.

3. License dated July 5, 1843, "Abstract of Licenses . . . ," Letter Received, Office of Indian Affairs, St. Louis Superintendency, National Archives, Washington, D. C.

4. George Simpson dated a letter from Pueblo in November, 1844 as "Fort Spaulding A[rkansas] R[iver]" (Barclay Papers), as did Lancaster Lupton a month later (letter of Lupton dated "Fort Spaulding, Dec. 31, 1844," Lupton Papers). Charles Bent referred to "Publo or fort Spalding" in a letter of April 8, 1846 (Alvarez Papers), and Tom Boggs, who first came west in 1844, remembered "Spaulding & Fisher's Fort" (Tom Boggs, "Dictation," MS, Colo. Hist. Soc.). For data on Spaulding, see Chap. 10, note 8.

5. Barclay diary, Nov. 12, 1847, Barclay Papers; "A Scrap of Pueblo History," *Pueblo* (Colo.) *People*, March 30, 1872. The fort was not listed as an asset in either Turley's or Doyle's estates.

6. Examples of communal action at Pueblo will appear in Chapters 9, 16 and 18.

7. Sage, *Scenes in the Rocky Mountains*, 172; George F. Ruxton, *Adventures in Mexico*, 271.

8. Sage, *Scenes in the Rocky Mountains*, 172; Bonner, *Life and Adventures of James P. Beckwourth*, 320–21; Parkman, *The Oregon Trail*, 301; John Brown's Journal in LeRoy R. Hafen and Frank M. Young, "The Mormon Settlement at Pueblo, Colorado, During the Mexican War," *Colorado Magazine*, Vol. IX (1932), No. 4, 125.

9. Alexander Barclay to George Barclay, Arkansas River, December, 1845, Barclay Papers.

10. Barclay diary, July 29, 1846, Barclay Papers; Garrard, *Wah-to-yah and the Taos Trail*, 90, 169–70, 183, 311; Maria R. Audubon, *Audubon and His Journals*, (New York, 1900), II, 106; Ruxton, *Adventures in Mexico*, 208, 264–65; Gregg, *Commerce of the Prairies*, XX, 275; John C. Luttig, *Journal of a Fur-Trading Expedition on the upper Missouri, 1812–1813* (New York, 1964), 62n.

11. Barclay diary, July 23 and Sept. 7, 1846, Feb. 15, Oct. 24 and Dec. 18, 1847; Alexander Barclay to George Barclay, Arkansas River, 1845 (Barclay Papers); Garrard, *Wah-to-yah and the Taos Trail*, 192; Gregg, *Commerce of the Prairies*, XIX, 327; Ruxton, *Adventures in Mexico*, 218, 249.

12. Barclay diary, Sept., 1846, Feb. 20, 1847, Barclay Papers; Sage, *Scenes in the Rocky Mountains*, 173.

13. Thomas J. Farnham, *Travels in the Great Western Prairies* [1843], Vol. XXVIII in R. G. Thwaites, *Early Western Travels, 1748–1846*, 184; Abert, *Western America in 1846–1847: The Original Travel Diary of Lieutenant J. W. Abert*, 19, 21; Ruxton, *Adventures in Mexico*, 239–40.

14. H. L. Conard, *"Uncle Dick" Wootton*, 160–62. On p. 166 of this book, Wootton tells of another less disastrous meeting with a grizzly while he was hunting with Kinkead. Barclay has his grizzly story, too—see his letter of June 26, 1844, to George Barclay, Barclay Papers.

15. Barclay diary, July 2, 1846, Aug. 31, 1846, Barclay Papers; Favour, *Old Bill Williams*, 149; Lupton account book under "Marcelino Baca," Lupton Papers.

16. See account of Frémont's visit to Pueblo in Chapter 14.

17. Barclay diary, July, 1846, Sept. 1, 1846, Feb. 16, Mar. 23, Nov. 2, 1847, and others, Barclay Papers. Neither John Brown's account book (Henry E. Huntington Library, San Marino, Calif.) nor Barclay's diary mention any liquor other than whiskey.

18. For description of fandangos, see *The Personal Narrative of James O. Pattie* [1831] in Vol. XVIII, R. G. Thwaites, *Early Western Travels 1748–1846*, 84; Madame Calderon de la Barca, *Life in Mexico during a residence of two years in that country* (New York, 1946), 120 157–59; *Western America in 1846–1847: The Original Travel Diary of Lieutenant J. W. Abert*, ed. John Galvin, 34–35; "Extracts from the Journal of Lt. Emory," *Niles National Register*, Nov. 7, 1846, p. 159, c. 3; James A. Bennett, *Forts and Forays: The Diary of James A. Bennett*, ed. Clinton E. Brooks and Frank D. Reeve (Albuquerque, 1948), 196–98; Lt. Kribben in *Täglicher Anzeiger des Westens*, Sept. 26, 1846 quoted in George Rutledge Gibson, *Journal of a Soldier Under Kearny and Doniphan, 1846–1847*, ed. Ralph P. Bieber (Glendale, Calif., 1935), 216–17n.

19. See note 18, and also *Matt Field on the Santa Fe Trail*, ed. John E. Sunder, 239.

20. Garrard, *Wah-to-yah*, 129, describing a fandango at Bent's Fort.

21. Ruxton, *Adventures in Mexico*, 173; John Brown's account book.

22. Barclay's diary under dates of April 29, 1846, Sept. 13, 1846, Nov. 18, 1848, Nov. 20, 1848, July 19, 1846, Barclay Papers.

23. Ruxton, *Life in the Rocky Mountains*, 196–98.

24. Alexander Barclay to George Barclay, Arkansas River, December, 1845, Barclay Papers.

CHAPTER 7

1. Senex [George Simpson], "Pah-U-Tah," *Trinidad* (Colo.) *Daily News*, May 18, 1882, p. 2, c. 1–3; May 21, 1882, p. 2, c. 1–2; May 30, 1882, p. 2, c. 1–3.

2. *Ibid.*, *Trinidad* (Colo.) *Daily News*, July 15, 1883, p. 3, c. 2–3.

3. Janet Lecompte, "John Poisal," *Mountain Men*, Vol. VI (1968).

4. Lecompte, "Calvin Briggs," *Mountain Men*, Vol. II (1966); Lecompte, "John J. Burroughs," *Mountain Men*, III (1966); Ann W. Hafen, "Lancaster P. Lupton," *Mountain Men*, II (1966); Lecompte, "Marcelino Baca," *Mountain Men*, III (1966); Lecompte, "Charles Autobees," *Colorado Magazine*, Vol. XXXV (1958), 140; Stan Hoig, *The Western Odyssey of John Simpson Smith* (Glendale, 1974) mentions Watoola, Zarepta and Na-to-mah as Smith's wives (see index) but he gives them no separate entities, and they may all be the same woman as Ann W. Hafen assumes in

her sketch, "John Simpson Smith," *Mountain Men*, V (1968); for Guerrier's wife, F. W. Cragin's notes of an interview with Tom Autobees, Avondale, Colo., Nov. 8, 1907, Cragin Coll.; his three half-Cheyenne children, Edmund, Rose and Julia, were given 640 acres of land at the treaty of the Little Arkansas, Oct. 14, 1865, six years after Guerrier's death (Charles J. Kappler, *Indian Affairs. Laws and Treaties* [Washington, D.C., 1904], Vol. II, p. 889).

5. For Mitchell's wives, see F. W. Cragin's notes of an interview with Pedro Sandoval, Mora River, N. M., June 12, 1908, Cragin Collection; Lecompte, "Maurice LeDuc," *Mountain Men*, VI, 1968; Fitzpatrick's report, Bent's Fort, Sept. 18, 1847, with report of the Comm'r of Ind. Aff., 30th Cong., 1st Sess., S. *Exec. Doc. 1* (Ser. 503), 245; Lecompte, "John Hawkins," *Mountain Men*, IV (1966); Lecompte, "William Tharp," *Mountain Men*, III 1966.

6. Testimony of Calvin Jones, April 9, 1885, Trinidad, Colo., *Transcript of Record, Maxwell Land Grant and Railway Co.* et al. v. *Guadalupe Thompson* et al. Supreme Court, Territory of N. M., July term, 1894, no. 581.

7. Barclay diary, Dec. 4 and 15, 1845; Oct. 22, 1846 (Barclay Papers); Lupton account book, Lupton Papers; John Brown's account book, Henry E. Huntington Library, San Marino, Calif.

8. Cragin's notes of an interview with Tom Autobees, Nov. 8, 1907, and with Mrs. Felipe Ledoux, Las Vegas, N. M., June 17, 1908, Cragin Coll.; Senex [George Simpson], "Colorado—1840," *Trinidad* (Colo.) *Daily News*, Aug. 30, 1881.

9. Cragin's notes of an interview with Jesse Nelson, Smith Canyon Ranch, Colo., July 9, 1908. Gallegos's wife at one time was Cruz Padilla, later Mrs. Geo. Bent. Well known in his native Taos as El Gallegon, his strength was legendary. He once broke through the thick adobe wall of a Taos tavern when drunk. He had been to California and was killed at about the age of fifty by an arrow in the back in the Navajo country (Cragin's notes of interviews with Ignacio Santistevan, Taos, May 15, 1908, and Baptiste Lacroix, Mora, March 10, 1908, Cragin Collection).

10. George Simpson to George Sibley, Arkansas River, Feb. 7, 1844, Sibley Papers, Missouri Historical Society, St. Louis; Alexander Barclay to George Barclay, Arkansas River, 1845, December, Barclay Papers; Ruxton, *Adventures in Mexico*, 274.

11. Letter of Alexander Barclay to George Barclay, Oct. 14, 1838, Barclay Papers; diary of Orville Pratte, summer, 1848, Yale University Library.

12. Barclay Diary, Dec. 8, 1845, Dec. 10, 1847, March 25, 1847, Nov. 6, 1847.

13. Barclay diary, Dec. 22, 1845; testimony of José María Jimines, March 23, 1843, Secretaría de la Defensa Nacional, Dirección de Archivo Militar, Primer Tomo. XI/481.2/1714, Frac. 1.a, Operaciones Militares, Archivo General de la Nación, Mexico. Francis Parkman noted eye disease among Indian women and attributed it to dirt and direct exposure to the sun (*Letters of Francis Parkman*, ed. Wilbur R. Jacobs [Norman, 1960], I, 43).

14. Ruxton, *Adventures in Mexico*, 202; letter of N. P. Hill, Costilla, Colo., July 19, 1864, in "Nathaniel P. Hill Inspects Colorado," *Colorado Magazine*, Vol. XXXIII (1956), No. 4, 272.

15. Cragin's notes of an interview with Mrs. Jesús Chacon (Catarina Ryder), Trinidad, Colo., June 6, 1908, Cragin Coll. Barclay's diary notes the deaths of Wootton's child, a Julia Ives and Garmin's woman, and the murders of Wells's woman, her lover, and Ed Tharp. The diary records the births of two Doyle children (both dead by 1850), one Simpson child and a baby belonging to "Louis"

(Barclay Papers). Other children born on the Arkansas were Mathilda Poisal (U. S. Census, 1860, Denver, Colo. Territory, p. 357); Elena Baca, born 1846 at Hardscrabble (Cragin's notes of an interview with Elena Baca Autobees, Pueblo, Colo, Oct. 31, 1907); John Brown's children, Mathilda (1844), Lola (1846), John (1847) and Joseph (1848) (Los Angeles County, Calif. Census, 1852, p. 49; U.S. Census, 1870, San Bernardino, Calif., #185); Gethro New, born 1838 on the Greenhorn, and Jane New, born 1844 on the Arkansas (U.S. Census, 1850, Taos Co., N.M.); Juliana Jones, born 1844 on the Arkansas and living with the Lucien Maxwells at Cimarron in 1860 (U. S. Census, 1860, N. M.); Baptiste Lacroix (1845?) and his sister Mary (1847?) at Pueblo, children of a French-Canadian hunter who guided an emigrant party to California and was never heard of again. Both Lacroix children were taken by their mother, part-Indian María Salazar, to Embudo for baptism, for at that time there was no priest at Taos (Cragin's interview with Baptiste Lacroix, Taos, March 10, 1908).

16. For Ed Tharp's grave, see Cragin's notes of an interview with Jacob Beard, El Paso, Texas, Oct. 31, 1904; for Rumaldo Córdova's, see Cragin's notes of an interview with Tom Autobees, Avondale, Colo, Nov. 8, 1907; for massacre victims, see Chapter 23; for the possible site of the Mormon graveyard, see Cragin's notes of an interview with Thomas A. Bradford, Pueblo, Colo., Oct. 23, 1907 (Cragin Coll.).

17. Charles Bent letter of 1843, enclosed with a letter to Manuel Alvarez, Taos, March 30, 1845, Alvarez Papers.

18. *St. Louis Weekly Reveille,* May 18, 1846, p. 866, c. 1–2. Alexander Barclay found them unfit even for these chores, too stupid and stubborn to do the simplest task without supervision, yet diligent and clever in stealing, lying and cheating (letter to George Barclay, Barclay's Fort, Feb. 20, 1850, Barclay Papers).

19. Baptismal records of Elfego Jaramillo (Feb. 5, 1837), María Estefana Jaramillo (Aug. 4, 1839), María Teresa Jaramillo (Oct. 26, 1841), María Virginia Jaramillo (Aug. 24, 1845), who died as a child, as did George Jaramillo, born Jan. 9, 1844, died Jan. 21, 1844, who does not appear on the baptismal records (Taos Baptismal Records; Bent Family Bible, Museum of N. M., Santa Fe, courtesy of Dr. Myra Ellen Jenkins). St. Vrain's mistresses were María Dolores de Luna, mother of Vicente, born May 10, 1827; María Ignacia Trujillo, mother of Joseph Felix, born Nov. 1, 1844 (Cragin's notes of an interview with Joseph Felix St. Vrain, Walsenburg, Dec. 9, 1907, Cragin Coll.); and Luisa Branch, mother of Felicité, mentioned in St. Vrain's will, recorded in Mora County, N. M. records, book III, pp. 54–55. George Bent's will is recorded in St. Louis Co., Mo. records, Book R⁴-471. His estate is Probate Court records, St. Louis County, Mo., #2462.

20. In El Paso del Norte in 1822, the census shows 161 married couples and 3,000 single adults; in the same year, Albuquerque had 398 married couples and 1,500 single adults (Lansing Bartlett Bloom, "New Mexico under Mexican Administration," *Old Santa Fe,* Vol. 1, No. 1 (July 1913), 33n; W. H. H. Davis, *El Gringo, or, New Mexico and Her People,* 221–22; Alfred S. Waugh, *Travels in Search of the Elephant: The Wanderings of Alfred S. Waugh, Artist, in Louisiana, Missouri, and Santa Fe, in 1845–1846,* ed. John Francis McDermott (St. Louis, 1951), 121.

21. George Wilkins Kendall, *Narrative of the Texas Santa Fe Expedition* (New York, 1844), I, 321.

22. Ruxton, *Adventures in Mexico,* iv; Sage, *Scenes in the Rocky Mountains,* 175.

23. Obituary of George S. Simpson, *Trinidad* (Colo.) *Daily News*, Sept. 11, 1885; address of S. W. DeBusk, Las Animas Co. pphlt 359/243, Colorado Historical Society; "Frontier Sketches," *Field and Farm*, April 21, 1917, Dawson Scrapbook, VIII, 454, Colorado Historical Society.

24. Cragin's notes of an interview with Albert Tison, Wagon Mound, N. M., March 14, 1908 and with Mrs. Felipe Ledoux, June 17, 1908, Cragin Coll. The 1841 Taos census gives Antonia Luna's age as thirty, her husband as 51-year-old Francisco Turcote, her two daughters as María Ines, aged 12, and Dolores, aged 9 (Mexican Archives of New Mexico, microfilm publication roll 30, frame 402.)

25. For the Wells murder, see Chapter 16; for Nicolasa see Sage, *Scenes in the Rocky Mountains*, 161, Cragin's notes of an interview with Tom Autobees, Nov. 8, 1907, and with Mrs. Felipe Ledoux, June 17, 1908 (Cragin Coll.). David Weber writes me about "a mean character" named José Santos Susome, vagrant of French descent, who killed Rafael López in a fight in 1831. He appears in Fray Angélico Chávez, "New Names in New Mexico, 1820–1850," *El Palacio*, Vol. LXIV, Nos. 11 and 12 (Nov., Dec., 1957), p. 376, as "Supaume." For the Waters-Tharp fight, see Chapter 19.

CHAPTER 8

1. There were lapses in the peace. In the summer of 1842, half-Iroquois trapper Louis Ambroise was killed in South Park by Cheyenne who insisted they had killed him out of compassion after he had been mortally wounded by the Utes; in 1841 Arapahos made threats to traders at Bent's Fort, and in 1844, they drove stock from the post (Sage, *Scenes in the Rocky Mountains*, 162; Frémont, *Report*, 120, 283, 287; Leonard K. Smith, "On the Old Frontier, Fragments of Forgotten History," MS loaned to me by the author; Alexander Barclay to George Barclay, Fort William, March 12, 1841, Barclay Papers.

2. *The Journal of Jacob Fowler*, ed. Elliott Coues, 50–100, in particular pp. 58, 70, 93.

3. Virginia Cole Trenholm, *The Arapahoes, Our People* (Norman, 1970), 3–14.

4. Parkman, *The Oregon Trail*, 304; Barclay diary, April 16 to 19, Sept. 1–10, 1846, Feb. 9, 1847, Barclay Papers.

5. Parkman, *The Oregon Trail*, 301–302.

6. *The Journals of Theodore Talbot, 1843 and 1849–52*, ed. Charles H. Carey, 25–27.

7. For Barclay's trips east, see letters of June 30, 1843, June 26, 1844, June 11, 1845, and his diary from May 9 to Sept. 24, 1847 (Barclay Papers). Barclay and Doyle were partners in the spring of 1845, with Barclay going east for the goods (James J. Webb, *Adventures in the Santa Fe Trade, 1844–1847*, 133). By February, 1846, Doyle and William Tharp were partners (Charles Bent to Manuel Alvarez, undated letter [c. Feb. 4 to Feb. 9, 1846], Alvarez Papers), and in the summer of 1846 Doyle and J. B. Guerin were partners (Abstract of License, Doyle & Guerin, July 2, 1846, Letters Received, Office of Indian Affairs, St. Louis Superintendency, National Archives). In the spring of 1847, Tharp was Dick Wootton's partner, Wootton furnishing ten and twelve mules, Tharp taking Wootton's furs to market (Conard, *"Uncle Dick" Wootton*, 107–8). With characteristic disregard for dates, Dick says this was in 1843, but the circumstances indicate 1847. From summer to fall of 1848, Doyle's partner was William Guerrier (31st Cong., 1st Sess., *Sen. Doc.*

4 [Ser. 553], 212), after which Barclay and Doyle were partners until Barclay's death in 1855.

8. Chouteau Collection, Missouri Historical Society, St. Louis.

9. Sage, *Scenes in the Rocky Mountains*, 172. In 1811, Manuel Lisa's men learned at the Arapaho village where they had come to trade, that every year Spaniards traded there also (Herbert E. Bolton, "New Light on Manuel Lisa and the Spanish Fur Trade," *Southwest Historical Quarterly*, Vol. XVII, No. 1 [1913] 63); Hugh Glenn and Jacob Fowler found a party of Mexican traders on the Arkansas near the mouth of the Fountain in 1822 (*Journal of Jacob Fowler*, 71–2) and Col. Dodge found Mexicans trading whiskey and flour to Indians opposite Bent's Fort in 1835 ("Report of the Expedition of Dragoons . . . "). See also H. Picotte, Fort Pierre, to P. Chouteau Jr. & Co., Fort Pierre Letter Book, Mar. 11, 1846, Chouteau Coll., and Andrew Drips' letters about Taos whiskey traders, quoted in Chapter 9.

10. Sage, *Scenes in the Rocky Mountains*, 163; *Farnham's Travels*, Vol. XXVIII in R. G. Thwaites, *Early Western Travels, 1748–1846*, 182.

11. Sage, *Scenes in the Rocky Mountains*, 163–64. A *fanega* is about 140 pounds, or 1.6 bushels.

12. John Bidwell, *Echoes of the Past about California*, ed Milo M. Quaife (Chicago, 1928), 35; John Bidwell, *A Journey to California. . ." 1841*, (San Francisco, 1937), 19–20.

13. J. C. Frémont, *Report*, 12, 40–41, 116.

14. Matthew C. Field, *Prairie and Mountain Sketches*, ed. Kate L. Gregg and John Francis McDermott (Norman, 1957), 29; J. Bridger (by E. S. Denig) to P. Chouteau Jr. & Co., Fort Union, Dec. 10, 1843, Chouteau Coll. Dale L. Morgan, *The Great Salt Lake* (Indianapolis, 1947), 118–19, says this post for emigrants was the third and final location for Fort Bridger.

15. For early and late examples of Pueblo described as a trappers' rendezvous, see Wilbur F. Stone, "Pueblo," (Pueblo) *Colorado Chieftain*, June 17, 1880, and State Historical Society of Colorado *Newsletter*, Oct., 1963. Careers of most of these trappers have been sketched in LeRoy R. Hafen's ten-volume series, *The Mountain Men and the Fur Trade of the Far West*. Unfortunately, the most frequently cited source for Bill Williams' trapping activities is probably fraudulent. William T. Hamilton's *My Sixty Years on the Plains*, ed. Donald J. Berthrong (Norman, 1960), tells of trapping with Bill Williams between 1842 and 1845 in an account so spattered with errors that its credibility is zero. Hamilton or his ghost writer may perhaps be excused for such blunders as having Cherry Creek on the North Platte River, Fort Laramie on the South Platte, Navajos in skin lodges at a Brown's Hole rendezvous with Utes and Shoshones in 1842, fur companies that never existed, and Mormons camped on the North Platte a year before any came west. But how can any man who really trapped during the lean and hungry 1840's have said, "In those days beaver brought $8 to $16 a hide" ("hide," indeed), or "a great many trappers, such as Carson and Bent, resorted to Las Vegas and Santa Fe. There was a great rivalry among fur buyers at those places"? Neither Carson nor any of the Bents were trappers in the 1840's, nor was Las Vegas then, or ever, a fur market. Needless to say, the name of William T. Hamilton shows up in no fur-trade records of the period except his own book.

16. Ramsay Crooks to Pierre Chouteau, Jr., New York, Feb. 23, 1841 and July 10, 1842, Chouteau Coll.; Book EE, Chouteau Coll., p. 246, values 2,319 pounds of beaver from Bent's Fort at $4.37½ per pound. In 1842 Antoine Robidoux paid

Charles Bent a debt with 650 pounds of beaver worth $2.75 a pound (Bent to Alvarez, Taos, Oct. 11, 1842, Alvarez Papers). The price was probably lower yet when the Bents sent only four packs east in 1844 (George Ehninger to C. M. Lampson, March 11, 1844, *Calendar of the American Fur Company's Papers*, Part II, pp. 1269–70).

17. Barclay to Mary Barclay, Fort George, Dec. 12, 1842 and Jefferson City, Aboard the Steam Boat Mary Tompkins, Missouri River, June 30, 1843, Barclay Papers.

18. P. St. George Cooke met Bent's wagons and "cattle raised at the foot of the Rocky Mountains" which he was taking to a Missouri farm on June 14, 1843 ("A Journal of the Santa Fe Trail," *Mississippi Valley Historical Review*, Vol. XII, No. 1 [1925], 85). Shortage of grass will be treated in Chapter 18.

19. Abert, *Report of Lieutenant J. W. Abert of his Examination of New Mexico . . . 1846–'47*, p. 8; Fort Leche's farming has been described in Chapter 2. Rufus Sage mentions no farming at Pueblo in September, 1842 (*Scenes in the Rocky Mountains*, 172). Farming in the Arkansas Valley predates the coming of the Spaniards by hundreds of years. A village of Indians on the Purgatory around 1300 A.D. planted crops in the flood plains (information from Jenny Anderson who helped excavate the site in the summer of 1967). In historic times, the Apaches at Cuartelejo on the Arkansas did a little farming. The Comanche settlement at San Carlos de los Jupes on the Arkansas, probably at the mouth of the St. Charles, was meant to be supported by farming (Thomas, *After Coronado*, 65–66; Thomas, "San Carlos, a Comanche Pueblo on the Arkansas River, 1787" *Colorado Magazine*, Vol. VI (1929), No. 3.

20. F. W. Cragin's notes of an interview with Vicente Trujillo, Nov. 9, 1907, Cragin Coll.

CHAPTER 9

1. Abstract of license, July 5, 1843, Letters Received, Office of Indian Affairs, St. Louis Superintendency, National Archives.

2. Mitchell to Major R. W. Cummins, Council Bluffs, July 1, 1843, William Clark Papers, Kansas State Historical Society, Topeka, Kan.

3. Janet Lecompte, "Simeon Turley," *Mountain Men*, VII (1969), 304.

4. F. W. Cragin's notes of an interview with Tom Autobees, Avondale, Colo., Nov. 8, 1907, Cragin Collection; for Fisher and Spaulding as Turley's agents, see letter of Fisher to Turley, Fort Spaulding, March 13, 1843, quoted in Chapter 10. On Jan. 28, 1844, Autobees traded Lupton 147 pounds of flour at $12 per *fanega*, a sack of corn ($14) and 16 gals. of whiskey at $4 per gal. in exchange for 2 steers at $10, 5 cows at $12, and 3 calves at $4 (Lupton Papers).

5. Lecompte, "Simeon Turley," *Mountain Men*, VII (1969), 304–308.

6. Henry Dodge, "Report of the Expedition of Dragoons under Colonel Henry Dodge," p. 140.

7. Letter of William Clark, Dec. 3, 1831, William Clark Papers, Vol. IV, pp. 306–307.

8. Account of Sarpy & Fraeb, May 10, 1837, Chouteau Coll., Mo. Hist. Soc.; Bent, St. Vrain & Co. account, 1838, Book Z, p. 433, Chouteau Coll.; John Brown's Account Book, Henry E. Huntington Library, San Marino, Calif.; F. A. Wislizenus, *A Journey to the Rocky Mountains in the year 1839* (St. Louis, 1912), 84–91;

LeRoy R. Hafen, "Fort Jackson and the Early Fur Trade on the South Platte," *Colorado Magazine*, Vol. V (1928), No. 1, 14; Bonner, *Life and Adventures of James P. Beckwourth*, 297, 303–309.

9. F. X. Matthieu, "Refugee, Trapper & Settler," MS, Salem, Oregon, 1878, Bancroft Library, Univ. of Calif., Berkeley; Rufus Sage, *Scenes in the Rocky Mountains*, 82–86; Father Pierre-Jean de Smet, *Life, Letters and Travels . . .* , ed. Chittenden and Richardson (New York, 1905), I, 172–77; D. D. Mitchell to the Commissioner of Indian Affairs, Oct. 25, 1841, Letters Received, Office of Indian Affairs, St. Louis Superintendency, National Archives, and Mitchell to Superintendent of Indian Affairs, Sept. 12, 1842, 27th Cong., 3d Sess., *Sen. Doc. 1* (Ser. 413), 431.

10. "An Act to regulate trade and intercourse with the Indian tribes, and to preserve peace on the frontier," *United States Statutes at Large*, IV, 682–83.

11. *Ibid.*

12. J. J. Astor to Gen. W. H. Ashley, April 2, 1822, quoted by H. M. Chittenden, *The American Fur Trade of the Far West*, I, 26–27; E. E. Rich, *Hudsons' Bay Company, 1670–1870* (New York, 1960), III, 476–481.

13. Letter of D. D. Mitchell, March 16, 1842, Letters Received, Office of Indian Affairs, St. Louis Superintendency; John B. Sarpy to A. Drips, Dec. 31, 1842, Drips Papers; Daniel Miller, Bellevue, Council Bluffs Agency, April 22, April 29, July 2, 1842, William Clark Papers, Vol. VIII, pp. 54–55, 65–66.

14. J. C. Frémont, *Report of the Exploring Expedition . . .* , 39–40.

15. D. D. Mitchell to Commissioner of Indian Affairs, St. Louis, Oct. 25, 1841; P. Chouteau Jr. & Co. to Colin Campbell, St. Louis, Aug. 23, 1841; D. D. Mitchell to Commissioner of Indian Affairs, St. Louis, March 16, 1842; all in Letters Received, Office of Indian Affairs, St. Louis Superintendency.

16. Charles Larpenteur, *Forty Years a Fur Trader on the Upper Missouri*, ed. Elliott Coues (Minneapolis, 1962), 416–17; D. D. Mitchell to Commissioner of Indian Affairs, St. Louis, June 8, 1842, Letters Received, Office of Indian Affairs, St. Louis Superintendency.

17. Jacob Halsey to P. Chouteau Jr. & Co., Fort Pierre, Oct. 10, 1842, Letters Received, Office of Indian Affairs, St. Louis Superintendency.

18. A. Drips to D. D. Mitchell, Fort Pierre, Jan. 2, 1843, William Clark Papers, Vol. VIII, 91–92; D. D. Mitchell to T. Hartley Crawford, Commissioner of Indian Affairs, Washington, D. C., Feb. 27, 1843, with endorsements including that of the Secretary of War, April 7, 1843, Letters Received, Office of Indian Affairs, St. Louis Superintendency.

19. Report of D. D. Mitchell, St. Louis, Sept. 29, 1843, with Report of the Commissioner of Indian Affairs for 1843, 28th Cong., 1st Sess., *Sen. Doc. 1* (Ser. 431), 386–88; H. Picotte to Pierre Chouteau Jr. & Co., Fort Pierre, Jan. 4, 1844, Chouteau Coll.; Joseph V. Hamilton To D. D. Mitchell, Fort John [Laramie], March 7, 1844, Letters Received, Office of Indian Affairs, Upper Missouri Agency; Jos. V. Hamilton to T. H. Harvey, St. Louis, July 5, 1844, William Clark Papers, VIII, 171–72.

20. Drips to Harvey, St. Louis, July 6, 1844, William Clark Papers, VIII, 172–73; H. Picotte to P. Chouteau Jr. & Co., Fort Pierre, Jan. 4, 1844 and Dec. 7, 1845, Chouteau Coll.; P. Chouteau Jr. & Co. to Messrs. T. H. Harvey & T. G. Gantt, St. Louis, Jan. 12, 1849, Letters Received, Office of Indian Affairs, St. Louis Superintendency; Larpenteur, *Forty Years*, 189–95, 208, 229–30; deposition of

Joseph A. Sire, April 13, 1848, District Court of Missouri, Letters Received, Office of Indian Affairs, St. Louis Superintendency; Drips to T. H. Harvey, cited by Chittenden, *The American Fur Trade of the Far West*, I, 372n; Picotte to James Kipp, Fort Pierre, Dec. 18, 1845, Chouteau Coll. For a different view of Chouteau's actions, see Chittenden, *The American Fur Trade*, I, 367–80; Annie H. Abel, *Chardon's Journal at Fort Clark, 1834–1839* (Pierre, S. D. 1932), xli–xliii; John E. Sunder, *The Fur Trade on the Upper Missouri, 1840–1865* (Norman, 1965), 47–51, 69–72, 80–84, *passim*. Drips was removed from office in March, 1846 because of protests from the opposition that he had used Chouteau posts and interpreters on the Upper Missouri (F. Cutting to Superintendent Harvey, Fort George, Sept. 16, 1844, and Drips to Superintendent Harvey, June 1, 1845, Letters Received, Office of Indian Affairs, Upper Missouri Agency). Drips immediately went to work for his old employers, in whose service he died some years later.

21. Fort Pierre, April 11, 1845, Drips Papers.

22. J. F. A. Sanford to Drips, St. Louis, July 10, 1842, Drips Papers; Benjamin Clapp to P. Chouteau Jr., St. Louis, Sept. 4, 1842 and March 7, 1843, Chouteau Coll.; W. D. Hodgkiss to A. Drips, March 25, 1843, Drips Papers.

23. William Clark Papers, Vol. VIII, 92–93.

24. *Congressional Globe*, 26th Cong., 2d. Sess, Vol. IX (Washington, 1841), 89–90.

25. Bent to Alvarez, Taos, Sept. 19, 1842, Alvarez Papers.

26. Caja 1825–1849. Comercio. Serie Segunda, Archivo General y Publica, Secretaría de las Relaciones Exteriores, Herbert E. Bolton, *Guide to Materials for the History of the United States in the Principal Archives of Mexico* (Washington, D.C., 1913), 263; "Dec. 22, 1843, Santa Fe. Franco, Bernardo Vasquez, Secretaria de la Command.ª Gral. del Dep.to de N.M.," Ritch Collection.

27. Bent to D. D. Mitchell, Bent's Fort, Jan. 1, 1843, William Clark Papers, Vol. VIII, 92–93.

28. Bent to Mitchell, Arkansas River, May 4, 1843, Letters Received, Office of Indian Affairs, St. Louis Superintendency; Alvarez to Webster, Independence, Mo., July 1, 1843, Consular Despatches, Santa Fe, Vol. I, RG 59, National Archives; statement of Antonio José Martínez, Taos, Nov. 28, 1843, 39th Cong., 2d Sess., *Sen. Report 156*, (Ser. 1279), Appendix, p. 362. Bent still did not give up. He wrote the Superintendent of Indian Affairs in September urging the necessity of a sub-agent on the Upper Arkansas, but the Commissioner of Indian Affairs decided against it (Letters Received, Office of Indian Affairs, St. Louis Superintendency).

29. South Dakota Historical Society, *Collections*, Vol. IX (1918), 177–79.

30. Vol. I, pp. 368–69.

31. Harold H. Dunham, "Governor Charles Bent: Pioneer and Martyr," *The Westerner's Brand Book, 1951* (Denver, 1952), 242.

CHAPTER 10

1. John Francis McDermott, *Travels in Search of the Elephant: The Wanderings of Alfred S. Waugh* (St. Louis, 1951), 5. Warfield trapped for Wyeth in 1835 (Fort Hall Account Books, Oregon Historical Society; James B. Marsh, *Four Years in the Rockies, or, The Adventures of Isaac P. Rose* [New Castle, Penna., 1884], 44); for the American Fur Company from 1836–1838 in Bridger's brigade (Ledger AA,

289, Chouteau Collection; Matt Field, *Prairie & Mountain Sketches* [Norman, 1957], 153); for Bent, St. Vrain & Co. in 1839 (LeRoy R. Hafen, *To the Rockies and Oregon, 1839–1842* [Glendale, 1855], 57, 75, 105–106; Bonner, *The Life and Adventures of James P. Beckwourth*, 183–84, 314).

2. His wife was Margaret Ellen Hammond of St. Louis, and she died at Bloomington on September 14, 1841 (*St. Louis New Era*, Oct. 2, 1841, p. 3, c. 7); P. St. George Cooke, "A Journal of the Santa Fe Trail," *Mississippi Valley Historical Review*, Vol. XII (1925), No. 2, 227–36.

3. *Niles' National Register*, March 11, 1841, pp. 18–19; William Campbell Binckley, "The Last Stage of Texan Military Operations Against Mexico, 1843," *Southwestern Historical Quarterly*, Vol. XXII (1919), No. 3.

4. "Correspondence with Mexico and Texas on the Subject of Annexation," Message from the President . . . , *House Exec. Doc. 2*, 28th Cong. 2d Sess. (Ser. 463), 99–100; W. D. Hodgkiss to A. Drips, Platte River, Mar. 25, 1843, Drips Papers.

5. Solomon Sublette to William Sublette, Independence, Mo., Oct. 31, 1842, Sublette Papers, Missouri Historical Society, St. Louis.

6. Affidavit of Alexander Montgomerie, Santa Fe, May 19, 1843, Archive #7241, Mexican Archives of New Mexico, State Records Center and Archives, Santa Fe; Rufus Sage, *Scenes in the Rocky Mountains*, 244.

7. Declarations of David Spaulding and José María Jimines, Taos, March 23, 1843, Partes de la Comandancias Génerales de Chihuahua y Nuevo Mexico relacionados con la invación de Tejanos al Departamento de Nuevo Mexico. Secretaría de la Defensa Nacional, Primer Tomo, XI/481.3/1714, Frac. 1.a Operaciones Militares. Nicholas P. Hardeman, "Charles Warfield," *Mountain Men*, Vol. VII (1969), 358, lists sixteen mountain men enrolled in Colorado, including some later Pueblo men—James Grieves and "Brown" who was probably John Brown.

8. Partes de la Comandancias Génerales . . . relacionados con la invación de Tejanos . . . Secretaría de la Defensa Nacional, Primer Tomo, XI/481.3/1714. At the time he gave his testimony at Taos, David Spaulding was thirty-three years old, married, a farmer and resident of "el río del Almagre," and had just come from trading with the Arapahos ("*come perros*"). A native of Vermont, Spaulding first turns up in New Mexico in 1841 when he refused to pay a $30 surcharge to the priest Leyva for a marriage license, and complained to the American consul at Santa Fe, Manuel Alvarez, who added his letter to a file of them against Mexican treatment of Americans. Spaulding ("Espolen" in Mexican records) was finally married to María Gerónima García by Padre Martínez at Taos on March 20, 1842. Their first child was born in December, 1842, and baptized at Taos (Fray Angélico Chávez, "New Names in New Mexico, 1820–1850," *El Palacio*, Vol. 64 (1957), Nos. 11 and 12, p. 376; Alvarez to Daniel Webster, Feb. 2, 1842, Consular Despatches, Santa Fe, Vol. I, pp. 10–11, RG 59, National Archives, Washington, D.C.). He seems to have been at Pueblo in 1843 and 1844 only.

9. Affidavits of José Portalans and Alexander Montgomerie, Santa Fe, May 19, 1843, Archive #7241, Mexican Archives of New Mexico, State Records Center and Archives, Santa Fe.

10. *Daily People's Organ* (St. Louis), Sept. 30, 1843, p. 4, c. 1; *Niles' National Register*, May 13, 1843, p. 163, c. 2–3; Thomas James, *Three Years Among the Indians and Mexicans* (Philadelphia, 1962), 100.

11. D. D. Mitchell to Secretary of War J. M. Porter, St. Louis, April 21, 1843, Letters Received, Office of Indian Affairs, St. Louis Superintendency; letters of the

Judge of Mora to Manuel Armijo, May 11 and May 14, 1843, and General Armijo's "diary of operations," May and June, 1843, Ritch Collection; Sage, *Scenes in the Rocky Mountains*, 262–67; *Niles' National Register*, July 22, 1843, p. 323, c. 2.

12. *Niles' National Register*, Oct. 12 [21], 1843, p. 123, c. 3.

13. Circular of Donaciano Vigil to the people of the Territory, Santa Fe, Feb. 12, 1847, 30th Cong., 1st Sess., *House Exec. Doc.* 70 (Ser. 521), 23–24; Charles Bent to Manuel Alvarez, Taos, Dec. 17, 1845, Alvarez Papers; Frémont, *Report*, 116.

14. Fremont, *Report*, 111.

15. *Ibid.*, 115–16.

16. *Ibid.*, 30, 116.

17. *Ibid.*, 116.

18. *Ibid.*, 116–17. See sketches of Briggs, Burroughs, Maxwell, Carson and Town in Hafen, *The Mountain Men and the Fur Trade of the Far West*.

19. Frémont, *Report*, 287; Charles Preuss, *Exploring with Frémont* (Norman, 1958), 138.

20. *Niles' National Register*, Aug. 5, 1843, p. 353, c. 2–3 and Nov. 11, 1843, p. 166, c. 3; 28th Cong., 1st Sess., *Sen. Doc. 1* (Ser. 431), 36.

21. (St. Louis) *Daily Evening Gazette*, Jan. 5, 1844; *Niles' National Register*, Jan. 13, 1844, p. 320, c. 3; Feb. 17, 1844, p. 386, c. 2–3; testimony of Richens L. Wootten, Las Vegas, N.M., May 20, 1885, *Transcript of Record, U.S. v. Maxwell Land Grant Co.* et al, U. S. Supreme Court (Oct. term, 1886), no. 974, pp. 688, 690, 696; complaints of Antonio José Martínez, May 26, 1844 and June 8, 1844 in "Cuaderno de oficios dirigidos al Sec. del Gob.[no] Sup.[r]," Decree of Feb. 27, 1844, Archive #7533, Mexican Archives of New Mexico; Proceedings of Gov. Martínez, April 18, 1844, Archive #1169 and Territorial Assembly Journal [1844], Archive #150, Mexican Archives of New Mexico, State Records Center and Archives, Santa Fe; Rich & Wilson, Fort Lancaster, Jan. 28, 1844, receipt for whiskey to S. Turley per C. Ortibiz, Lupton Papers, Colorado Historical Society, Denver.

22. Maurice Garland Fulton, *Diary & Letters of Josiah Gregg* (Norman, 1941), I, 139.

23. Drips's Account Book for 1843, Drips Papers.

24. *Niles' National Register*, June 29, 1844, p. 276, c. 1; letters of Solomon Sublette, Fort William, May 5, 1844 and Fort Lancaster, June 6, 1844, Sublette Papers, Missouri Historical Society, St. Louis.

25. F. W. Cragin's notes of an interview with Mrs. George Simpson, El Paso, Texas, Oct. 31, 1904, with Jacob Beard, El Paso, Texas, Oct. 29, 1904, and with Felipe Cisneros, Pueblo, Oct. 19, 1907, in the Cragin Coll.; Barclay diary, Barclay Papers.

26. F. W. Cragin's notes of an interview with Jacob A. Betts, Sept. 29, 1907 [Pueblo], and with Edward Pauls, Canon City, Colo., Nov. 16, 1907, Cragin Coll. See sketches of William LeBlanc and Maurice LeDuc in Hafen, *Mountain Men*. The site was undisturbed until the 1880's. In 1886 a boy of twelve named Fred Walters discovered the ruins, now melted down to a few stands of adobe wall and some half-buried roof beams. Around and in the ruins were trade beads, percussion caps, arrowheads, pipe stems, pig lead and other relics of trading days. The boy paced off the ruins and made a diagram of the site, which shows a rectangular courtyard measuring 54' by 48' and one outside wall measuring 84' by 90'. The outer walls were probably fourteen or more feet high, for Walters described a remaining piece of wall as story-and-a-half in height. Later Walters gave his little

diagram to a young engineer who made a blueprint of it, dressing it up with a surrounding octagonal stockade fence, eight log watch-towers and a lookout post, like forts he remembered from his history books. The blueprint was filed in the Colorado State Historical Society, where it has since persuaded writers that "Fort LeDoux" (as the young engineeer christened the post) was uniquely eight-sided, log-stockaded and 144 feet in diameter. Unfortunately, the letter Fred Walters wrote the Historical Society denying that the blueprint was in any way descriptive of the ruins of the fort, was filed in a different place in the Historical Society. (Interview of Janet Lecompte with Fred Walters, Wetmore, Colo., Sept. 26, 1953; letter of Mr. Walters, Wetmore, May 5, 1954 enclosing his original diagram, now in possession of this writer; see also Harry Chalfant, "The Forgotten Trappers' Fort," *Frontier Times* (June-July, 1964).)

CHAPTER 11

1. Edwin James, *Account of an Expedition from Pittsburgh to the Rocky Mountains, performed in the Years 1819, 1820* [1823], Vol. XVI in R. G. Thwaites, *Early Western Travels, 1748–1846*, 36.

2. *Ibid.;* J. C. Frémont, *Report of the Exploring Expedition*, 110, 113, 115.

3. Solomon Sublette to Andrew Sublette, Fort William, May 5, 1844, Sublette Papers, Missouri Historical Society, St. Louis; *St. Louis Reveille*, June 6, 1844, quoted in *Colorado Magazine*, Vol. XI (1934), No. 6, 223; A. J. Weston, "Historical Notes on Floods at Pueblo and Precipitation in the Arkansas Valley West of Pueblo," MS (1921), Colorado Historical Society.

4. Sibley Papers, Missouri Historical Society, St. Louis. The letter is addressed to George C. Sibley, St. Charles, Missouri, "per fav Mr J B L Doyle."

5. Taos Matrimonial Records, 1833–1845, p. 270; Lancaster Lupton to Senator Benton, Pueblo, Nov. 28, 1848, in LeRoy R. Hafen and Ann W. Hafen, *Frémont's Fourth Expedition* (Glendale, 1960), 28–29; and see Chapter 20, note 8.

6. Senex [George Simpson], "Colorado—1840," *Trinidad* (Colo.) *Daily News*, Aug. 28, 1881, p. 1, c. 2–3.

7. Barclay to the British Minister to Mexico, Barclay's Fort, Nov. 22, 1852, Barclay Papers. Other parts of this letter show that Barclay was well aware of laws governing Mexican land grants.

8. *Niles' National Register*, June 21, 1845, p. 249, c. 2–3, reprinted from the *St. Louis New Era*. The Shoshone women were probably the wives of John Burroughs and Calvin Briggs.

9. Barclay to George Barclay, Arkansas River, Dec., 1845, Barclay Papers.

10. Drips to Thomas Harvey, Fort Pierre, April 6, 1845, Letters Received, Upper Missouri Agency, Office of Indian Affairs, RG 75, National Archives, Washington, D. C.; Report of Thomas Fitzpatrick, Bent's Fort, Arkansas River, Sept. 18, 1847, 30th Cong., 1st Sess., *Sen. Exec. Doc. 1* (Ser. 503).

11. Captain B. F. Rockafellow, "History of Fremont County," in *History of the Arkansas Valley, Colorado* (Chicago, 1881), 545. Maurice was also reported to have said the post was built in 1830 and abandoned in 1838 after a Ute attack. It was superseded, according to Maurice, by an American settlement founded in 1840 by "Gov. Bent, Mr. Lupton, Col. Ceren St. Vrain, Beaubien and Lucien B. Maxwell." The settlement was managed by Beaubien and supplied the needs of trappers in the vicinity until 1846, when all but Maurice moved to other localities (see Janet

Lecompte, "The Hardscrabble Settlement, 1844–1848," *Colorado Magazine*, Vol. XXXI (1954), 84–85, for an attempt to disentangle these snarled errors). Maurice's description of the plaza tallies with that of Richard Kern in 1848. Kern says, "about a dozen houses Corn Cribs and Corrals . . . the houses are built of Adobes . . . ." ("Diary of Richard Kern," ed. Hafen and Hafen, *Frémont's Fourth Expedition*, Vol. XI in *Far West and Rockies Historical Series*, 118). Other descriptions of Hardscrabble are fragmentary and nearly useless. Fitzpatrick said the wall was, like Pueblo's, twelve feet high, but there is doubt that either Pueblo's or Hardscrabble's wall was that high (Report of Thomas Fitzpatrick, Bent's Fort, Sept. 18, 1847, 30th Cong., 1st Sess., *Sen. Exec. Doc. 1* [Ser. 503], 245). A man who grazed cattle on the Hardscrabble in 1859 said the remains of the plaza showed "an old square of adobe buildings around a court of 20 to 60 feet, exact dimensions forgotten (Cragin's notes of an interview with Jack Templeton, Pueblo, Aug. 27, 1903, Cragin Coll.). The legal description of the approximate site of the post is SE ¼ of the NE ¼, Sec. 11, Twp. 20 S. of R. 69W (Cragin's notes of an interview with Henry Burroughs, Hardscrabble Creek, Sept. 27, 1907, Cragin Coll.).

12. George Simpson to George Sibley, letter quoted above; *Niles' National Register*, June 21, 1845, p. 249; Alexander Barclay to George Barclay, Arkansas River, December, 1845, Barclay Papers; Report of Thomas Fitzpatrick, Bent's Fort, Sept. 18, 1847; Senex [George Simpson], "Colorado—1840"; Cragin's notes of an interview with Mrs. George Simpson, El Paso, Texas, Oct. 31, 1904, Cragin Coll.

13. Annie H. Abel, ed., *The Official Correspondence of James C. Calhoun* (Washington, D.C., 1915), 68.

14. Various letters of Alexander Barclay in the Barclay Papers.

15. Alexander Barclay to Mary Barclay, St. Louis, Nov. 19, 1836, July 14, 1837 and Sept., 1837, Barclay Papers.

16. F. W. Cragin's notes of an interview with Edward Frank Mitchell, Trinidad, Colo., Dec. 25, 1907, Cragin Coll.; Alexander Barclay to Mary Barclay, St. Louis, Nov. 19, 1836, July 14, 1837 and Sept., 1837, and to George Barclay, St. Louis, July 20, 1838 (Barclay Papers).

17. Alexander Barclay to George Barclay, Fort William, Arkansas River, March 10, 1840 and May 1, 1840, Barclay Papers.

18. George Barclay to Alexander Barclay, London, Nov. 1, 1840; Alexander Barclay to Mary Barclay, Fort William, April 1, 1841, Westport, Sept. 1, 1842, Fort George, Platte River, Nov. 27, 1842 (Barclay Papers).

19. Alexander Barclay to Mary Barclay, Fort George, Dec. 12, 1842; to George Barclay, Westport, Sept. 1, 1842, Jefferson City, Aboard the Steam Boat Mary Tompkins, Missouri River, June 30, 1843 (Barclay Papers).

20. Alexander Barclay to George Barclay, Barclay's Fort, Mora River, Nov. 1, 1853; watercolor sketch of Teresita painted by Barclay (Barclay Papers).

21. Alexander Barclay to George Barclay, Jefferson City, Aboard the Steam Boat Mary Tompkins, June 30, 1843 (Barclay Papers).

22. *Rocky Mountain News Weekly*, March 24, 1864, p. 4, c. 4. A number of his letters are in the J. M. Francisco Papers, Colorado Historical Society, Denver. See also F. W. Cragin's notes of an interview with A. W. Archibald, Trinidad, Colo., Dec. 25, 1907, Cragin Collection. Doyle's portrait may be found in H. L. Conard, *"Uncle Dick" Wootton*, 310.

23. Inscription on gravestone, Huerfano County, Colo. The inscription errs in

his birthplace, given as "la Ciudad de Lafayette." There is no city of Lafayette in Shenandoah County; "Lafayette" was part of Doyle's name. See also Cragin's notes of an interview with Florence Ann Doyle Richards, Pueblo, April 10, 1916; John W. Wayland, *A History of Shenandoah County, Virginia* (Strasburg, Va., 1927), 12, 147, 252, 469, 522; Cragin's notes of an interview with E. F. Mitchell, Trinidad, Colo., Dec. 25, 1907, Cragin Coll.

24. Book GG, pp. 43, 165, 322 and Book HH, p. 106, Chouteau Coll., Missouri Historical Society, St. Louis; Solomon Sublette to A. W. Sublette, Fort William, April 18, 1844, A. W. Sublette to William Sublette, Westport, May 21, 1844, Sublette Papers, Missouri Historical Society, St. Louis; Alexander Barclay to George Barclay, St. Louis, June 26, 1844, Barclay Papers; Harvey L. Carter, "Joe Doyle," *Mountain Men*, Vol. III (1966).

25. George F. Ruxton, *Life in the Far West* (New York, 1849), 23, 193; Janet Lecompte, "Marcelino Baca," *Mountain Men*, Vol. III (1966).

26. Lecompte, *loc. cit.*

27. Lecompte, "John Poisal," *Mountain Men*, Vol. VI (1968).

28. Cragin's notes of an interview with Mrs. Jacob Beard (Isabel Simpson), Oct. 30, 1904, El Paso, Texas, Cragin Coll. The plaque erected in Pueblo to the Mormon Battalion says, "here were born the first white children in Colorado"; Arthur Mitchell of Trinidad has shown me pictures of both Isabel and Juana, and they are both, in Mitchell's word, "lookers."

29. "A Mountain is His Tomb," *New York Sunday World*, June 17, 1888, p. 22, c. 3. Although this became Simpson's obituary, it is obviously written by him or with the use of his materials.

30. Senex [George Simpson], "Colorado—1840," *Trinidad* (Colo.) *Daily News*, Aug. 30, 1881, p. 1, c. 2–3. Simpson remembers Asa Estes on this trip, but Estes was back at Pueblo by October 9, when Solomon Sublette took his note for $10.50 (Sublette Papers, Missouri Historical Society, St. Louis).

31. Senex [George Simpson], "Colorado—1840," *Trinidad* (Colo.) *Daily News*, Aug. 28, 1881. Other travelers over the Sangre de Cristo Pass at about the same time were Lucien Maxwell, Kit Carson and Timothy Goodale who went from Pueblo to Taos in one day. Camped on the Culebra at this time were Santa Fe traders James J. Webb, Eugene and Tom Leitensdorfer and T. J. Caldwell, on their way to Taos (J. J. Webb, *Adventures in the Santa Fe Trade 1844-1847*, 65).

32. Taos Baptismal Records, 1844–1847, p. 10, and Taos Matrimonial Records, 1833–1845, p. 270. The marriage record, translated, reads as follows: "In this parish of Taos on the fourteenth day of the month of October, eighteen hundred forty-four, I, the priest D. Antonio José Martínez, having concluded a proper marriage ceremony at the solicitation of George S. Simpson of St. Louis, Missouri, and living in San Carlos de Napeste, of the Roman Catholic religion, legitimate son of Robert S. Simpson and Maria Bricia, with Anna-María Suaso, legitimate daughter of José Manuel Suaso, deceased, and María Teresa Sandoval, native of this parish of Taos and citizen of San Carlos; after marriage banns published in this parish, three days of festivities *inter Misarem solemne* held on the 6th, 9th and 14th of this month, and wholly satisfied that no impediment exists to the marriage, after confession and communion I married them *in facie Ecce*. Sponsors were Luis Lee and María de la Luz Tafoya; witnesses were Manuel Miera and Pablo Sandoval, all residents of the plaza of Our Lady of Guadalupe with the rest of those present I sign
[signed] Ant° José Martínez.

33. George Simpson to Alexander Barclay, Hardscrabble, Nov., 1844; note of Barclay to Boggs, Fort William, Nov. 11, 1844, Barclay Papers; F. W. Cragin's notes of an interview with Tom Autobees, Avondale, Colo., July 29, 1908, and with Mrs. Felipe Ledoux, Las Vegas, N. M., June 17, 1908, and with Albert Archibald, Trinidad, Colo., Dec. 25, 1907, Cragin Coll.

34. Alexander Barclay to George Barclay, Missouri River, June 11, 1845, Barclay Papers. Lewis Garrard describes a duel at Pueblo in 1846–1847 caused by a jealous husband who suspected his squaw of cherishing greater affection for a handsome young fellow. The husband sent the young fellow a challenge, which was accepted, and resulted in the death of the young man. This duel does not quite fit any duel known to have happened at Pueblo (Lewis H. Garrard, *Wah-to-yah*, 191).

CHAPTER 12

1. J. C. Frémont, *Report of the Exploring Expedition*, 143–45; Frank Gilbert Roe, *The North American Buffalo* (Toronto, 1951), 269–71, 501, 541, 549; Alexander Barclay to George Barclay, Arkansas River, December, 1845, Barclay Papers.

2. George Catlin's paintings and exhibits in the United States and Europe, and his 1841 book entitled *Letters and Notes on the Manners, Customs, and Condition of the North American Indians* had no little part in stimulating interest in buffalo calves and Indians. Notice of buffalo calf hunters is found in the *Daily National Intelligencer* (Washington, D.C.) June 24, 1842, reprinted in Dale L. Morgan's newspaper transcripts, "The Mormons and the Far West," Henry E. Huntington Library, San Marino, Calif.; LeRoy R. Hafen and Francis M. Young, *Fort Laramie* (Glendale, 1938) 78–80; "A Fragmentary Journal of William L. Sublette," *Mississippi Valley Historical Review* VI (1919), 110; Rufus B. Sage, *Scenes in the Rocky Mountains*, 27; P. St. George Cooke, "A Journal of the Santa Fe Trail," *Mississippi Valley Historical Review*, Vol. XII (1925), 85; *Niles' National Register*, July 1, 1843, p. 275.

3. William Clark Papers, Vol. VII, p. 265, Kansas Historical Society, Topeka, Kansas; Louise Barry, *The Beginning of the West*, 504, 519–20.

4. See many letters between Stewart and William Sublette in the Sublette Papers, Missouri Historical Society, St. Louis, especially Stewart to W. Sublette, London, July 3, 1844; Theodore Talbot, *Journals*, 43–44. For Warfield, see Chapter Ten.

5. Letters of Solomon Sublette, Fort Lancaster, Platte River, June 6, 1844 and Fort William, May 5, 1844, Sublette Papers.

6. Note in the amount of $10.50, dated "Fort Puerblo Oct 9 1844" from Asa Estes, to be credited on a note given in favor of Solomon P. Sublette "now in hands of D. A. Staton. Witness, W. Adamson"; Andrew Sublette to William Sublette, Arkansas River, April 6, 1845, Sublette Papers.

7. Alexander Barclay to George Barclay, dated "Aboard the Steam Boat Mary Tompkins, Missouri River," June 30, 1843, at Independence, July 19, 1844, and at St. Louis, June 26, 1844, Barclay Papers.

8. Alexander Barclay to George Barclay, June 26 and July 19, 1844, Barclay Papers.

9. Alexander Barclay to George Barclay, Missouri River, June 11, 1845, Barclay Papers.

10. Cooke, "A Journal of the Santa Fe Trail," 85; Sage, *Scenes in the Rocky*

Mountains, 294; Solomon Sublette to Andrew Sublette, Bent's Fort, May 5, 1844, Sublette Papers; John James Audubon, *Audubon and his Journals*, ed. Maria E. Audubon and Elliott Coues (New York, 1900), 499–500.

11. Sage, *Scenes in the Rocky Mountains*, 294; *St. Louis Daily Evening Gazette*, June 13, 1844, p. 2, c. 2; J. W. Abert, *Report of Lieut. J. W. Abert, of his Examination of New Mexico*, 7.

12. H. Picotte to P. Chouteau Jr. & Co., Fort Pierre, Jan. 4, 1844, Chouteau Collection; Solomon Sublette to William Sublette, Fort William, April 18, 1844, Sublette Papers; Alexander Culbertson to P. Chouteau Jr. & Co., Fort John [Laramie], Oct. 16, 1843, Chouteau Coll.; Klauke to P. Chouteau Jr. & Co., June 27, 1843, Nov. 28, 1843 and Jan. 26, 1844, American Historical Association, *Calendar of the American Fur Company's Papers*, Part II, 1317, 1347, 1354.

13. J. J. Webb, *Adventures in the Santa Fe Trade*, 121; Ceran St. Vrain to C. Bent, Fort William, Feb. 11, 1845, Alvarez Papers.

14. *Niles' National Register*, June 7, 1845, p. 224, c. 2–3 and August 3, 1844, p. 378, c. 2; *St. Louis Weekly Reveille*, Sept. 22, 1845, p. 498, c. 1, June 1, 1846, p. 878, c. 1; *St. Louis Daily Evening Gazette*, June 19, 1844, p. 2, c. 1; Alexander Barclay to George Barclay, June 11, 1845 and June 13, 1845, Barclay Papers; J. J. Webb, *Adventures in the Santa Fe Trade*, 133–35; Ceran St. Vrain to Charles Bent, Fort William, Feb. 11, 1845, Alvarez Papers.

15. *Niles' National Register*, June 28, 1845, p. 258, c. 2; H. Picotte to P. D. Papin, Fort Pierre, Dec. 14, 1845, Fort Pierre Letter Book, Chouteau Coll.; LeRoy R. Hafen, "Fort St. Vrain," *Colorado Magazine*, Vol. XXIX (1952).

16. Talbot, *Journals*, 24.

17. Louis Pelzer, "A Frontier Officer's Military Order Book," *Mississippi Valley Historical Review*, Vol. VI (1919), 265; "Report of the Expedition of Dragoons under Colonel Henry Dodge," *American State Papers*, Military Affairs, Vol. VI, 130; Ann W. Hafen, "Lancaster P. Lupton," *Mountain Men*, Vol. II (1965).

18. William Lupton to Lancaster Lupton, Elkhorn, Wis., July 29, 1850, Lupton Papers; license issued to Hiram Rich, Nov. 2, 1837 and Nov. 10, 1840, Letters Received from the Office of Indian Affairs, St. Louis Superintendency; John Brown, *Mediumistic Experiences*, 23, 188–89.

19. Sage, *Scenes in the Rocky Mountains*, 155; Frémont, *Report*, 35; O. Sarpy to Major A. Drips, Fort Pierre Sept. 7, 1843, Drips Papers; Louise Barry, *The Beginning of the West*, 387, 433–34; receipt of Rich & Wilson to L. Maxwell, Fort Lancaster, Jan. 13, 1844 for 28 gallons and 3 pints of whiskey, on the back of which is written, "Deduct 7 gal for private use of L. P. Lupton, Esq." (Lupton Papers). Pratte & Cabanné was the fur company that owned Fort Platte, and Sibille and Adams were its chief traders, a distinction often ignored with resulting confusion. For Wilson's Houses, see A. Drips, Fort John, Dec. 4, 1843 in "Fort Tecumseh and Fort Pierre Journal and Letter Books," South Dakota Historical Society *Collections*, Vol. IX (1918), 186–87; abstract of license issued to Albert G. Wilson, Aug. 31, 1843, Letters Received, Office of Indian Affairs, St. Louis Superintendency; Barclay Diary, Jan. 2, 1847, Barclay Papers; Solomon Sublette to A. W. Sublette, Fort Lancaster, June 6, 1844, Sublette Papers; Lupton's Account Book, Lupton Papers. The town of Fort Lupton grew up around the old trading post, but the post itself was always called Fort Lancaster.

20. Lupton Papers.

21. Lancaster Lupton to Charles Town, Fort Spaulding, Dec. 13, 1844, and list

of employees in 1841–42, Lupton Papers. Others on the list are Prodom, Godey, Murray, Pierre, LeClerc, Louis Trokey, Steel, Seminary, Sutton, Fallon, Austin Loyd, Barry, Cave and Rice, and an "H" Brown as well as a "J" Brown.

22. Janet Lecompte, "Archibald Charles Metcalf," *Mountain Men*, Vol. IV (1966).

23. Dale L. Morgan, "Miles Goodyear and the Founding of Oregon," *Utah Historical Quarterly*, Vol. XXI (1953), No. 217; P. St. George Cooke, *Scenes and Adventures in the army*, 243; E. M. Kern to A. Robidoux, Taos, Feb. 11, 1849, in LeRoy R. Hafen and Ann W. Hafen, *Fremont's Fourth Expedition* (Glendale, 1960), 222; Lieut. E. G. Beckwith, *Report of Explorations for a Route for the Pacific Railroad*, 41–42; Gwinn Harris Heap, *Central Route to the Pacific* (Philadelphia, 1854), 30; F. W. Cragin's notes of an interview with L. W. Curry, Ouray Ute Agency, Fort Duchesne, Utah, Sept. 3, 1902, Cragin Coll.

24. "Manifiesto que el Governador del Departamento de Nuevo-Mexico hace a sus habitantes, Sept. 8, 1844," L. Bradford Prince Papers, State Records Center and Archives, Santa Fe. See also Lansing Bartlett Bloom, "New Mexico under Mexican Administration," *Old Santa Fe*, Vol. II (1915), 225; (Washington, D.C.) *Daily National Intelligencer*, Nov. 11, 1844, in Dale L. Morgan's newspaper transcripts, "The Mormons and the Far West"; *St. Louis Reveille*, Oct. 31, 1844, quoted in *Colorado Magazine*, Vol. XI (1934), 226–27, which errs in having the Indians returning to Albuquerque after the fight instead of Abiquiu.

25. F. W. Cragin's notes of an interview with Mrs. Felipe (Luz Trujillo Metcalf) Ledoux, Las Vegas, N. M. June 17, 1908, Cragin Coll. (Mrs. Ledoux was the daughter of José Francisco Trujillo); A. W. Sublette, Taos, Oct. 20, 1844, Sublette Papers; Juan Andrés Archuleta, Taos, Dec. 26, 1844, Archive #7999, Mexican Archives of New Mexico, State Records Center and Archives, Santa Fe.

26. "Manuel Ruis, Manuel Pais, Miguel Ruibali, Jose my Payute Boy and Felipe Archuleta will please to deliver to Mr. W. Subletz my mules, seven in nomber, three rifles, riding sadles, pack sadles, rops & powder horn, one tomahawk.—Mr. Subletts his fully authorize by me, and in my name to perseau or Receive any part or all the above mention property, as the said property has been stolen from me on Green Rever October last. Given at Larama Fort on the 4th July 1845. [signed] A. Robidoux" (Sublette Papers). On June 29, 1845, Robidoux was on the North Platte River three days west of Fort Laramie where he remarked that he had come by this route because the Indians had killed eight of his men in the Spanish country (Dale L. Morgan and Eleanor Towles Harris, *The Rocky Mountain Journals of William Marshall Anderson* [San Marino, 1967], 383).

27. Statement of Alexander Montgomerie, Taos, Dec. 25, 1844, Archive #7999, Mexican Archives of New Mexico. First reports of the massacre said that the fort attacked was not Uncompaghre but Uintah. So Frémont understood (*Report*, 279) and also Montgomerie, who said in the above cited statement, which I have translated, "I met several peons from Señor Rubidu's Fort Uintah (*Fuerte de Ullinte*) who were taking refuge at Hardscrabble (*el pueblo de las piedras amarillas*) who told me what the enemy Yutas had done at said fort . . . . " Robidoux himself indicates it was Fort "Tampagarha" in an account in the Fayette, *Missouri Democrat*, Sept. 17, 1845, in Dale L. Morgan's transcripts, "The Mormons and the Far West." The article states there were three Mexicans massacred in the fort and one American spared, who was sent to Robidoux 120 miles away. Dale Morgan helped me clarify this confusing incident.

28. Barclay Diary; John Brown's account book; Janet Lecompte, "Charles Autobees," *Colorado Magazine*, Vol. XXXV (1958), 142; Cragin's notes of an interview with Luz Trujillo Metcalf Ledoux, Cragin Coll.

29. Abstract of licenses issued to Bent, St. Vrain & Co., July 25, 1842, and to P. Chouteau Jr. & Co., Aug. 31, 1843, Letters Received, Office of Indian Affairs, St. Louis Superintendency; sketches of Hawkins and Tharp in *Mountain Men*, Vols. III (1966) and IV (1966).

30. Barclay diary, Barclay Papers.

CHAPTER 13

1. A. B. Thomas, *Forgotten Frontiers* (Norman, 1932), 123–29.

2. *Adventures in Mexico and the Rocky Mountains*, 216–17.

3. Charles Autobees testified in 1873 that the Greenhorn Valley "was occupied in the year 1841 or 1842 by Archibald Metcalf, John Brown, William New and Marcelin Baca. They occupied it until the year 1858" (Colorado Private Land Claim #17, Vigil & St. Vrain Grant, Records of the General Land Office, National Archives, Washington, D. C.). The latter date is erroneous, for by 1858 Metcalf and New had been gone for six or seven years, John Brown had been living in California for nine years, and Baca had been in New Mexico for three years. In June, 1844 the Governor of New Mexico listed "Huerfano" as a settlement in the County of Taos which extended to the Arkansas River. "Huerfano" had for half a century or more referred to the little volcanic butte beside the Huerfano River just over the hill from Greenhorn. There was no settlement at "Huerfano" in 1844; the Governor was probably referring to the mountain men's early camp at Greenhorn (Gov. Mariano Martinez to the president of the Departmental Assembly, Santa Fe, June 17, 1844, Mexican Archives of New Mexico, quoted in translation in Lieut. Abert's *Examination of New Mexico*, 62). In 1863 O. J. Goldrick, who had accompanied Joe Doyle west in the summer of 1859, wrote that "Green Horn Mountain was used by Maxwell as a grazing tract over twenty years ago" (*Rocky Mountain News* (weekly), Dec. 23, 1863, p. 3, c. 5); Dick Wootton told Frank Hall in the late 1880's that John Brown located on the Greenhorn about 1843 (Frank Hall, *History of the State of Colorado*, II [1890], 226).

4. *L. A. Ingersoll's century annals of San Bernardino county, 1769–1904* (Los Angeles, 1904), 649–50. John Brown is probably the fellow George Simpson called "Cut Rock Brown" and characterized as the "tiresome teller of the same story" (Leonard K. Smith, "On the Old Frontier, Fragments of Forgotten History," MS loaned to me by author). There were no fewer than three John Browns who located on the Huerfano and Greenhorn in the nineteenth century. First was this John Brown; then a John M. Brown who was murdered with his wife Sarah in La Veta in 1876 (Pueblo) *Colorado Chieftain*, Nov. 30, 1876, p. 1, c. 4) and last, John Henry Brown, an early settler on the Huerfano interviewed by F. W. Cragin at Walsenburg in 1907 (Cragin's notes of the interview, Dec. 7, 1907, Cragin Collection).

5. *Mediumistic Experiences . . .* , 23.

6. *Ibid.*, 37–38, 41–42, 45–46.

7. *Ibid.*, 24, 37–42, 45–47, 51–52.

8. Testimony of Alexander Hicklin, Dec. 26, 1871, of Thomas Oliver Boggs, Jan. 11, 1873, and of others, showing that Ceran St. Vrain believed to his dying day

that Greenhorn was part of his grant (Colorado Private Land Claim #17, Vigil & St. Vrain Grant). In later years the Greenhorn Valley was determined to be outside the boundaries of the grant. For the Mexican inspector, see the next chapter.

9. Barclay diary, Barclay Papers; John Brown's Account Book, Henry E. Huntington Library, San Marino, Calif.

10. John Brown's Account Book; Barclay diary entry of July 18, 1846 shows Brown returning from "North Fork [of the Platte]."

11. John Brown's Account Book.

12. *Ibid.*

13. *Ibid.*

14. *Ibid.;* Lieut. E. G. Beckwith, *Report of Explorations for a Route for the Pacific Railroad . . .*, 34–35. Lieut. Beckwith passed the settlement in 1853, after Brown and most of his customers had left. At that time Beckwith estimated that the size of farming operations at Greenhorn was equal to that of a small eastern farmer who cultivated his own fields. The maximum yield of the Greenhorn Valley came to no more than 200 *fanegas* of wheat, 50 of corn, and small amounts of beans and watermelons.

15. John Brown's Account Book; Harvey L. Carter, "Calvin Jones," *Mountain Men*, Vol. VI (1968).

16. Frank Hall, *History of the State of Colorado*, II, 236.

17. F. W. Cragin's notes of an interview with John Henry Brown, Walsenburg, Dec. 7, 1907, Cragin Coll.; John Brown's Account Book. White, bolted flour cost $4 per barrel at St. Louis in 1845 (*St. Louis Weekly Reveille*, July 7, 1845); in Santa Fe in November, 1846, Taos flour (coarse, dark and unbolted) cost $2.50 per *fanega* (Abert, *Examination of New Mexico*, 39) and by 1847 flour was up to $9 per *fanega* at Taos (Garrard, *Wah-to-yah*, 276). At Fort Laramie in 1843, Matt Field paid 25¢ per pound for Taos flour brought north by pack train (*Prairie and Mountain Sketches*, 81). Farther into the mountains the price doubled and quadrupled: at Fort Bridger, Fort Hall and Fort Boise, flour was 50¢ per pound in 1843 (Marcus Whitman to the Secretary of War, Oregon Pioneer Association, *Transactions*, I [1891], 70); at Green River in 1841 the Bidwell party paid some trappers 50¢ per cup (Bidwell, *A Journey to California*, 18); and at Fort Lancaster in 1844, flour was $12 per *fanega* (receipt of Charles Ortibus, Jan. 28, 1844, Lupton Papers).

18. John Brown's Account Book. The three faithful peons were "Charno," "Tucksender," and "Scapoolar" or "Esquipoola." For peons in Mexico, see J. J. Webb, *Adventures in the Santa Fe Trade*, 102–103; Josiah Gregg, *Commerce of the Prairies*, XX, 30–31.

19. John Brown's Account Book; Lancaster Lupton's Account Book, Lupton Papers.

20. Samuel Eliot Morison and Henry Steele Commager, *The Growth of the American Republic* (New York, 1962), I, 504; John Brown's Account Book.

21. John Brown's Account Book.

22. *Adventures in Mexico and the Rocky Mountains*, 216–17. There were a few more "cares to annoy them" than Ruxton knew of. In the summer of 1846, Jicarilla Apaches stole twenty horses from "Mais Leduke, Browne and Murry" on the Greenhorn, as Charles Bent tells us in a letter to Manuel Alvarez, June 11, 1846, Alvarez Papers.

23. Ruxton, *Adventures in Mexico and the Rocky Mountains*, 217.

24. Barclay Papers.

CHAPTER 14

1. Charles Bent to Manuel Alvarez, Rio Arriba, Jan. 24, 1845, Alvarez Papers.

2. George L. Rives, *The United States and Mexico, 1821–1848* (New York, 1913), I, 700, 716.

3. Louise Barry, *The Beginning of the West*, 563; *Niles' National Register*, June 7, 1845, p. 224, c. 2–3; Hamilton Gardner, "Captain Philip St. George Cooke and the March of the 1st Dragoons to the Rocky Mountains in 1845," *Colorado Magazine*, Vol. XXX (1953), No. 4.

4. Lieut. J. Henry Carleton, *The Prairie Logbooks: Dragoon Campaigns to the Pawnee Villages in 1844, and to the Rocky Mountains in 1845*, 195; Col. S. W. Kearny, "Report of a summer campaign to the Rocky Mountains &c. in 1845," 29th Cong., 1st Sess., *House Exec. Doc.* 2 (Ser. 480) 210–13. Simpson and Lieut. Franklin had missed the command at Fort Leavenworth and had ridden 217 miles in five and a half days to catch up.

5. P. St. George Cooke, *Scenes and Adventures in the Army: or, Romance of Military Life* (Philadelphia, 1859), 284, 415–16.

6. Kearny, "Report of a summer campaign," 213.

7. Cooke, *Scenes and Adventures*, 417.

8. Gardner, "Captain Philip St. George Cooke . . . ," *Colorado Magazine*, Vol. XXX (1953), No. 4, p. 263.

9. *Op. cit.*, 251, 268–69. This was not the first dragoon march to the Rocky Mountains. For Dodge's 1835 expedition, see *American State Papers, Military Affairs*, Vol. VI, 130–146.

10. Allan Nevins, *Fremont, the West's Greatest Adventurer* (New York, 1928), I, 235.

11. Thomas S. Martin, "Narrative of Frémont's Expedition in 1845–6"; Harvey Lewis Carter, *'Dear Old Kit': The Historical Christopher Carson* (Norman, 1968), 95–96; Nevins, *Frémont*, I, 238–39; Lieut. James W. Abert, *Through the Country of the Comanche Indians in the Fall of the Year 1845 . . .* , ed. John Galvin, 17–19.

12. Martin, "Narrative of Frémont's Expedition"; Nevins, *Frémont*, 238–39, cites Jesse Benton Frémont's manuscripts as authority for the number of twelve prize rifles. Dates of Frémont's stay at Pueblo and Hardscrabble are determined from his accounts in "Selected Records of the General Accounting Office relating to Frémont Expeditions and the California Battalion, 1842–1890," National Archives Microfilm Publication, T-135, roll 1.

13. "Selected Records of the General Accounting Office relating to Frémont Expeditions . . . ," *loc. cit.*, and Martin, "Narrative . . . ." Martin calls Pueblo "Hardscrabble" but locates it more or less properly sixty miles above Bent's Fort.

14. "Diary of Edward Kern, 1845–6, with Frémont," *Life*, April 6, 1959, pp. 96–97. Kern wrote a description of Frémont's expedition at Pueblo, but when a section of his journal was published in *Life*, the Pueblo part was omitted. The journal is at present in private hands; if it is ever published we may hope to see a fine description of Pueblo.

15. *St. Louis Weekly Reveille*, June 1, 1846, p. 878, c. 5, under date of May 30, and copied from the *National Intelligencer*. The letter without the editorial note is in Frémont's *Memoirs of My Life*, Vol. I (Chicago, 1887), 452.

16. L. B. Bloom, "New Mexico Under Mexican Administration," *Old Santa Fe*, Vol. II (1915), 231.

17. Archive #1128, Mexican Archives of New Mexico. The document is dated Sept. 20, 1845, and the translation is with the archive.

18. Exp. XI/481.3/2081. Designación del Gral. Francisco García Condé, como Jefe de 5/a division . . . Archivo Histórico Militar, Mexico; Governor's letter book, 1845–46, Archive #8126, Mexican Archives of New Mexico. Luis Lachoné, the only name not familiar to us on García Condé's list, was from St. Louis, son of Santiago Lachoné and Elena Varon (or Bisonette). He was married in Taos to Dolores García on April 26, 1841 and had children born in 1842, 1845, 1847, 1850 and 1853, all baptized at Taos. (Chávez, "New Names in New Mexico, 1820–1850," *El Palacio*, Vol. LXIV [1957], 311). However, he was probably not a resident of Hardscrabble, for he is not mentioned in Barclay's diary, John Brown's account book or the Lupton Papers. Nor, surprisingly, is he in Charles Bent's list of residents of the Valley of Taos as of January 30, 1841, Alvarez Papers.

19. Charles Bent to Manuel Alvarez, Taos, Feb. 5, 1846, Alvarez Papers.

20. Barclay Papers.

21. See letters of Charles Bent to Manuel Alvarez, Alvarez Papers.

22. Cragin's notes of an interview with Luz Metcalf (Mrs. Felipe Ledoux), Las Vegas, June 17, 1908, Cragin Coll.; Lieut. Col. W. H. Emory, "Notes of a Military Reconnoissance, from Fort Leavenworth, in Missouri, to San Diego, in California . . . ," 30th Cong., 1st Sess., Sen. Doc. 7 (Ser. 505), 14. Other ladies at the fort, according to Luz, were Rumalda Luna Boggs, aged fifteen and the bride of Tom Boggs; Rumalda's mother Ignacia Jaramillo, wife of Charles Bent; Ignacia's sister Josefa, wife of Kit Carson; and Cruz Padilla, wife of George Bent.

23. John T. Hughes, *Doniphan's Expedition* (1847), reprinted in William E. Connelley, *Doniphan's Expedition and the Conquest of New Mexico and California* (Topeka, 1907), 178; Parkman, *The Oregon Trail*, 317; Barclay's diary, April 19 and 20, 1847, Barclay Papers.

24. *St. Louis Weekly Reveille*, Sept. 14, 1846, p. 1001, c. 1–2; Barclay's diary, May 28, 1846, Barclay Papers; Testimony of Calvin Jones, Trinidad, Colo., Oct. 31, 1883, *Transcript of Record, U. S. v. Maxwell Land Grant Co.* et al, U. S. Supreme Court, no. 974 (Oct. term, 1886), 169; T. D. Bonner, *The Life and Adventures of James P. Beckwourth*, 328. The joke was, of course, that the horses had been stolen several months before war was declared.

25. (St. Louis) *Missouri Republican*, July 17, 1846, quoted in Morgan, *Overland in 1846*, II, 645.

26. Charles Bent to Manuel Alvarez, Fort William, June 11, 1846, Alvarez Papers. More horses and mules arrived later with Solomon P. Sublette and Joseph Walker, who had left Los Angeles at the end of May in a party of ten men driving four or five hundred horses and mules (*New York Weekly Tribune*, Sept. 26, 1846, quoted in Morgan, *Overland in 1846*, II, 647). They drove their horses east to Fort Bridger, where the company split. One party consisting of Sublette, Walker, Reddick, Taplin and another man arrived at Pueblo about the middle of August and Bent's Fort on August 17 (*New York Weekly Tribune*, Sept. 26, 1846, *St. Louis Weekly Reveille*, Sept. 14, 1846, quoted in Morgan, *Overland in 1846*, II, 647); the other party consisting of Joseph Walker, Tim Goodale and others arrived at Hardscrabble on August 20, leaving for Pueblo on August 22 (Barclay diary, Barclay Papers) and arriving at Bent's Fort three or four days later with sixty mules. There was no pasture left near Bent's Fort, so Walker camped eight miles north of the fort

and waited for the volunteers under Colonel Price to arrive, in order to sell his animals to them (Lieut. J. W. Abert, "Examination of New Mexico . . . ," 30th Cong. 1st Sess., *Sen. Exec. Doc. 23* [Ser. 506], 4, 16).

27. John Brown's Account Book.

28. Barclay diary, Barclay Papers.

CHAPTER 15

1. Report of T. P. Moore, Upper Missouri Indian Agent, Sept. 21, 1846, 29th Cong. 2d Sess., *House Exec. Doc. 4* (Ser. 497), 293. Francisco Conn described himself as a Navajo trader in 1846 (Morgan, ed., *Overland in 1846: Diaries and Letters of the California-Oregon Trail*, II, 652).

2. Abstract of Licenses, Letters Received, Office of Indian Affairs, St. Louis Superintendency, National Archives, Washington, D. C. Other traders in Doyle's and Barclay's company were William Adamson, Jim Cowie, Gurteau and William Guerrier.

3. Barclay diary under dates of Dec. 30, 31, 1845 and Jan. 7, 1846, Barclay Papers. Although Joe Doyle was Barclay's principal partner, Barclay's partnership with Levin Mitchell was typical of Arkansas Valley traders who frequently combined their assets in a single wagonload of goods, or in some other project of limited amount, time or purpose. See Chapter 8, footnote 8.

4. Charles Bent to Manuel Alvarez, Taos, March 19, 1846, Alvarez Papers.

5. Barclay diary, Jan. 13, 1846 to March 24, 1846, Barclay Papers.

6. *Ibid.*

7. Lewis H. Garrard, *Wah-to-yah and the Taos Trail*, 173–74; Barclay diary, Barclay Papers; Janet Lecompte, "William Tharp," *Mountain Men*, III (1966).

8. F. W. Hodge, *Handbook of American Indians North of Mexico* (Washington, D. C., 1907), II, 874–76; Alfred B. Thomas, *After Coronado*, 9, 18, 21, 26–27, 171 *passim;* W. H. H. Davis, *The Spanish Conquest of New Mexico* (Doylestown, Pa., 1869), 404–405; H. H. Bancroft, *History of Arizona and New Mexico, 1530–1888, Works,* XVII (San Francisco, 1889), 165, 171; Alfred B. Thomas, *The Plains Indians and New Mexico*, 2–30, 32 *passim;* Thomas, *Forgotten Frontiers*, 125–27, 132, 139 *passim;* LeRoy R. Hafen and Ann W. Hafen, *Old Spanish Trail, Santa Fe to Los Angeles* (Glendale, 1954), 263; Ralph Emerson Twitchell, *The Spanish Archives of New Mexico* (Cedar Rapids, Iowa, 1914), I, 25–26, II, 208; Josiah Gregg, *Commerce of the Prairies*, XX, 83; Don Pedro Bautista Pino, *Exposición*, in H. Bailey Carroll and J. Villasana Haggard, *Three New Mexico Chronicles* (Albuquerque, 1942), 133–34.

9. Thomas James, *Three Years Among the Indians and Mexicans* (Philadelphia, 1962), 90–92; Dale L. Morgan, *The West of William H. Ashley* (Denver, 1964), 115, 141, 277–78, 281–82. Nathaniel Wyeth and Capt. Bonneville each took out licenses to trade with the Utes, Wyeth's dated April 2, 1834 and Bonneville & Co.'s dated April 16, 1834 (23d Cong., 2d. Sess., *Sen. Doc. 69* [Ser. 268]), but there is no indication either actually traded with them ("The Correspondence and Journals of Captain Nathaniel J. Wyeth, 1831–6," *Sources of the History of Oregon*, ed. F. G. Young, I [Eugene, 1899]); Washington Irving, *The Adventures of Captain Bonneville U. S. A. in the Rocky Mountains and the Far West*, ed. Edgeley W. Todd (Norman, 1961).

10. For Robidoux and his forts, see Chapter 12; abstract of license issued to Bent,

St. Vrain & Co., July 30, 1839, Letters Received, Office of Indian Affairs, St. Louis Superintendency; Thomas J. Farnham, *Travels in the Great Western Prairies*, Vol. XXVIII in Thwaites, *Early Western Travels, 1748–1846*, 166–67 describes Ute treatment of Bent traders; Alexander Barclay to George Barclay, Fort William, March 12, 1841, Barclay Papers describes the Utes' visit to Bent's Fort. By 1842 and 1843 the Utes were named in trading licences of Bent, St. Vrain & Co. (July 28, 1842), of P. Chouteau Jr. & Co. (Aug. 22, 1842) and of Joseph Robidoux (July 24, 1843) who was licensed to trade "at Grand river of Ocompagras [Fort Uncompah-gre], at Green river eighteen miles above the mouth of Winty [Fort Uintah], and at Lake Tempanago," all on Spanish soil (abstract of licenses, Office of Indian Affairs, St. Louis Superintendency); Theodore Talbot, *Journals*, 42–44.

11. Letter of Diego Lucero, Prefect, 2d district, March 22, 1845, #8065, Mexican Archives of New Mexico, State Records Center and Archives, Santa Fe; Charles Bent to Manuel Alvarez, Rio Arriba, Jan. 24 [1845], Alvarez Papers; *Niles' National Register*, May 31, 1845, p. 193, c. 1; *St. Louis Weekly Reveille*, March 23, 1845, p. 800, c. 5. When certain Americans got hold of the story, the number of soldiers increased to 800 or even 1500, the number of Utes diminished to 40 or 50, and the Mexicans were ignominiously routed in a skirmish (*St. Louis Weekly Reveille*, May 18, 1846, p. 859, c. 4–5; Maurice Garland Fulton, ed., *Diary & Letters of Josiah Gregg: Southwestern Enterprises, 1840–1847* [Norman, 1941], 168–169).

12. Bent to Alvarez, April 1, 1846, Alvarez Papers.

13. Alexander Barclay to George Barclay, Missouri River, June 11, 1845, Barclay Papers.

14. *St. Louis Weekly Reveille*, March 30, 1846, p. 805, c. 4; Bent to Alvarez, Taos, March 4, 1846, Alvarez Papers.

15. Barclay diary, Barclay Papers.

16. *Ibid.*

17. H. L. Conard, *"Uncle Dick" Wootton*, 108–111; Frank Hall, *History of the State of Colorado*, II, 237–38. Mules were about $25 in Missouri in 1844, $60 to $80 in 1846 (*St. Louis Weekly Reveille*, Sept. 30, 1844, p. 96, c. 2 and March 23, 1846, p. 796, c. 5).

18. Barclay diary, Barclay Papers. South Park's peculiar bilingual name of Bayou Salado combines the Mississippi French word for lake or creek with the Spanish word for salty.

19. John T. Hughes, *Doniphan's Expedition* (1847) in W. E. Connelley, *Doniphan's Expedition and the Conquest of New Mexico and California* (Topeka, 1907), 72, 251.

20. Barclay diary, Barclay Papers; F. W. Cragin's notes of an interview with Mrs. Felipe Ledoux (Luz Trujillo Metcalf), Las Vegas, N. M., Feb. 13, 1908, Cragin Collection. Maurice LeDuc had a far more romantic memory of the battle, which he was said to have described as occurring in 1838 while he was at Buzzards' Roost on Adobe Creek. On the approach of the Sioux and Arapahos, the people of Hardscrabble took refuge in Maurice's fort. When the Indians demanded Maurice's Ute squaw, he parlayed with them until a courier sent to the Ute camp in the Wet Mountain Valley brought the Utes, who defeated the Arapahos and Sioux on the mesa south of Adobe Creek (Capt. B. F. Rockafellow, "History of Fremont County," *History of the Arkansas Valley, Colorado* [Chicago, 1881], 545).

21, Barclay diary, Barclay Papers; John Brown's account book.

22. Edwin Bryant, *What I Saw in California*, 112–13.

23. *Ibid.*, 113.

24. Morgan, ed., *Overland in 1846: Diaries and Letters of the California-Oregon Trail*, II, 652; Barclay diary, Barclay Papers.

25. Bryant, *What I Saw in California*, 143. Goodale was with Joseph R. Walker who had just returned from California with a supply of horses. See note 26, Chapter 14.

CHAPTER 16

1. Alexander Barclay diary, December, 1845, Barclay Papers.

2. Alexander Barclay to George Barclay, Arkansas River, December, 1845, Barclay Papers.

3. Barclay diary, Barclay Papers.

4. *Ibid.*

5. F. W. Cragin's notes of an interview with Mrs. Felipe Ledoux (Luz Trujillo Metcalf), Las Vegas, N. M., Feb. 13, 1908 and June 17, 1908, Cragin Collection; Barclay diary, Barclay Papers. Wells' identity is obscure. An Englishman named Welles joined Bryant's party of California emigrants on July 3, 1846 on the North Platte. A vigorous, athletic man of sixty, Welles claimed a captain's commission in the British army, which his bearing, manners and intelligence confirmed although he was dressed in trapper's buckskins. After leaving Bryant's party at Fort Bridger, Welles joined Miles Goodyear in establishing an emigrant trading post on Weber River which later became the city of Ogden, Utah (Edwin Bryant, *What I Saw in California*, 119; Dale L. Morgan, "Miles Goodyear and the Founding of Ogden," *Utah Historical Quarterly*, Vol. XXI [1953], 213–14, 315). Another Wells, recently from North Carolina, was met in New Mexico by Lieut. Emory in August, 1846 on the Mora River where he had been living for six months. He was dressed in the full regalia of Mexican dragoons—broad sombrero, gold-striped blue pantaloons, lace-trimmed jacket (Lieut. W. H. Emory, "Notes of a Military Reconnoissance...," 25). Another possibility was "Tomas el matador [murderer]," otherwise known as Tom Whittlesey or Whittle or Wilson, who turned up years later at the Huerfano settlement with an ugly reputation and a new woman (see Chapter 22).

6. Barclay Papers.

7. J. C. Frémont, *Report of the Exploring Expedition . . .* , p. 111 tells of Lupton's farm; Howard Egan's account, Journal History, June 2, 1847, p. 1, Church of Jesus Christ of the Latter Day Saints, Church Historian's Office, Salt Lake City, tells of Fort Laramie's farm; letter of A. R. Bouis to F. A. Chardon, Fort Pierre, Aug. 17, 1845, "Fort Clark, Fort Pierre Letter Book," Chouteau Collection, tells of Fort Pierre's cornfield, and letter of Honoré Picotte to P. Chouteau Jr. & Co., Fort Pierre, March 11, 1846, tells of the Taos peddlers. Unless otherwise indicated, all the material on Barclay's summer of 1846 is from his diary in the Barclay Papers.

8. *St. Louis Weekly Reveille*, Aug. 10, 1846, p. 957, c. 1.

9. Doyle arrived at Bent's Fort alone on the evening of Sept. 6 and hurried on (*Western America in 1846–1847: the Original Travel Diary of Lieutenant J. W. Abert . . .* , ed. John Galvin, 22); Guerrier and the six wagons arrived Sept. 8 (*ibid.*, 23 and *St. Louis Weekly Reveille*, Sept. 7, 1846, p. 989, c. 5).

10. George Simpson describes the site of Barclay's "Houses" in Senex, "Old

Time Recollections," *Trinidad* (Colo.) *Daily News*, June 8, 1881, p.1, c. 2–3.

CHAPTER 17

1. Francis Parkman, *The Oregon Trail*, 93–94.
2. Mason Wade, ed., *The Journals of Francis Parkman* (New York, 1947), II, 467–73; Parkman, *Oregon Trail*, 282–300.
3. Parkman, *Oregon Trail*, 300.
4. *Ibid.*, 301.
5. Sage, *Scenes in the Rocky Mountains*, 172.
6. Parkman, *Oregon Trail*, 302.
7. *Ibid.*, 303–305; Wade, *The Journals of Francis Parkman*, II, 473. The injured man was George W. Therlkill, hurt on August 6 (LeRoy R. Hafen and Frank M. Young, "The Mormon Settlement at Pueblo, Colorado, During the Mexican War," *Colorado Magazine*, Vol. IX [1932], p. 126).
8. Parkman, *Oregon Trail*, 303–304.
9. *Ibid.*, 305.
10. For a strong gentile opinion of the Mormons, see Bernard De Voto, *The Year of Decision, 1846* (Boston, 1943).
11. Charles L. Camp, ed., *James Clyman, Frontiersman* (Portland, Ore., 1960), 226; "John Brown's Journal," Hafen and Young, "The Mormon Settlement at Pueblo, Colorado, During the Mexican War," *Colorado Magazine*, Vol. IX (1932), p. 124.
12. Kate B. Carter, *The Mormon Battalion*, 8, 14, 15, 117; Parkman, *Oregon Trail*, 305. I have arrived at the number detached by subtracting Mrs. Carter's roster of 525 men and 33 women who left Winter Quarters from P. St. George Cooke's enumeration of 448 men and 25 women who reached Santa Fe ("Report of Lieutenant Col. P. St. George Cooke of His March from Santa Fe, New Mexico, to San Diego, Upper California," 30th Cong., 1st Sess., *House Exec. Doc. 41* [Ser. 517], 551–52). Dale Morgan points out, however, that some men enlisted at Fort Leavenworth, so my figures are on the low side. None of the accounts mentions the pregnancy of the women, but records show that six children were born to Mormon women between September, 1846 and May, 1847, four being children of men detailed to escort the detachment to Pueblo (Carter, *Mormon Battalion*, 14–15; Hafen and Young, "The Mormon Settlement at Pueblo, Colorado, During the Mexican War," *Colorado Magazine*, Vol. IX [1932], p. 127n; Sgt. Daniel Tyler, *A Concise History of the Mormon Battalion in the Mexican War, 1846–1847*, 165; "Journal History," Sept. 16, 1846, Church of Jesus Christ of the Latter Day Saints, Church Historian's Office, Salt Lake City; "John Steele's Day Book").
13. "Journal History," *loc. cit.*, Oct. 18, 1846, p. 4; Oct. 31, 1846, p. 2; Nov. 24, 1846, p. 3; Nov. 17, 1846, p. 3; Dec. 31, 1846, p. 6–7; Tyler's *Concise History*, 171; "John Steele's Day Book," 39; "Extracts from the Journal of John Steele," *Utah Historical Quarterly*, Vol. VI (1933), p. 14 (these extracts differ considerably from the manuscript journal cited above).
14. "Journal History," *loc. cit.*, Dec. 31, 1846, p. 6–7. A roster of Lieut. Willis' men may be found in Tyler, *Concise History*, 190.
15. George F. Ruxton, *Life in the Far West*, 261–62; "John W. Hess, with the Mormon Battalion," *Utah Historical Quarterly*, Vol. V (1931), p. 52; "Extracts from

the Journal of Henry W. Bigler," *Utah Historical Quarterly*, Vol. V (1932), p. 42. Hess said the houses were made of "cottonwood logs split in halves and the pieces all joined together in the form of a stockade," and Bigler remembers dust blowing through the crevices between the logs, covering food and everything else in the cabins.

16. John D. Lee, "Diary of the Mormon Battalion Mission," ed. Juanita Brooks, *New Mexico Historical Review*, Vol. XLII (1967), 188–89; *New York Weekly Tribune*, Sept. 26, 1846, quoted by Dale Morgan, *Overland in 1846*, II, 647; J. W. Abert, "Examination of New Mexico," 30th Cong., 1st Sess., *Sen. Exec. Doc. 23* (Ser. 506), 14; "John Steele's Day Book," 43; Barclay diary, Barclay Papers. John Steele tells of Capt. James Brown picking up fourteen yoke of oxen and one mule belonging to government contractors on the Santa Fe Trail and giving only seven yoke back when the contractors came to find them. "And," says Steele, "many other kettle & mules ware picket up & kept," of which he gives further examples ("John Steele's Day Book," 38, 55, 58).

17. Carter, *Mormon Battalion*, 80, 89, 101, 117; Tyler, *Concise History*, 196, 365; Hafen and Young, "The Mormon Settlement at Pueblo," *Colorado Magazine*, Vol. IX (1932), p. 134n; "Journal History," Nov. 9, 1846, p. 2, Church of Jesus Christ of the Latter Day Saints, Church Historian's Office, Salt Lake City. The annual mortality rate in the U. S. in 1852 was between 1.24 and 1.55 of the population, or one death to every 73 living ("Report of the Superintendent of the Census, Dec. 1, 1852," in 32d Cong., 2d Sess., *House Doc. 1* [Ser. 673], 649–50).

18. "Pioneer, Near Century Mark, Recalls Early Utah Days," *Salt Lake Tribune*, March 10, 1938 (J. R. Korns's interview with Mrs. Manomas Andrus, courtesy of the Utah Historical Society).

19. John Hess wrote, "Here we passed the winter in drilling and hunting and having a good time generally" ("John W. Hess, with the Mormon Battalion," *Utah Historical Quarterly*, Vol. 5 [1932], p. 52); Henry Bigler wrote, "The men and families, too, were tolerably well supplied with food, so that none needed to suffer from hunger," (Hafen and Young, "The Mormon Settlement at Pueblo," *Colorado Magazine*, Vol. IX [1932], p. 130); John Steele wrote at the end of their stay on the Arkansas, "our boys are all well and hearty" ("John Steele's Day Book," 55; Barclay diary, Barclay Papers).

20. Frank Hall, *History of the State of Colorado*, II, 237; Ruxton, *Life in the Far West*, 214.

21. Ruxton, *Life in the Far West*, 215; Barclay diary, Barclay Papers.

22. Interview with Manomas Lavina Gibson Andrus, Utah Historic Records Survey, 1936, Utah Historical Society, Salt Lake City.

23. Ruxton, *Life in the Far West*, 228–30; Carter, *Mormon Battalion*, 61, 110; Harriet D. Munnick, "Louis Labonte," *Mountain Men*, Vol. VII (1969) and Ann Woodbury Hafen, "Lewis B. Myers, 'La Bonte,' " *Mountain Men*, Vol. VII.

24. J. R. Korns, interviewer of Manomas Andrus, told Dale Morgan of the marriage (letter of Morgan to writer, Berkeley, Calif., Sept. 6, 1968). Jesse Nelson saw Bill New living at Greenhorn in the summer of 1848 (Cragin's notes of an interview with Nelson, Smith Canyon Ranch, Colo., July 9, 1908, Cragin Coll.), and the 1850 census of Taos County shows William New, aged 48 from Illinois, living with Mary New, aged 25 from South Carolina, and their children Gethro, female, aged 12, born on the Greenhorn, Nancy, 12, born on the Platte, and Jane, 10, born on the Arkansas. The 1860 census of Taos County shows only William New,

aged 4, born at Mora, and Gethro New, male, aged 12, living in the household of Lucien Maxwell at Rayado. I assume that Gethro was Mary's child (a marvelous child of changeable gender and eternal youth) and that William New, born six years after his father's death, was an error of the census taker, or of Mary.

25. "John Steele's Day Book," 52.

26. Ruxton, *Life in the Far West*, 90–91, 217; Janet Lecompte, "Valentine Johnson ("Rube") Herring," *Mountain Men*, Vol. IX, (1972). Another convert at Pueblo was mountain man Lewis B. Myers. See Ann Woodbury Hafen, "Lewis B. Myers 'LaBonte,' " *Mountain Men*, Vol. VII (1969).

27. Carter, *Mormon Battalion*, 133.

28. "John Steele's Day Book," 41, 44–50; George Deliverance Wilson Diary, transcript by Juanita Brooks, Utah Historical Society, Salt Lake City.

29. "John Steele's Day Book" 55–56. After his arrival at Salt Lake, Capt. Brown repeated this speculation, going to California to collect monies due other Mormon soldiers. He returned with a profit of $2,000 in the form of 3,000 Spanish doubloons, which he paid to Miles Goodyear in November, 1847 for his ranch on Weber River. (Carter, *Mormon Battalion*, 100).

30. "John W. Hess, with the Mormon Battalion," 53; "Journal History," May 16, 1847, p. 2; July 29, 1847, p. 1, Church of Jesus Christ of the Latter Day Saints, Church Historian's Office, Salt Lake City; "John Steele's Day Book," 56.

31. The Gibson family was probably that of Thomas Gibson, Company C, Mormon Battalion; the other may have been that of deserter T. Barnes or Thomas R. Burns, Company E, who stayed at Pueblo with Rebecca Smith, widow of Elisha Smith who died on his way to California (Barclay diary, Barclay Papers; "The Journal of Nathanial V. Jones," *Utah Historical Quarterly*, Vol. IV (1931), p. 8; "The Journal of Robert S. Bliss," *Utah Historical Quarterly*, Vol. IV (1931), p. 80; Benjamin Kern's diary reprinted in LeRoy R. Hafen and Ann W. Hafen, eds., *Frémont's Fourth Expedition* (Glendale, 1960), 91–92; Charles Edward Pancoast, *A Quaker Forty-Niner: The Adventures of Charles Edward Pancoast on the American Frontier* (Philadelphia, 1930), 200.

32. Carter, *Mormon Battalion*, 7–8; "Journal History," July 29, 1847, p. 1, Church of Jesus Christ of the Latter Day Saints, Church Historian's Office, Salt Lake City; "John Steele's Day Book," 38, 55, 58.

33. Carter, *Mormon Battalion*, 129; Tyler, *Concise History*, 318; *Utah: A Guide to the State*, American Guide Series (New York, 1941), 246. Dale Morgan calls my attention to the fact that Gwinn Harris Heap, traveling through the Santa Clara Valley in 1853, was given some wild wheat by a Piute Indian. It was the same wheat domesticated by New Mexicans and called "Taos Wheat" (Gwinn Harris Heap, *Central Route to the Pacific* [Philadelphia, 1854], 100). See also LeRoy Hafen's footnote to his edition of Heap's journal in his *Far West and Rockies Historical Series*, VII, 179n.

CHAPTER 18

1. Barclay diary, Barclay Papers. Pueblo's Northside Reservoir covers the site now.

2. Barclay diary, Sept. and Oct. 1846 and April 4, 5, 9, 10 and 13, 1847, Barclay Papers. The press could have been a robe press, but the fact that it had a gate (diary, April 21, 1847) and that there is frequent mention hereafter of branding and

steering cattle and little mention of robes, leads me to think it a cattle press.

3. *Historic Sketches of the Cattle Trade of the West and Southwest* (Glendale, Calif., 1940), 401.

4. Barclay diary, June 6, 1848, July 9, 1849, Nov. 13, 1847, Nov. 27, 1847; Alexander Barclay to George Barclay, Arkansas River, December, 1845 (Barclay Papers).

5. Barclay diary, November, 1845, Barclay Papers.

6. George R. Ruxton, *Adventures in Mexico and the Rocky Mountains*, 238–39. While looking for his strayed animals, Ruxton met Barclay at his Houses on Feb. 22, 1847, an encounter Barclay recorded (calling Ruxton "Roxbarn") but Ruxton, unfortunately, did not (Barclay diary).

7. Ruxton, *Adventures in Mexico*, 217, 270. For a different version, saying the woman was ransomed by William Bent and turned over to her husband, see Dwight L. Clarke, ed., *The Original Journals of Henry Smith Turner With Stephen Watts Kearny to New Mexico and California, 1846–1847* (Norman, 1966), 67.

8. Ruxton, *Adventures in Mexico*, 271.

9. *Ibid.*, 218.

10. *Ibid.*, 218–20. One of the Arapaho brothers was probably Left Hand, brother-in-law of John Poisal (see Janet Lecompte, "John Poisal," *Mountain Men*, Vol. VI (1968).

11. Ruxton, *Adventures in Mexico*, 220.

12. Barclay diary, April 22–24, 1847, Barclay Papers.

13. *St. Louis Weekly Reveille*, Dec. 28, 1846, p. 1116, c. 2; Jan. 4, 1847, p. 1124, c. 4.

14. Barclay diary, Dec. 16, 1846 through March 15, 1847, Barclay Papers.

15. Barclay diary, Barclay Papers.

16. Barclay diary, March 15 and 16, 1847, Barclay Papers.

17. "John Steele's Day Book."

18. LeRoy R. Hafen, "John D. Albert," *Mountain Men*, Vol. II (1965), p. 21.

19. *Ibid;* Ruxton, *Adventures in Mexico*, 226–230; Louis B. Sporleder MS quoted by LeRoy R. Hafen, "Mountain Men—John D. Albert," *Colorado Magazine*, Vol. X (1933); *Trinidad* (Colo.) *Weekly Advertiser*, Feb. 2, 1885.

20. "John Steele's Day Book," 45–49; Lewis H. Garrard, *Wah-to-yah and the Taos Trail*, 181. Dr. Hempstead at Bent's Fort wrote on Feb. 1, 1847 that the Mormon offer of troops "speaks well of them as soldiers, whatever may be said of them as citizens," (*Niles' National Register*, April 3, 1847, p. 73, c. 1).

21. Ruxton, *Adventures in Mexico*, 226; Louis B. Sporleder MS quoted by LeRoy R. Hafen, "Mountain Men—John D. Albert," *Colorado Magazine*, Vol. X (1933).

22. Barclay diary, Jan. 27 to Feb. 1, 1847, Barclay Papers.

23, Barclay diary, Barclay Papers.

24. L. B. Prince, *Historical Sketches of New Mexico* (Kansas City, 1883), appendix; Report of Col. Price, Santa Fe, Feb. 15, 1847 and letter of Lt. A. B. Dyer, Santa Fe, Feb. 14, 1847, both in *Niles' National Register*, April 24, 1847, pp. 121–22; Ruxton, *Adventures in Mexico*, 217; Barclay diary, Jan. 29, 1847, Barclay Papers; Report of Thomas Fitzpatrick, Bent's Fort, Sept. 18, 1847, 30th Cong., 1st Sess., *Sen. Exec. Doc. 1* (Ser. 503), 246; *Niles' National Register* July 3, 1847, p. 275; Richard W. Cummings to Major Thos. H. Harvey, Fort Leavenworth Agency, July 19, 1847, Letters Received, Office of Indian Affairs, St. Louis Superintendency, National Archives. Dick Wootton was not at the battle of Taos despite the vivid

description he gives of it. Barclay's diary shows that Dick never left the Arkansas in January and February of 1847.

25. Janet Lecompte, "Archibald Charles Metcalf", *Mountain Men*, Vol. IV (1966).

26. Ruxton, *Adventures in Mexico*, 225–26.

27. *Ibid.*, 230–253.

28. *Ibid.*, 270–273. Fisher's Hole is now the resort town of Beulah.

29. Clyde and Mae Reed Porter, *Ruxton of the Rockies*, ed. L. R. Hafen, (Norman, 1950), 307–309.

CHAPTER 19

1. Barclay diary, Feb. 5–6, Oct. 18, 21, 24, 29, 30, Nov. 4, 1847, Barclay Papers; Report of Thomas Fitzpatrick, Bent's Fort, Sept. 18, 1847, with the report of the Commissioner of Indian Affairs, 30th Cong., 1st Sess., *Sen. Exec. Doc. 1* (Ser. 503); F. W. Cragin's notes of an interview with Tom Autobees, Avondale, Colo., Nov. 10, 1907, Cragin Collection. Tom Autobees says the St. Charles farm was begun in 1846 and lasted a year, but evidence in Barclay's diary (Oct. 29, 1847) and in John Brown's account book and elsewhere shows it was farmed in 1847 for one summer only. See Janet Lecompte, "Charles Autobees," *Colorado Magazine*, Vol. XXV (1958), 279–80.

2. Barclay diary, Nov. and Dec. 1, 1847, Barclay Papers.

3. Statement of Calvin Jones before Judge E. J. Hubbard in the Matter of the Adjudication of Priorities of right to the use of Water in Water District no. 19, Trinidad, Colo., March 6, 1885 (copy in Cragin Coll.). See also Frank Hall, *History of the State of Colorado*, Vol. IV (1895), p. 193; Lewis H. Garrard, *Wah-to-yah and the Taos Trail*, ed. Bieber (Glendale, 1938), 305, 316–18.

4. Barclay diary, Dec. 13, 1847, Feb. 4, 1848, Barclay Papers; Report of Thomas Fitzpatrick, Bent's Fort, Dec. 18, 1847, reprinted by Alvin M. Josephy, Jr., ed. "Another Letter from Broken Hand," *The Westerner's Brand Book*, New York Posse, Vol. X (1963), p. 76; *Niles' National Register*, Jan. 9, 1847, p. 304, c. 1.

5. Janet Lecompte, "William Tharp," *Mountain Men*, Vol. III (1966). See Chapter 15 for details of his license.

6. George F. Ruxton, *Adventures in Mexico and the Rocky Mountains*, 272–73.

7. Lecompte, "William Tharp," *Mountain Men*, Vol. III (1966).

8. Louise Barry, *The Beginning of the West*, 722.

9. Barclay diary, May 15, 1847 to June 10, 1847, Barclay Papers; "The W. M. Boggs Manuscript About Bent's Fort, Kit Carson, the Far West and Life Among the Indians," ed. LeRoy R. Hafen, *Colorado Magazine*, Vol. VII (1930); Report of Thomas Fitzpatrick, Bent's Fort, Sept. 18, 1847, p. 242.

10. Barclay diary, May 15 to June 13, 1847, Barclay Papers; Louise Barry, *The Beginning of the West*, 688; Garrard, *Wah-to-yah*, 349–50, 351–52.

11. Barclay diary, June 13 to Sept. 20, 1847; letter of Barclay [no addressee] dated St. Louis, July 20, 1847 (Barclay Papers). The destruction of Turley's mill would have caused Barclay to buy more of his whiskey at St. Louis.

12. Records of the St. Louis Superintendency of Indian Affairs, Kansas Historical Society, Topeka, Vol. IX, 286.

13. Report of Thomas Fitzpatrick, Bent's Fort, Sept. 18, 1847, with the report of the Commissioner of Indian Affairs, 30th Cong., 1st Sess., *Sen. Exec. Doc. 1* (Ser. 503).

14. Letter of Fitzpatrick to Abert, no date, no place [c. May, 1847], copy in the Colorado Historical Society, Denver.

15. Barclay diary, Barclay Papers.

16. Thomas Fitzpatrick to Alexander Barclay, Bent's Fort, Dec. 18, 1847, in LeRoy R. Hafen, *Broken Hand: The Life of Thomas Fitzpatrick: Mountain Man, Guide and Indian Agent* (Denver, 1973), 257. Two more of Col. Gilpin's companies were stationed at Fort Mann. Gilpin's command camped among the Cheyennes and Arapahos until early in March when it went to Mora and thence down the Canadian. Gilpin recommended four permanent posts to control Indians: at Pawnee Fork, the crossing of the Arkansas, "Beautiful Encampment" on the Arkansas, and on the Canadian. He also recommended the purchase of Bent's Fort and a post at La Junta de los Rios, later site of Barclay's Fort (letter of Lt. Col. W. Gilpin, Head-quarters, Battalion of Missouri Volunteers, Fort Mann, Aug. 1, 1848, 30th Cong., 2d Sess., *House Exec. Doc. 1* [Ser. 537], 136–40).

17. *Jefferson* (Mo.) *Inquirer*, April 1, 1848, in Dale L. Morgan's transcripts, "The Mormons and the Far West." Tom Autobees says the woman in the case was Nicolasa, but Luz Metcalf Ledoux and her brother Vicente Trujillo both say it was Candelaria, and they were present (Cragin's notes of interviews with Tom Autobees, Avondale, Colo, Nov. 8, 1907; with Mrs. Felipe Ledoux, Las Vegas, N. M., Feb. 13, 1908; and with Vicente Trujillo, Avondale, Colo., Nov. 9, 1907, Cragin Coll.)

18. Mrs. Ledoux says it was Metcalf who fostered his friend Waters, but if so it was after Feb. 12, 1848, when Metcalf returned from the Platte (Cragin's notes of an interview with Mrs. Ledoux, Feb. 13, 1908, Cragin Coll.; and Barclay diary, Feb. 12, 1848, Barclay Papers).

19. John Brown's Account Book; with accounts of 1848 are undated memos that Brown "paid Waters," and that "James Watters" ground 49 "almores" *(almudes)* of corn; letters of Thomas Fitzpatrick, Bent's Fort Feb. 13, 1848 and St. Louis, June 24, 1848, Letters Received, Office of Indian Affairs, Upper Platte and Arkansas Agency, National Archives.

20. *Jefferson, Mo. Inquirer*, April 1, 1848; Louise Barry, *The Beginning of the West*, 740.

21. Barclay diary, Barclay Papers.

22. *Ibid.*, April 14 to 18, 1848.

CHAPTER 20

1. F. W. Cragin's notes of an interview with Mrs. Jacob Beard (Isabel Simpson), El Paso, Texas, Oct. 30, 1904, Cragin Coll.; Senex [George Simpson], "Old Time Recollections," *Trinidad* (Colo.) *Daily News*, June 8, 1881, p. 1, c. 2; Barclay Diary, May and June, 1848, Barclay Papers.

2. Cragin interview with Mrs. Beard; Senex [George Simpson], "Old Time Recollections," *Trinidad* (Colo.) *Daily News*, June 8, 1881, p. 1, c. 2; Barclay diary, June, 1848, Barclay Papers; *Santa Fe Republican*, May 15, 1848, p. 2, c. 2; George S. Simpson's testimony in *Transcript of Record, U. S. v. Maxwell Land Grant Co.* et al, U. S. Supreme Court, No. 974 (Oct. term, 1886), 142–43.

3. Letter of Thomas Fitzpatrick, Bent's Fort, Dec. 18, 1847, Letters Received, Office of Indian Affairs, Upper Platte and Arkansas Agency, National Archives; Charles Bent to Manuel Alvarez, Taos, March 2, March 4 and March 6, 1846, and

list of Louis Joseph Crombeck's goods, Alvarez Papers; *Santa Fe Republican*, May 13, 1848, p. 2; Barclay diary, Nov. 9, 1847, Barclay Papers; *Jefferson* (Mo.) *Inquirer*, Dec. 25, 1847, in Dale L. Morgan, "The Mormons and the Far West"; *Matt Field on the Santa Fe Trail*, ed. John E. Sunder, 190.

4. John Brown's Account Book; F. W. Cragin's notes of an interview with Mrs. Felipe Ledoux (formerly the wife of Metcalf), Las Vegas, June 17, 1908, Cragin Coll.; L. A. Ingersoll, *Ingersoll's century annals of San Bernardino county, 1769–1904* (Los Angeles, 1904), 651; "Claims for Indian Depredations in New Mexico," 35th Cong., 1st. Sess., *House Exec. Doc. 122* (Ser. 929), 11. Maxwell's claim was for 30 mules, 50 horses and 600 buckskins stolen by Jicarilla Apaches on June 12, 1848, but it was not filed until 1854 and was not allowed. Maxwell also tells the story of the attack: He wrote his father-in-law Beaubien from Greenhorn on June 4 that the party left Greenhorn on June 1 with 60 horses and 400 deerskins. At the foot of Raton Pass they saw Apaches and turned back towards Greenhorn, the Indians following. About two miles south of Apache Creek the Indians caught up, shouting that they were Utes and friendly. Their yells frightened the traders' horses, thirty of which got away and were captured by the Indians who promised to return them if the Americans would visit their village. The Americans returned to Greenhorn and raised eighteen men. The next day they started for the village at the foot of Raton Pass. The Indians came out to meet them and repeated their promise, but the Americans refused to visit the village. After a little skirmish during which one or two shots were fired, the Americans returned to Greenhorn with the Indians following them (*St. Louis Daily Union*, July 20, 1848, in Morgan, "The Mormons and the Far West").

5. Maxwell's letter of June 4, 1848, above; Report of Major W. W. Reynolds, Don Fernando de Taos, Aug. 5, 1848, RG 94, National Archives; *Santa Fe Republican*, Aug. 1, 1848.

6. Janet Lecompte, "The Manco Burro Pass Massacre," *New Mexico Historical Review*, Vol. XLI (1966), No. 4.

7. "Key to the view of Barclay's Fort," Barclay Papers; Advertisement in *Santa Fe Weekly Gazette*, Feb. 19, 1853, p. 1, c. 1; F. W. Cragin's notes of an interview with Mrs. Frank M. Jones (Fanny Kroenig), Las Vegas, June 26, 1908, Cragin Coll.

8. Barclay diary, May, 1848 to Feb., 1850, Barclay Papers.

9. Alexander Barclay to George Barclay, Barclay's Fort, Dec. 28, 1851, Barclay Papers. William Carr Lane wrote in September, 1853, "The Mora Valley is beautiful but the seasons are too late for productive ag. tre." "William Carr Lane Diary," *New Mexico Historical Review*, Vol. XXXIX (1964), 289–90.

10. Robert W. Frazer, ed., *Mansfield on the Condition of the Western Forts, 1853–54* (Norman, 1963) 14n; draft of a letter of Alexander Barclay to Senator John S. Phelps (Mo.), no date, Barclay Papers. Barclay and Doyle built a log store at the edge of what had been designated "military reserve" to establish their claim and to sell soldiers whiskey in trade for government stores. Col. Sumner arrested Barclay and Doyle and ordered their building destroyed. Then he increased the "military reserve" around Fort Union to four miles square, to obviate another such "store" (John Greiner, "Memorandum," Ritch Papers, Huntington Library, San Marino, California; Mora County, N. M. Records, Book C, 269). Barclay and Doyle filed a $30,000 damage suit against Sumner and the United States for trespass and destruction of property (Chris Emmett, *Fort Union and the Winning of the Southwest* [Norman, 1965], 138–42) which led to acknowledgment of their ownership of the

land and to a lease of the Fort Union Reservation to the U. S. for $1,200 a year, signed March 31, 1854 (Mora County, N. M. Records, Book C, 269).

11. Barclay and Doyle had each brought $4,000 in cash to New Mexico, along with other property, and they invested $11,000 in the fort. The farm around it did not serve to feed the huge summer population or even the reduced winter staff of 32. One to two thousand pounds of meat and flour had to be bought in Mora every month, and in 1851 six wagonloads of grain (30,000 pounds) as well as $2,000 worth of staples had to be brought in. Four men with 2 wagons and 4 yoke of oxen were employed 5 months a year in obtaining firewood (Alexander Barclay to George Barclay, Feb. 20, 1850, Jan., 1851, March 21, 1851, Dec. 28, 1851, March 27, 1852; Mora County N. M. Records, Book I, p. 98; *Santa Fe Weekly Gazette*, Feb. 9, 1853, p. 1, c. 1.

12. Annie Heloise Abel, ed., "Indian Affairs in New Mexico under the Administration of William Carr Lane. From the Journal of John Ward," *New Mexico Historical Review*, Vol. XVI (1941), 222; letter of Alexander Barclay, Barclay's Fort, Nov. 1, 1853, Barclay Papers. The bridge had been built in 1851 by John Richard and others in cooperation with the U. S. Army (Merrill J. Mattes, "Seth E. Ward," *Mountain Men*, Vol. II [1966] 365).

13. William Adamson to A. G. Barclay, Junta de los Ríos, March 15, 1850; Alexander Barclay to George Barclay, Mora, Aug. 25, 1852, J. B. Doyle to Barclay, La Junta, Nov. 12, 1852; Barclay Papers.

14. Barclay diary, Oct. 1, 1848 and *passim;* B[recia] S[impson] to Barclay, St. Louis, Oct. 3, 1849, Barclay Papers; Senex [George Simpson], "Pencillings," Watrous, N. M., June 30, 1882, *Trinidad* (Colo.) *Daily News*, July 4, 1882, p. 4, c. 3.

15. F. W. Cragin's notes of an interview with Jesse Nelson, Smith Canyon Ranch, Colo., July 9, 1908, Cragin Coll.; "William Carr Lane Diary," *New Mexico Historical Review*, Vol. XXXIX (1964), 290. Cruz Doyle signed an affidavit with her mark as late as May, 1864 (administration papers on estate of Joseph B. Doyle, Records of the Probate Court, Pueblo, Colo.).

16. Alexander Barclay, fragment of a draft of a letter [probably to Joe Doyle], undated, Barclay Papers; Harvey L. Carter and Janet S. Lecompte, "George Semmes Simpson," *Mountain Men*, Vol. III (1966), 298, n. 50.

17. Alexander Barclay to George Barclay, Barclay's Fort, Nov. 1, 1853.

18. William C. Mitchell to Alexander Barclay, Independence, March 23, 1854; Alexander Barclay to George Barclay, Barclay's Fort (n. d., c. Aug., 1854); Herbert George Yatman to George Barclay, On the Mississippi, Nov. 28, 1856; Barclay Papers.

19. "Reminiscences," *Field and Farm*, Vol. VI, No. 11 (Sept. 15, 1888), 6.

20. Herbert George Yatman to George Barclay, On the Mississippi, Nov. 28, 1856, Barclay Papers.

CHAPTER 21

1. *Niles' National Register*, June 19, 1847, p. 248, c. 1; John E. Sunder, *The Fur Trade on the Upper Missouri, 1840–1865* (Norman, 1965), 104.

2. This picture of conditions in the Arkansas Valley of 1848 is drawn from reports of Thomas Fitzpatrick dated Bent's Fort Feb. 10 and Feb. 13, 1848, and St. Louis, June 24 and Oct. 6, 1848, in Letters Received, Office of Indian Affairs,

Upper Platte and Arkansas Agency, National Archives. In an earlier letter of Dec. 18, 1847 from Bent's Fort, after talking to Alexander Barclay there, Fitzpatrick reported the Indian trade "greatly on the decline" due to excessive competition and scarcity of buffalo, but a few months later he reversed this opinion. Barclay's gout and general depression apparently colored not only his own but Fitzpatrick's thinking about the condition of the robe trade. For specific events of 1848, see Louise Barry, *The Beginning of the West* (Topeka, 1972), 714–15, 720, 732–33, 755.

3. F. W. Cragin's notes of an interview with Jesse Hodges Nelson, Smith Canyon Ranch, Colo., July 9, 1908, Cragin Coll.

4. Cragin's notes of an interview with Nelson, above. George Simpson had a log cabin at the trail crossing of the St. Charles in 1843 (Cragin's notes of an interview with Jesús Pando, Avondale, Colo., Nov. 7, 1907, Cragin Coll.); Dick Wootton said he built another in 1846 where he spent the summer farming (Frank Hall, *History of the State of Colorado*, II, 237); Calvin Jones wintered there in 1846–47 (testimony of Calvin Jones, Trinidad, Colo., Oct. 31, 1883, *Transcript of Record, U. S. v. Maxwell Land-Grant Co.* et al, pp. 169–71); and in the summer of 1847 Charles and Tom Autobees, Levin Mitchell, Blackhawk and Labonte had a farm (see Chapter 19).

5. Lancaster Lupton Papers; Barclay diary, March 5, 1847, Barclay Papers. The quotation is from Shakespeare's *Julius Caesar* and was in frequent use among speculators from all sections of 19th century America.

6. Benjamin Kern's diary and Richard Kern's diary in LeRoy R. Hafen and Ann W. Hafen, eds., *Frémont's Fourth Expedition* (Glendale, 1960), 91–92, 118.

7. Charles Preuss, *Exploring with Frémont*, 143; Benjamin Kern diary, "Extracts from the Journal of J. H. Simpson," Letter of Lancaster P. Lupton to Senator Benton, Pueblo on the Upper Arkansas, Nov. 28, 1848, Hafen and Hafen, *Frémont's Fourth Expedition*, pp. 91–92, 247, 284; Micajah McGehee, "Frémont's Fourth Expedition," *Outdoor Life*, May, 1910; *L. A. Ingersoll's century annals of San Bernardino county, 1769–1904* (Los Angeles, 1904), 650.

8. Richard Kern's diary, Hafen and Hafen, *Frémont's Fourth Expedition*, p. 118. Lupton's letter of Nov. 28, 1848 (*ibid.*, 284–85) tells of buying provisions and horses at Pueblo; Frémont's notes written much later in preparation for a second volume (never written) of his *Memoirs*, say that he bought corn here also (*ibid.*, 298), but contemporary diaries contradict him. Frémont probably used a letter of Fitzpatrick to Jesse Benton Frémont, dated Bent's Fort, Jan. 3, 1849 (*ibid.*, 286–87) to refresh his memory, but Fitzpatrick erroneously states that Frémont procured forage at Pueblo. Frémont confused Pueblo with Hardscrabble; his notes say, "Halt at Pueblo (San Carlos?) on the Fontaine qui Bouit" (*ibid.*, 298), and Richard Kern's map, drawn for Lieut. Parke in 1851, locates "Pueblo de S. Carlos" at the mouth of the Fountain, and an unnamed settlement meant to be Hardscrabble on the east side of the mouth of the Hardscrabble ("Map of the Territory of New Mexico compiled by Bvt. 2nd Lt. Jno. G. Parke, U.S.T.E. assisted by Mr. Richard H. Kern . . . Santa Fe, N.M., 1851," National Archives). But Pueblo San Carlos was Hardscrabble and not Pueblo, as Lupton makes clear in his letter to Senator Benton written from "Pueblo on the Upper Arkansas, November 28, 1848," when he writes, "Col. Frémont passed this place (near the mouth of Fontaine qui Bouit) on the 22d instant . . . At the Pueblo San Carlos, twenty five miles above . . ." (Hafen and Hafen, *Frémont's Fourth Expedition*, 28–29, 91–92.)

9. Thomas Breckenridge, in his "Memoirs," says Burroughs and Briggs were

the only residents, but Lupton's account book indicates many others at Hardscrabble then. See Hafen and Hafen, *Frémont's Fourth Expedition*, 91–92, 200, 217, 284. On seeing the Sangre de Cristo range, Dick Wootton is said to have exclaimed, "There is too much snow ahead for me," and to have returned to Hardscrabble (Breckenridge, "The Story of a Famous Expedition," *Cosmopolitan*, Vol. XXI, p. 400), but this is one adventure Dick did not claim for himself. He was sheriff of Taos at the time and met Frémont when he arrived at Taos in January, 1849 (Conard, *"Uncle Dick" Wootton*, 197–98).

10. John Brown's Account Book; Cragin's notes of an interview with Mrs. Felipe Ledoux, Las Vegas, N. M., June 17, 1908, Cragin Coll.; *L. A. Ingersoll's annals*, 650–52.

11. More complete accounts of these men may be found in sketches under their names in Hafen's *Mountain Men* (see index).

12. Richard Martin May, "Sketch of a Migrating Family to California," MS, Bancroft Library, Berkeley, Calif.

13. Cragin's notes of an interview with Mrs. Frank M. (Fanny Kroenig) Jones, Las Vegas, N. M., June 28, 1908, and with Jacob Beard, El Paso, Texas, Oct. 29, 1904, Cragin Coll.; Mora County, N. M. Records, Book IV, p. 352, Book V, p. 23, Cragin's notes of an interview with Tom Autobees, Avondale, Colo., Nov. 7, 1907, Cragin Coll.; for family tradition about Teresita's death and burial, see Richard L. Luna, *Lady of Taos* (Colorado Springs, 1974), 257. For Andrés' death see *Santa Fe New Mexican*, July 9, 1908.

14. Ceran St. Vrain to Lieut.–Col. Eneas McKay, July 21, 1847, and letter of Thos. J. Jessup, QMG, Oct. 14, 1847, Old Fort Lyon Abandoned Military Reservation File, War Dept. Records, RG 98, National Archives; St. Louis, Mo. County Records, Books M4–116, M4–151, N4–43; David Lavender, *Bent's Fort*, 315–18.

15. Barclay's diary indicates some of these men on the Arkansas (Jan. 28, Feb. 9, March 9, March 30, April 1, April 11, June 18, July 19, 1849); others will be found in this chapter.

16. Grant Foreman, *Marcy & the Gold Seekers* (Norman, 1939), 75, 332–39; Louise Barry, *The Beginning of the West*, 878.

17. Foreman, *Marcy & the Gold Seekers*, 66–82; Ralph P. Bieber, ed., *Southern Trails to California in 1849* (Glendale, 1937), 333–47.

18. Charles Edward Pancoast, *A Quaker Forty-Niner: The Adventures of Charles Edward Pancoast on the American Frontier*, 185, 200–202; Barry, *The Beginning of the West*, 853–60; "Statement of W. C. Randolph," MS, Bancroft Library, Berkeley, Calif.

19. Pancoast, *A Quaker Forty-Niner*, 204, 206; letter of Geo. W. Withers, Salt Lake City, Aug. 12, 1849 in Robert H. Miller Envelope, 1849, Missouri Historical Society, St. Louis; Hafen and Hafen, supplement to *Journals of the Forty-Niners, Salt Lake to Los Angeles* (Glendale, 1954), 15–26.

20. Letter from Santa Fe, Aug. 9, 1849, *Daily Missouri Republican*, Sept. 12, 1849, quoted by Ralph P. Bieber, *Southern Trails to California in 1849* (Glendale, 1937), 378–79; Elisha Douglass Perkins, *Gold Rush Diary*, ed. Thomas D. Clark (Lexington, Ky, 1967), 175.

21. Letter of Geo. W. Withers, cited.

22. Pancoast *A Quaker Forty-Niner*, 204; Louise Barry, *The Beginning of the West*, 858–59; Barclay's diary (March 30, April 1, 1849) shows that Kinney left Taos

for the Arkansas via Barclay's Fort on April 1 with Dennis and Jim Dickey.

23. Foreman, *Marcy*, 102–104; "The Journal of John Lowery Brown, of the Cherokee Nation en Route to California in 1850," ed. Muriel H. Wright, *Chronicles of Oklahoma*, Vol. XII (1934), 188–90.

24. Notes of Superintendent Alfred Cummings, Washington, D. C., April 28, 1853, Letters Received, Office of Indian Affairs, Central Superintendency, National Archives.

25. William Kroenig, Sr., "Autobiography."

26. (St. Louis) *Missouri Republican*, Oct. 2, 1849, quoted *Colorado Magazine*, Vol. XXXIII (1956), 278.

27. LeRoy R. Hafen and Francis Marion Young, *Fort Laramie and the Pageant of the West, 1834–1890* (Glendale, 1938), 166.

28. Senex [George Simpson] article in the *Trinidad* (Colo.) *Daily News*, July 15, 1882, Dawson Scrapbook I, 407, Colorado Historical Society, Denver; Harvey Lewis Carter *'Dear Old Kit,'* 127–28.

29. *The Official Correspondence of James S. Calhoun*, ed. Annie H. Abel (Washington, D. C., 1915), 288, 450.

CHAPTER 22

1. Janet Lecompte, "Charles Autobees," *Colorado Magazine*, Vol. XXXV (1958), 55.

2. *Ibid.*, Vol. XXXIV (1957), 287–88; XXXV (1958), 51–60.

3. *Ibid.*, Vol. XXXIV (1957), 288–89.

4. *Ibid.*, Vol. XXXV (1958), 53–56; Charles Irving Jones, "William Krönig, New Mexico Pioneer," *New Mexico Historical Review*, Vol. XIX (1944), 290–92.

5. Lecompte, "Charles Autobees," *Colorado Magazine*, Vol. XXXV (1958), 51–52.

6. Jones, "William Kronig," *New Mexico Historical Review*, Vol. XIX (1944), 294–97.

7. *Ibid.*, 212–13.

8. *Ibid.*, 296–300.

9. Beckwith, *Report of Explorations for a Route for the Pacific Railroad* . . . *House Exec. Doc. 91*, 33d. Cong., 3d Sess. (Ser. 792), 34–35.

10. *Ibid.*

11. *Ibid.*

12. *Ibid.*

13. Janet Lecompte, "Marcelino Baca," *Mountain Men*, Vol. III (1966); F. W. Cragin's notes of interviews with Vicente Trujillo, Avondale, Colo., Nov. 9, 1907, Cragin Coll.: Felipe Cisneros, Florence, Colo., Sept. 27, 1907, and Pedro Sandoval, Mora River, June 12, 1908, Cragin Coll. The cornfield was where the Pueblo stockyards are now.

14. Cragin's notes of an interview with Mrs. R. L. Wootton, Trinidad, Colo., Dec. 14, 1907, Cragin Coll.; Garrard, *Wah-to-yah*, 246–47; Fray Angélico Chávez, "New Names in New Mexico, 1820–1850," *El Palacio*, Vol. LXIV (1957), 312, 379; District Court Records, Taos, N. M., 1847–1855, Book C–1 n.p.; testimony of Charles Williams, Trinidad, Colo., Nov. 2, 1883, *Transcript of Record, U. S. v. Maxwell Land Grant Co.* et al, U. S. Supreme Court no. 974 (Oct. term), 188; Conard, *"Uncle Dick" Wootton*, 205–206.

15. Lecompte, "Charles Autobees," *Colorado Magazine*, Vol. XXXV (1958), 58–59.

16. Lecompte, "Levin Mitchell," *Mountain Men*, Vol. V (1968).

17. Lecompte, "Charles Autobees," *Colorado Magazine*, Vol. XXXV (1958), 58–59.

18. Alexander Barclay to George Barclay, Barclay's Fort, Nov. 1, 1853, Barclay Papers; testimony of Calvin Jones, Trinidad, Colo., Oct. 31, 1883, *U. S.* v. *Maxwell Land Grant Co.* et al, p. 171.

19. Lecompte, "Charles Autobees," *Colorado Magazine*, Vol. XXXV (1958), 61.

20. *Ibid.*, 64.

21. *Ibid.*, 62–64. Between January and March, 1853 a man named Whittle stabbed four Mexicans at a fandango in Taos. He was arrested and imprisoned, but escaped. He seems to have been apprehended again before turning up at Huerfano, if indeed this is the same man (William Carr Lane's endorsement on voucher #17, Abstract A, Wm. Carr Lane Papers, Missouri Historical Society, St. Louis).

22. Lecompte, "Charles Autobees," *Colorado Magazine*, Vol. XXXV (1958), 62–64.

23. *Ibid.*

24. Deposition of Juan Isidro Landoval [Sandoval], Court of Claims, Dec. 5, 1891, against the United States and the Ute Indians. Copy in "Pioneer Envelope," Cragin Coll.; Cragin's notes of an interview with Pedro Sandoval, cited.

CHAPTER 23

1. John T. Hughes, *Doniphan's Expedition* reprinted in William E. Connelley, *Doniphan's Expedition and the Conquest of New Mexico and California*, 72, 251; letter of Colonel Doniphan in the *Missouri Republican*, reprinted in *Niles' National Register*, Dec. 19, 1846, pp. 241–42.

2. Report of E. A. Graves, agent, and D. Meriwether, governor, with 33d Cong., 2d Sess., *House Exec. Doc. 1* (Ser. 777) 166–84; D. Meriwether to the Commissioner of Indian Affairs, Santa Fe, Sept. 15, 1855, Letters Received, Office of Indian Affairs, New Mexico Superintendency, National Archives.

3. *Niles' National Register*, Nov. 6, 1847, p. 155, c. 1–2; testimony of George S. Simpson, Trinidad, Colo. Oct. 29, 1883, *Transcript of Record U. S.* v. *Maxwell Land Grant Co.* et al, U. S. Supreme Court no. 974 (Oct. term, 1886), 144; F. W. Cragin's notes of an interview with Jesse Nelson, Smith Canyon Ranch, Colo., July 9, 1908, Cragin Coll.

4. Report of Lieut. J. H. Whittlesey, March 15, 1849, 31st Cong., 1st Sess., *Sen. Exec. Doc. 24* (Ser. 554), 11–13; report of Auguste Lacome, March 15, 1850 and letter of James S. Calhoun, Nov. 15, 1849 in *The Official Correspondence of James S. Calhoun*, ed. Annie H. Abel, 169; John Greiner's notes entitled "Whittlesey's expedition to the Cerro del Olla Against the Utes" and "Capt. Chapman and Coniachi" with a sheaf of notes entitled "Overawing the Indians" in the William E. Ritch Collection; Greiner's interview with Dr. Bowman, Jan. 22, 1852, Ritch Coll. *Missouri Republican*, July 7, 1849 in Dale Morgan's "The Mormons and the Far West."

5. Reports of Lieut.–Col. J. M. Washington, May 29, 1849 and June 4, 1849, 31st Cong., 1st Sess., *H. Exec. Doc. 5* (Ser. 569), 107–109, Charles J. Kappler,

Indian Affairs; Laws and Treaties, Vol. II (Wash., D. C., 1904) 585–87.

6. *Correspondence of James S. Calhoun*, 281, 388–89, 438, 530. This short chapter on the Utes is merely the sketchiest outline of the available material. Besides the specific references cited I have used a large number of documents from the Ritch Collection, including John Greiner's notes and a batch of military reports of contacts between U. S. soldiers and Ute Indians from 1849 to 1854 (RI 381, 383, 397, 400, 415, 540, 635, 636, 640, 646, etc). I have also used documents in Letters Received, Office of Indian Affairs, New Mexico Superintendency, 1849–1857, National Archives.

7. David V. Whiting to William Carr Lane, Washington, D. C., Aug. 5, 1852 and John Greiner to William Carr Lane, Dec. 31, 1852, in Letters Received, Office of Indian Affairs, New Mexico Superintendency; Robert W. Frazer, ed., *Mansfield on the Condition of the Western Forts, 1853–54* (Norman, 1963), 17–19.

8. Kappler, *Indian Affairs. Laws and Treaties*, II, 440–42, 600–602, 585–87. "Coniache" is also spelled "Conniach," "Kaneatche" and other variants.

9. John Greiner to William Carr Lane, Dec. 31, 1852, Letters Received, Office of Indian Affairs, New Mexico Superintendency.

10. M. Steck to William Carr Lane, Feb. 7, 1853 and William Carr Lane to Superintendent of Indian Affairs, Feb. 24, 1853, Letters Received, Office of Indian Affairs, New Mexico Superintendency.

11. Charles Irving Jones, "William Kronig, New Mexico Pioneer, from his memories of 1849–1860," *New Mexico Historical Review*, Vol. XIX (1944), 215–220; *Correspondence of James S. Calhoun*, 170; DeWitt C. Peters, *Pioneer Life and Frontier Adventures*, 328–29; letters of David Meriwether, Sept. 19, 1853 and Oct. 30, 1853 in Letters Received, Office of Indian Affairs, New Mexico Superintendency; James H. Quinn, "Notes of a Spy Company under Col. Cooke," Ritch Coll.

12. Kappler, *Indian Affairs. Laws and Treaties*, Vol. II, 598–600; report of David Meriwether, Superintendent of Indian Affairs for New Mexico, Sept. 1, 1854, 33d Cong., 2d. Sess., *House Exec. Doc. 1* (Ser. 777), 166–67.

13. Lieut. James Henry Carleton, HQ, Column in the Field, Camp in the Raton Mountains, June 5, 1854, Ritch Coll.; Meriwether to Superintendent of Indian Affairs, March 17, 1854, Letters Received, Office of Indian Affairs, New Mexico Superintendency.

14. Reports of C. Carson, March 21, 1854 and D. Meriwether, March 17, 1854, Letters Received, Office of Indian Affairs, New Mexico Superintendency.

15. Letters of William Carr Lane, May 26, 1853 and John Greiner, March 25, 1852, Letters Received, Office of Indian Affairs, New Mexico Superintendency. Charles Beaubien testified in 1858 that he had distributed land at Conejos in 1832 or 1833 which could not maintain settlement because of Navajo hostility (statement of Jan. 18, 1858, Blackmore Papers, #0023, State Records Center and Archives, Santa Fe). In 1842, land on the Conejos was granted by the Mexican government to eighty settlers who were prevented from living there by the Utes (Blackmore Papers, #0023; "Schedule of Documents relating to grants of land . . . ," Report of the Surveyor General of New Mexico, Sept. 30, 1856, 34th Cong. 3d Sess., *House Exec. Doc. 1* (Ser. 893), 431; Ralph Carr, "Private Land Claims in Colorado," *Colorado Magazine* Vol. XXV (1948), 20–21); John Greiner's diary of a trip to Fort Massachusetts in July, 1852, in the course of which he passed Costilla, Culebra and Conejos Creeks, mentions no settlements at any of these places. Probably San Luis

on the Culebra, said to have been established in 1851, was not populated until at least 1853 (Annie H. Abel, ed., "Journal of John Greiner," *Old Santa Fe*, Vol. III (1916), No. 2, 231–32).

16. J. S. Calhoun, Feb. 2, 1851 and Nov. 10, 1851, *Correspondence of James S. Calhoun*, 288, 450–51.

17. F. W. Cragin's notes of an interview with Mrs. William Walker (Eliza Ann Wootton), Trinidad, Colo., June 2, 1908, Cragin Coll.; letter of Charles Ortibi, Huerfano, Oct. 22, 1854, Kit Carson Papers, Bancroft Library, Berkeley, Calif., courtesy of Dale Morgan; Janet Lecompte, "Charles Autobees," *Colorado Magazine*, Vol. XXXV (1958), 140–42. Much of what the Utes considered their land was covered by Mexican land grants, a fact beyond the knowledge or comprehension of either Superintendent Calhoun or the Utes, or in fact many modern investigators. It was another half century before the validity of these grants was determined, and there are still those who do not consider the matter closed.

18. Letter of Meriwether, Oct. 29, 1854, Letters Received, Office of Indian Affairs, New Mexico Superintendency; F. W. Cragin's notes of an interview with Felipe Cisneros, Pueblo, Colo., Sept. 7, 1907, Cragin Coll.

19. Meriwether, *My Life in the Mountains and on the Plains*, 201.

20. Letter of Meriwether, Nov. 30, 1854, Letters Received, Office of Indian Affairs, New Mexico Superintendency; Harvey Lewis Carter, *'Dear Old Kit': The Historical Christopher Carson* (Norman, 1968), 143.

21. Meriwether, *My Life in the Mountains*, 228. Peters, *Pioneer Life*, 473, describes Blanco very differently as having "every feature about his face as regular as if it had been carved for sculptured perfection." Peters represents him as having a high forehead, active brain, a man of vast superiority and latent greatness. Peters was surgeon at Fort Massachusetts in 1854 and may have been acquainted with Blanco, but I believe he is describing the handsome Capote chief Tamouche (Amuche), often in Chico Velasquez's company. W. H. H. Davis says of Tamouche, "his features were regular and classic . . . finest specimen of a wild, untutored Indian I have ever met" (*El Gringo; or, New Mexico and Her People*, 283). Meriwether describes Tamouche as "the most gentlemanly Indian in his manners that I ever met with," but goes on to say he succeeded Chico Velasquez as Muache head chief, which is in error (Meriwether, *My Life in the Mountains*, 202).

22. Peters, *Pioneer Life*, 499.

CHAPTER 24

1. F. W. Cragin's notes of an interview with Pedro Sandoval, Webber P. O., Mora River, N. M., June 12, 1908, Cragin Coll. The material in this chapter first appeared, without references, in Janet Lecompte, "Pueblo Massacre," Westerners Brand Book (Denver, 1954).

2. H. L. Conard, *"Uncle Dick" Wootton*, 297–301.

3. Cragin's notes of an interview with Felipe ("Chico") Cisneros, Florence, Colo., Sept. 27, 1907 and Nov. 14, 1907, Cragin Coll. Cragin also interviewed Felipe ("Grande") Cisneros, hence the distinction.

4. Cragin's notes of an interview with Mrs. Mariano (Elena Baca) Autobees, Pueblo, Colo., Oct. 31, 1907, Cragin Coll.

5. Cragin's notes of interviews with Felipe ("Chico") Cisneros and Elena Baca Autobees, Cragin Coll.

6. Cragin's interviews with Cisneros and Elena Baca Autobees, Cragin Coll. José Barela was the brother of Ramona Barela, who was Teresita and Benito Sandoval's mother. An 1845 census shows that in April, 1845 he was living in Mora with his wife Dolores Sandoval, aged 50, and their son Juan, aged 25. He was then 85 years old, which would make him 94 or 95 at the time of the Pueblo massacre (Census of Valle de San Antonio de Mora, April, 1845, Mexican Archives of New Mexico, State Archives and Records Center, Santa Fe).

7. Cragin's notes of interviews with Elena Baca Autobees and with Juana Suaso Simpson, El Paso, Texas, Oct. 31, 1904, Cragin Coll.

8. Cragin's notes of an interview with Felipe ("Chico") Cisneros, Sept. 27, 1907, Cragin Coll. Baca's claim for indemnity showed that the Indians took 73 head of cattle, 13 horses and 2 mules valued at $4,015 ("Claim for Indian Depredations in New Mexico," 35th. Cong., 1st. Sess., *House Exec. Doc. 123* [Ser. 959], 62). Fifty years later, Felipe Cisneros, Baca's horse-herder, remembered that Baca had 13 horses and 500 head of cattle (Cragin's interview with Cisneros). An affidavit made by Baca before Governor Meriwether on Jan. 13, 1855 states his losses as ten yoke of American oxen worth $100 per yoke, 53 American cows at $30 per head, 13 horses and 2 mules at $95 per head, driven off by a hundred Indians, principally Utes (Letters Received, Office of Indian Affairs, New Mexico Superintendency).

9. Cragin's interview with Felipe Cisneros, Nov. 14, 1907, Cragin Coll.

10. Cragin's interview with Cisneros, *loc. cit.*, and with Elena Baca Autobees, Oct. 31, 1907, Cragin Coll.

11. Cragin's interviews with Cisneros and Elena Baca Autobees, *loc. cit.*

12. *Ibid.*, and Cragin's interview with Pedro Sandoval, June 12, 1908, Cragin Coll.

13. Cragin's interviews with Cisneros and Elena Baca Autobees, *loc. cit.*

14. Cragin's interviews with Pedro Sandoval, Webber P. O., Mora River, N. M., June 12, 1908, and with Mrs. Ira Miller (Alvina Sandoval, daughter of Felix), Trinidad, May 25, 1908, Cragin Coll. For other versions of the massacre, see Appendix C, "Sources for an Account of the Pueblo Massacre."

15. Cragin's interviews with Felipe ("Chico") Cisneros, Sept. 27 and Nov. 14, 1907, with Pedro Sandoval, June 12, 1908; with Elena Baca Autobees, Oct. 31, 1907; with Tom Autobees, Avondale, Colo., July 29, 1908; and with Mrs. William Adamson (Cecilia Sandoval), Trinidad, Colo., May 23, 1908; Cragin Coll.

16. Cragin's interviews with Tom Autobees, Pedro Sandoval, Felipe Cisneros, as above, and with Mrs. William Walker (Eliza Ann Wootton), Trinidad, Colo., Dec. 15, 1907, Cragin Coll. The burial party from down the Arkansas included Charles Autobees, Tom Suaso, Francis Yara, Levin Mitchell, Jesús Pando, Jean–Baptiste Charlefou, Charley Carson (Cragin's interview with Jesús Pando, Nov. 7, 1907, Cragin Coll.), J. W. Atwood and John Jurnegan (W. A. Nichols to Col. T. T. Fauntleroy, Santa Fe, Jan. 11, 1855, Dept. of New Mexico Orders, Vol. IX, National Archives, copy from the collection of the late James W. Arrott, Sapello, N. M.). Jesús Pando says fourteen of the massacre victims were buried inside the fort; Felipe Cisneros says some were buried near the county bridge over the Fountain, some near Baca's. Tom Autobees and Jesús Pando, whom Cragin interviewed together, agreed that "18 people were killed in this massacre [19 counting Chepita

M.]. Five men were buried outside of the fort in front [that is, east of the north half of it], and about twice that number were buried in the S. E. part of the fort." In 1892 workmen excavating a trench for a pipeline on Union Avenue directly in front of the Fariss Hotel, dug up one or more old skeletons and some logs at a depth of ten feet below present street level (Elliott Coues, ed., *The Expeditions of Zebulon Montgomery Pike*, II, 453n).

17. Cragin's interviews with Jesús Pando and Tom Autobees, Nov. 7, 1907 and with Elena Baca Autobees and Pedro Sandoval, *loc. cit.*

18. Cragin's interviews with Mrs. Ira Miller (Alvina Sandoval), Mrs. William Adamson (Cecilia Sandoval) and Juan Andrés Sandoval, Trinidad, May 23, 1908, Cragin Coll. According to Dick Wootton, the Arapahos were urged to attack the Utes by Wootton and Autobees. Their victory had evil consequences, for the Arapahos caught smallpox from blankets stolen from the Utes and suffered heavily from the disease *("Uncle Dick" Wootton*, 304).

19. Cragin's interviews with Mrs. William Adamson (Cecilia Sandoval), and Juan Andrés Sandoval, Trinidad, May 23, 1908 (Cragin Coll.).

20. Cragin's interviews with Pedro Sandoval, Webber P. O., Mora River, N. M., June 12, 1908, and Elena Baca Autobees, Oct. 31, 1907 (Cragin Coll.); claim of Levin Mitchell with "Claims for Indian Depredations in New Mexico," 35th. Cong., 1st. Sess., *House Exec. Doc. 123* (Ser. 959), pp. 61–62; DeWitt C. Peters to his sister, Fort Massachusetts, Jan. 14, 1844, in DeWitt Peters Papers, Bancroft Library, Berkeley, Calif.

21. W. A. Nichols, AAG, Santa Fe, to Col. T. T. Fauntleroy, Fort Union, Jan. 11, 1855 and to Maj. G. A. H. Blake, Camp Burgwin, and other letters in Dept. of N. M. Orders, Vol. IX, pp. 265–281, RG 98, National Archives, courtesy of James W. Arrott.

22. Conard, *"Uncle Dick" Wootton*, 302.

23. *Ibid.*, 303.

24. W. A. Nichols to Col. Fauntleroy, Santa Fe, Feb. 6, 1855, Dept. of N. M. Orders, Vol. IX, 292–93. On this foray the Utes took 117 *fanegas* of Baca's corn, 30 cows and 9 horses belonging to Tom Suaso, 7 horses and a wagon of William Kroenig's ("Claims for Indian Depredations in New Mexico," 35th Cong., 1st. Sess., *House Exec. Doc. 123* (Ser. 959), pp. 61–62).

25. Morris F. Taylor, "Action at Fort Massachusetts: The Indian Campaign of 1855," *Colorado Magazine*, Vol. XLII (1965).

26. Cragin's interviews with Tom Autobees, July 29, 1908, with José de Jesús Valdez, Walsenburg, Colo. Dec. 8 and 9, 1907, and with Elena Baca Autobees, Nov. 8, 1907, Cragin Coll.

27. Cragin's interviews with Tom Autobees, Nov. 8, 1907 and with Mrs. William Walker (Eliza Ann Wootton), Dec. 15, 1907, Cragin Coll.

28. Conard, *"Uncle Dick" Wootton*, 390–91; Edward W. Wynkoop, "Unfinished History," MS, library, Colorado Historical Society, Denver; *Reminiscences of General William Larimer and of his son William Larimer* (Lancaster, Pa., 1918), 77, 153, 206; "Diary of Samuel A. D. Raymond, 1859," MS, Colorado Historical Society, Denver. Not all the adobes of Pueblo were used in new buildings. *The Pueblo Weekly Chieftain* reported in 1874 that remains of the adobe walls still stood (Dec. 31, 1874, p. 4, c. 2), and in 1891 Frank Hall wrote that "the quadrangular foundations of the adobe walls are still visible on the west side of Union avenue, a

few rods southeast of the depot of the Atchison, Topeka & Santa Fe Railway" (*History of the State of Colorado*, III, 447).

CHAPTER 25

1. David Lavender, *Bent's Fort;* Janet Lecompte, "Charles Autobees," *Colorado Magazine*, Vol. XXXVI (1959).

2. The sale of Fort Barclay is recorded in the Taos County, N. M. Records, Book A–1 (1852–1870), p. 116; for Kroenig's marriage and bereavement see *History of New Mexico* (Pacific States Publishing Co., 1907), II, 956, and F. W. Cragin's notes of an interview with Mrs. Frank M. Jones (Fannie Kroenig), Las Vegas, N. M., June 26, 1908, Cragin Coll.; Pedro Sandoval (in an interview with Cragin, Webber P. O., N. M., June 12, 1908) tells of the graveyard and is himself buried there, his headstone reading that he was born Jan. 31, 1838 and died Aug. 30, 1930.

3. H. L. Conard, *"Uncle Dick" Wootton*, 319–373.

4. "The First Gold Find," *Denver Daily Times*, July 5, 1883, p. 2. Simpson's discovery was only one of several on Cherry Creek in 1858.

5. Wm. M. Slaughter, "Dictation," 1886, Bancroft Library, Berkeley, Calif.; "Reminiscenses of W. H. H. Larimer," Dec., 1909, Dawson Scrapbook IV, p. 45, Colorado Historical Society Library, Denver; Andrew Sagendorf in *Commonwealth Magazine*, quoted by L. W. Cutler in "Reminiscences," *Field & Farm*, April 13, 1889, Vol. VII, no. 15, p. 6; Conard, *"Uncle Dick" Wootton*, 383–84; Pueblo County, Colo. Records, Book I, p. 2; testimony of Richens L. Wootton, Las Vegas, N. M., May 20, 1885, *Transcript of Record, U.S. v. Maxwell Land Grant Co.* et al, U. S. Supreme Court, no. 974, Oct. term, 1886, p. 689. Some accounts say Wootton brought his family with him from New Mexico, but his daughter says that Mrs. Wootton gave birth to Joseph at Barclay's Fort in December, 1858 (Cragin's notes of an interview with Mrs. William Walker [Eliza Ann Wootton], Trinidad, Colo., Dec. 4, 1907, Cragin Coll.).

6. "Passing Away," *Rocky Mountain News Daily*, Jan. 1, 1873, p. 4, c. 2.

7. Hall, *History of the State of Colorado*, III, 342, 449; R. M. Stevenson, "History of Pueblo County" and Capt. B. F. Rockafellow, "History of Fremont County," in *History of the Arkansas Valley, Colorado, 1881*, 550, 766; Irving Howbert, *Memories of a Lifetime in the Pikes Peak Region* (New York, 1925), 44.

8. "Correspondence 1868–1914," Records of the General Land Office, Colorado Private Land Claim #17 (Vigil & St. Vrain Grant), RG 49, National Archives; William A. Bell, *New Tracks in North America* (London, 1869), I. 124; (Pueblo) *Colorado Chieftain*, Jan. 18, 1872, p. 4, c. 4.

9. Taos County, N. M. Records, Book B–3, pp. 82–83; O. J. Goldrick "From Denver to Santa Fe," *Rocky Mountain News Weekly*, Dec. 30, 1863, p. 1, c. 2–4.

10. *Rocky Mountain News Weekly*, March 5, 1864, March 23, 1864, p. 4, c. 4.

11. Administration papers, estate of Joseph B. Doyle, Pueblo County Records. The Doyle children were James Quinn, born 1849, died 1885; Frances Teresa, born Dec. 5, 1852, married A. P. Berry; Florence Ann, born 1855, married George Richards; Alexander Greene, born Sept. 26, 1858, died 1864; Elizabeth Matilda, died about 1867.

12. Cragin's notes of interviews with Mrs. William Walker (Eliza Ann Wootton), Trinidad, Colo., Dec. 4, 1907, and with Mrs. Richens L. Wootton (Maria Paula

Lujan), Trinidad, Dec. 4, 1907, Cragin Coll.; (Pueblo) *Colorado Chieftain*, April 22, 1869, p. 3, c. 4; June 15, 1871, p. 3, c. 3; Jan. 18, 1872, p. 4, c. 7; May 20, 1869, p. 3, c. 3; *Trinidad Daily News*, May 2, 1882, p. 3, c. 1; *Denver Republican*, Aug. 23, 1893, p. 1, c. 4. Wootton claimed in 1888 that he had fathered twenty children, lost eight, and at that time had 22 living descendants. After Dolores LeFevre died in 1855, he married Mary Ann Manning in 1858, by whom he had two children, Joseph and William. Mary Ann died in Denver in 1861 at the latter child's birth. Wootton married Fanny Brown at Doyle's ranch in 1863; she died in 1864 at the birth of Frances Virginia. His last wife, cousin of his first wife, outlived him (Cragin's interviews with Mrs. William Walker and Mrs. Richens L. Wootton, cited above).

13. Las Animas County, Colo. Records, Book I, pp. 8, 71, *Trinidad* (Colo.) *Daily Times*, Oct. 18, 1887, cited in DeBusk Memorial, Colorado Historical Society, p. 293–94; DeBusk on George Simpson, DeBusk Memorial, pp. 295–96; E. B. Sopris, "Colorado Before and During the Civil War," MS in Colorado Historical Society; Cragin's notes of an interview with Jesse Nelson, Smith Canyon Ranch, Colo., July 9, 1908, Cragin Coll.; WPA interview with Nicholas Vigil, Trinidad, Colo., Dec. 7, 1934, Las Animas Co. Pam. 359/12, Colorado Historical Society; Sister Blandina Segale, *At the End of the Santa Fe Trail* (Milwaukee, 1948), 48; WPA interview with Teodoro Abeyta, Las Animas Co., Pam 359/5, Colorado Historical Society. Simpson was buried on "Simpson's Rest," a mesa overlooking Trinidad where he was supposed to have been besieged by Indians in the early days. Simpson himself never bothered to deny the story and in fact he retold it for tourists, although it appears to have been untrue (WPA interview with Teodoro Abeyta; E. B. Sopris, "Colorado Before and During the Civil War," MS).

14. Segale, *At the End of the Santa Fe Trail*, 24, 63; Luis Baca, "The Guadalupita Colony of Trinidad," *Colorado Magazine*, Vol. XXI (1955), 26–27.

APPENDIX A

1. F. W. Cragin's notes of an interview with Mrs. George Simpson, El Paso, Texas, Oct. 31, 1904, Cragin Coll.

2. Book GG, pp. 189, 322, Chouteau Collection, Missouri Historical Society, St. Louis.

3. Testimony of George Simpson, Trinidad, Colo., Oct. 29, 1883, *Transcript of Record, U. S. v. Maxwell Land-Grant Company* et al, U. S. Supreme Court no. 974, p. 142.

4. Brown, *Mediumistic Experiences of John Brown, the Medium of the Rockies*, 23.

5. Hall, *History of the State of Colorado*, II, 233–34.

6. Vol. I, p. 167.

7. "Autobiography," typescript, Denver Public Library, Denver, Colo.

8. *Rocky Mountain News Weekly*, Dec. 23, 1863, p. 3, c. 4.

9. Cragin's notes of an interview with Pedro Sandoval, Mora River, June 12, 1908, Cragin Coll.

10. Cragin's notes of an interview with Tom Autobees, Avondale, Colo., Nov. 8, 1907, Cragin Coll.

11. Inman, *The Old Santa Fe Trail*, 252.

12. Dale L. Morgan, *The West of William H. Ashley* (Denver, 1964), 27–28, 30.

NOTES: APPENDIX C

13. Books V and X, Chouteau Coll.

14. Annie H. Abel, *Chardon's Journal at Fort Clark, 1834–1839* (Pierre, S.D., 1932), 291n.

15. Willis Reed, "The Fight at Battle Mountain, as told by Jim Baker," *El Porvenir*, Vol. III (1904), 163–175; "An Indian Fight in 1841, A Scrap of History as told by Jim Baker," *The Trail*, Vol. IX (1917), 12–15.

16. Fray Angélico Chávez, "New Names in New Mexico, 1820–1850," *El Palacio*, Vol. LXIV (1957), 317; A. R. Bouis to Joseph Picotte, Aug. 30, 1845, "Fort John, Fort Pierre Letter Book," Chouteau Coll.

APPENDIX B

1. F. W. Cragin's notes of an interview with G. W. Bilby, Pueblo, Colo., Oct. 15, 1907, Cragin Coll.

2. Cragin's notes of an interview with J. W. Smith, Pueblo, July 25, 1908.

3. "Draft to show the old crossing of Arkansas River 1863. (Drawn in 1907 by John A. Thatcher)," sketch in Cragin Coll.

4. (Pueblo) *Colorado Chieftain*, June 17, 1880, p. 1, c. 1.

5. Judge Wilbur F. Stone, "Early Pueblo and the Men Who Made It," *Colorado Magazine*, Vol. VI (1929), 201–202.

6. Elliott Coues, ed., *The Expeditions of Zebulon Montgomery Pike*, 453n.

7. Glenn R. Scott to writer, Denver, Jan. 18, 1967.

8. Map in the Land Office Books at Pueblo, drawn by William Ashley in 1869; Standard Par. by A. Z. Sheldon, 1863; Arkansas River meandered by Geo. H. Hill, 1872; traced copies in the Cragin Coll.; John A. Thatcher, "Draft to show old crossing of Arkansas River 1863 . . . ." Cragin Coll.

9. A map made by H. M. Fosdick for the Probate Judge dated "March, 1869," shows the meander reaching as far north as First Street, its most westerly point lapping the very edges of Cragin's hypothetical site of the Pueblo. But Fosdick made another map for the County Commissioners dated "Feb. 27, 1869" which shows the river lapping in another direction three blocks south. Except for the names of the streets, the two Fosdick maps have nothing in common, leading one to suspect fraud.

10. "Complete Map of the City of Pueblo, Colorado, compiled from actual surveys and the official records by Wm. Peach, City Engineer, August, 1900," tracing in the Cragin Coll.

11. *Ibid.*

12. Unidentified map in the Cragin Coll.

13. For instance, Frémont's 1848 party reached Mormon Town before Pueblo as it traveled up the Arkansas (see Chapter 21), as did John Albert the year before (see Chapter 18). Francis Parkman said Mormon Town was half a mile from the Pueblo, yet it took him half an hour to get there on horseback (Parkman, *The Oregon Trail*, p. 305).

APPENDIX C

1. W. A. Nichols, AAG, Santa Fe, to Col. T. T. Fauntleroy, Fort Union, Dept. of N. M. Orders, Vol. IX, p. 265, RG 98, National Archives, courtesy of James W. Arrott.

2. DeWitt Peters to his sister, Fort Massachusetts, Jan. 14, 1855, DeWitt Peters Papers, Bancroft Library, Berkeley, Calif.

3. Senex [George Simpson], "Pah-U-Tah," *Trinidad* (Colo.) *Daily Advertiser,* undated clipping c. 1884 in Dawson Scrapbook X, p. 298, Colorado Historical Society, Denver Colo.

4. Cragin's notes of an interview with Mrs. George Simpson, El Paso, Texas, Oct. 31, 1904; Cragin's Chapter XXVII, typescript in the Cragin Coll. (see Dorothy P. Shaw, "The Cragin Collection," *Colorado Magazine,* Vol. XXV [1948]); letter of Jacob Beard in *The Trail,* Vol. V (1912), 25–26.

5. "A Scrap of Pueblo History," *Pueblo People,* March 30, 1872.

6. *History of the Arkansas Valley, Colorado* (Chicago, 1881), 765; Hall, *History of the State of Colorado,* I, 168n.

7. F. W. Cragin's notes of interviews with these informants.

8. W. A. Nichols to Col. T. T. Fauntleroy, Santa Fe, Jan. 11, 1855; Bvt. Brig. Gen. John Garland to his Excellency D. Meriwether, Santa Fe, Jan. 22, 1855; Gen. Garland to Lt. Col. L. Thomas, Jan. 31, 1855; W. A. Nichols to Col. Fauntleroy, Santa Fe, Feb. 5, 1855, all from the Dept. of N. M. Orders, Vol. IX, pp. 265–293, RG 98, National Archives, courtesy of James W. Arrott; petition of José Marcelino Baca, Jan. 13, 1855, Letters Received, Office of Indian Affairs, New Mexico Superintendency, National Archives.

Selected Sources
for the Early History
of the Arkansas Valley

Abert, J. W. "Journal of Lieutenant J. W. Abert, from Bent's Fort to St. Louis, in 1845." *Message from the President of the United States, . . . communicating a report of an expedition led by Lieutenant Abert, on the upper Arkansas and through the country of the Camanche Indians, in the fall of the year 1845.* 29th Cong., 1st Sess., S. *Doc. 438* (Ser. 477). Reprinted, beautifully, as *Through the Country of the Comanche Indians in the fall of the year 1845: The Journal of a U.S. Army Expedition led by Lieutenant James W. Abert of the Topographical Engineers, Artist extraordinary whose paintings of Indians and Their Wild West illustrate this book.* Edited by John Galvin. San Francisco, 1970.

——. *Report of Lieut. J. W. Abert, of his Examination of New Mexico, in the years 1846–'47.* With Report of the Secretary of War, 30th Cong., 1st Sess., *Sen. Exec. Doc. 23* (Ser. 506).

Abert's diary, from which this report was drawn, has been magnificently published as *Western America in 1846–1847: The Original Travel Diary of Lieutenant J. W. Abert who mapped New Mexico for the United States Army.* Edited by John Galvin. San Francisco, 1966.

Alvarez, Manuel. Papers. Benjamin M. Read Collection, State Records Center and Archives, Santa Fe, N.M.

Charles Bent's letters in this collection have been published in the *New Mexico Historical Review*, beginning Vol. XXIX, No. 3 (July, 1954).

American Historical Association. *Calendar of the American Fur Company's Papers.* Vols. II and III in *Annual Report . . . For the Year 1844 in three volumes.* Washington, D. C., 1945.

Anderson, William Marshall. *The Rocky Mountain Journals of William Marshall Anderson.* Edited by Dale L. Morgan and Eleanor Towles Harris. San Marino, Calif., 1967.

Contains 45 superb sketches of mountain men in an appendix.

Arrott, James W. Papers. Highlands University, Las Vegas, N. M. Transcripts from War Department records in the National Archives relating to the U. S. Army in New Mexico, and some to the Arkansas Valley.

Bancroft Library. *A Guide to the Manuscript Collections of the Bancroft Library.* Edited by Dale L. Morgan and George P. Hammond. Vol. I,

Pacific and Western Manuscripts (except California). Berkeley, 1963. The section on New Mexico lists many documents and collections important to the history of the Arkansas Valley.

Barclay, Alexander. Papers. Bancroft Library, Berkeley, California. Including letters, 1834–1854, and diary, 1845-1850. Many of these papers have been published in George P. Hammond, *The Adventures of Alexander Barclay Mountain Man* . . . (Denver, 1976).

Barry, Louise. *The Beginning of the West.* Topeka, Kansas State Historical Society, 1972.
Careful, detailed chronology with much concerning the Arkansas Valley.

Beckwith, Lieut. E. G. *Report of Explorations for a Route for the Pacific Railroad, by Capt. J. W. Gunnison, Topographical Engineers, near the 38th and 39th parallels of North latitude, from the Mouth of the Kansas River, Mo., to the Sevier Lake, in the Great Basin,* in *Reports of Explorations and Surveys, to ascertain the most practicable and economical route for a railroad from the Mississippi River to the Pacific Ocean.* Made under the direction of the Secretary of War, in 1853–4, According to acts of Congress of March 3, 1853, May 31, 1854, and August 5, 1854. Volume II. 33d Cong., 3d Session, *House Exec. Doc. No. 91* (Ser. 792), Washington, D. C., 1855.

Bell, Captain John R. *The Journal of Captain John R. Bell, official Journalist for the Stephen H. Long Expedition to the Rocky Mountains, 1820.* Edited by Harlin M. Fuller and LeRoy R. Hafen. The Far West and the Rockies Historical Series, 1820–1875, Vol. IV. Glendale, Calif., 1957.

Bieber, Ralph P., and Leroy R. Hafen, eds. *The Southwest Historical Series.* 12 vols. Glendale, Calif., 1931–1942.
Includes Josiah Webb's *Adventures in the Santa Fe Trade* and Lewis Garrard's *Wah-to-yah and the Taos Trail.* A fine index helps locate many references to the Arkansas Valley in other volumes.

Blackmore, William. Papers. State Records Center and Archives, Santa Fe. Material on claimants to the Mora Grant, and on early land grants in Colorado. Used by Herbert O. Brayer in preparing his *William Blackmore: Early financing of the Denver and Rio Grande Railway and Ancillary Land Companies, 1871–1878.* 2 vols. Denver, 1949. Volume I is on the Spanish-Mexican land grants, and contains material on the Arkansas Valley.

Boggs, Thomas Oliver. "Dictation," Springer, N.M., 1885. Bancroft Library, Berkeley, Calif.
An old-timer (1844) in the Arkansas Valley.

Boggs, William M. "The W. M. Boggs Manuscript About Bent's Fort, Kit Carson, The Far West and Life Among the Indians," edited by LeRoy R. Hafen. *Colorado Magazine,* Vol. VII (1930).

Bolton, Herbert Eugene. *Guide to Materials for the History of the United States in the Principal Archives of Mexico.* Washington, D.C., 1913.

SELECTED SOURCES

Some documents listed concern the Arkansas Valley.

———. *Spanish Exploration in the Southwest, 1542–1706*. New York, 1916.

———. "French Intrusions into New Mexico, 1749–1752." In *Bolton and the Spanish Borderlands*, edited by John Francis Bannon. Norman, 1964.

Bonner, T. D. *The Life and Adventures of James P. Beckwourth* [1856]. Edited by Bernard De Voto. New York, 1931.

Breckenridge, Thomas. "Memoirs." Western Historical Manuscripts Collection. Missouri State Historical Society Library. Columbia, Mo. Frémont in the Arkansas Valley, 1845.

Brown, John. *Mediumistic Experiences of John Brown, the Medium of the Rockies*. Edited by J. S. Loveland. Third Edition, San Francisco, 1897.

———. Account Book. Manuscript Copy in the Henry E. Huntington Library. San Marino, Calif.

Bryant, Edwin. *What I Saw in California: Being the Journal of a Tour, By the Emigrant Route and South Pass of the Rocky Mountains, Across the Continent of North America, The Great Desert Basin, and Through California, in the Years 1846, 1847*. New York, 1849. Pueblo traders on the North Platte.

Buckman, George Rex. "An Historical Rocky-Mountain Outpost," *Lippincott's Magazine of Popular Literature and Science*, Vol. XXVI (Dec., 1880). One of the earliest if least reliable accounts of Pueblo.

Calhoun, James S. *The Official Correspondence of James S. Calhoun while Indian Agent at Santa Fe and Superintendent of Indian Affairs in New Mexico*. Edited by Annie Heloise Abel. Washington, D. C., 1915.

Carleton, Lieut. J. Henry. *The Prairie Logbooks: Dragoon Campaigns to the Pawnee Villages in 1844, and to the Rocky Mountains in 1845*. Edited by Louis Pelzer. Chicago, 1943.

Carroll, H. Bailey and J. Villasana Haggard, translators and editors. *Three New Mexico Chronicles: The Exposición of Don Pedro Bautista Pino, 1812; the Ojeada of Lic. Antonio Barreiro 1832; and the additions by Don José Agustín de Escudero 1849*. Quivira Society Publications, Vol. XI. Albuquerque, 1942. Excellent contemporary descriptions of New Mexico.

Carter, Harvey Lewis. *'Dear Old Kit': The Historical Christopher Carson*. With a New Edition of the Carson Memoirs. Norman, 1968.

Carter, Kate B. *The Mormon Battalion*. Published by the Daughters of Utah Pioneers, assisted by Clara B. Steele, [Salt Lake City], 1956. Biographies of many Mormons at Pueblo, 1846–47.

Chávez, Fray Angélico. "New Names in New Mexico, 1820–1850." *El Palacio*, Vol. LXIV (1957). Invaluable data about "Americans" in New Mexico, drawn from Church records.

Cheetham, Francis T. "The First Term of the American Court in Taos, New Mexico." *New Mexico Historical Review*, Vol. I (1926).
Trials of the rebellion leaders, 1847.
Chittenden, Hiram Martin. *The American Fur Trade of the Far West: A history of the pioneer trading posts and early fur companies of the Missouri Valley and The Rocky Mountains and of the Overland Commerce with Santa Fe*. Three volumes. New York, 1902.
Still the best and most readable history of the fur trade.
Chouteau Collection. Missouri Historical Society, St. Louis.
Ledgers of the firm of P. Chouteau Jr. & Co., and letters from traders and bourgeois at company posts. Much of the collection indexed.
Clark, William. Papers. Records of the St. Louis Superintendency of Indian Affairs, Kansas Historical Society, Topeka.
Colorado, State Historical Society of. *The Colorado Magazine*. Vols. I–XLVI (1923–1969). Two indexes: one for Vols. I–XXV (Denver, 1950); the other for Vols. XXVI–XXXVIII (Denver, 1964).
Conard, Howard Louis. *"Uncle Dick" Wootton: The pioneer frontiersman of the Rocky Mountain region*. Chicago, 1890.
A charming biography, studded with errors.
Connelley, William E. *Doniphan's Expedition and the Conquest of New Mexico and California*. Topeka, 1907.
Contains a reprint of John T. Hughes, *Doniphan's Expedition* [1847].
Cooke, Philip St. George. "A Journal of the Santa Fe Trail," edited by William E. Connelley. *Mississippi Valley Historical Review*, Vol. XII (1925).
Soldiers on the trail in 1843.
———. *Scenes and Adventures in the army: or, Romance of Military Life*. Philadelphia, 1859.
Including an account of Kearny's 1845 expedition to the mountains.
Coues, Elliott, ed. *The Expeditions of Zebulon Montgomery Pike, to Headwaters of the Mississippi River, through Louisiana Territory, and in New Spain, During the Years 1805–6–7*. New York, 1895.
Valuable for Coues' own investigation of the route in the footnotes.
Cragin, Francis Whittemore. Collection. Pioneers' Museum, Colorado Springs. Includes twenty-eight small notebooks containing notes of interviews; typescript chapters of an unfinished book on Colorado history; letters from George Bent; Will Boggs' drawing of Bent's Fort in 1844; tracings of maps from Pueblo County records. For a description, see Dorothy P. Shaw, "The Cragin Collection," *Colorado Magazine*, Vol. XXV (1948).

Davis, W. W. H. *El Gringo: or, New Mexico and her People*. New York, 1857.
Dawson, Thomas F. Scrapbooks. Colorado State Historical Society, Denver.

Vast, disorganized treasure-house of clippings, many from lost newspapers.

DeBusk, Samuel W. Memorial Interviews, Las Animas County, Colo. Colorado State Historical Society, Denver.

DeMun, Julius. Letter to Gov. William Clark, St. Louis, Nov. 25, 1817. Missouri Historical Society *Collections*, Vol. V (1928).
Details of a fur-trader's woes on the Arkansas, 1815–17.

Dodge, Henry. "Report on the Expedition of Dragoons under Colonel Henry Dodge." *American State Papers, Military Affairs*, Vol. VI. Washington, D. C. 1836.

Drips, Andrew. Papers. Missouri Historical Society, St. Louis.
A few of his letters deplore the Pueblo liquor trade.

Emory, William H. *Notes of a Military Reconnoissance, from Fort Leavenworth, in Missouri, to San Diego, in California, including part of the Arkansas, Del Norte, and Gila Rivers . . . Made in 1846–7, with the Advanced Guard of the "Army of the West."* 30th Cong., 1st Sess., H. Exec. Doc. 41 (Ser. 517).

Farnham, Thomas J. *Travels in the Great Western Prairies, the Anahuac and Rocky Mountains, and in the Oregon Territory* [1843]. Vols. XXVIII and XXIX in R. G. Thwaites, *Early Western Travels 1748–1846*. Cleveland, 1906.
The Arkansas Valley in 1839.

Favour, Alpheus H. *Old Bill Williams, Mountain Man*. Norman, 1962.

Field, Matt. *Matt Field on the Santa Fe Trail*. Collected by Clyde and Mae Reed Porter. Edited by John E. Sunder. Norman, 1960.
The Arkansas Valley in 1839.

Ford, Lemuel. "Captain Ford's Journal of an Expedition to the Rocky Mountains." Edited by Louis Pelzer. *Mississippi Valley Historical Review*, Vol. XII (1926).
With Henry Dodge in 1835.

Foreman, Grant. *Marcy & the Gold Seekers: The Journal of Captain R. B. Marcy, with an Account of the Gold Rush over the Southern Route*. Norman, 1939.
Prospectors at Pueblo, 1849.

Fort Lyon, Old. Abandoned Military Reservation File. RG 49, National Archives.
Some early history of the Arkansas Valley.

Fowler, Jacob. *The Journal of Jacob Fowler Narrating an Adventure from Arkansas through the Indian Territory, Oklahoma, Kansas, Colorado and New Mexico to the Sources of the Rio Grande Del Norte, 1821–22*. Edited by Elliott Coues. New York, 1898.

Frémont, Brevet Captain J. C. *Report of the Exploring Expedition to the*

Rocky Mountains in the year 1842, and to Oregon and North California in the years 1843-'44. Washington, D.C., 1845.

————. Selected Records of the General Accounting Office relating to the Frémont Expeditions and the California Battalion, 1842–1890. RG 217, National Archives. National Archives Microfilm Publication, T-135, roll 1.
Fiscal details of Frémont's 1843–44 expedition.

Garrard, Lewis H. *Wah-to-yah and the Taos Trail.* Edited by Ralph P. Bieber. Southwest Historical Series, Vol. VI. Glendale, Calif., 1938.

Gregg, Josiah. *Commerce of the Prairies, or the Journal of a Santa Fe Trade, During Eight Expeditions Across the Great Western Prairies, and a Residence of Nearly Nine Years in Northern Mexico* [1845]. Vols. XIX and XX in R. G. Thwaites, *Early Western Travels 1748–1846.* Cleveland, 1905.

Grinnell, George Bird. "Bent's Old Fort and Its Builders." Kansas Historical Society *Collections,* Vol. XV (1923).

————. *The Cheyenne Indians.* Two vols. New Haven, 1923.

Hafen, LeRoy R. "When Was Bent's Fort Built?" *Colorado Magazine,* Vol. XXX (1954).

————, ed. *The Mountain Men and the Fur Trade of the Far West.* Ten vols. Glendale, Calif., 1965–1972.
Sketches by Harvey Carter, Ann W. Hafen, LeRoy R. Hafen, and Janet Lecompte are especially pertinent to the Arkansas Valley, and a fine index will locate other references.

———— and Frank M. Young. "The Mormon Settlement at Pueblo, Colorado, During the Mexican War." *Colorado Magazine,* Vol. IX (1932).

———— and Ann W. Hafen. *The Far West and the Rockies Historical Series, 1820–1875.* Fifteen vols. Glendale, Calif., 1954–1961.
Another valuable and well-indexed Hafen series containing Capt. Bell's Journal (1820), Sage's *Scenes in The Rocky Mountains* (1842), E. H. Heap's journal (1853), and accounts of Frémont's Fourth Expedition (1848–49), all of importance to the Arkansas Valley.

Hall, Frank. *History of the State of Colorado, Embracing Accounts of the Pre-Historic Races and their Remains; the Earliest Spanish, French and American Explorations; the Lives of the Primitive Hunters, Trappers and Traders; The Commerce of the Prairies; the First American Settlements Founded; the Original Discoveries of Gold in the Rocky Mountains; the Development of Cities and Towns, with the Various Phases of Industrial and Political Transition, from 1858 to 1890.* Four vols. Chicago, 1889–95.

Hilger, Sister M. Inez. *Arapaho Child Life and Its Cultural Background.* Bureau of American Ethnology, Bulletin 148. Washington, D.C., 1952.

Hill, Nathaniel P. "Nathaniel P. Hill Inspects Colorado: Letters Written in 1864." *Colorado Magazine*, Vols. XXXIII and XXXIV (1956 and 1957).
Describes some Mexican customs of the Arkansas Valley.
History of the Arkansas Valley, Colorado. O. L. Baskin & Co., Chicago, 1881.
Antique and unscholarly, but still important, especially Charles W. Bowman's "Bent County" and Capt. B. F. Rockafellow's "Fremont County."
Huerfano County (Colorado) Records. Walsenburg, Colo.
Many old–timers—Autobees, Wootton, Jones, etc.—turn up here.

Indian Affairs, Office of. Letters Received, 1824–1881. RG 75, National Archives.
From the Upper Platte and Arkansas Agency, 1846–1856; St. Louis Superintendency, 1824–1849; Upper Missouri Agency, 1824–1874; New Mexico Superintendency, 1849–1857; Central Superintendency, 1851–1856. The student must see these. They are published inexpensively as a National Archives Microfilm Publication.
Inman, Colonel Henry. *The Old Santa Fe Trail: The Story of a Great Highway.* New York, 1897.
Useful only in determining where later writers obtained their misinformation.

Jablow, Joseph. *The Cheyenne in Plains Indian Trade Relations 1795–1840.* Monographs of the American Ethnological Society, edited by Marian W. Smith, Vol. XIX. New York, c. 1950.
James, Edwin. *Account of an Expedition from Pittsburgh to the Rocky Mountains, performed in the Years 1819, 1820* [1823]. Vols. XIV–XVII in R. G. Thwaites, *Early Western Travels 1748–1846.* Cleveland, 1905.
An account of Stephen H. Long's expedition.

Kearny, Stephen W. *Report of a summer campaign to the Rocky Mountains &c., in 1845.* 29th Cong., 1st Sess., H. Exec. Doc. 2 (Ser. 480).
Kern, Edward. "Diary of Edward Kern, 1845–6, with Frémont." *Life*, Vol. XLVI (April 6, 1959), 96–97.
The other Kern brothers, Benjamin and Richard, left diaries also, which are reprinted in Hafen and Hafen, *Frémont's Fourth Expedition*, Vol. XI, *Far West and Rockies Historical Series.*
Kroenig, William. "Autobiography." Typescript. Denver Public Library.
Published, with confusing alterations, by Charles Irving Jones, as "William Kronig, New Mexico Pioneer from his memories of 1849–1860." *New Mexico Historical Review*, Vol. XIX (1944).

Larpenteur, Charles. *Forty Years a Fur Trader on the Upper Missouri:*

The Personal Narrative of Charles Larpenteur, 1833–1872. Edited by Milo M. Quaife. Chicago, 1933.
Methods of the traders.
Lavender, David. *Bent's Fort.* New York, 1954.
The classic work on the early Arkansas Valley.
Lecompte, Janet. "Charles Autobees." *Colorado Magazine,* Vols. XXXIV–XXXVI (1957–1959).
———. "Gantt's Fort and Bent's Picket Post." *Colorado Magazine,* Vol. XLI (1964).
———. "The Manco Burro Pass Massacre." *New Mexico Historical Review,* Vol. XLI (1966).
———. "The Hardscrabble Settlement, 1844–1848." *Colorado Magazine,* Vol. XXXI (1954).
———. "Bent, St. Vrain and Company Among the Comanche and Kiowa." *Colorado Magazine,* Vol. XLIX (1972).
Luna, Richard L. *Lady of Taos.* Colorado Springs, 1974.
The lady is Teresita. The treatment is fictional, but some family history appears here.
Lupton, Lancaster P. Papers. Colorado State Historical Society, Denver.
Receipts for liquor at Fort Lancaster; a letter of Lupton to Charles Town; account book at Hardscrabble, 1848.

Martin, Thomas S. "Narrative of Frémont's Expedition in 1845–6." Manuscript. Bancroft Library, Berkeley, Calif.
Meriwether, David. *My Life in the Mountains and On the Plains.* Edited by Robert A. Griffen. Norman, 1965.
Valuable for Meriwether's tenure as Governor and Superintendent of Indian Affairs for New Mexico, 1853–1854.
Mexican Archives of New Mexico. State Records Center and Archives, Santa Fe. All manuscript; all in Spanish. Documents of general interest have been used by Lansing Bartlett Bloom, "New Mexico under Mexican Administration," *Old Santa Fe,* Vols. I–II (1913–1915). David J. Weber has used others in *The Taos Trappers: The Fur Trade in the Far Southwest, 1540–1846* (Norman, 1971).
Morgan, Dale. *Overland in 1846: Diaries and Letters of the California-Oregon Trail.* Two vols. Georgetown, Calif., 1963.
Pueblo traders on the North Platte.
———. "The Mormons and the Far West." Transcripts from American newspapers. Unpublished collection in the Henry E. Huntington Library, San Marino, Calif.; in the Beinecke Rare Book and Manuscript Library, Yale University; in the Utah State Historical Society, Salt Lake City; and in the Bancroft Library, Berkeley, Calif.

Niles' National Register, Vols. XXXI-LXXIII. Baltimore and Washington, D.C., 1826–1848.

Many items reprinted from St. Louis and New Orleans papers regarding the West.

Pancoast, Charles Edward. *A Quaker Forty-Niner: The Adventures of Charles Edward Pancoast on the American Frontier.* Edited by Anna Paschall Hannum. Philadelphia, 1930.
A California emigrant at Pueblo.

Parkman, Francis. *The Oregon Trail: Sketches of Prairie and Rocky Mountain Life.* Boston, 1894.

Parke, Lt. Jno. G. "Map of the Territory of New Mexico compiled by Bvt. 2nd Lt. Jno. G. Parke, U.S.T.E., assisted by Mr. Richard H. Kern. Santa Fe, N.M., 1851." National Archives.
The best contemporary map of the early Arkansas Valley, southern part.

Peters, DeWitt C. *Pioneer Life and Frontier Adventures: An Authentic Record of the Romantic Life and Daring Exploits of Kit Carson and His Companions, from his Own Narrative.* Boston, 1883.
Expands and romanticizes Carson's autobiography. Some material from Dr. Peters' own knowledge of the West.

Pike, Zebulon Montgomery. *The Journals of Zebulon Montgomery Pike, With Letters and Related Documents.* Edited and annotated by Donald Jackson. 2 vols. Norman, 1966.

Preuss, Charles. *Exploring with Frémont: The Private Diaries of Charles Preuss, Cartographer for John C. Frémont on His First, Second, and Fourth Expeditions to the Far West.* Translated and edited by Erwin G. and Elisabeth K. Gudde. Norman, 1958.

(Pueblo) *Colorado Chieftain.* 1868–1886.
An occasional item about the old Pueblo's history.

Pueblo County Records. Pueblo, Colorado.
The Arkansas Valley in the sixties and seventies.

Ritch, William G. Collection. Henry E. Huntington Library, San Marino, Calif.
Mexican passports, customs house records, naturalization papers, 1823–1848; military reports of actions against New Mexico Indians, 1849–1855; notes of John Greiner, Indian Agent, 1848–1853; and many other items.

Rocky Mountain News (weekly). 1860–64. Denver, Colorado.
Occasional descriptions showing the importance of Arkansas Valley farms to the development of the Territory.

Ruxton, George Frederic. *Adventures in Mexico and the Rocky Mountains.* New York, 1848.
———. *Life in the Far West.* New York, 1849.

Sage, Rufus. *Scenes in the Rocky Mountains, and in Oregon, California, New Mexico, Texas, and the grand prairies.* Philadelphia, 1846.

St. Louis Superintendency of Indian Affairs. Records. Kansas Historical Society, Topeka.
Also known as the William Clark Papers. Many documents here are not found in the Indian Office files.

Seger, John H. *Early Days Among the Cheyenne and Arapahoe Indians.* Edited by Stanley Vestal. Norman, 1934.

Steele, John. "John Steele's Day Book." Office of the Church Historian, Church of Jesus Christ of Latter-Day Saints, Salt Lake City, Utah.
Used with kind permission of Kenneth Jensen, Northridge, Calif. A Mormon's diary at Pueblo, 1846–1847.

Stone, Wilbur F. "Pueblo." (Pueblo) *Colorado Chieftain*, June 17, 1880.
———. "Early Pueblo and the Men Who Made It." *Colorado Magazine*, Vol. VI (1929).

Sublette Papers. Missouri Historical Society, St. Louis.

Sunder, John E. *The Fur Trade on the Upper Missouri, 1840–1865.* Norman, 1965.

Talbot, Theodore. *The Journals of Theodore Talbot, 1843 and 1849–52, With The Frémont Expedition of 1843 and with the First Military Company in Oregon Territory, 1849–1852.* Edited by Charles H. Carey. Portland, Oregon, 1931.

Taos County Records. Taos, New Mexico.
Especially Book C-1, "Diario de la Corte de Pruebas, 1847-1855," which are the earliest records in the County Clerk and Recorder's office (earlier ones were destroyed in the rebellion of 1847).

Taos, New Mexico. Church of Nuestra Señora de Guadalupe, Matrimonial Records, 1833–1845, and Baptismal Records, 1827–1850. State Records Center and Archives, Santa Fe, N. M.

Taylor, Morris F. *Trinidad, Colorado Territory.* Pueblo, 1966.
This fine scholar has published many articles on the Arkansas Valley of a later period, in the *Colorado Magazine, New Mexico Historical Review* and elsewhere.

Thomas, Alfred Barnaby, ed., "Documents Bearing Upon the Northern Frontier of New Mexico, 1818–1819." *New Mexico Historical Review*, Vol. IV (1929).
———. "San Carlos—A Comanche Pueblo on the Arkansas River, 1787." *Colorado Magazine*, Vol. IV (1929).
———. "An Anonymous Description of New Mexico, 1818." *Southwestern Historical Quarterly*, Vol. XXXIII (1929).
———. *Forgotten Frontiers: A Study of the Spanish Indian Policy of Don Juan Bautista de Anza, Governor of New Mexico, 1777–1787.* Norman, 1932.
———. *After Coronado: Spanish Exploration Northeast of New Mexico, 1696–1727.* Norman, 1935.

SELECTED SOURCES

————. *The Plains Indians and New Mexico, 1751–1778.* Albuquerque, 1940.
Thwaites, Reuben Gold. *Early Western Travels 1748–1846.* Cleveland, 1904–1907. Thirty-two volumes of annotated reprints, including Farnham's *Travels*, Gregg's *Commerce of the Prairies*, Edwin James' *Account of an Expedition* . . . .
Trinidad (Colo.) *Daily News.*
   Files from 1881–1885 have many important articles by "Senex" [George Simpson].
Turley family. Papers. Missouri Historical Society, St. Louis.
   Letters, Receipts, *aduana* declarations, etc. Two valuable letters from this collection are published in Janet Lecompte and Lester F. Turley, "The Turleys from Boonslick," Missouri Historical Society *Bulletin*, Vol. XXVIII (1972).
Tyler, Sgt. Daniel. *A Concise History of the Mormon Battalion in the Mexican War, 1846–1847* [1881]. Reprinted, Chicago, 1964.

United States *v.* Maxwell Land Grant Company *et al. Transcript of Record*, U.S. Supreme Court, October term, 1886, no. 974.
   Testimony of Calvin Jones, Charles Williams, Richens L. Wootton, George Simpson, Jesús Silva, etc.
United States Congress. Senate Documents and Executive Documents. 22d Congress, 1st Session through 35th Congress, 1st Session (1831–1858).
————. House Executive Documents. 22d Congress, 1st Session through 35th Congress, 1st Session (1831–1858).
   Searching the thousand pertinent volumes of these "serials" is made easier by an index of document titles at the beginning of each volume. Reports and Journals of both houses are occasionally useful.

[Vigil and St. Vrain Land Grant]. Colorado Private Land Claim #17. Records of the General Land Office, RG 49, National Archives.
   Considerable material on the early Arkansas Valley.
Voelker, Frederic E. "Ezekiel Williams of Boon's Lick." Missouri Historical Society *Bulletin.* Vol. VIII (1951).
   Very early traders on the Arkansas.

Webb, James Josiah. *Adventures in the Santa Fe Trade, 1844–1847.* Edited by Ralph P. Bieber. Southwest Historical Series, Vol. I. Glendale, Calif., 1931.
Wheat, Carl I. *Mapping the Transmississippi West, 1540–1861.* Five Vols. San Francisco, 1957–1963.

INDEX

218848
2-16-79